GREAT

SURVEYS

of the

AMERICAN

WEST

THE AMERICAN EXPLORATION AND TRAVEL SERIES

GREAT
SURVEYS
of the
AMERICAN
WEST

by Richard A. Bartlett

UNIVERSITY OF OKLAHOMA PRESS : NORMAN

By Richard A. Bartlett

Great Surveys of the American West (Norman, 1962)

The Yellowstone National Park, by Hiram Martin Chittenden (editor) (Norman, 1964)

Nature's Yellowstone (Albuquerque, 1974)

The New Country: A Social History of the American Frontier, 1776-1890 (New York, 1974)

Freedom's Trail (with Clare Keller) (Boston, 1979)

Rolling Rivers: An Encyclopedia of America's Rivers (editor) (New York, 1984)

Yellowstone: A Wilderness Besieged (Tucson, 1985)

Library of Congress Catalog Card Number: 62-16745

ISBN: 0-8061-1653-6

Great Surveys of the American West is Volume 38 in *The American Exploration and Travel Series.*

Acknowledgments

SOME TWENTY MILES northwest of Boulder, Colorado, about halfway between the plains and the icy crags of the Front Range, lies Cooke Mountain. Years ago a couple of boys and a mongrel dog, exploring thereabouts, stumbled upon a bronze plaque cemented into a large boulder, commemorating the death there of a lost Captain Cooke. The boys conjectured while catching their breaths until the dog took out after a chipmunk, and then dog, chipmunk, and boys were on their way again.

From the summit of Cooke Mountain they saw the jagged peaks spread northwestward to perhaps Mount Richtofen, southward to Mount Evans or even to Lieutenant Pike's "Blue Mountain." Nearly due west, looming mightiest of all, was Longs Peak. Eastward lay foothills and the great high plains of Colorado. There was Denver, far to the southeast; Boulder was hidden by intervening ridges; but Longmont was easily sighted, and other patches of civilization dotted the view. An occasional automobile windshield flashed in the sun. West was nature, wild and untamed; east was dull civilization.

West was where the boys went on Saturdays. They explored the old mines and forced open more cabin doors than they should have. They knew the decaying mining camps of Magnolia, Wall

Street, Sugar Loaf, Gold Hill, Sunshine, Caribou, Nederland, Eldora, Hesse, Ward, and Jim Town. Sometimes they hitched rides with the hard-rock miners—proud characters who preferred sifting old mine dumps to going on Relief in those dismal days of the 1930's. Or they trekked into the high country with classmates who lived "in the hills" and who could identify gold-bearing ore even though they had never read a book on geology. The boys really had fun.

So perhaps acknowledgments should go all the way back to those days, for I was one of those boys, and my curiosity about the explorers and miners who first were in those hills blended naturally with my increasing absorption in American history.

I owe a debt of gratitude posthumously to Colin B. Goodykoontz, my major professor at the University of Colorado, whose excellent guidance aided my original research into the Surveys. Aid was extended to me by Mrs. Opal Harber and Mrs. Alys Freeze of the Western History Room of the Denver Public Library, and by Mrs. Nan V. Carson, librarian of the State Historical Society of Colorado. In The National Archives I give special thanks to the aid of Herman Friis, chief archivist of the Technical Records Division, and to Charles Dewing, who serviced Interior Department records while I was there. Other archivists who offered special attention and showed unusual interest in my project were Oliver Wendell Holmes, Miss Josephine Cobb, and Miss Katherine Murphy.

I received help from the capable men of the Manuscripts Division of the Library of Congress as well as from Milton Kaplan of the Division of Prints and Photographs. Terry Bender and Julian Barclay of the Bender Room, Stanford University Special Collections, gave me every possible aid during the weeks Survey. I had help concerning Clarence King from the Huntington Library and information on Wheeler and King from Hunting Library and information on Wheeler and King from the Bancroft Library. While there I also examined Francis Farquhar's collection on King and Gardner, which materially deepened my understanding of those men. (Mr. Farquhar was then in Europe: I trust he will accept my belated gratitude.)

For further information on Gardner and Hayden I am indebted to Mrs. Anne Gardiner Pier of Williamstown, Massachusetts, to Juliet Wolohan of the New York Public Library at Albany, to Margaret Butterfield, in charge of Special Collections at the University of Rochester, to Leonidas Dodson of the Archives of the University of Pennsylvania, and to John Saeger, reference librarian at Oberlin College. I am indebted to Aubrey L. Haines, park historian, Yellowstone Park, for pertinent information about that region, and to Bruce Woodard of Denver, Colorado, for aid in my research on the Diamond Hoax. Useful aid was extended to me at the Smithsonian Institution and by the curator of the National Collection of Fine Arts in Washington, D. C. Significant information about all the Surveys was culled from dozens of other sources, but space prevents more than a sincere thanks to those many informants.

I owe a special debt of gratitude to the entire staff of the Robert Manning Strozier Library at the Florida State University, and especially to the director of libraries, N. Orwin Rush. His western background made his criticism of parts of the manuscript most helpful. The Florida State University Research Council, under the chairmanship of Dean Werner Baum and later of Dean John K. Folger, helped with funds, and from J. Paul Reynolds, dean of the College of Arts and Sciences, and from W. Tyree Jordan, chairman of the Department of History, I received encouragement. Roland W. Eves gave unstintingly of his time in the preparation of the maps.

In a more personal vein I wish to acknowledge my heartening discussions with the Reverend Harcourt Waller, formerly of the Episcopal Chapel of the Resurrection at F. S. U. To the patience and faith and encouragement of my wife, Marie Cosgrove Bartlett, and to Richard, Margaret, Mary Ellen, and Thomas, whose father was lost to Clio for long periods of time, my debt can never be repaid.

Richard A. Bartlett

THE FLORIDA STATE UNIVERSITY
TALLAHASSEE, FLORIDA

Introduction

"In the morning the strawberry can be seen in full bloom, at noon fully developed, and at night ripe and falling from the stem."—"Captain" Sam Adams speaking of the valleys of the Colorado River, in the Washington (D.C.) *Chronicle,* March 25, 1872.

WHEN THE AGONY of the great Civil War was ended, the victorious North flexed its muscles, eyed its tremendous resources in cheap labor, bustling industry, and investment capital, and cast its covetous—nay, rapacious—eyes westward.

What lay out there?

Way out there was California, and Oregon, and the gentle waters of the Pacific. Soon the transcontinental railroad would carry passengers to California at the incredible speed of thirty miles an hour. But what lay, say, between the Front Range of the Rockies and the eastern slope of the Sierra Nevadas? Gold? Silver? Diamonds? Coal? Could the land be profitably broken to the plow? Was there anything out there worth looking into?

Now of course something was known of the general area. But like a pretty dress to a pretty girl, the maps of the area and the knowledge of its contents intrigued without divulging the mysteries. The government had sent out many explorers. Lewis and Clark, Zebulon Pike, Stephen H. Long, and John C. Frémont are perhaps the best known of the government men who conducted explorations in the decades prior to the Civil War. From 1851 through 1853, Jefferson Davis, the secretary of war, had encouraged the so-called Pacific Railroad Surveys, aimed at finding the most practicable route across the continent. These surveys numbered among their personnel a few scientists, but still they merely whetted the appetite for more knowledge of the Great West.

Then came the Civil War, and with its end a tremendous expansive impulse. The West seemed the obvious place for investment, for settlement, for exploitation, for health. So great was the curiosity about it that newspapers published the most incredible stories as if they were fact.

There was a "Captain" Sam Adams who claimed that he had explored the Colorado River, that it was freely navigable for six hundred miles from its mouth, that in one of the valleys—appropriately named "Paradise Valley"—wild oats, timothy, clover, and rye were seen, "the latter growing over seven feet in height." He described veins of gold, silver, copper, and lead appearing in the canyon walls or extending far up the side canyons. "We saw oil floating on a number of small streams entering the main river," he boasted. "Occasionally a spot could be seen on the land, composed of a sticky, tarry substance, where we found that a number of birds and squirrels had perished in endeavoring to extricate themselves."[1]

Preposterous? Certainly. Yet what else could people believe? Rumors about this fabulous river and its tributaries were fantastic because the truth was—and is today—incredible enough. And in 1872, Powell had not yet published his beautiful narration of his journey down the Colorado. Not only were "Captain" Sam Adams' letters published, but that psychopath prevailed upon the Committee on Claims of the House of Representatives to compensate him to the extent of $20,000 for his alleged hazardous explorations! The bill—H.R. 2565, 41 Cong., 3 sess.—was actually printed, but, fortunately for our faith in government, "Captain" Adams never received a cent.

There were rumors—had been for years—about an area in the Northwest where boiling hot water spouted up in great fountains and living streams of molten brimstone endangered the explorer,

[1] "Captain" Sam Adams' narration, for what it is worth, appears in a series of eleven letters to the Washington (D.C.) *Chronicle*, March and April, 1872.

and where there were "small craters from four to six inches in diameter from which streamed a blaze and a whistling sound." Explorers related how "the hollow ground resounded beneath their feet as they traveled, and every moment seemed to break through." Nor was there a living thing to be seen in the area. By 1867, it was clear that something strange and wonderful existed up there in the vicinity of the Yellowstone River, but exactly *what?*[2]

There were stories of Indians down in the southwestern deserts who lived in strange adobe apartment houses. It was believed that they were the last remains of the sanguinary Aztecs of Mexico. In Denver's saloons shabby prospectors related stories of cliff dwellings, long deserted, in the walls of piñon-covered canyons in the far southwestern corner of the Territory. And what about the rumored "Holy Mountain" deep in the Colorado Rockies, displaying to the rising sun an enormous, nearly perfect cross of white snow?

Then there was the question of mineral wealth. Investors demanded more than a prospector's story and a couple of fist-sized specimens of ore. They weren't going to invest large sums on such flimsy evidence—at least the smart ones weren't! They wanted the careful appraisals of professional geologists. What was needed was a general geological survey of the West, with topographers making reliable maps as the survey progressed. Only then could the western lands be safely exploited.

If, for the sake of science, they wanted to take along some zoologists, botanists, biologists, ornithologists, entomologists and paleontologists, let them. Someone had to assemble the foundations for the knowledge of the flora and fauna of the West, make the original collections, and do the classifying; and why should they not be individuals attached to the geological and geographical surveys?

Let them take along painters, too, and possibly experts in the new-fangled magic of photography. A few journalists might go along to narrate their adventures. And then, pretty soon, the mysteries of the West would be solved; pioneers, investors, rail-

[2] New York *Times*, September 14, 1867, p. 1. Quoted from the Montana *Post*.

road builders, timber barons, and mining engineers, could take over. The West would be populated and, sometimes, rapaciously exploited. Like the pretty girl with the pretty dress, what was hidden would become known, but all would still remain incredibly beautiful, mysterious, wonderful. The West is still, even today, the Wonderful West.

The results of this quest for knowledge about the American West after the Civil War were four geographical and geological surveys conducted over large areas of the West from 1867 until 1879, when the United States Geological Survey, which is still in existence, took over. Two of these surveys were under the administration of the War Department: the United States Geological Exploration of the Fortieth Parallel, headed by a civilian, Clarence King, and the United States Geographical Surveys West of the One Hundredth Meridian, led by Lieutenant George Montague Wheeler. The other two surveys were under the administration of the Department of the Interior: the United States Geological and Geographical Survey of the Territories, directed by Ferdinand Vandeveer Hayden, and the United States Geographical and Geological Survey of the Rocky Mountain Region, led by John Wesley Powell.

In government agencies, these four surveys are often grouped together and referred to as "the Great Surveys." They were great in the sense of the vast territories they examined, in their breadth —embracing topography, geology, and the natural sciences—and in the span of years in which they operated. Their contributions to the knowledge of the American West were enormous. The *Checklist of United States Public Documents, 1787–1901*[3] lists eight publications for the King Survey (not including the brief annual reports), forty for the Wheeler Survey, about fifty for the Hayden Survey (the exact number depends upon the treatment given various editions and supplements), and eighteen for the Powell Survey. For purposes of indexing, the four surveys have been grouped together by government catalogers.[4]

[3] "List of Congressional and Departmental Publications," *Checklist*, I, 467–70, 1272–73, 1276–78.

[4] Laurence F. Schmeckebier, *Catalogue and Index of the Hayden, King, Powell, and Wheeler Surveys.*

Finally, the Hayden, Wheeler, and Powell surveys were consolidated in 1879 into the United States Geological Survey, the King Survey having completed its work just prior to that time. For all of these reasons the four surveys are usually considered together as the Great Surveys.

In the years that have passed since 1879, the voluminous reports issued by the Great Surveys have been allowed to gather dust in the reference libraries of the world. Much, perhaps most, of the work done by the surveys, which laid the basis for the knowledge of the geology and natural history of the West, has been superseded by subsequent research. Their wonderful maps, compiled after so much physical labor, are now useless, save to historians and collectors. It may be commonly known, in a vague sort of way, that the Hayden Survey was instrumental in creating the Yellowstone National Park, that it was the organization whose employee, William Henry Jackson, first photographed the Mount of the Holy Cross in Colorado, and that men attached to the Hayden Survey first reported the cliff dwellings of the Mesa Verde region to the world. Perhaps Clarence King is known as the man who exposed the diamond hoax in northwestern Colorado in 1873. Some may know that Marshall Pass in south central Colorado is named for a member of the Wheeler Survey who had a toothache and had to get to Denver in a hurry to have the tooth removed—he took a short cut, and the pass over which he trod bears his name to this day. Powell is undoubtedly remembered as the one-armed explorer who went down the Colorado River canyons in boats in 1869 and 1871. But generally speaking, these men "who built up the knowledge which establishes the habits of millions of Americans, shapes their businesses, and in fact makes possible the way they live" have been ignored by the writer and the historian.[5]

That the great work being done by members of the Hayden, King, Powell, and Wheeler Surveys was going unnoticed save by scientists bothered some individuals as far back as 1874. "The invaluable results of these investigations for the most part lie hidden away in costly volumes among the archives of the govern-

[5] Bernard De Voto, *The Year of Decision: 1846,* 359.

ment in Washington," commented the New York *World*. "But it is almost a shame that no sympathetic and entertaining writer has given to the public such a book, let us say, upon the passes of the Rocky Mountains as Tyndall has given us upon the peaks of the Alps, or as Clarence King has given us upon the Sierra Nevada."[6]

In spite of the recognized need for a chronicle of their achievements, no such literary work was forthcoming. Journalists often accompanied the surveys for a field season or two—Ernest Ingersoll wrote about his adventures with Hayden, and William H. Rideing narrated a summer with Wheeler. But neither of these men ever grasped the surveys as complete entities. In this absence of a chronicler with literary talent, the Great Surveys have been for the most part forgotten, and an important story in the history of the American West has never been told.

Now, with deep humility, and ofttimes feeling the fool treading where sensible angels would not, I have attempted to resurrect the Great Surveys from their stack-area tombs where their reports lie gathering dust. From the 212-page list of their publications I have tried to choose their most notable contributions; from the ranks of their constantly fluctuating personnel I have endeavored to pull out and flash a historical spotlight upon important scientists, journalists, painters, photographers; from their known achievements I have tried to emphasize the more important as well as the more interesting of their accomplishments.

All of this should lead to a full-course intellectual dinner. We shall discover where the grasshopper which plagued the prairies was hatched; we will learn a little about Odontornithes, those hideous toothed birds that once lived in today's Wyoming. With Thomas Moran we shall paint the Grand Canyon of the Yellowstone; with William H. Jackson we shall photograph the Mount of the Holy Cross. With A. D. Wilson, Henry Gannett, James T. Gardner, and Franklin Rhoda we shall take barometric readings, sometimes in snowstorms, and we shall make careful triangulations while Indians threaten us with arrows. We shall make magnificent maps of the Rockies—maps that are expensive collector's

6 Quoted in the *Rocky Mountain News*, July 30, 1874, p. 2.

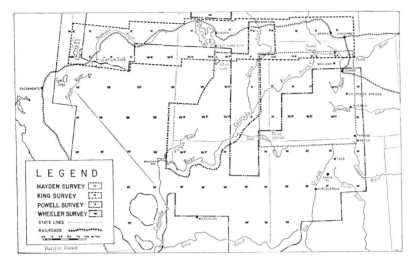

The Great Surveys of the American West

items today. We shall study birds with the seventeen-year-old ornithologist Robert Ridgway, braving the wilds with King in 1867. We shall name mountain peaks by the score, challenge the swirling waters of the Colorado with Powell, and expose the Great Diamond Hoax with King. We'll have our fill of the cantankerous army mule, and once in a while we may even find time to shoot a grizzly b'ar!

Here, then, is a humble attempt at what a Tyndall or a King or a Powell should have done eighty years ago. Here is the story of the Great Surveys of the American West.

Contents

Illustrations

GREAT SURVEYS *of the* AMERICAN WEST

Maps

PART ONE

Exploring with Hayden

I

Hayden and His Men

THE SIOUX of the Northern Plains knew him well, and they let him go about his business without molestation. Sometimes they spotted him as he trod briskly alongside a limitless buffalo herd, a telltale American raven hovering ceaselessly above him, hour after hour, giving his position away and croaking in such an ominous way as to raise the flesh at the nape of the man's neck. On other occasions some of the young braves crept up to watch him huddled by his little fire at night, his only company a yellow-eyed long-eared owl which hooted ominously nearby while coyotes and prairie wolves howled from farther off. The Sioux also spied the lone white man from afar, standing alone in the blood-red blaze of a prairie sunset, watching a red-tailed hawk hovering effortlessly over the waving sea of grass, head poised downward, nearly motionless against the sunset as it searched for prey.

Once, in the cold month of January, the solitary figure lost his course and wandered two days without food before stumbling upon a small Indian lodge. The inhabitants welcomed him as a friend and fellow sufferer and offered him some roast wildcat, for they knew he was the harmless one they had heard about around their campfires. He was the slim, bearded, white man who always carried a bag over his shoulder and a little pick in his right

3

hand and who darted from one dry run to another, climbed up buttes and escarpments, picked at the rocks, and then went hastily on. Once, a party of braves had surrounded him and dumped the contents of his bag onto the ground. It had contained nothing but rocks. So, thinking him loco, they had given him a name that meant "man-who-picks-up-stones-running" and let him go.

His real name was Ferdinand Vandeveer Hayden, M.D.

How did a young medical doctor happen to be collecting geologic specimens in the wilds of the trans-Missouri country in the 1850's? The story deserves a brief narration, for it took unusual motivation to become a scientist in the middle years of the nineteenth century. Even though science was well on its way to a sacrosanct position, and although it was considered "smart" to know about scientific theories, it was still not quite respectable for a young man to enter science as his chosen profession. If he possessed the drive and the intelligence necessary for a career in geology, or botany, or ornithology, then let him take a degree in medicine and pursue his other interests as a hobby. Any man who proposed to be a scientist entered that difficult career amidst dismal predictions from most of his advisers.

Ferdinand Vandeveer Hayden solved the problem in a most remarkable way. He was born on September 7, 1829, in Westfield, in southwestern Massachusetts, but when his father died and his mother remarried, he was sent to live with an uncle on a farm near Rochester, New York. At sixteen he began teaching, and at eighteen he enrolled at Oberlin College, in Ohio. He graduated from there in the spring of 1850, a quiet, nervous, dreamy young man who no one believed, the class historian recalled twenty years later, "would . . . conquer in practical life."[1]

Small wonder they thought this way, for Oberlin was militantly abolitionist and religiously fundamentalist; its personnel, both faculty and student, was hardly inclined toward young Hayden's interests. He found his friendships in outsiders, especially in Dr. John Newberry, a physician who was also in-

[1] Charles D. Walcott, "Ferdinand Vandeveer Hayden," U.S. Geological Survey, *Ninth Annual Report, 1887–1889*, 32.

terested in geology. From him Hayden got the idea of taking a degree in medicine, and it was through him that he met James Hall, of Albany, New York, the leading paleontologist of the time. That meeting was the turning point in Hayden's life. He entered the Albany Medical School, lived at Hall's house, and gained an education in geology and paleontology while earning the title of M.D., which was granted him in the spring of 1853.[2]

By all the customs of the day, the time had now come for Ferdinand Vandeveer Hayden, M.D., to find a likely town full of ailing people and hang out his shingle. But he was not yet twenty-four, and try as he would the love of geology remained uppermost in his mind. Then Hall asked him to spend a season making a collection of the tertiary and cretaceous fossils of the White River Bad Lands. The trip promised Indians, wild animals, and the outdoor life of an American frontiersman. This was heady wine, and Hayden promptly accepted the offer. Ailing humanity would just have to wait.

This, then, is how one young man in the mid-nineteenth century broke into a lifetime career as geologist. Hayden joined an older man, the invertebrate paleontologist Fielding Bradford Meek, and the two railroaded west to St. Louis. From there aboard the Missouri River steamer *Robert S. Campbell*, they embarked for Fort Pierre, sixteen hundred miles up the turbulent river.[3] For four weeks the river boat was their home. Life got dull, but the air one breathed from the bow was sweet and fresh and full of promise. The new grass on the prairies was growing tall and green; cottonwoods and willows waved languorously along the banks; deer, antelope, bison, jack rabbits, prairie dogs, meadow larks, hawks, and even an occasional eagle paused from concern with nature's iron law of life and death to spy on the lumbering steamboat, an ugly anomaly on the roily waters of the wide Missouri.[4]

[2] John M. Clarke, *James Hall of Albany, Geologist and Palaeontologist, 1811–1898*, 243.

[3] *Ibid.*, 246–49.

[4] The interesting details of this trip can be found in the letters from Meek to Hall, in George P. Merrill, *The First One Hundred Years of American Geology*, 699–707.

At Fort Pierre (across the river from present-day Pierre, South Dakota), the scientists assembled their gear and then, late in June, struck a route southwest by west until, after about one hundred miles, they arrived at that strange "part of Hell with the fires burned out," as General Custer described it. Millions of years ago it had been a great marsh in which living things had lived and died. Then the land had dried up, erosion had set in, peaks, pinnacles, and mesas had appeared, and finally prehistoric skeletons were exposed.[5]

There they pitched camp, slung their sacks over their shoulders, and with picks in hand eagerly sought after fossil remains. It was lonesome work in the unearthly, labyrinthine passages of the prehistoric graveyard, but each day offered exciting new finds. All too soon, Hayden thought, their little cart was full, and the time had arrived for them to turn southeastward across the prairie toward Council Bluffs, from whence they would travel by steamboat back to St. Louis. From there they would ship the invertebrate fossils to Hall and the vertebrates to a specialist in the field, Joseph Leidy, of Philadelphia.[6]

But when the time came for Hayden to entrain for the East, he tarried. The prospect of a quiet life administering opiates, delivering babies, and setting broken bones had lost whatever appeal it had ever held for him. He kept casting his eyes northward up the Missouri and westward to where the prairie and the great sky met on the horizon. He yearned for the panoramas, the blazing sun, the bluffs and buttes and river cuts out there in what later became Nebraska and the two Dakotas. He had decided that, one way or another, he would devote himself to its geographical and geological exploration.

And Hayden succeeded admirably. In 1854 and 1855, financed

[5] Today, much of the Bad Lands area is embraced by the Badlands National Monument. See *A South Dakota Guide*, 318–19.

[6] F. V. Hayden and F. B. Meek, "Notes on the Geology of the Mauvaises Terres of the White River, Nebraska," *Proceedings of the Academy of Natural Sciences of Philadelphia*, Vol. IX (June, 1857), 154–56. F. V. Hayden, "On the Geology and Natural History of the Upper Missouri," *Transactions of the American Philosophical Society*, New Series, Vol. XII (1862), 4. Merrill, *American Geology*, 35n.

by such individuals as Charles Chouteau, of the American Fur Company, and Major Vaughan, an Indian agent, and by such organizations as the St. Louis Academy of Sciences, the Academy of Natural Sciences of Philadelphia, and the Smithsonian Institution, Hayden explored the great expanse from the Missouri westward to the Rockies. Sometimes he was accompanied by an Indian guide and a packer or two; other times he worked alone, using the fur company steamboat as his base of operations.[7]

In 1856 and 1857, he accompanied young, slender Gouverneur K. Warren, a lieutenant in the Topographical Engineers, into Dakota; in 1858, the geologist and his old friend Meek explored on their own; and in 1859 and 1860, Hayden was back again with the military, this time with Captain W. F. Raynolds, Topographical Engineers, on a two year expedition to the region drained by the Yellowstone River.[8]

These were years of training and preparation for the young geologist. Year after year he pieced together parts of the geological puzzle of the vast Missouri River watershed. He learned how to handle soldiers and packers, Indians and mountain men. Cloudbursts and voracious mosquitoes, rattlers and coyotes, catamounts and grizzlies became familiar things; the vast prairies and the mountain solitudes lost whatever terror they had once held for him. According to Captain Joseph La Barge, upon whose steamboat, the *St. Mary*, Hayden and Lieutenant Warren had traveled north to the Yellowstone in 1856, the geologist during these years was "a man of rather small stature, talkative and companionable, well informed, and very energetic and

---

[7] Charles A. White, "Memoir of Ferdinand Vandeveer Hayden, 1829–1887," National Academy of Sciences, *Biographical Memoirs*, III, 399. Edward Drinker Cope, "Ferdinand Vandeveer Hayden, M.D., LLD.," *The American Geologist*, Vol. I (February, 1888), 111–12. For further mentions of Hayden in this period, see *Transactions of the Academy of Sciences of St. Louis*, Vol. I (1856–60), 17, 107.

[8] Letters from Warren to Hayden, in Merrill, *American Geology*, 711–13. G. K. Warren, "Preliminary Report of the Explorations of Nebraska and Dakota," *Annual Report of the War Department*, 35 Cong., 2 sess., Sen. Exec. Doc. 1, 627–28. W. F. Raynolds, *Report of the Exploration of the Yellowstone and Missouri Rivers, in 1859–1860*, 40 Cong., 1 sess., Sen. Doc. 77. White, "Memoir," *Biographical Memoirs*, III, 401.

eager in his work."[9] Geology and the natural sciences were his all-consuming passion, and his increasing maturity as a scientist was displayed in the growing list of articles being published by him in various scientific journals.[10]

By the autumn of 1860, Ferdinand Hayden had served his apprenticeship as scientific explorer. Even as the war clouds gathered, and he set aside his pick to devote himself to medicine for the duration of the conflict, he knew what to do next, when he was free to go West again. He wanted to explore the headwaters of the Yellowstone, for he had heard tall tales about it, but had only succeeded in reaching the fringes of that exotic region. He also desired to explore the central Rockies, for he had only covered the high plains along the Front Range south as far as Pikes Peak. And finally, he had already gained a concept of a government-financed geological survey which might, he had written, "lay before the public such full, accurate, and reliable information . . . as will bring from the older states the capital, skill, and enterprise necessary to develop the great natural resources of the country."[11]

From May, 1862, until June, 1865, Hayden was in the Union Army, ending his military career as post surgeon and surgeon in chief to the Twenty-second Division of Cavalry, and with a brevet rank of lieutenant colonel.[12] Yet so well known had he become that in 1863 the University of Rochester awarded him an honor-

[9] Hiram Martin Chittenden, *History of Early Steamboat Navigation on the Missouri River*, I, 208–10.

[10] Examples of Hayden's work in these years: "Descriptions of New Fossil Species of Mollusca Collected by Dr. F. V. Hayden in Nebraska Territory; Together with a Complete Catalogue of All the Remains of Invertebrata Hitherto Described and Identified from the Cretaceous and Tertiary Formations of that Region," *Proceedings of the Academy of Natural Sciences of Philadelphia*, Vol. VIII, No. 6 (November, 1856), 265–86; "Explorations Under the War Department," *Proceedings of the Academy of Natural Sciences of Philadelphia*, Vol. IX (May 26, 1857), 148; "Sketch of the Geology of the Country about the Headwaters of the Missouri and Yellowstone Rivers," *American Journal of Science and Arts*, Second Series, Vol. 37, No. 81 (March, 1861), 229–45.

[11] White, "Memoir," *Biographical Memoirs*, III, 401. Hayden, "On the Geology and Natural History of the Upper Missouri," *Transactions of the American Philosophical Society*. New Series, Vol. XII (1862), 59–60.

[12] Merrill, *American Geology*, 525.

ary A. M. degree, and after he left the army in 1865, he accepted an appointment as professor of mineralogy and geology on the auxiliary faculty of the Medical Department of the University of Pennsylvania, a position he kept until 1872, when his other activities made his resignation necessary.[13]

Certainly, Hayden never hung up his geologist's pick for long. The upper Missouri country beckoned him like a magnet, and in 1866, with a six-mule team and wagon and a few soldiers, guides, and helpers, he headed toward the Bad Lands again. For 52 days in the late summer and early fall they were out, covering nearly 650 miles and filling the wagon full of fossils. Special care was taken of several nearly perfect fossilized turtles.[14]

Now it was 1867. Andrew Johnson was president of the United States. The Union Pacific was pushing inexorably westward, while the Central Pacific was breaking through the high Sierras. The Indians watched the rails extending further and further into the continent: it was like a nightmare, condemning the proud red man to the status of the white man's ward. The American buffalo approached the shining rails, sniffed and snorted and pawed the earth, and then turned tail and fled. The rails split the herd, gave transportation to its killers, made its end a certainty. Down in Texas, cattle were being raised, and soon they would spread over the Great Plains, filling the vacuum left by the shaggy buffalo. In the East and in Europe, interest in the American West had never been greater, and an age that was trying desperately to be "scientific" about all things was anxious to possess scientific knowledge about the vanishing frontier. The time was propitious for experienced scientists to step in and exploit the situation. Four of them did, and Ferdinand Vandeveer Hayden was one of the four.

Hayden's opportunity to have his own survey, free of the army

[13] Correspondence with Margaret Butterfield, assistant librarian in charge of special collections, University of Rochester Library. F. V. Hayden, Letter of Resignation from Hot Springs, Yellowstone Valley, July 26, 1872, University of Pennsylvania Archives.

[14] F. V. Hayden, "Exploration of the 'Bad Lands' or 'Mauvaises Terres' of the Upper Missouri Region," *American Journal of Science and Arts,* Second Series, Vol. 42, No. 126 (November, 1866), 425.

but still well supported, came about through a combination of politics and western expansion. When Nebraska attained statehood in 1867, a small sum of money was left from what had been appropriated to defray the expenses of her territorial legislature. Congress, in a moment of generosity, had granted this unexpended sum "for the purpose of procuring a geological survey of Nebraska, said survey to be prosecuted under the direction of the Commissioner of the General Land Office."[15] Hayden applied for the position of geologist in charge just as soon as his friend Spencer Baird, secretary of the Smithsonian Institution, had alerted him that money had been set aside for the survey. Hastily, the geologist contacted Gouverneur K. Warren, General A. A. Humphreys, chief of the Army Engineers, and the paleontologist Othniel Charles Marsh to write letters in his behalf.[16] And Hayden's friend General John A. Logan, of Illinois, soon to be a powerful Republican senator in Washington, pulled all the wires his politicking fingers could reach to get Hayden into the field.[17] The pressure was sufficient, and Hayden received the position of geologist in charge of the Geological Survey of Nebraska. His letter of appointment summarized the task before him. Besides studying the geology of Nebraska, he was to search for and examine "all the beds, veins, and other deposits of ores, coals, clays, marls, peat and such other mineral substances as well as the fossil remains of the various formations," to make barometric observations, and to gather "ample collections in geology, mineralogy, and paleontology to illustrate the notes taken in the field and transmit them to this office to be embodied in its next annual report." Since Nebraska was a farming area, his examination was invited of "its soil, and subsoils and description of their adaptability to particular crops, and the best methods of preserving and increasing their fertility." Finally, since the new state was nearly treeless, he was to look into the feasibility of introducing certain forest trees there. A little later in the season he was requested to

15 *U.S. Statutes at Large*, Vol. 14, 470.

16 National Archives, R.G. 57, Hayden Survey, General Letters Received (Chronological), Vol. I, 1867–69.

17 "James Stevenson," U.S. Geological Survey, *Ninth Annual Report, 1887–1889*, 42.

submit "graphic illustrations" of striking and beautiful land-scapes for inclusion in the annual reports of the General Land Office.[18]

In essence, Hayden was requested to make a general natural history survey of Nebraska, with emphasis upon the practical aspects of such a survey—to search out the possibilities for human use and exploitation of the land. This was the concept which he kept uppermost in his mind through the years, as his organization became the biggest and best known of all the Great Surveys. But in 1867, and on through the season of 1870, the survey was a modest undertaking with little indication of its later phenomenal growth.

Its beginning was certainly modest enough. The "unexpended balance" turned out to be about $5,000, and with this Hayden was to pay himself, a professional assistant, and three collectors, as well as provide the necessary equipment and provisions for a season in the field. But the geologist was used to exploring on a tight budget, and he used every means to augment the little appropriation—horses and supplies from the quartermaster at Omaha, aid from the Smithsonian Institution, and the help of his old friend Fielding Bradford Meek, who was employed as the professional assistant.[19]

Hayden also took along with him twenty-seven-year-old James Stevenson, who had accompanied him on most of his expeditions since the first Warren exploration in 1856. Stevenson was a brown-haired, slender Kentuckian. Because of his proven ability in the field, he became Hayden's right-hand man. He was the executive officer of the Hayden Survey throughout its existence and was the first man to hold that position in the new United States Geological Survey. Quiet and reserved like the traditional frontiersman, Stevenson only spoke when necessary, and when he did speak he got action. He loved the West, and he never let his duties prevent his active participation in the explo-

[18] National Archives, R.G. 57, Hayden Survey, General Letters Received, Box 11, J. S. Wilson, commissioner of the General Land Office, to Hayden, April 29, 1867, and May 10, 1867.

[19] *Ibid.* See also *Annual Report of the Smithsonian Institution*, 40 Cong., 3 sess., *House Exec. Doc. 83*, 25.

rations. As the years went on, his interests narrowed on the field of ethnology, and in the last years of his life he concentrated on the Zuni and Hopi tribes of the Southwest, with whom he and his wife spent many summers. He was one of the few members of the Great Surveys to die as a result of his western activities. He caught the dreaded "mountain fever"—Rocky Mountain spotted fever—while out West in 1887. He never fully recovered from it, and he died the following summer. But this was twenty-one years after the first year of the survey.[20]

During the late spring and the summer of 1867, Hayden, Meek, and Stevenson concentrated on western Nebraska and Wyoming and Colorado east of the Front Range. In Nebraska, sections of artesian well borings down to four hundred feet were examined, but in no case were veins revealed of sufficient thickness to warrant their exploitation as a source of coal. Nebraskans would have to rely upon the coal from the Laramie beds along the Union Pacific or upon the lignite from south Boulder in Colorado. When Hayden discovered that there were iron ore deposits in the region near the lignite, he predicted that since the one could smelt the other, they could "exert the same kind of influence over the progress of the great west that Pennsylvania exerts over all the contiguous states."[21]

Such glowing predictions became the trade-mark of Hayden's reports, and they furnish a key to his popularity among the western people. They loved to hear just such rosy predictions. Whether they were based upon sound judgment or thorough research did not really matter. In the frontiersman's mind there was

[20] "James Stevenson," U.S. Geological Survey, *Ninth Annual Report, 1887–1889*, 42. "James Stevenson," *American Anthropologist*, New Series, Vol. XVIII (1916), 552–59.

[21] F. V. Hayden, "Notes on the Lignite Deposits of the West," *American Journal of Science and Arts*, Second Series, Vol. 45, No. 134 (March, 1868), 204. See also F. B. Meek, "Remarks of Prof. Geimitz's Views Respecting the Upper Paleozoic Rocks and Fossils of Southeastern Nebraska," *American Journal of Science and Arts*, Vol. 44, No. 132 (November, 1867), 327; and the official report, *First, Second, and Third Annual Reports of the United States Geological Survey of the Territories for the Years 1867, 1868, 1869, Under the Department of the Interior*, 9–15. In 1871, Hayden published the completed *Final Report of the United States Geological Survey of Nebraska and Portions of the Adjacent Territories*, 42 Cong., 1 sess., *House Exec. Doc. 19.*

always a great day coming, and any scientist who confirmed that opinion would meet with consistent support. (And in the economic history of Colorado and Wyoming both the coal and the iron deposits did enrich the inhabitants.)

The results of the first season of the Hayden Survey were small indeed. They consisted for the most part of the sixty-four-page *First Annual Report* and a few articles. Yet the *Report* fulfilled his official obligations and was well received. Armed with it, Hayden began his secondary role in the story of his survey—his activities as a lobbyist. In the spring and early summer of 1868, he worked on key congressmen and senators for another $5,000 for the continuance of his scientific activities in the West. When the Sundry Civil Expense Act was passed on July 20, 1868, the pertinent clause was still there intact, the survey was continued as a general survey of all the territories, and Hayden's first adventure into lobbying was a complete success.[22]

This time Hayden planned to begin operations along the Union Pacific near where he had stopped the year before, pushing on westward to Fort Bridger, then backtracking and working south again along Colorado's Front Range. His survey, he informed the commissioner of the General Land Office, would also investigate prospects for grazing and agriculture and would assemble much technical data obtained from railway engineers, ranchers, and miners.[23] As it was thus proposed, it would publish material that would be of immediate usefulness to settlers and businessmen. Hayden ardently believed in this pragmatic approach to his scientific work, and this trait separated him considerably from the more purely scientific approaches of his rival scientists in the field.

Actually, Hayden was still restricted in his activities, for the $5,000 was hardly enough to launch an ambitious program. He entrained for the West, having gathered together a party of nine, plus four riding animals, a two-horse ambulance, a four-mule covered wagon, three tents, and other necessary camp equipage,

[22] *U.S. Statutes at Large*, Vol. 15, 119.
[23] National Archives, R.G. 57, Hayden Survey, General Letters Received, Hayden to Wilson, July 9, 1868, Wilson to Hayden, July 28, 1868.

and clattered westward along the line of the Union Pacific.[24] He knew that the civilized East was watching the progress of the Great Transcontinental with avid interest, and so he capitalized on it.

His most interesting explorations of the season were several side trips from his main line of march. In company with Major General John Gibbon, commander of the Rocky Mountain District, and the irascible New York paleontologist, James Hall, he explored the "Last Chance" diggings in the Snowy Mountains southwest of Laramie. The value of the mines was questionable, but the beauty of the land was a certainty. The timberline meadows were covered with light-green grasses and delicately colored, fragile flowers. Wild strawberries grew in abundance, and little streams of sparkling snow water started on their way to the sea. Range after range of mountains were in view, interspersed with idyllic parklands. All of this was unknown and unexplored from a scientific point of view. Before he left, Hayden vowed to return to these mountains.

But for the present he went to Fort Sanders, south of Laramie, through pine forests where the staccato chop of the woodsman's ax and the buzz of his saw warned of the foolish exploitation of America's natural resources. Men were cutting ties for the Union Pacific, concentrating on the stately spruce trees, which made the best ties, but using the pine trees too, floating them down the Big and Little Laramie, Rock Creek, and the Medicine Bow. One man alone was reported to have held a contract for 550,000 ties, which he was floating down from the mountains at a cost of one to three cents per tie. A perfect place, thought Hayden, "for a peculiar class of people, like the lumbermen of Maine and Michigan."[25]

Hardly had he returned to Fort Sanders before the opportunity arose to plunge into the wilderness again. General Francis Preston Blair, Democratic candidate for vice-president in 1868, and General G. M. Dodge, chief engineer of the Union Pacific,

24 F. V. Hayden, "Geological Explorations in Wyoming Territory," *Second Annual Report*, 76.
25 *Ibid.*, 83.

were organizing a hunting party to go into Colorado's North Park, and Hayden was invited along. Accompanied by another officer or two and a few packers and camp men, the party started southward up the Big Laramie River until they hit the obscure, overgrown Old Cherokee Trail. This they followed westward for twenty-five miles into North Park.[26]

It was past the middle of August when they reached the park, and autumn was already in the air. The party gazed down from the high mountains into an oval about thirty miles wide by forty miles long, with a rather rugged surface but with broad bottoms along the streams. Scarcely a tree dotted the park, although the timber was thick in the surrounding mountains. Grass grew abundantly, and, Hayden wrote, "myriads of antelope were quietly feeding in this great pasture-ground like flocks of sheep."[27]

The temptation to stay on in North Park was great, but with proper diligence Hayden returned to the main line of the Union Pacific. By September 25, he was able to report that he had covered the land as far west as Fort Bridger and had collected a sizable quantity of fossils which impressed both James Hall and Louis Agassiz, who was working with Hall that summer.[28]

Anxiously, for the season was late, Hayden turned southward. Before he returned East he had obligations to fulfill that hinged on a successful exploration in Colorado. For one thing, he had obtained aid for this part of his work from the Smithsonian Institution, and it expected him to produce specimens for its collections.[29] Hayden had also committed himself to an English entrepreneur, William Blackmore, whose extensive land holdings in the Sangre de Cristo grant in the mountain and park country

[26] *Ibid.*, 84–87. The Old Cherokee Trail was cut by a party of Cherokees who came through in 1848 on their way to California. Ansel Watrous, *History of Larimer County, Colorado,* 109–10.

[27] Hayden, "Geological Explorations in Wyoming Territory," *Second Annual Report,* 87. North Park became a ranching region and is the state's main source of wild hay. *Colorado: A Guide to the the Highest State,* 215.

[28] Hayden, "Geological Explorations in Wyoming Territory," *Second Annual Report,* 88.

[29] *Annual Report of the Smithsonian Institution,* 40 Cong., 3 sess., Departmental Edition, 25.

of southern Colorado and northern New Mexico justified the expense of a general survey of the area. This survey, which Hayden had agreed to conduct, was to be made immediately.[30]

So the geologist advanced southward rapidly, re-examining coal deposits on the way. He collected the necessary specimens for the Smithsonian and in October felt free to do the work for Blackmore. Four days' ride southwest from Denver brought him to Fort Garland, a remote but strikingly situated army post in the San Luis Valley. From here he conducted his investigations. Hayden's report, written in New York the following December, was highly exaggerated in its statements about minerals, climate, roads, and farming opportunities. He predicted fantastic profits. "It is believed," he wrote for Blackmore, "that sheep will yield an annual income of 90 per cent; cattle 50 to 60 per cent."[31]

With this obligation fulfilled, Hayden returned East and submitted a brief, thirty-five-page preliminary report. It was of negligible quality, but combined with his lobbying activities it was sufficient to carry the issue with Congress. The appropriation for 1869, $10,000, was double that of each of the preceding two years. The survey was taken out of the hands of the commissioner of the General Land Office and placed directly under the authority of the secretary of the interior. It also acquired a formal title: "The United States Geological Survey of the Territories." The Hayden Survey was showing its first signs of growth.[32]

In 1869, Hayden began employing several other professional men to accompany him and to submit their own reports. This was the first year in which he had the money to pay for such men. He hired six professional assistants as well as three teamsters, a cook, and a general laborer.[33] Since in its twelve years

[30] Herbert O. Brayer, *William Blackmore: A Case Study in the Economic Development of the West*, I, 73, 196–97.

[31] *Ibid.*, I, 74. That Blackmore was pleased and wished for more help is apparent from the Blackmore-Hayden correspondence in the National Archives, R.G. 57, Hayden Survey, General Letters Received. But Hayden never again worked for Blackmore, although the two men often explored the Rockies together and remained friends until Blackmore's death.

[32] *U.S. Statutes at Large*, Vol. 15, 306.

[33] F. V. Hayden, "Letter to the Secretary," *Third Annual Report*, 105.

the Hayden Survey employed well over two hundred men, ranging from cooks and packers through journalists and artists to
experts in paleontology and entomology, it is of course impossible to mention very many of them. But Hayden's choices in 1869
give us some insight into the quality of men he tried to hire.

For the artist of the survey, he chose twenty-three-year-old
Henry W. Elliott, the private secretary to Professor Joseph
Henry of the Smithsonian Institution. For three successive seasons he accompanied Hayden, drawing sketches of terrain and
sections of geologic formations, and in 1871 he made a circuit
of Yellowstone Lake, sketching the entire shore line.[34] In later
years Elliott became a leading expert on the fur seal industry of
Alaska, finally drawing up the fur seal treaty ratified in 1911 by
Japan, Russia, Canada, and the United States.[35] His sketches,
which provide the illustrations for the 1870 and 1871 reports of
the survey, are acceptable even if not artistically outstanding.
Considering the low pay and the rigorous life demanded of survey members in the field, Elliott was a good choice.

Another of Hayden's appointees was Cyrus Thomas, ethnologist, botanist, agriculturalist, and anthropologist. He had
grown up in the trans-Allegheny region, and fundamentalist,
antebellum Tennessee was hardly friendly ground for a precocious lad whose greatest interest was in insects. "His early years
of constant warfare against intellectual indifference and opposition developed a strongly marked argumentative tendency,"
wrote one of his biographers, "but those who knew him best were
aware that it concealed a kindly disposition."[36]

He had attended the village school and the academy at Jones-
boro, Tennessee, and had then gone up to Illinois and practiced
law. But natural history was always his first love, and he was

[34] *The Biographical Dictionary of America* (ed. by Rossiter Johnson), III.
F. V. Hayden, "Letter to the Secretary," [*Fifth Annual*] *Preliminary Report of
the United States Geological Survey of Montana and Portions of Adjacent Territories; Being a Fifth Annual Report of Progress* (hereafter cited as *Fifth Annual
Report*), 5.
[35] New York *Times*, May 22, 1930, p. 29.
[36] "Cyrus Thomas," *American Anthropologist*, New Series, Vol. XII (April–
June, 1910), 337–43.

the principal founder in 1858 of the Illinois Natural History Society. His reputation earned for him the appointment in 1869 (when he was forty-four years old) of entomologist and botanist for Hayden. During the four years in which he was with the survey, he championed its cause with verve and became a mainstay of the entire organization.

In later years—while he was a professor of natural history at Southern Illinois Normal, the state entomologist, a member of the United States Entomological Commission (which tried to cope with the grasshopper plagues), or a member of the Bureau of American Ethnology—he remained a stalwart defender of the Hayden Survey. Still, it is true that he became a difficult old cuss who occasionally wrote most unscientifically about scientific matters. Defender of the survey that he was, he may have earned it more enemies than friends.[37]

Hayden's choice as mining engineer and metallurgist was Percifor Frazer, Jr. He was a bright young man of twenty-five, a scientist's son who had been through the Civil War and had completed his education at the Royal Saxon School of Mines at Freiburg, Germany. With Hayden, he did good work, writing a competent technical report, "Mines and Minerals of Colorado."[38] In 1870, he was appointed instructor in natural philosophy and chemistry at the University of Pennsylvania and succeeded his father as the head of the department in 1872.[39]

The other two professional men, not including James Stevenson, were E. Campbell Carrington, Jr., zoologist, and B. H. Cheever, general assistant, neither of whom are as well known. Still we have positive evidence that four of the six men hired in 1869 were men who in their future careers proved to be above average.

This is not to say that all appointments in all categories were good. In the survey's twelve years, there were a few poor scientists. There were also good packers, like Steve Hovey and Shep Madera, and poor ones; good cooks, like "Potato John" Raymond,

[37] *Ibid.* See also *Dictionary of American Biography* (ed. by Allen Johnson), XVII, 426.

[38] *Third Annual Report*, 201–28.

[39] *Dictionary of American Biography*, VII, 4–5.

and poor ones. There were a few congressmen's sons, like W. S. Holman, Jr., son of William S. Holman, of Indiana, and the young son of Congressman John P. C. Shanks, of the same state. In at least one season, 1874, there was J. S. Delano, son of the secretary of the interior, Columbus Delano. But the number of these political appointees was small compared to the total personnel of the survey, and the common criticism leveled against Hayden, that he packed his organization with congressmen's sons, was simply not true.

In 1869, Hayden continued his policy of using army supplies, usually obtained at Fort D. A. Russell, in Wyoming. There he picked up wagons (often an old army ambulance gave admirable service), pack supplies, blankets, cooking utensils, and nearly everything else that was necessary for a season in the West. Most important of all, he obtained all the mounts he needed. The survey used some castoff army horses, but the men preferred the sure-footed army mule, even if the critter had been rejected and put out to pasture. Cantankerous, full of the devil, unpredictable, quarrelsome, and kicking hell-for-leather toward the sky, those army seconds served the Hayden Survey throughout all its operations.

Having enlisted his personnel and outfitted his party from army stores, Hayden, in 1869, set out to make a geological survey of Colorado and New Mexico. His entire party consisted of about a dozen men, eighteen mules and horses, two large covered wagons, and an ambulance. It was already well into summer—June 29, 1869—when the little expedition left Fort D. A. Russell and headed south.[40]

But this only spurred on the nervous, intense man with the geologist's pick and specimen bag. It was in his very nature to advance rapidly and let someone else come along later to make a slower, more methodical examination. Hayden knew that there was more than a lifetime of geological exploration to be done in the Great West, but he proposed to accomplish his full share —and then some—if at all possible. As more meticulous scientists came along in the 1870's, his methods were subjected to severe

[40] F. V. Hayden, "Geological Report," *Third Annual Report*, 115.

criticism. Yet Hayden was simply of the old school that had found a virgin wilderness waiting to be scientifically examined. To him, in a geological way, the West was like Christmas every day that he was in the field, with new and fascinating formations ever appearing along his path. Hayden dealt with the big questions and left the finer points to his successors.

Such an approach to his work led him naturally to a reportorial style in describing his explorations. By 1869, he had formed his technique, and he used the same "slant" for the next decade. Hayden took his readers on an annual geological "Cook's Tour" of the territories, never tarrying anywhere for long, but commenting briefly, posing problems, admitting controversial questions, then hastily moving on again.

Thus in the *Third Annual Report* the reader follows Hayden's explorations in itinerary style, the chapter headings indicating the route: "From Cheyenne to Denver," "From Santa Fe to Taos," and so on, until after about 90 pages a round trip has been completed. Then it is early October, the supplies are being stored for the winter at Fort D. A. Russell, and the season is over. With Percifor Frazer's "Mines and Minerals of Colorado" and Cyrus Thomas' "Agriculture in Colorado," the finished *Report* added up to 146 pages.[41]

The results of Hayden's reportorial techniques were not brilliant. Because he covered so much ground, he could always lay claim to many discoveries which he had briefly mentioned in passing. Superficially, he geologized to the horizon. He worked with a telescope instead of with a microscope. He worked so rapidly and published so quickly that shoddiness became the hallmark of his reports. Save to a geologist, most of his writings are a bore. They are pedestrian, dull, poorly organized, and inaccurate in details—even though on questions of geology Hayden was often correct in his conclusions.

---

[41] Impressive fossil and geologic collections, along with dried and otherwise preserved birds, animals, plants, and insects, were sent to the Smithsonian. *Annual Report of the Smithsonian Institution,* 41 Cong., 3 sess., *House Exec. Doc. 153,* 30.

As would be expected, he published the reports of others without making careful study of them, so that unscientific statements, poor organization, and errors in judgment often appeared. A case in point in 1869 was Cyrus Thomas' monograph on agriculture. One error in it was used as "Exhibit A" in criticism of the entire Hayden Survey in the years to come.

The erroneous statements concerned the question of rainfall. As Thomas traveled from the Cache la Poudre in northern Colorado southward along the base of the Front Range to Las Vegas, New Mexico, he found evidence everywhere of more water than man in that region had ever before seen. The Poudre had been sending down more water; Cherry Creek, in Denver, which had been so dry that shacks had been built along its sandy bed, had carried off the shacks in a flood; and the Arkansas was more swollen than ever before. For six to seven years prior to 1869, there had been a gradual increase in rainfall. Thomas had just been witness to the most bountiful harvest in the white man's history in those parts. "It is a common expression of the Mexicans," he commented, "that the Americans bring rain with them."

The good Reverend (for he was an ordained Lutheran minister) then explained that since the coming of the rain coincided with the coming of civilization, it was his "firm conviction . . . that it is in some way connected with the settlement of the country; and that, as the population increases, the amount of moisture will increase. . . . This is the plan [he wrote] which nature herself has pointed out. The perpetual snows of the great central axis are the sources of the various streams which rush down upon the margin of these plains, but chiefly sink in their effort to cross it. Let the population gather around the points where these burst from the mountains, and as it increases pushing out on the plains eastward, I believe the supply of water will accompany it."[42]

Although Thomas submitted this argument merely as a theory, he should have known better. The belief that "rain follows the plow" was common throughout the West at the time, but as a

[42] Cyrus Thomas, "Agriculture in Colorado," *Third Annual Report*, 236–37.

21

competent scientist Thomas should never have allowed himself to become a victim of it. Nor is Hayden above reproach, for he allowed the report to be published with the popular theory intact. A few years later, when the climatic cycle changed, there were some agonizing reappraisals.[43]

If Hayden was aware of these weaknesses caused by haste and bad judgment, he never admitted it. On the contrary, he was proud of his achievements, and he emphasized the practical value of his reports. Testifying before a congressional committee in 1874, he boasted that within three weeks of the time the *Third Annual Report* was published, the eight thousand copies ordered printed were so much in demand that he "was unable to procure a copy." He also gave his survey the credit for the construction of the Denver and Rio Grande Railroad which, he said, "was started by friends of mine who say, to this day, that they were stimulated to that enterprise by the report which was the result of that expedition."[44] He also insisted that his organization was partly responsible for stimulating the settlement of Colorado, which began to grow so rapidly that the 1870's have been called Colorado's "Boom Decade."[45]

By 1870, Hayden was well entrenched both in the West and in Washington. He loved his work, was proud of his survey, and was becoming adept at wringing money from tight-fisted congressmen, for if the Congress of the early 1870's was quick to dispense gifts to robber barons, it was still reluctant to appropriate money in the interests of science. Yet by his sincerity, by the respect he commanded merely by being a scientist in a world otherwise dedicated to the acquisition of material wealth, he won his way with Congress, season after season. In 1870, he obtained $25,000, this time for a survey of Wyoming and adjacent territories.[46]

[43] For an exhaustive study of this theory, see Henry Nash Smith, "Rain Follows the Plow: The Notion of Increased Rainfall for the Great Plains," *Huntington Library Quarterly*, Vol. X, No. 2 (February, 1947), 169–94.

[44] *Geographical and Geological Surveys West of the Mississippi River*, 43 Cong., 1 sess., *House Report 612*, 31.

[45] S. D. Mock, "The Effects of the 'Boom Decade,' 1870–1880, Upon Colorado Population," *Colorado Magazine*, Vol. XI, No. 1 (January, 1934), 31.

[46] *U.S. Statutes at Large*, Vol. 16, 306.

In Wyoming, old trappers said that there were just two seasons—winter and the Fourth of July. Hayden knew this was an exaggeration, but still he had to work fast if he was to accomplish $25,000 worth of exploring before the snow fell, for it was already late in July. Hastily, he entrained for the West.

On the way he stopped off at Omaha, walked over to the corner of Douglas and Fifteenth streets, and entered the business establishment of Jackson Brothers, Photographers. Hayden had met young William Henry Jackson out on the Union Pacific the previous summer, and the fellow's contraptions had started the geologist thinking. Photography, especially stereoptican photography, could show people what the West really looked like and could be used for lobbying purposes too. Now, in 1870, Hayden had the money to hire a photographer, and he was quite sure that Jackson was the perfect man for the job. *If* he could be persuaded to undertake it.

Jackson was twenty-seven years old when Hayden approached him, and he already knew the West well. An easy-going, pleasant man, young William had already been through a lifetime's stock of adventure. Born at Keeseville, New York, in 1843, he had grown up in a rural atmosphere and had early displayed ability in painting and sketching. In his late teens his artistic flair had won for him employment as a photographer's artist, first at Troy, New York, and later at Rutland, Vermont. Although his task was primarily that of a touch-up artist, it was in these jobs that Jackson first became acquainted with photography.

Then came the war. In August, 1862, he joined Company "K" of the Twelfth Vermont Volunteers, attracted a colonel's attention for his sketching ability, and held a virtual carte blanche as an artist until he was honorably discharged in 1864. Months later, when still only twenty-three years old, he had a senseless argument with his sweetheart, and with the impetuousness of youth he packed up and went West to forget it all.

His adventures in 1866 and 1867 were most unusual. How he worked his way, first as a novice bullwhacker to Salt Lake, then with a wagon train to Los Angeles, then eastward again herding a band of 150 wild horses to Julesburg, Colorado Territory, is a narration delightfully told in his autobiography, *Time Exposure,* and in his diaries.[47]

Jackson and his brother had finally set up shop in Omaha, and while his young wife Mollie and brother Ed looked after the studio, Jackson followed the shining rails of the Union Pacific. He took scenic views of the Weber Canyon, the Wasatch Mountains—and a few portraits in Cheyenne of Madame Cleveland's painted ladies. It was while photographing scenes along the railroad that Jackson met Hayden, and now, on July 23, 1870, the results of this chance meeting the previous summer bore fruit.

> He spent a long time studying my Union Pacific pictures and the Indian groups I had photographed near Omaha [Jackson later wrote]. Then, with a sigh, he remarked, "This is what I need. I wish I could offer you enough to make it worth your while to spend the summer with me."
>
> "What *could* you offer," I asked quickly.
>
> Dr. Hayden smiled and shook his head.
>
> "Only a summer of hard work—and the satisfaction I think you would find in contributing your art to science. Of course, all your expenses would be paid, but . . ."
>
> At that moment my wife walked into the reception room. . . .
>
> "Dr. Hayden has just been outlining his plans for Wyoming," I explained, introducing him.
>
> "And telling your husband how much I would like to take him with me, Mrs. Jackson," he said emphatically.
>
> Mollie looked at Dr. Hayden for a moment, then at me. Then she laughed—and I knew that everything, so far as she was concerned, was arranged.[48]

Thus did Hayden add to his entourage the best photographer in the West. Jackson shared in all the glories that came to the survey and lived to be honored and respected for achievements in the realms of American photography and art. His was a long and active life. Finally one evening in 1942 he put down his

[47] LeRoy and Ann W. Hafen, *The Diaries of William Henry Jackson.* Details of Jackson's life up to his employment with Hayden are taken from *Time Exposure* and this book.

[48] Jackson, *Time Exposure,* 187–88.

pallet and went about his normal evening's activities, retired, and quietly died in his sleep—ninety-nine years old.

Besides Jackson, Hayden had Stevenson, Elliott, and Cyrus Thomas along as usual, plus several other professional and camp men. The party numbered twenty in all. Along as a guest was the distinguished landscape painter, Sanford Robinson Gifford, who had come west with another party but had left it in favor of a season with Hayden. Gifford was of the Hudson River school; he painted a wide range of subjects, making his sketches in the field and then, months later in the privacy of his studio, using them as models for his completed works. However, of his 734 paintings that have been listed, none of the outstanding ones were based upon his trip west with Hayden in 1870.[49]

On August 6, the Hayden Survey left Camp Carlin, the quartermaster depot, for Fort D. A. Russell. It was well outfitted for a two-month tour, with four heavy wagons for food, tents, and other camp paraphernalia, and two army ambulances for use on side trips. Army "seconds" carried the men. Jackson recalled their mess outfit as being absolutely superb, and he gave considerable credit for the success of the expedition to the cook, six-foot, four-inch "Potato John" Raymond. This leathery old camp man had earned his sobriquet by vainly attempting to boil potatoes to a palatable softness at an altitude of 12,000 feet—something nearly impossible to do.

The party proposed to work a belt of country north of the Union Pacific by way of the North Platte River, Red Buttes, the Sweetwater River, South Pass, and on southwest to Fort Bridger. On their return east they planned to work south of the railroad, exploring Henry's Fork and part of Green River, even going down into Brown's Park, then east again via Bitter Creek, Bridger's Pass, the Medicine Bow Mountains, and on to Cheyenne.[50]

Potato John and the camp men clattered along the trail with

[49] Virgil Baker, *American Painting: History and Interpretation*, 436. Edgar P. Robinson, *Painting in America: The Story of 450 Years*, 227.

[50] F. V. Hayden, "Report of F. V. Hayden," [*Fourth Annual*] *Preliminary Report of the United States Geological Survey of Wyoming and Portions of Contiguous Territories, (Being a Second Annual Report of Progress)* (hereafter cited as *Fourth Annual Report*), 81.

the wagons while the professional men digressed north and south, now a mile or two, now several miles, or even several days, from the provision wagons. "For every mile on the map," Jackson commented, "we covered between two and three on the ground—up mountainsides, down stream beds, across country—to gather rock specimens, to survey and map, and to paint and photograph."[51]

As they went along, Hayden recorded everything that seemed to him worth mentioning, not only about geology, but about the flora and fauna, and even the beauty of the country. One evening, he remembered, the sun had set directly behind the summit of Laramie Peak, creating a halo of gold, and "the whole range was gilded with a golden light, and the haziness of the atmosphere gave to the whole scene a deeper beauty." Later they camped at Independence Rock, the great landmark for the Oregonians and the forty-niners; then they explored down the Sweetwater River that flowed along with a "low, gentle murmur . . . a soothing music not common to mountain streams." Climbing to the summit of the Sweetwater Range they could see, in the lonely, lonely country "far to the westward . . . the Wind River range, and feel the cool breeze, ladened with the icy chill from the snow-clad summits."

On September 1, they were at Fort Stambaugh, about three miles from the mining community of Atlantic City and not many miles east of South Pass. From there, Hayden and most of the professional men made a short trip to the Wind River Mountains, rising darkly and threateningly in the distance.

We made our camp [wrote Hayden] at night near the foot of Fremont's Peak, by the side of a spring of the purest crystal water, surrounded with a thick growth of fresh green grass, that gave a manifest delight to our animals. We were on the Pacific slope, and as the waters of the little spring passed by us, within a few feet of our camp-fire, in the stillness of the night, we imagined we could hear in its rippling music the faint echo of the great ocean to which it was hastening. Among the numerous plants which grew here,

[51] Jackson, *Time Exposure*, 189.

many of them with handsome flowers, I was attracted by the great abundance of a species of trifolium, with a white blossom, about the size of our domestic red clover of the States. There was also a large species of allium which I have not observed before in the West.[52]

One of the very busiest of the Hayden men was William Henry Jackson. Everywhere there were things for him to photograph—Indians, mountains, and geologic formations. Fortunately for him, his photographic work along the Union Pacific in 1869 had prepared him well for his work with Hayden. In 1870, he was assigned an army ambulance, and he happily deposited 300 pounds of equipment in it. This included a portable dark room of Jackson's own design—a wooden box 30x6½x8½ inches, fitted with pans and trays and a canopy. His cameras were a double-barreled stereo and a 6½x8½-inch wet-plate outfit. He carried 400 glass plates. When the terrain got too rough for the ambulance, Jackson used a fat little mule with cropped ears which the photographer had promptly dubbed Hypo. "Carrying my cameras, tripod, dark box, chemicals, water keg, and a day's supply of plates, all loaded in big, brightly painted rawhide containers called parfleches, Hypo was good for as many miles as my horse was, and together we covered an enormous amount of ground off the road from the wagon party," Jackson reminisced.[53]

By September 12, they were at Fort Bridger, the western terminus of their explorations. With this little outpost of civilization as a base, Hayden made explorations into the east-west-running Uinta Mountains, up to the sources of the Muddy and Bear rivers in the heart of the range, where the aspen groves were colored with autumn's melancholia. On still another trip they marched south about thirty miles to the place where Henry's Fork emerges from the Uintas. It was the first week of October, and the crisp frosts of mid-autumn spurred the men into vigorous activity. They worked upstream toward Gilbert's Peak, the highest point in the Uintas, and then climbed it. Hayden found the as-

[52] Hayden, "Report of F. V. Hayden," *Fourth Annual Report*, 37.
[53] Jackson, *Time Exposure*, 191.

cent well worth the effort. "From this high elevation," he wrote, "with such a vast area of country within our range of vision, one could glance back into the abyss of time, and trace, step by step, the origin and slow erosion of these wonderful, gorge-like valleys, one thousand to twelve hundred feet deep, and speculate upon the beginning and growth of this beautiful mountain itself."[54]

They followed Henry's Fork down to its junction with Green River, then followed the Green down through canyons twelve to fifteen hundred feet deep to Brown's Hole. This spot, five miles wide and thirty miles long, and well protected from the elements, was filled with some twenty-two hundred Texas cattle being wintered there before being driven on to California. From Brown's Hole the Hayden party turned northward to Green River Station on the Union Pacific then worked eastward as planned toward Cheyenne, where they arrived November 1. For two more months field work continued until they entrained for Washington. There, where offices were provided, they completed their season's work and turned over sixty boxes of fossils and specimens to the Smithsonian Institution.[55]

Most of the extra money that Hayden had at his disposal that year went into the *Fourth Annual Report*, which increased in size from the pamphlet it had been in previous years to a substantial volume of 511 pages. His own contribution comprised about two-fifths of the total; the rest of the material reflected Hayden's policy of including reports by leading scientists. In later years he expanded this policy until tremendous tomes, separate volumes unto themselves, were issued under the imprint of the Hayden Survey.

Often as not, the authors of these works had never even been in the field with Hayden, nor did they receive any pay. Quite likely, however, collections of flora and fauna, or of fossils and geologic specimens, were temporarily turned over to them for study and classification, in exchange for the rights of publica-

[54] Hayden, "Report of F. V. Hayden," *Fourth Annual Report*, 57.

[55] *Ibid.*, 180. *Annual Report of the Smithsonian Institution*, 42 Cong., 1 sess., *House Exec. Doc. 20*, 29.

tion by the Survey. In this way—and much to the chagrin of his opponents—Hayden added the names of leading scientists to his survey roster.[56]

Hayden's line of reasoning in including these monographs and listings of flora and fauna was clear and defensible. Of what use to man was, say, a listing of carboniferous fishes if the report on them lay gathering dust on a shelf in a paleontologist's study? The report *must* be published, so that for centuries to come it might serve as one of the foundation stones of man's knowledge of the geologic past. But publication had always been a problem; even a paper published by a little natural history society could easily be lost. So why not publish information in government reports? *There* was a method of achieving wide-spread dissemination. "Without this technical work," Hayden testified to a congressional committee in 1874, "we could not have the popular information descending down into the school-books—just as a watch, which is of such importance to us, is the result of hundreds of years of brainwork, and of the most abstruse astronomical calculations."[57]

The *Fourth Annual Report* contained a monograph by Cyrus Thomas on agriculture, along with a list and description of orthoptera, especially the hated grasshopper of the Great Plains. It also included nine special reports on various scientific or economic aspects of the West. These included a paleontological report by Fielding Bradford Meek and a report about some vertebrate fossils by Joseph Leidy. In addition, three important newcomers to the Hayden Survey made contributions. These men were giants in their fields, and their influence, adverse or beneficial, became important in the history of the Hayden Survey.

The first of these men was John S. Newberry, the medical-doctor-turned-geologist who had been Hayden's friend of Oberlin days. In the mid-1850's, Newberry had thrown in his fortunes with the Topographical Engineers, being employed as surgeon

[56] For criticism of this policy, see A. Hunter Dupree, *Science in the Federal Government*, 198.

[57] *Geographical and Geological Surveys West of the Mississippi River*, 43 Cong., 1 sess., *House Report 612*, 37.

and naturalist, first by Lieutenant Wilkinson, who surveyed a railroad route from California to Oregon, and then by Lieutenant Ives on his expedition from the mouth of the Colorado up as far as a steamboat could go. Newberry did not like the life much —he found it terribly monotonous, and he hated the food and the sand that permeated everything on the Colorado—but he loved the geological exploration. Later he accompanied Captain Macomb into western Colorado, and after the Civil War he settled down as a professor in the School of Mines at Columbia University.[58]

The second newcomer to the Hayden Survey was the paleo-botanist Leo Lesquereux. This gentle, compassionate little man "with inexhaustible powers of life" became known as "the Nestor of American paleobotanists." Lesquereux was a Swiss, one of the trio of scientists, including Louis Agassiz and Arnold Guyot, who left Switzerland during the revolutionary years of 1846–48 for the promise of America. Europe lost and America gained from this migration.

Lesquereux settled in Columbus, Ohio, where his family opened a jewelry store and where Leo continued his work as paleobotanist and bryologist (an expert on mosses). He was closely associated until the early 1870's with two well-known American botanists, William Starling Sullivant and Asa Gray. His reputation grew rapidly, centering upon his great knowledge of fossil plants and coal measures. In a nineteenth-century world in which coal for steam power was as important to society as uranium or petroleum is today, Lesquereux's contributions were significant.[59]

Lesquereux had patience and sympathy with the layman, and in one of his papers for Hayden he explained his work and its

[58] Merrill, *American Geology*, 363–65, 684. Newberry's monograph was: "The Ancient Lakes of Western America: Their Deposits and Drainage," *Fourth Annual Report*, 329–39.

[59] The best biography of Lesquereux is in Andrew Denny Rodgers III, *"Noble Fellow": William Starling Sullivant*, 191–204. See also the Editor's Preface to Leo Lesquereux, "The Flora of the Dakota Group," U.S. Geological Survey, *Monographs*, XVII, 15–17.

importance clearly, lucidly, and uncondescendingly: Since "vegetation is in absolute relation with atmospheric circumstances, the fossil plants are, indeed, the written records of the atmospheric and physical conditions of our earth at the epochs they represent." Thus from the fossil record of the Middle Devonian he was able to describe the landscape: "A black muddy surface covered with an atmosphere darkened by vapors, where nothing is distinguishable, but perhaps at wide intervals, a group of some trees emerging from the muddy bottom and breaking the universal gloom. No trace of animal life appears above the waters. All is dismal and silent." But later, he went on to explain, vegetable life predominated, with immense forests, thick swamps, and a tangle of greenery almost inconceivable. These absorbed the atmospheric humidity, the carbonic acid, cleaned the atmosphere, and prepared it for animal life, and from them the great coal beds were formed.[60]

Only after suitable explanation did Lesquereux begin his cataloging of fossilized plants. Here he reigned as supreme authority. This was his work, his world. Living in a foreign land, speaking a new language mastered after he was deaf (so that he was always quite inarticulate in English), he pursued his work in the silence of his study. Most of his colleagues knew him by his correspondence—page after page of small, neat, detailed script. His work for Hayden extended throughout the history of the survey and included several large volumes of detailed classifications of geologic flora. "I have lived with nature," Lesquereux once wrote, "the rocks, the trees, the flowers. They know me, I know them. All outside are dead to me."[61]

The third newcomer, who was honored with three reports on vertebrates in the *Fourth Annual Report,* was Professor Edward Drinker Cope. He was one of a triumvirate of great nineteenth-century vertebrate paleontologists, the other two of whom were

[60] Leo Lesquereux, "On the Fossil Plants of the Cretaceous and Tertiary Formations of Kansas and Nebraska," *Fourth Annual Report,* 373–74.

[61] Letter quoted in Editor's Preface, Lesquereux, "The Flora of the Dakota Group," U.S. Geological Survey, *Monographs,* XVII, 15.

Joseph Leidy and Othniel Charles Marsh. Cope, who worked rapidly and produced an amazing quantity of material, appeared continually in the Hayden publications, one of his volumes alone running to over one thousand pages.

He was born in 1840 of a prominent, well-to-do Philadelphia Quaker family. He grew up amidst nature, books, and the religion of the Friends. "I have been at a Museum," he wrote, at the age of six, to his grandmother, "and I saw a Mammoth and Hydrarchas, does thee know what that is? It is a great skeleton of a serpent. It was so long that it had to be put in three rooms."[62] Before he was ten, young Edward was keeping notebooks filled with sketches of birds and animals, and his love of nature was apparent to all.

His formal education consisted of some time in a Quaker boarding school, a year's work with Joseph Leidy, and some work with Spencer Baird. Such excellent tutoring, coupled with travel abroad, prepared Cope for his life's work. From 1867 until he accepted a professorship at the University of Pennsylvania in 1889, he was concerned entirely with exploration and research in the field of vertebrate paleontology. From 1870 until 1879, save for the year 1874 when he was with Wheeler, Cope was attached to the Hayden Survey.

It is unfortunate that the Quaker paleontologist's professional life was darkened by his near psychotic jealousy of his rival, Othniel Charles Marsh, of Yale. Marsh himself contributed in no small part to this animosity. Both men were wealthy, and both desired the credit for every new prehistoric fish, animal, or bird that came into their hands. Other scientists reminded the two that there were plenty of fossils for everybody, but this never deterred Cope and Marsh in their hatred of each other, their accusations and counter accusations. Scientists of the day were either pro-Cope or pro-Marsh. They could not be both.[63]

Hayden's report was ready in time to impress Congress before

[62] Henry Fairfield Osborn, *Cope: Master Naturalist,* 40.

[63] Osborn, *Cope.* See also Charles Schuchert and C. M. LeVene, *O. C. Marsh: Pioneer in Paleontology.* The scientific journals of the period are full of the charges hurled back and forth by these two men.

it adjourned on March 4, 1871. It aided an enlarging group of western solons who were giving him their complete support. They knew that his survey reflected the philsophy of a man who loved the American West with his heart and soul, a man who saw the West in its potential greatness, and who wanted to help it on its way, trying to unite man and the land in a harmonious relationship. "Never has my faith in the grand future that awaits the entire West been so strong as it is at the present time," Hayden wrote, "and it is my earnest desire to devote the remainder of the working days of my life to the development of its scientific and material interests, until I shall see every Territory, which is now organized, a State in the Union."

The Westerners loved him for it, and railroad men, mining officials, newspaper editors, ranchers, and men of the lonely army posts gave him willing aid. "Every dollar that could be saved," Hayden noted, "I have regarded as so much power given me to place before the world in a proper light the magnificent resources, scientific and practical, of our vast domain in the West."

For their favors to the survey he thanked Stanford, Huntington, and Crocker of the Central Pacific, General G. M. Dodge of the Union Pacific, and lesser officials of the Kansas Pacific and Denver Pacific Railroads. He reminded them, however, that *they*, not the poorly paid scientists, would be the recipients of the material benefits gained from the surveys. But he added that "generosity on the part of such corporations towards men who are devoted to the advancement of knowledge or the good of the world, may be regarded as the index of their tone and character."

He made his position with regard to these men crystal clear. Under no circumstances would he compromise with facts, for "he was obliged to speak the truth as [he] read it in the great book of nature, whether it [was] in accordance with the preconceived notions of a district or not." And finally, practical scientist that he was, he emphasized his desire to bring his work to as wide an audience as possible, using the least-technical terminology possible. Perhaps he failed here, but at least he had a clear-cut concept of the aims of his survey, all of which he expressed succinctly in

33

his "Letter to the Secretary" accompanying his report for 1870.[64]

Now the Hayden Survey was prepared for its greatest years. The groundwork was laid, and in 1871 and 1872 large and well-outfitted parties explored the fabulous region of northwestern Wyoming—the legendary Yellowstone area and the magnificent Teton Mountains.

[64] *Fourth Annual Report*, 6–8.

2

Yellowstone and the Tetons

WHEN the Oregonians approached South Pass, their gaze was attracted northwest across the greasewood- and sage-covered plateau to where a great mountain barrier looms skyward, dark blue and hazy in the distance. The mountains look cold, stormy, formidable. They warn the traveler to stay away, leave them alone. They are like some great wall protecting hidden treasures within.

And the Wind River Range, for that is the name given these mountains, is just that—a wall, a barrier, a protective fortress on the southeast side of a narrow rectangle of land which extends northward into Montana, westward into Idaho, then southward down to the Utah line, and eastward again to where the Wind River Mountains begin. Almost everywhere the land inside the rectangle is protected by mountains. When the Wind River Range gives out in the north, the Gros Ventres, then the Shoshonis, then the mighty Absarokas, and finally the Snowy Range furnish the protective walls on the east; on the narrow east-west side of the rectangle the Gallatin and Madison ranges fill in across southwestern Montana and into Idaho; and then southward the Tetons loom, landmarks to travelers ever since the days of the mountain men. The narrow south side of the rectangle is made up of badlands and high plateaus.

This enormous area, said the Indians, was the summit of the world. Within its borders were places where the Great Spirit had not yet completed his work, where sulphurous steam spewed out of clefts in the earth, boiling hot water spouted high into the air, and pools of mud bubbled away neverendingly, moon after moon after moon.

The summit country was also the wellspring of the great rivers of the land. There the Yellowstone (a principal tributary of the Missouri), the Snake (a principal tributary of the Columbia), and the Green (a principal tributary of the Colorado) arose and began rippling toward sea level. At Two Ocean Pass, streams within sight of one another flowed westward to the Pacific, or eastward to the Gulf and the Atlantic.

Today, this region includes Yellowstone National Park and Grand Teton National Park. But in 1871, when Hayden led the first official government expedition into the area, it was still a virtual terra incognita—almost the last such area within the continental boundaries of the United States and its territories. The migrations to California and Oregon had passed it by, and even the gold discoveries in Montana had failed to bring about its exploration.

While at first thought this situation seems strange, a little background history clarifies the facts. What few passes do exist through its mountain bastions are filled with snow from late September to June. (Captain Raynolds' party, of which Hayden was a member, attempted to get through in 1860, but failed because of snow.) Furthermore, before men went exploring for exploring's sake, there were no valid reasons for anyone to enter "the summit of the world." Although fur-bearing animals were there, they were even more abundant elsewhere in more accessible places. Therefore, Indian trappers and white or half-blood mountain men ignored the area. Nor was it necessary to pass through the Tetons or the Absarokas or the geyser basins in order to get from one place to another. The principal Indian trails, and

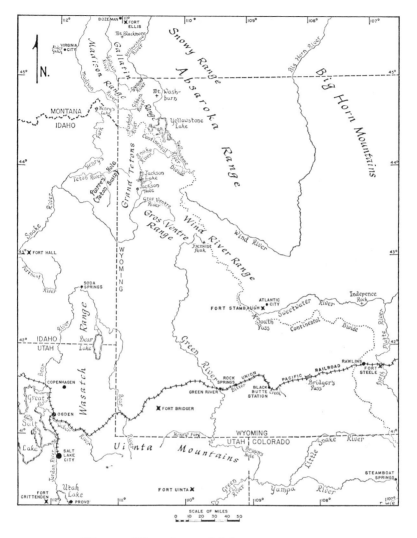

Western Wyoming and Adjacent Territories

later the trails of the Montana argonauts, naturally went elsewhere. What man-made trails there were (and there were a few
Indian trails), were used relatively little.

Nor did anyone of importance live there. The land was Sho-

shoni land, but the only real inhabitants were a deteriorating half-miserable-animal, half-miserable-human type known as the Sheepeaters. These Indians, who ate berries and roots and ferreted out rodents, remained hidden in the thick timber and never caused trouble. They were too despicable to be worth raiding or hunting down, even by lusty young Blackfeet, Crow, or Sioux braves hell-bent for scalps. Their tribes, although they lived on the periphery of "the summit of the world," had very few superstitions about the region. They simply knew nothing about it.

In time, a few white men did go in, and they emerged with stories. Rumors about the geysers, the hot springs, and the Grand Canyon of the Yellowstone were carried eastward as with the westwinds, and here and there they left imprints upon the minds of men, as dust devils left slight imprints on the plain. Tales were told and retold around buffalo-chip fires until facts and fiction blended as the great sky blended with the earth at the horizon.

Historically, the knowledge of the Yellowstone area goes back to Thomas Jefferson and that pompous rascal, Brigadier General James Wilkinson. From his duty post at St. Louis, Wilkinson had heard rumors of the Yellowstone wonders at least as early as September, 1805. Later that fall, he sent a Captain Stoddard with some Indians to see the President, and the Captain carried with him (as Wilkinson's letter of introduction said) "a Savage delineation on a Buffalo Pelt, of the Missouri and its South Western Branches, including the Rivers Plate and Lycorne or Pierre jaune; this Rude Sketch without scale or compass . . . is not destitute of interests . . . among other things a little incredible, a volcano is distinctly described on Yellow Stone River."[1]

The mountain man John Colter, who had been with Lewis and Clark and had turned back toward the mountains in 1806 or 1807, may or may not have seen the geysers, but latter-day historians with a flare for the romantic have claimed, probably erroneously, that "Colter's Hell" was indeed the Yellowstone. There is also substantial evidence that Old Bill Williams, Thomas

---

[1] "The Territories of Louisiana-Missouri, 1803–1806," *The Territorial Papers of the United States* (ed. by Clarence Edward Carter), XIII, 199, 243.

Fitzpatrick, Milton Sublette, Jim Bridger, and some of the Astorians had certainly seen parts of the region before 1860.[2]

Hayden had heard rumors about the Yellowstone during his lone explorations of the upper Missouri country in the 1850's, and Jim Bridger had reinforced the scientist's interest with many a tall tale during the long winter of 1859–60 along the Platte. The failure of the Raynolds party to break through the mountains into the land where hell spouted up had only served to whet his appetite to see the region.[3]

With the occupation of Montana by the gold seekers, curiosity about the Yellowstone increased. Several parties entered the region, but failed to find gold, or anything else of interest, and left without comment. But a professional surveyor named Walter W. DeLacey was sufficiently impressed from what he saw to publish a map in 1865, which, though fairly accurate, seems to have had little influence.[4]

Yet the coming of civilization to Montana made exploration of the region inevitable, and in 1869 a small party led by two men, Cooke and Folsom, explored up the Yellowstone River to Yellowstone Lake, crossed westward over the divide into the geyser basin of the Madison River, then made their way back out into Montana. Their stories spurred a group of Montana boosters to make a more detailed exploration. This was the Washburn Party of 1870, named for its leader, General H. D. Washburn, surveyor general of Montana. It numbered nine civilians including Truman C. Everts, who became United States assessor for Montana, Walter Trumbull, son of Senator Trumbull, of Illinois, and Nathaniel P. Langford, who wrote and lectured extensively on his experiences. Langford was with Hayden in 1872 and later became the first superintendent of the Yellowstone National Park.[5]

[2] Merrill J. Mattes, "Behind the Legend of Colter's Hell: The Early Exploration of Yellowstone National Park," *Mississippi Valley Historical Review,* Vol. XXXVI, No. 2 (September, 1949), 251–82.

[3] F. V. Hayden, "Letter to the Secretary," *Fifth Annual Report,* 7–8.

[4] Mattes, "Behind the Legend of Colter's Hell," *Mississippi Valley Historical Review,* Vol. XXXVI, No. 2 (September, 1949), 282.

[5] N. P. Langford, "The Wonders of the Yellowstone," *Scribner's Monthly,*

In addition, cooks, camp men, and five cavalrymen, led by the able and literate Lieutenant Gustavus C. Doane, upped the number in the party to nineteen. With the precision of a good military man, Doane recorded the progress of the party, up the valley of the Yellowstone to Yellowstone Lake and from there over the divide into what was later called the Upper Geyser Basin, along the Firehole River. They gave Old Faithful her name.[6] But then one of the members, Truman Everts, got lost. This put a damper on the party, and after searching for the missing man for a week they gave up and went back. Thirty-seven days after he was missed, Everts was found, safe but exhausted, and the exploration was finally considered successful in every way.[7]

During the winter of 1870–71, Langford lectured in the East on the wonders of the Yellowstone. He had a tendency to exaggerate until truth and fiction became a fine blend, and there is reason to believe that he made the incredible just a little more so. Meanwhile, Washburn's papers (he had died suddenly) were being read in Washington. Interest was running high by the spring of 1871, when James G. Blaine and Ferdinand Vandeveer Hayden pooled their activities and brought about a lush appropriation of $40,000 from Congress for an expedition into the Yellowstone. This would be the first, official government scientific expedition into the region.[8]

Stevenson quickly entrained for the West to make the necessary preparations at Ogden, Utah Territory, where the expedition was to rendezvous early in June. Fortunately, most of the personnel were veterans of past Hayden expeditions. Henry

---

Vol. II, No. 1 (May, 1871), 1–17, No. 2 (June, 1871), 113–28. See also N. P. Langford, *The Discovery of Yellowstone Park, 1870,* and W. T. Jackson, "The Washburn-Doane Expedition into the Upper Yellowstone, 1870," *Pacific Historical Review,* Vol. X, No. 2 (June, 1941), 189–208.

[6] Gustavus C. Doane, *The Yellowstone Expedition of 1870,* 41 Cong., 3 sess., *Sen. Exec. Doc. 51.*

[7] *Ibid.,* 23. Truman C. Everts, "Thirty-seven Days of Peril," *Scribner's Monthly,* Vol. III, No. 1 (November, 1871), 1–17.

[8] W. T. Jackson, "Governmental Exploration of the Upper Yellowstone, 1871," *Pacific Historical Review,* Vol. XI, No. 2 (June, 1942), 187–200. *U.S. Statutes at Large,* Vol. 16, 503.

National Archives

Hayden Survey en route, 1871.

Hayden Survey at Red Buttes, Wyoming Territory, August 24, 1870. Hayden is sitting at the table, hatless and facing the camera. Stevenson stands directly to his left and Jackson stands at the right, closest to the wagon. The man in the right foreground is Cyrus Thomas.

W. H. Jackson photograph
Bancroft Library

Dr. Hayden on the trail.

Dr. Hayden, James Stevenson, Frank Bradley, and Mrs. Hayden
in camp at Salt Lake City, 1872.

Moose Camp, Teton Canyon, 1872 (Hayden Survey).

National Archives

Grand Canyon of the Yellowstone from the east bank, 1871
(Hayden Survey).

W. H. Jackson photograph
Bancroft Library

Mount Hayden, 1872.

Jackson's photographic outfit at the summit of Mount Washburn, Yellowstone Park (Hayden Survey). The packer is not identified.

Elliott, William Jackson, and Potato John were all asked to come along. One of the new men was Dr. Albert C. Peale, who was employed as mineralogist. He spent several years with the survey and became a respected geologist. Another new man was a German named Anton Schonborn, who was employed in a new capacity for the survey—chief topographer. This marked the beginning of the topographic work of the Hayden Survey. Unfortunately, Schonborn committed suicide in Omaha on the way back to Washington. However, an engraver for the Coast Survey, Mr. E. Hergesheimer, took Schonborn's notes and drew fairly accurate maps of some parts of the Yellowstone.[9]

With Hayden that year as a guest was one of the outstanding landscape painters of the nineteenth century, Thomas Moran. Today, the modernists have tried to forget him. His paintings are in storage in art museum basements. It is said that his attempts to paint the realities of the Grand Canyon of the Yellowstone, the Grand Canyon of the Colorado, and the Mount of the Holy Cross were all failures, and anyway, painting has now passed far beyond attempts merely to convey an accurate scene. Yet in the 1870's, Moran's work was judged among the finest, and Congress twice appropriated $10,000 for the purchase of his western scenes. One of them, of Yellowstone Falls and the Grand Canyon, hung for years in the Capitol. "It captured more than any other painting I know, the color and atmosphere of spectacular nature," said Jackson, himself an artist of some ability. But the paintings deteriorated and, though restored, no longer hang in the Capitol.[10]

If painters ever return to reality, to a respect for the man who can make authentic paintings of authentic subjects, then a reappraisal of Moran may bring him back from the limbo of discarded artists. He boldy tried to convey on canvas the most majestic scenes in the entire American West, and some of his work —his painting of Yellowstone Falls and the Grand Canyon of the

[9] Hayden, "Letter to the Secretary," *Fifth Annual Report*, 5.

[10] Jackson, *Time Exposure*, 200. The two paintings now hang in the lobby of the Interior Department auditorium, fifth floor, New Interior Building, Washington, D.C. Jackson's paintings of the Great Surveys hang in the main lobby of this building.

Yellowstone, for example—is breath-taking in concept, majesty, and color. Writing to Hayden about the Yellowstone painting early in 1872, he expressed his objectives. Most artists, he said, had considered it next to impossible to make good pictures of strange and wonderful scenes in nature, and the most that could be done with such material was to give it topographical or geological characteristics. "But I have always held that the grandest, most beautiful, or wonderful in nature, would, in capable hands, make the grandest, most beautiful, or wonderful pictures," he wrote, "and that the business of a great painter should be the representation of great scenes in nature. All the above characteristics attach to the Yellowstone region, and if I fail to prove this, I fail to prove myself worthy the name of painter. I cast all my claims to being an artist, into this one picture of the Great Canyon and am willing to abide by the judgement upon it."[11]

Moran was thirty-four years old in 1871, tall, gaunt, and cadaverous, but compassionate, helpful, and level headed. He had never mounted a horse before, but he rode the creatures all day long from the very beginning and accepted his sore posterior as part of his sacrifices for the sake of art. He was one of that rare breed of men that have some knowledge about almost everything. He taught the old camp men how to wrap trout in wet paper, bury them beneath the fire, and uncover them baked and delicious half an hour later. He was interested in photography, and he gave unstintingly of his artistic knowledge, especially with regard to the problems of composition.[12]

It must always be kept in mind that Hayden's primary interests were in the field of geology. This explains his choice of Ogden as the rendezvous point in 1871. In previous years he had taken his geologic explorations to the Salt Lake valley, and now, starting from Ogden, Hayden could extend his work without a break northward into Idaho Territory, eastward into southern Montana Territory, and then up the Yellowstone or the Gardiner River. Such a route was already sufficiently well known to assure

[11] National Archives, R.G. 57, Hayden Survey, General Letters Received, Moran to Hayden, March 11,1872.

[12] Jackson, *Time Exposure,* 200–201.

Hayden that no insurmountable geographic barriers would prevent his party from fulfilling its mission.[13]

From Ogden, then, on June 11, the Hayden Yellowstone expedition set out. Mules heehawed in protest, men cursed as aparejos slipped, and the sun was approaching the meridian as the twenty-one horsemen and their seven clattering wagons strung out over a quarter of a mile and headed northward. Four hundred and twenty-nine miles away lay Fort Ellis in Montana, the point from which they would enter the Yellowstone. Better than three weeks of hard travel lay ahead of them before they would get there, and Yellowstone Lake, they discovered later, was another 118 miles from Fort Ellis.

But the trip through Idaho and southern Montana was not without interest. Northern Utah, with its beautiful little parks and cold, clear springs, and its little communities like Copenhagen, settled by Danish Mormons, made the early stages of the long journey pleasant and interesting. Geologically, Hayden could trace the lakes which had once covered the region to points one thousand feet above the floors of the valleys.

Soon they were advancing down the Port Neuf River, enjoying its music as the water splashed over the little rapids three to six feet high that broke the continuity of the basaltic floor. The party moved on, northward past Robber's Roost City, up the Snake River Valley, then turned off into Lincoln Valley toward the newly constructed Fort Hall, 176 miles from Ogden. They arrived there on June 21. Hayden found it a small "but exceedingly neat post . . . located in a beautiful, fertile, grassy valley, among the foothills of the east side of the Snake River Basin." Irrigation ditches flowed through the grounds, making the fort an oasis of cool green in the parched plain. In winter, water was obtained from some warm springs two miles distant which never froze over, and the whole valley was protected from cold winds. It was an ideal place for a fort.[14]

As usual, the lonely officers and men at the post were glad to

[13] F. V. Hayden, "Report of F. V. Hayden," *Fifth Annual Report*, 13.
[14] This was forty miles east of the site of old Fort Hall, known to the thousands of Oregonians of the 1840's.

see the expedition arrive, for visitors broke the humdrum monotony. This always worked to Hayden's advantage, for his party was well treated, and the supplies of the commissary and the quartermaster's depot were made available to him. Finally, on the afternoon of June 23, the survey left the hospitality of Fort Hall and headed northward again, bound for Taylor's Bridge across the Snake River. The route was then, and is today, over a drab, forsaken land—a dry plain of basalt topped by a fifty-foot thickness of volcanic dust which, during the dry season, became "a sort of impalpable powder," as Hayden described it, "filling the air with clouds to such an extent as almost to suffocate man and beast." But even this useless plain interested Peale and Hayden, for it was full of potholes and great caves, such as "Hole in the Wall," which was used as a stage station. Entire rivers—the Camas, the Medicine Lodge, and the Godins, for example—disappeared into the porous basalt never to be seen again.[15]

When the men raised their eyes eastward, they could see the Tetons looming up "like shark's teeth" seventy to eighty miles away. North of the Tetons, and distinctly visible, was the majestic Mount Madison. On the morning of June 29, they left the valley of the Snake River behind them and entered the broken, rocky country that was part of the watershed of the Jefferson Fork of the Missouri. Swinging east, they crossed several peaks and pushed over a pass into Alder Gulch and down to the mining town of Virginia City, Montana Territory. Here, in the twelve-mile length of Alder Gulch, nearly thirty million dollars' worth of gold had been extracted since 1863. Virginia City itself had already passed from boom-town youth into roaring maturity and was now in its dotage, tired and full of recollections, save for the little Chinese who were busy reworking the gravel beds.[16] Not until several years later did the town vigilantes purge the community by hanging their sheriff, Henry Plummer, western rogue

[15] Hayden, "Report of F. V. Hayden," *Fifth Annual Report*, 13–159. A. C. Peale, "Report of A. C. Peale, M.D., On Minerals, Rocks, Thermal Springs, Etc.," *Fifth Annual Report*, 165–96. Unless otherwise noted, information on the 1871 expedition comes from the above sources.

[16] Jackson, *Time Exposure*, 197.

and bad man supreme. Meanwhile, some prospectors had found copper, "which," Peale speculated, "will no doubt one day add much to the prosperity of Montana."

From Virginia City they crossed the hills to the Madison River Valley, then passed through the Gallatin Valley, the "garden valley of Montana," to the town of Bozeman. Three miles beyond this was Fort Ellis, at the head of the valley. There they pitched camp and enjoyed a welcome every bit as warm as the one at Fort Hall.

From there on into Yellowstone, the expedition cheerfully accepted the protection of a small military escort. A few army engineers under the command of Colonel J. W. Barlow and Captain D. P. Heap also accompanied them during some of the actual exploration.[17]

On the morning of July 15, the Hayden expedition headed out from Fort Ellis "nearly due east for about thirty miles," Hayden later narrated, "when we came to the valley of the Yellowstone, and then ascended the valley for ten miles farther, and pitched our permanent camp near Bottler's Ranch."[18] Actually it took the expedition three days to reach Bottler's, for the terrain was rough and rocky, and at times they had to construct the road for the wagons. But when they did reach the ranch, the Yellowstone River stretched before them, its valley, about four miles wide at that point, green and inviting.

The three Dutch Bottler brothers, "laughing, hearty fellows who kept bachelor hall in a big log house" and augmented their cattle and fur business by serving occasional guests, welcomed the Hayden men and helped them transfer their goods from the wagons to pack animals, storing the surplus in safety at the ranch.[19] While these changes were being made, Hayden climbed the nearby buttes and assessed the terrain, delineating where the

[17] J. W. Barlow, *Reconnaissance of the Yellowstone River,* 42 Cong., 2 sess., *Sen. Exec. Doc. 66.*

[18] Hayden, "The Wonders of the West—II: More About the Yellowstone," *Scribner's Monthly,* Vol. III, No. 4 (February, 1872), 388.

[19] Jackson, *Time Exposure,* 197. Harold R. Driggs and William H. Jackson, *The Pioneer Photographer,* 105–108.

waves of a thirty-mile-long lake had once lapped at the mountains and noting how the floor of the valley now carried the Yellowstone on its way to the Missouri. He also noticed, as a portent of the wonders to come, the hundreds of springs bubbling out of the terraces above the ranch, in one case fifty of them in a single mile creating a substantial tributary to the Yellowstone.

By the morning of July 20, the mules were packed and the expedition started up the Yellowstone. The only wheeled vehicle along was the odometer, a two-wheeled oddity made from a couple of wagon wheels and pulled by a mule chosen for her gentleness. Fifteen miles up the river they reached the lower canyon where the fast flowing water turned a bright green color with snow-white ripples. From it they landed hundreds of pounds of firm, white-meated, speckled trout. Green pines and quaking aspens embroidered the general view, and the hillsides were dotted with black or reddish rocks. Peale found a few crystals of calcite and beautiful specimens of chalcedony which contained crystals of quartz, opal, and agate. Beautiful chips of obsidian were also prevalent.

Soon, Cinnabar Mountain appeared, so named for its distinctive reddish color, which was due not to cinnabar but to iron. Then they passed the Devil's Slide, "two masses of rock in almost vertical position, perfectly defined as two walls. They are," Peale described them, "fifty feet in width each, and 300 feet high, reaching from the top of the mountain to its base. They are separated from each other about 150 feet, the intervening softer material having in the lapse of time washed away." At one point a few miles farther on, the strata of limestone were found so contorted that within the space of 200 feet they dipped in three different directions. A thrill of anticipation swept through the party. These were not "just mountains"—these were formations reminiscent of recent violence. There was something different, unfinished, about the region.

Ten miles farther on they reached the mouth of the Gardiner River. The guides had reported some hot springs on this tributary, and the expedition started up to investigate. On the hillsides Hayden's trained eyes cited volcanic debris mixed with the older cretaceous clays. "Indeed," he said, "the entire surface looks much like the refuse about an old furnace."

The rounded hilltops, covered with fragments of basalt and conglomerate, were splashed with somber colors, giving the landscape an appearance of desolation. Depressions that looked like volcanic vents, fifty to one hundred yards wide, lay full of stagnant water. The bottomland was covered with a whitish, calcareous crust. A sizable tributary came into view, its channel toward the river clearly revealed by the steam from its waters. And then the first hot springs appeared, with a few invalids camped close by, "most emphatic in their favorable expressions in regard to the salutary effects."

Now the party angled up a hill, the horses' hoofs making a hollow sound upon the whitened earth. Hayden and his men crested a ridge and halted momentarily to drink in the view, for directly in front of them lay a snowy-white mound two hundred feet high, covered with terraces and hot springs. "It had the appearance of a frozen cascade," said the geologist.

They pitched camp by the side of the stream that carried off the water from the springs. The closer they examined, the more they marveled. Great semicircular basins ornamented the steep sides, with margins varying in height from a few inches to six to eight feet. And the margins were "so beautifully scalloped and adorned with a kind of beadwork," Hayden wrote, "that the beholder stands amazed at . . . nature's handiwork. Add to this, a snowy-white ground, with every variety of shade, of scarlet, green, and yellow, as brilliant as the brightness of our aniline dyes."

The largest spring was at the top, and its water was "so perfectly transparent that one [could] look down into the beautiful ultramarine depth to the bottom of the basin." The sides were "ornamented with coral-like forms, with a great variety of shades, from pure white to a bright cream-yellow," and the blue sky reflected in the transparent water added immeasurably to the enchanting effect. They drank of the water and cooked with it, and

47

all "enjoyed the luxury of bathing in these most elegantly carved natural bathing pools, and it was easy to select, from the hundreds of reservoirs, water of every variety and temperature."[20]

The Hayden Survey is generally given credit for the discovery of Mammoth Hot Springs, although guides and some local residents of the Yellowstone valley must have already known of its existence—else how would the invalids have got there? Jackson was particularly delighted, for it was a certainty that the Hot Springs had never been photographed, and they were excellent subjects. Making use of water at a hot 160°, he found that he could dry his plates in half the usual time.[21]

Happy and exhilarated by their discoveries, the expedition left White Mountain Hot Springs (as they named them) on July 24, crossing the branches of the Gardiner and working southeast towards the right bank of the Yellowstone. High mountains and broad vistas spread before them as they climbed. The meadows in the midsummer were densely covered with green grass and colorful flowers, and aspen groves occasionally broke the more somber monotony of the dark pine woods. "The climate was perfect," Hayden thought, "and in the midst of some of the most remarkable scenery in the world, every hour of our march only increased our enthusiasm."

As they approached the Yellowstone, they paused along the rim of the Devil's Den, the name they gave to the dark and gloomy ten-mile-long canyon down which Tower Creek wound like a silver thread in the darkness. They marveled at the beauty of Tower Falls, where the creek plunges over a 132-foot precipice into a rounded basin cut out of solid limestone. At the foot of the falls Jackson put in one of his hardest days, photographing there and scrambling up to his dark box above with his plate wrapped in a damp towel. If the plate dried before he got it into the chemicals, it would be ruined. Five times he made the trip, and five times he succeeded.[22]

---

[20] Hayden, "The Wonders of the West—II: More About the Yellowstone," *Scribner's Monthly*, Vol. III, No. 4 (February, 1872), 390.

[21] Jackson, *Time Exposure*, 198.

[22] *Ibid.*, 199.

Again, the expedition left the Yellowstone River and turned westward, crossing the northern rim of the Yellowstone Basin. But the wonders of the land were never far away. Here and there hot springs and vapor vents appeared, and the unpleasant rotten-egg odor of sulphurated hydrogen filled the air. There were ravines and canyons filled with hundreds of pinnacles and columns "resembling Gothic spires."

Now they were on the side of Mount Washburn, and time was spared to climb to the top of this highest point to view the country around. To the south were the Tetons, "rising high above all the rest, the monarchs of all they survey, with their summits covered with perpetual snow." Southwest were 150 miles of dense black pine forest stretching to the Madison Mountains. Due west were the bold peaks of the Gallatin Range, extending northward as far as the eye could see. To the north lay the valley of the Yellowstone, and east of north, chaotic, rugged peaks pierced the clouds. But the greatest beauty of the landscape was Yellowstone Lake, in full view to the southeast, "set like a gem amid the high mountains, which are literally bristling with peaks."

They descended the south side of Mount Washburn through thick pine timber interspersed with meadows and aspen groves. At one point they found a large field of sulphur, copper, alum, and soda springs, with occasional mud-pots adding their obscene sounds to the mysterious land. Then a distant roar was heard, like far-off thunder, growing louder and louder as they marched along.

Soon they were once more on the banks of the Yellowstone. Here it flowed "through a grassy, meadow-like valley, with a calm, steady current, giving no warning, until very near the falls, that it is about to rush over a precipice 140 feet and then, within a quarter of a mile, again to leap down a distance of 350 feet."[23]

Most pictures are of the Lower, or Great, Falls of the Yellowstone, but the Upper Falls run a close second in beauty, the water being hurled off the precipice with such force that "the mass

[23] Hayden's measurements were approximations; correct heights are 109 and 308 feet.

is detached into the most beautiful snow-white, bead-like drops, and as it strikes the rocky basin below, it shoots through the water with a sort of ricochet for the distance of 200 feet. The whole presents in the distance," Hayden wrote, "the appearance of a mass of snow-white foam."

Within a quarter of a mile, the river makes a turn northeastward, thus hiding the Upper from the Lower Falls, the channel contracts, and "the waters seem, as it were, to gather themselves into one compact mass and plunge over the descent 350 feet in detached drops of foam as white as snow; some of the large globules of water shoot down like the contents of an exploded rocket." And what kind of a chasm does it fall into? No language can do justice to the grandeur of the Lower Falls and the Grand Canyon that continues twenty miles on down the river, but Hayden made a valiant attempt: the "very nearly vertical walls, slightly sloping down to the water's edge on either side, so that from the summit the River appears like a thread of silver foaming over its rocky bottom; the variegated colors of the sides, yellow, red, brown, white, all intermixed and shading into each other; the Gothic columns of every form standing out from the sides of the walls with greater variety and more striking colors than ever adorned a work of human art."

Pictorially, as Jackson said, this was the climax of the expedition. Elliott and Moran sketched and painted, while Jackson and J. Crissman, a free-lance cameraman who had tagged along ever since Bozeman, took photographs alongside each other. There was photographic terrain enough for both of them. Too soon the word came into their camp at Cascade Creek, close to the Yellowstone and the falls, to pack up. The time had come to trek southward toward Yellowstone Lake. So far the expedition had been an outstanding success. What wonders lay ahead?

The trip from the falls to the lake took three days, until July 28, because so many springs, mud puffs, steam vents, and other unnatural sights enticed them along the way. They crossed a little creek of clear water strongly impregnated with alum; about ten miles above the falls they came to a group of springs that called to them through a steam vent that had "an impulsive noise like a high-pressure engine"—so they named it "Locomotive Jet." It was not much, but these curious men just had to pause from their journey and ride up to the jet and examine it, note its aperture (about six inches), its bright-yellow sulphur lining, and its white surface crust. Close by was a magnificent sulphur spring, its water in a continual state of agitation, sometimes rising as much as four feet into the air—"a huge caldron of perfectly clear water somewhat superheated." The decorations about its rim consisted of scalloping, the inner and outer surface covered with a sort of pearl-like bead work. "No kind of embroidering that human art can conceive or fashion could equal this specimen of the cunning skill of nature," Hayden proclaimed. They also found mud-pots. Hayden attempted to walk among a group of these simmering vents, but he broke through the surface up to his knees, covering himself with hot mud.

Camp for the night was at Mud Springs near the banks of the Yellowstone, about two miles above the Locomotive Jet and thirteen miles from their previous camp at the falls. Here were springs of every size and hue: the Grotto, roaring and steaming in the side of a hill and yet releasing barely ten gallons of clear water an hour; and the Giant's Caldron, shaking the ground with its constant roar, steam rising from its crater, and (when the wind swept the steam away) revealing its contents—mud in a constant state of agitation, "like an immense caldron of mush submitted to a constant, uniform, but most intense heat." The Giant's Caldron must have been of recent origin, for nearby pines still stood, dying from their coatings of mud from the caldron's occasional eruptive temperament.

On July 28, the Hayden Survey camped on the northwest shores of Yellowstone Lake in a grassy meadow. "The Lake," Hayden wrote, "lay before us, a vast sheet of quiet water, of a most delicate ultramarine hue, one of the most beautiful scenes I have ever beheld."

From the packs the men took the framework for a boat 12 feet long and 3½ feet wide, assembled it, applied tarred ducking, and attached the spars and a sail shaped like a blanket. In the stern a framework was attached for a lead and a line so that soundings of the lake's depths could be made.

She was christened the *Anna*—at Stevenson's suggestion—in honor of Miss Anna L. Dawes, daughter of H. D. Dawes, of Massachusetts, who had supported the Hayden Survey in Congress. On the morning of July 29, Stevenson and Elliott launched the little bark and rowed her over to the nearest island, which they explored. By common consent the survey christened the island in Stevenson's name, and it is still known as Stevenson's Island.

The *Anna* performed excellent service. Experience soon taught that the lake was usually calm in the morning, roily by noon, and rough by afternoon, with whitecaps and waves sometimes four to five feet high. Although the boat rode the waves well and performed well in the water, it was always kept close to the shore during the afternoons. Carrington (the zoologist of the expedition) and Elliott, working together, made a complete sketch of the shoreline and of the islands, a considerable task, since the lake is about twenty-two miles long and fifteen miles wide. It has many fingers to it and has occasionally been compared—though not very accurately—with the outline of a human hand. Soundings were made of depths up to three hundred feet. The two young explorers found the lake full of plant life and of trout, which, however, were infested with an ugly white intestinal worm that weakened them and made them unpalatable. Leidy later examined specimens, and his report on them was included in Hayden's annual report.[24]

Their next camp was established at the hot springs on the southwest arm of the lake. It was here that some of the members enjoyed the luxury of catching a trout and then cooking it in a boiling spring without removing it from the hook. (This sounds like a "fish story" since a trout cooked before cleaning could

24 Joseph Leidy, "Notice of Some Worms Collected during Professor Hayden's Expedition to the Yellowstone River in the Summer of 1871," *Fifth Annual Report*, 381–82.

hardly be considered palatable. Yet the yarn proved intriguing to the outside world, and it died hard.)

On July 31, Hayden, Peale, Elliott, Schonborn, and Jackson left camp to cut southwest to the geyser basin of the Firehole River, one of the headwaters of the Madison. The thirty-one-mile hike was a nightmare of fallen timbers, and when they did reach the river, it proved to be the East Fork of the Madison instead of the Firehole. This proved fortunate, however, for it revealed a series of springs which they would not otherwise have seen. They camped along this fork, whose valley resembled an alkali flat. On August 1, they followed the valley down to the Firehole Basin, a distance of about six miles, noticing the temperature of the stream—a tepid 76°, and clear and insipid to the taste. Camp on August 2 and August 3 was in what has become known as the Lower Geyser Basin. In the cool of the early morning the scene reminded them of an industrial city, with the smoke rising from a thousand chimneys.

They took the temperatures of the springs (sixty-seven separate readings were made in the Lower Basin alone), and they gave names to the more outstanding or beautiful ones; such as White Dome and Fountain Geyser, as they slowly worked down the Firehole River, then back up its west fork. Sometimes pines had fallen into the hot springs and had lain so long and so still that the cones and twigs had become petrified; once removed from the spring and dried, they provided beautiful collector's items.

About noon on August 4, the party left their camp in the Lower Basin and proceeded on up the Firehole, stopping that evening in the Upper Geyser Basin.[25] It is a smaller area of only about three square miles, with fewer, but far more active, springs, most of them conveniently located near the banks of the river. The Washburn and Doane groups had camped there the year before, giving names and information about the wonders

[25] *Fifth Annual Report,* 116, 185. Hayden says it was August 5, while Peale says it was August 4. Peale's date has been accepted, because Hayden's dates have continually proved wrong.

of the area. For Hayden and the men of 1871, the wonders were not long in coming.

Hardly had camp been established before "a tremendous rumbling was heard, shaking the ground in every direction, and soon a column of steam burst forth from a crater near the edge of the river. Following the steam, arose, by a succession of impulses, a column of water, apparently six feet in diameter, to the height of 200 feet, while the steam ascended a thousand feet more." For twenty minutes the display continued, appropriately named "the Grand," before it settled back into its basin. Thirty-one hours later it erupted once more while the men were still camped close by.

Hayden was particularly impressed by what he called the central springs—the large springs that occupy the highest mounds in the basin. One of these he named the Bathtub, one the Punch Bowl, and one the Dental Cup, for their resemblances to those containers. He described them thus:

> The continual but very moderate overflow of [these springs] uniformly on every side, builds up slowly a broad-based mound, layer by layer, one-eighth to one-sixteenth of an inch thick; looking down into these springs, you seem to be gazing into fathomless depths, while the bright blue of the waters is unequaled even by the sea. . . . . The great beauty of the prismatic colors depends much on the sunlight, but about the middle of the day, when the bright rays descend nearly vertically, and a slight breeze just makes a ripple on the surface, the colors exceed comparison; when the surface is calm there is one vast chaos of colors, dancing, as it were, like the colors of a kaleidoscope. As seen through this marvellous display of colors, the decorations on the sides of the basin are lighted up with a wild, weird beauty, which wafts one at once into the land of enchantment; all the brilliant feats of fairies and genii in the Arabian Nights Entertainments are forgotten in the actual presence of such marvelous beauty; life becomes a privilege and a blessing after one has seen and thoroughly felt these incomparable types of nature's cunning skill.[26]

[26] Hayden, "Report of F. V. Hayden," *Fifth Annual Report*, 121.

By now, descriptions were becoming repetitive, but one geyser, noticed on the way out from the Firehole River, deserved special mention:

> Early in the morning, as we were leaving the valley, the grand old geyser which stands sentinel at the head of the valley gave us a magnificent parting display, and with little or no preliminary warning it shot up a column of water 6 feet in diameter to the height of 100 to 150 feet, and by a succession of impulses seemed to hold it up steadily for the space of fifteen minutes, the great mass of water falling directly back into the basin, and flowing over the edges and down the sides in large streams. When the action ceases, the water recedes beyond sight, and nothing is heard but the occasional escape of steam until another exhibition occurs. This is one of the most accommodating geysers in the basin, and during our stay played once an hour quite regularly. On account of its apparent regularity, and its position overlooking the valley, it was called by Messrs. Langford and Doane "Old Faithful." It has built up a crater about 20 feet high around its base, and all about it are decorations similar to those previously described.[27]

On August 6, the explorers split up. The Barlow-Heap exploring party, which had joined Hayden by Grand Geyser, went its own way, and Lieutenant Doane arrived from Fort Ellis with orders for the return of the military escort. Hayden and his small group, including the young lieutenant, left the Upper Geyser Basin and started back toward Yellowstone Lake. By August 9, they were again at the lake, camped on the main bay west of Flat Mountain. Hayden proposed to complete a circuit of that beautiful body of water. While Stevenson was en route to Bottler's for more supplies, the party ate the poor meat of a black-tailed deer, the only game the hunters could find. Speculation was that the heat of summer drove the game to the higher ridges where the swarms of flies were not so troublesome. And so with growling stomachs the party continued their tour, plung-

[27] *Ibid.*, 125.

ing through dense pines, over fallen timber, "sometimes in grassy glades, through marshes, or by lily-covered lakes."

At sunrise on August 10, the thermometer stood at fifteen degrees and Hayden found a quarter of an inch of ice covering his water pail. But they continued their circuit and pitched their tents that night "upon a sort of terrace on the east side of the southeast arm, eighty feet above the water level of the lake." During the next few days Hayden, Schonborn, and one or two others took a side journey or two to the Continental Divide, which Hayden wanted to be traced on the map; meanwhile the main party continued along the shores of the lake. By mid-August everyone was noting how the days were getting shorter, the shadows of the pines longer, the crispness in the air sharper. They had to hurry. Then one night they were frankly alarmed when their sleep was interrupted by several earthquake tremors —predictable phenomena of the region. On August 23, they turned away from the lake, trekked in a northeasterly direction up Pelican Creek, reached its source, and crossed the water divide over to the branches of the East Fork of the Yellowstone River. They followed these streams northwest to the Yellowstone and on August 25 crossed to the west side on the only bridge, built near the junction of the East Fork and the Yellowstone by miners working up the Clark's Fork to the east. On August 27, they arrived at their base camp at Bottler's. They had spent thirty-eight days in this land where nature had erred so beautifully.[28]

The wagons were quickly packed, and the Hayden Survey, all old hands now, retraced its route to Fort Hall and then struck eastward to Evanston on the Union Pacific. There the party disbanded on about the first of October. Thus ended one of the most successful field seasons in the history of the Hayden Survey. These men had ridden horses or mules over one thousand miles of western America and had examined every characteristic and every freak of nature with a childlike curiosity that befitted the youthful, unoccupied land.

[28] *Ibid.*, 173–191. Jackson, however, reported he spent "exactly forty days in the Yellowstone." *Time Exposure,* 202.

The permanent employees entrained for Washington, where manuscripts would be prepared, sketches of all the marvels they had witnessed would be engraved, and Jackson's photographs would be reproduced. Hayden had to work fast. If he was to return to the Yellowstone the next summer, he had to advertise his work and convince the right people of the wonders of the region, or else the money would not be forthcoming from Congress.

Then on October 27, he received a letter from A. R. Nettleton of the firm of Jay Cooke and Company and the Northern Pacific Railroad. "Judge Kelley," the letter read in part, "has made a suggestion which strikes me as being an excellent one, *viz.* Let Congress pass a bill reserving the Great Geyser Basin as a public park forever—just as it has reserved that far inferior wonder the Yosemite Valley and big trees. If you approve this, would such a recommendation be appropriate in your official report?"[29]

Not only was Hayden willing to do this, but he was willing to use all his lobbying powers, all his resources to get the park created. While a map of the proposed reserve was hastily completed, he ground out an article for *Scribner's Magazine* and he urged the passage of the park bill in the *American Journal of Science and Arts.*[30] Jackson's views of the hot springs, the geysers, and the falls and the canyon were reproduced in abundance. This ammunition, along with the ardent work of members of the Washburn Expedition of 1870, among whom the park idea originated, and the front-line tactics of William H. Clagett, territorial delegate from Montana, Senators Pomeroy and Trumbull, and Representative Dawes, all brought unusual success. On March 1, 1872, President Grant signed the Yellowstone Park Bill, after it had passed through both houses of Congress with unanimous consent.[31] "This noble deed," the geologist noted in his *Fifth Annual Report,* "may be regarded as a tribute from our legislators to science, and the gratitude of the nation and of

[29] National Archives, R.G. 57, Hayden Survey, General Letters Received, Vol. III, 1871. Judge Kelley was William Darrah "Pig Iron" Kelley, a representative from Pennsylvania.

[30] F. V. Hayden, "The Hot Springs and Geysers of the Yellowstone and Firehole Rivers," *American Journal of Science and Arts,* Third Series, Vol. III, No. 15 (March, 1872), 176.

[31] *U.S. Statutes at Large,* Vol. 17, 32.

men of science in all parts of the world is due them . . . ."

In later years, Hayden was wont to give himself full credit for the creation of the park. He flatly stated that "so far as is now known" the whole idea of a national park originated with him.[32] This claim has been completely refuted.[33] But at the same time an excellent argument could be submitted that without Hayden's vigorous activities in behalf of the park, the bill would have been pigeonholed or would have died in committee. It was the widespread publicity given the Yellowstone by the Hayden Survey that made the public conscious of it and interested in its protection. Jackson's photographs influenced doubtful congressmen, and Hayden's vigorous lobbying, and his influence among the higher officials of the Department of the Interior (under whose jurisdiction the park would be placed), brought the bill to successful passage. Thus Hayden's activities were crucial, even though his annual report for 1871 was not issued until after the bill was passed and Moran's great canvas of the Grand Canyon was not ready for public showing until April.

Hayden's own report was well received, but there were some unpleasant mutterings from professional men. Five pages of it, any five pages, would indicate why. Hayden rambled. He wrote like a man with a grasshopper mind. He was here and there and back again, pausing to discuss something here, forgetting where he had been or where he was going, thoroughly confusing his dates, his parties, his geographical places. The report was a confusing maze for scientist and lay reader alike. The man could certainly have done better, for on occasion his descriptions and explanations were superb. But in his haste to publish he had turned over his unedited, unchecked, and unrevised narration to the public printer. In 1871, he could get away with this, but in

[32] F. V. Hayden, "Letter to the Secretary," *Twelfth Annual Report of the United States Geological and Geographical Survey of the Territories: A Report of Progress of the Exploration in Wyoming and Idaho for the year 1878*, Part II, xvii.

[33] See W. T. Jackson, "The Creation of Yellowstone National Park," *Mississippi Valley Historical Review*, Vol. XXIX (June, 1942), 187–206, for a definitive paper on the passage of the Yellowstone Park Bill. New evidence is in Richard A. Bartlett, *Nature's Yellowstone* (Albuquerque, 1974), 194–210.

later years such haste and carelessness harmed his professional reputation, supplied his enemies with useful ammunition, and contributed to the demise of the survey.

All things considered, Jackson's photographs were the most important contributions of the 1871 expedition. They were wonderful, and they were the only ones. Crissman, the free-lance photographer who had come down the Yellowstone with him, never bothered to sell his photographs outside of Montana, and T. J. Hine, a photographer from Chicago who had accompanied the Barlow-Heap party, got back to his home town just in time to have every last negative consumed in the great Chicago fire. But Jackson still had his plates.[34]

And one other achievement should be chalked up for the Yellowstone expedition. In 1872, an impressed Congress, full of the publicity about the Yellowstone and tired of the Grant scandals, appropriated $75,000 for the continued work of the Hayden Survey.[35]

The year 1872 was the first of several years in which the Hayden Survey dominated the field. It was the best known of the Great Surveys, it had the largest funds at its disposal, it hired the best scientists, and it consistently maintained itself in the public eye through Jackson's photographs. The Government Printing Office produced hundreds of documents under the imprint of the survey, ranging from ten-page pamphlets to octavo and quarto volumes thousands of pages long. Even scientists who had never been associated with Hayden got their works published by him, while Cope, Leidy, Newberry, Lesquereux, Meek, and Thomas could count on ready acceptance of their material. Some of the work published was of poor quality and was cited as such by Hayden's critics. But much of it was sound, and its publication and subsequent availability to scientists and institutions of learning throughout the world constituted one of the great contributions of the Hayden Survey.

In the late spring of 1872, Hayden decided to divide his ex-

---

[34] Jackson, *Time Exposure*, 202–203.
[35] *U.S. Statutes at Large*, Vol. 17, 350.

pedition into two parties of about thirty men each. His own party would rendezvous at Fort Ellis, in Montana Territory, and return to the Yellowstone via the same general route used the year before. James Stevenson was to lead the other group, which was to head north from Ogden to Fort Hall, then plunge eastward across the sagebrush desert toward the Tetons. Then it was to explore Pierre's Hole (also known as the Teton Basin), cross over into Jackson's Hole, then head north for a rendezvous with Hayden's party at the Firehole Geyser Basin.[36]

The basic staff of both parties consisted of the old-timers—Stevenson, Peale, Jackson, the packer Shep Madera, and the cook Potato John Raymond. Hayden also invited a few guests along. William Blackmore was with his party, and Nathaniel P. Langford, who had been with Washburn in 1870 and who was now the first superintendent of Yellowstone National Park, accompanied Stevenson. Hayden also took along his bride of less than a year. (Blackmore's summer was marred by the death of his wife in Montana Territory.)

Besides the usual political appointees—"pilgrims," as Shep Madera called them—there were a few newcomers in 1872 who left their marks on the organization just as the survey left its imprint on them.

One of these men was Henry Gannett, listed in 1872 as an astronomer. He was recommended by Charles F. Hoffman, a recognized authority on topographical techniques who had done work with Josiah Dwight Whitney on the California Geological Survey.[37] Gannett was a graduate of the Lawrence Scientific School and the Hooper Mining School at Harvard, and he had

---

[36] F. V. Hayden, "Letter to the Secretary," *Sixth Annual Report of the United States Geological Survey of the Territories, Embracing Portions of Montana, Idaho, Wyoming, and Utah, Being a Report of Progress of the Exploration for the Year 1872* (hereafter cited as *Sixth Annual Report*), 5. Unless otherwise noted, the material in this section is based on "Report of F. V. Hayden," 11–85, and "Report of Frank H. Bradley, Geologist of the Snake River Division," 189–271, in the above. The latter, though slanted toward geology, still constitutes the best official report of the Teton exploration, since Stevenson made no report.

[37] Both Hoffman and Whitney figured in the lives of Clarence King and James T. Gardner.

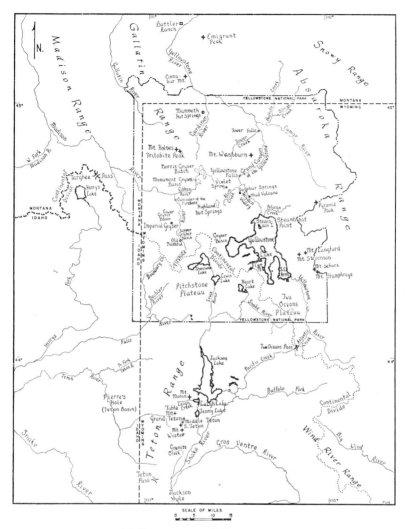

Yellowstone and the Tetons

later been one of Hoffman's students, working with him and Whitney in the Rockies in 1869. "I do not recommend him as a draughtsman," Hoffman wrote, "but he can make a decent looking map and you will find him of great service in field work."[38]

[38] National Archives, R.G. 57, Hayden Survey, General Letters Received, Hoffman to Hayden, February 1, 1872. See also "Henry Gannett," *National Geographic Magazine,* Vol. XXVI (December, 1914), 610.

Gannett stayed with Hayden until the end of the survey in 1879. He began work by determining astronomical positions (the latitude and longitude of geographic locations), heights of peaks and divides, the margin of timberline, and distances. For his work he used an astronomical transit, a zenith telescope, cistern barometers, and, when it was available, the telegraph. The work required some mathematical skill and a lot of patience.[39] Gannett possessed both.

In later years, he became chief topographer for the United States Geological Survey, was one of the six founders of the National Geographic Society (and at the time of his death in 1914, its president), and was a celebrated statistician. His maps for the Hayden Survey were never imaginative or particularly artistic, but they always showed good, solid workmanship. He was painstaking and precise, reticent and unusually cruel to his livestock.[40] Ambitious, with a reputation to make, he was a good choice.

Another new man with Hayden in 1872 was William Henry Holmes. Of medium build, brown-haired, and twenty-six years old he had hopes of becoming a successful artist. After graduating from McNeeley Normal School at Hopedale, Ohio, he came to Washington to study art. There he met Miss Mary Henry, daughter of the Smithsonian's Professor Henry, who subsequently recommended that young Holmes be appointed as successor to Henry Elliott, who had resigned from his position as artist with the survey. Thus began William Holmes's long career as artist, geologist, topographer, anthropologist, and as director of the National Collection of Fine Arts. Along with Story B. Ladd, George B. Chittenden (both of whom joined the survey in later years), and William Henry Jackson, Holmes completed a foursome of old veterans of the survey who until death finally parted them in the 1930's and 1940's often got together and talked over old times.[41]

[39] Henry Gannett, "Report on Astronomy and Hypsometry," *Sixth Annual Report*, 795–808.

[40] National Archives, R.G. 57, Hayden Survey, General Letters Received, Bechler to Hayden, July 13, 1878.

[41] William Henry Holmes, "Biography of William H. Holmes," Random

As a topographer he was unsurpassed. A lover of truth as any topographer must be, this man had an uncanny God-given ability to sketch what he saw with an accuracy unrivaled even by a photograph. To emphasize what the eye saw he could exaggerate, and his exaggeration only made the terrain look more real, more natural. Never has his topographic sketchwork been surpassed by an American artist.

Another topographer, Gustavus Bechler, joined the survey in 1872. "Gus" was an excellent map maker and a good mountaineer, and he stayed with Hayden until 1878, although his cantankerous ways and his jealousy of the other division leaders made him a difficult personality to handle.[42]

Frank Bradley, the geologist with the Teton party, had been a professor at Hanover College in southern Indiana. It was through his efforts that young John Merle Coulter went along. Coulter subsequently became one of the world's great botanists.[43] Another young member was sixteen-year-old C. Hart Merriam, who went along as ornithologist. In later years he became the first chief of the United States Biological Survey and a trustee of the National Geographic Society. And there were other members too numerous to mention. Sixty-one are identified in one of Jackson's photographs of the two groups together in the Firehole Basin.

Much of Hayden's work was of an administrative nature, and for that reason he excused himself from writing a long report in 1872. He concentrated upon places he had missed in 1871, such as the canyon of the Gallatin River, squeezed in between the Madison and the Yellowstone. The result was a brief and respectable narration.

Records, Vol. I. The Random Records consist of sixteen volumes of memoirs—photographs, newspaper clippings, personal notes and essays—which piece together his life. The volumes, of which the first six pertain to the years of the Hayden Survey, are in the custody of the Director of the National Collection of Fine Arts, New Museum Building, Washington, D.C.

[42] Bechler's grumbling appears in many of his letters. For a good example, see National Archives, R.G. 57, Hayden Survey, General Letters Received, Bechler to Hayden, July 8, 1875.

[43] Andrew Denny Rodgers III, *John Merle Coulter: Missionary in Science*, 10–11.

It is Stevenson's party that is worth watching in 1872. Ogden was again chosen as the rendezvous point, and on June 24 the expedition, consisting of thirty-seven mounted men, headed for their first destination, Fort Hall.[44] There the settled country ended. The well-traveled roads veered northwestward, but the Stevenson party planned to swing eastward. The wagons were turned in and, save for one heavy one, were replaced with ever-useful pack mules. On July 12, they arose early, spent hours packing the unhappy mules, and finally hit the trail in time to make just seven miles before dark.

Things went better the next day, and the mules finally accepted their places in the line of march so that the men could turn their attentions elsewhere. As they marched along in an easterly direction, they began to notice one great peak looming above the rest, appearing and then disappearing in clouds just above the eastern horizon. Soon they could make out three great pinnacles projected into the heavens, and later a whole range came into view, with ten to twelve jagged peaks piercing the sky.

These were the Tetons—landmarks for decades to the trappers, for centuries to the aborigines. From either east or west, their pinnacles appeared in the sky and helped give travelers along the lonely wastes a reckoning. To the sensuous half-blood trapper they resembled the soft breasts of a woman, so he called them *Les Grandes Tetones* or "the Paps." Washington Irving, in *Astoria*, called them "Pilot Knobs."[45] Hayden, seeing them closer, saw nothing soft or feminine about their jagged outlines, and he compared them to shark's teeth. Whatever their names, they were isolated, gigantic, foreboding. Now, for the first time, civilized men proposed to explore them, to define their geologic history, and even to climb the tallest of them.

The route east took the party to Henry's Fork of the Snake River, which they followed for some distance. The terrain appeared barren, but for the knowledgeable men of the West (including illiterate trappers, Indians, squaw men such as the party's guide, Beaver Dick Leigh), there were edible plants even

[44] *Ibid.*, 13–14.
[45] *Astoria*, 361.

in this barren country to keep a man alive and going. Camas and yamp plants, prized by the Indians for their food value, grew in great profusion.

On July 20, the Stevenson party left the valley of Henry's Fork. Following Beaver Dick's advice, they entered a rising, fertile, rolling country which led them to Pierre's River, where the Tetons loomed higher and closer, their inviting softness giving way to their true jagged nature. On July 21, the last rattlesnake was seen; wild strawberries grew in abundance, and the breeze bore the cool freshness of the high country.

They descended into Pierre's Hole (now known as the Teton Basin), a favorite summer retreat for the trappers. It was about twenty miles long and five to fifteen miles wide, hidden away among the mountains, bounded on three sides by snow-capped peaks. It was carpeted with heavy, luxurious bunch grass dotted with blue camas flowers and yamp, and in the lowlands and along the streams more strawberries grew. Like an oasis in the desert it offered good pasturage for the stock and good hunting for the men. Around a shallow pond fed by springs bursting out from the hills were the tracks of antelope, deer, and elk. Fresh meat provided by men who carried guns as they carried their hats kept the party in good shape for the work to come.

On July 23, still in Pierre's Hole, they camped at the mouth of the largest tributary of Pierre's River, known as Teton Creek, so named "because it heads directly toward the highest Teton and its valley gives a fine view of the peak." Fifteen to twenty rugged miles would take them to the crest of Grand Teton; over one hundred miles in the other direction was Fort Hall. Here Stevenson established a semipermanent camp and set out to explore the country.[46]

But always, as if drawn by some great primitive god who resided there, the men caught themselves gazing at the towering peaks. Fifty times a day, Bradley and Stevenson paused to look up at the shining mountains. Jackson was magnetized by their beauty and spent the days clambering over rocks and pinnacles

[46] For a useful map tracing the entire route of the Teton expedition, see the one facing page 255 in the *Sixth Annual Report*.

with his heavy equipment and his fragile glass plates, often camping alone all night so as to be at the right place at the right time the next morning to get just the right negative.

One day, Stevenson and Langford started up the canyon, studying Grand Teton and its approaches, analyzing its crags, snow fields, and cliffs. They finally figured out what they hoped would be a successful route to the summit. Then they took twelve men with them and started up the right fork of Teton Creek and established a base camp close enough, they believed, for a party to make it to the crest of the highest Teton and return between sunup and sundown.

At sunrise on July 29, 1872, the thermometer registered eleven degrees above zero. Fires were kindled, and the men ate a hearty breakfast. Compared to a modern mountain-climbing outfit, they were miserably equipped. Each man had only an alpine staff to help him upwards, a bacon sandwich for his noon meal, and determination in his heart. As the rays of the sun cast their first long shadows across the camp, and the odor of bacon frying and coffee boiling mixed with the pungence of the pine-knot fire, the ruddy faces of the awakening men turned again and again toward her: Grand Teton, Shark's Tooth, Grand Paps, or, as some of the men wished, Mount Hayden (the latter name never caught on).

The climb began. Bradley was entranced by the beauties of this alpine wonderland, where streams of snow water hurtled in beautiful cascades 200 to 300 feet over canyon walls, where the "kid-like bleat of the rare little coney, *Lagomys princeps*," could be heard beneath the roar, although the little fellow was rarely seen. They struck masses of snow in an alpine wonderland 10,500 feet above sea level and 300 to 400 feet above the timber line. The soft tundra was a mass of deep green plants and white, blue, purple, and crimson flowers. Buttercups grew right up to the snowbanks, even piercing through two to three inches of snow. Grasshoppers had fallen by millions onto the snow, and their warmth had melted them down into it. Bradley said that when the snow melted, the sun thawed out the 'hoppers, and

66

they emerged just as lively as ever, but this was probably more of an impression than a reality.

Gus Bechler sprained an ankle, and the rarefied atmosphere exhausted eight of the others, so only five of the original fourteen—Bradley, Langford, Stevenson, and two "pilgrims," Hamp and Spencer—reached a saddle just north of the Grand Teton. With a strong, cold west wind buffeting them, they munched on their cold bacon sandwiches and pondered their next move. Grand Teton loomed directly above. Then all but Bradley resumed the climb.

What followed must always be a mystery. In his report, Bradley merely states that others of the party of fourteen who had gone westward into a gorge, "report that Messrs. Stevenson and Langford reached the summit, while Messrs. Hamp and Spencer stopped 300 feet below."[47] Langford later wrote that the two younger men gave up about 300 feet below the summit, but that he and Stevenson reached it at about three o'clock. Langford's description of the summit of Grand Teton is significant:

> The main summit, separated by erosions from the surrounding knobs, embraced an irregular area of thirty by forty feet. Exposure to the winds kept it free from the snow and ice, and its bald, denuded head was worn smooth by the elemental warfare waged around it. With the unshorn beams of a summer sun shining full upon us, we were obliged to don our overcoats for protection against the cold mountain breeze.[48]

Langford also described a man-made rock enclosure which he and Stevenson found there, indicating that the Grand Teton had been used either for religious rites or as a lookout by the aborigines.

The trouble with Langford's description is that the summit of Grand Teton does not look like that. It is barely big enough

[47] Bradley, "Report of Frank H. Bradley," *Sixth Annual Report,* 222. Page 221 carries a sketch of the Tetons showing the apparent route of the climb.

[48] N. P. Langford, "The Ascent of Mount Hayden: A New Chapter in Western Discovery," *Scribner's Monthly,* Vol. VI, No. 2 (June, 1873), 129–37.

for three men to stand upon it. The man-made enclosure does in fact exist, but it is 1100 feet west and 500 feet below the summit.[49] And even Bradley, as early as 1873, expressed doubt about their having reached the summit. He wrote that there were "great discrepancies between the statements of the two persons who claim[ed] to have reached the summit," and he pointed out that Langford's description of a small pond of clear, frozen ice 12 to 15 feet thick was not in keeping with the rotten, opaque snow-ice that one sees there. And it must have taken sharp ears, he added, to have heard the murmur of a creek 1,200 feet beneath the snow—yet Langford claimed this.[50]

In August, 1898, six men led by William O. Owen set out to scale Grand Teton. After finding the stone enclosure, they crept up on a bench and found a narrow ledge about sixteen inches wide and twenty-five feet long. This was the key to the summit, and at four o'clock they were on the crest overlooking Jackson Hole to the east. There was no sign of a human being ever having been there—not a stone cairn, a piece of cloth, or an empty whisky bottle. So naturally the Owen party disputed the Langford-Stevenson claim and insisted instead that *they* were the first ones to have conquered Grand Teton.

In 1926, their claims were officially confirmed by the commissioners of Teton County, Wyoming, and in 1927 and 1929 the state legislatures of Wyoming further recognized the Owen achievement.[51] Although William Jackson supported the Langford-Stevenson claim, the evidence against the Hayden men is overwhelming. Whether the two explorers made their claim with a knowledge of its falsity, with a mere suspicion they might have made an error, or with an absolute belief that they had con-

49 Nolie Mumey, *The Teton Mountains: Their History and Tradition,* 373.

50 Frank H. Bradley, "Explorations of 1872: United States Geological Survey of the Territories, under Dr. F. V. Hayden, Snake River Division," *American Journal of Science and Arts,* Third Series, Vol. VI, No. 33 (September, 1873), 198n.

51 Mumey, *The Teton Mountains,* 371–81. Five arguments are submitted as evidence of the falsity of Langford's claim. They are much the same as Bradley's statements, and they also point out that Stevenson never officially claimed he had reached the summit.

quered the mountain is a question that must forever remain unanswered.[52]

Stevenson and his men had to hurry to keep the rendezvous with Hayden's party in the Upper Geyser Basin of the Firehole River. Originally, they had intended to cross Teton Pass into Jackson's Hole and then travel northward, but Beaver Dick insisted that the deep snows and swollen streams would prevent this. So, they decided to retrace their path to the camp on Teton Creek. After investigating the Tetons as long as possible—the dense spruce forests, deep canyons, cascading streams, abundant deer, elk, moose, white ducks, and geese—they got back to the camp on August 2. They had spent about a week on or about the Tetons.

From there the party worked northeastward to the headwaters of Henry's Fork, then made an easy trip over the Continental Divide by way of Targhee Pass into the drainage region of the Madison. For the most part, life on the trail was very pleasant. The mules caused trouble, of course. One of them rubbed her pack against every tree and stone along the trail, and within seven miles her packers readjusted her load twenty-five times! And occasionally progress was hindered by growths of young pine. But trout swam in the cold streams, and wild strawberries and large blue huckleberries tantalized the tastes of the mountaineers. It was August, and spring and fall flowers mingled in the upland meadows. Rich-colored little violets, blue, purple, and yellow monk's-hood, geraniums, and fringed gentians intermingled in the green velvety meadows. Nothing could compare with the beauty of nature's carpet. The aspens stood still, patiently awaiting summer's end, and the sky was a deeper blue. Only the saucy blue jay squawked in the quiet wilderness.

On August 14, the Stevenson and Hayden parties met at the rendezvous point on the Firehole River, and Shep Madera, who had spent much of the time with Stevenson, came up from Virginia City with a pack train of supplies. At this meeting, where all sixty-one men of the survey were briefly together, Grand

[52] Jackson, *Time Exposure*, 208. For cogent arguments in favor of Langford and Stevenson, see articles by William M. Bueler in *Off Belay* (June, 1976) and *American Alpine Journal* (1978).

Teton was named Mount Hayden (a name which did not endure), and another high Teton was dubbed Mount Moran (a name that has remained).

Among the new members at this meeting was William Henry Holmes. He had ridden a bumpy coach-and-four up to Fort Ellis from Ogden and had learned the painfulness of travel in the West in the first hours out from the fort. But Holmes rapidly adjusted to the outdoor life and came to like it. He was one of the first to climb Mount Blackmore, in the Gallatin Range, which had been named in honor of the Englishman's wife who had died and was buried nearby.

In later years, Holmes enjoyed recalling his early fear of bears, for by the time the survey was into the wilderness the old timers had filled him with all manner of dreadful stories. The one that bothered him most concerned the poor fellow who was squeezed so hard that he lost his breath and his eyes popped out. When he came to his senses, his first task was to find his eyes and replace them in their sockets! When Holmes actually did meet his first bear, he was on a mule, which straightaway turned around and high-tailed it with Holmes hanging on for dear life. When he returned to the scene, the footprints left by the bear showed that he had been equally frightened and had done a fast 180° turn also.[53]

In a few days, the parties separated again. Hayden left the area by way of Bottler's Ranch, Stevenson went to Virginia City for more supplies, and Bradley explored the geyser basins. When Stevenson returned, the party headed southward, leaving the Upper Geyser Basin on September 3. They searched out the sources of the Snake River, named Shoshone Lake, and trekked along the shores of Jackson Lake. The view across the lake, with the Tetons rising 7,000 feet above its western shores, filled the observers with a sense of sublimity. As they worked southward they also named Leigh Lake and Jenny Lake, both names which have remained. Leigh was Beaver Dick's last name; Jenny was the name of his wife.

[53] Holmes, Random Records, Vol. II, 15–39.

Autumn was upon them now. One morning the thermometer stood at 4.5 degrees above zero. Much of the time the peaks of the Tetons were protected by a soft brassière of gray-white cloud, and when the protective mantle was lifted a new, glistening cover of snow increased their beauty. Hastily, the party made its way down the upper Snake River, past the mouth of Salt Creek. The terrain was changing. With each mile, the timber diminished on the hillsides until scattered groves of cottonwoods and green serpentine traces of willows along the streams constituted the only foliage. Westward now, onto the sagebrush plain, the party worked its way until, on October 11, it arrived at Fort Hall. Within a few days, the men reached Ogden, where they disbanded. Thus ended the work of Stevenson's division, which had explored territory virtually unknown to the civilized world.

It was fortunate that Jackson had accompanied Stevenson, for in this year as in the previous season, some of Jackson's pictures did more to advertise the Tetons than thousands of words could have done. At one time, the photographer, with four aides and the usual pack animals, spent ten days apart from the main party, reaching a great plateau at between 10,500 and 11,000 feet and there setting up his outfit. "At one place," he wrote, "we had to pass around a narrow, high ledge, an extremely dangerous undertaking through the deep, sloping snow. But we made it, and . . . were rewarded with one of the most stupendous panoramas in all America. Thousands of feet below us lay the icy gorge of Glacier Creek, while on the eastern horizon the main range shimmered in the midmorning sun. Above all this towered the Grand Teton, nearly 14,000 feet above sea level."[54]

The usual accomplishments were credited to the expedition. Lesquereux, Meek, and Cope all submitted papers for the annual report on their analyses of fossils turned over to them by the survey, and Coleoptera (insects such as beetles and weevils), Orthoptera (grasshoppers, cockroaches), Odonata (dragon flies), and Mallophaga (bird lice) were all subjects of scientific re-

[54] Jackson, *Time Exposure*, 206–207.

ports. John Merle Coulter submitted a report on botany: 60 species of grasses, 53 of mosses, 66 of lichens, and a total listing of over 1,200 species of plants.

Sixteen-year-old C. Hart Merriam, the ornithologist, collected 313 bird skins and 67 bird's nests with eggs, all of which were later classified and stored at the Smithsonian, Professor Baird and young Robert Ridgeway contributing their knowledge to the work.

Sometimes the collectors erred. Merriam thought he had collected five rare little rabbits (Lepus bairdii, Hayden) which lived only in the Yellowstone-Teton area and were remarkable in that the males suckled the young.[55] Unfortunately, these "rare" rabbits soon turned out to be typical snowshoe rabbits that live in the high western country from Canada to New Mexico, are really hares rather than rabbits, and raise their young in a fairly normal manner.[56]

In still other fields beginnings were made. Topographical work was not yet very good, but the additions to survey personnel of Gustavus Bechler, Henry Gannett, and William Henry Holmes indicated that in another season such work might become outstanding.

Hayden would return again, one day, to "the summit of the world." In 1877 and 1878, he began an ambitious project of mapping Wyoming, Idaho, and Montana, as well as making the usual exhaustive geological and natural history survey of the region. Along with the topographers went Jackson with his camera and the usual entourage of scientists. Money in abundance was available for maps, etchings, and photographs, and the results of the expeditions of 1877 and 1878 were voluminous annual reports as well as special reports, bulletins, and tremendous monographs too numerous to mention. Geologists C. A. White, F. M. Endlich, A. C. Peale, Orestes St. John, and Hayden

[55] C. Hart Merriam, "Report on the Mammals and Birds of the Expedition," *Sixth Annual Report*, 667–68.

[56] Elliott Coues and J. A. Allen, *Monographs of North American Rodentia*, 310–13. William B. Davis, *The Recent Mammals of Idaho*, 355–57.

himself contributed their energies to the great project. In botany, Sir Joseph Hooker, director of the Gardens of Kew, England, and Professor Asa Gray, of Cambridge, contributed their
knowledge and their valuable time. Elliott Coues and J. A. Allen
contributed information about North American mammals. And
men of hardly less ability in other fields made their valuable
contributions. The annual report of 1878, in two volumes, totalled
1,312 pages. It did not appear until 1883 because of the work
demanded in its preparation.

These volumes all added to the basic knowledge of the American West, and in that sense they are just as important as are the
earlier ones. But by 1877 the terrain had already been covered,
and the glamour was missing from the work (although A. D.
Wilson's division was robbed of all its animals and part of its
outfit near Sawtelle's Peak in eastern Idaho in 1878).

Such was not the case with the activities of the survey in Colorado Territory, 1873–1876, when the Hayden men mapped the
rugged central Rockies, and mapped them well. They also discovered the Mount of the Holy Cross and the cliff dwellings. To
Colorado, then, we must next direct our attention.

3

Colorado

WHEN RUMORS PERSISTED, back in 1859, that the Pikes Peak gold discoveries were a gigantic hoax, Horace Greeley put on his white duster, his porkpie hat, and his sloppy black boots, adjusted his little glasses so that he could see better, and set off to investigate for himself. Having survived a stage trip across the plains that could have pleased only a chiropractor, Greeley appeared one day at Central City, center of the diggings, and asked to be shown.

The miners escorted him to a placer claim, handed him a pan, and let him wash the gravel away. The newspaperman's light-blue eyes blazed with excitement as the fine flakes of lustrous gold appeared at the bottom of the pan. Impressed, he went home to write glowing reports on the gold discoveries in Gregory Gulch, and the rush to the Rockies increased.

In his excitement, that day at Central City, Greeley had missed the knowing glances exchanged between the miners. Of course there was gold in the pan! The gravel had been permeated with gold dust blasted into it from a shotgun. The old technique of "salting" a claim had worked again.[1]

[1] *Colorado: A Guide to the Highest State*, 265.

74

A lot of people besides the New York publisher had been fooled by the Pikes Peak rush, and still more of them were persuaded to part with their money in sky-high Colorado gold mine stocks in the 1860's. The stocks soon proved worthless, and "Colorado Gold Mine Stock" became a loathsome phrase in financial quarters back East. The net result of these disappointments was that the census of 1870 gave to Colorado a population of 39,864, barely 5,000 more inhabitants than it had had in 1860.[2] Yet there was a curiosity about that rugged land that could not be quenched.

In the early 1870's, Colorado's people were concentrated in two areas. One of these centered around Denver and westward twenty-five miles, embracing the mining areas of Georgetown, Central City, Boulder, and Gold Hill. The miners who lived there knew that gold was in the hills, and fortunes were being made even then. (By 1940, over $67,000,000 in gold had been taken from the mines around Central City alone.)[3] The second area, like the first, hugged the Front Range, but extended far to the south, and included Colorado Springs and Pueblo.[4]

To railroad promoters, mining engineers, and English investors in ranchlands, it was clear that the natural resources of Colorado had barely been touched. Yet she lay in the very heartland of the American West, about midway between the Canadian boundary and the Mexican border, with her high Central Rockies acting as a barrier between the Great Plains and the great interior basin beyond. If nothing else, her climate offered hope to the thousands suffering from consumption, the "white man's plague" which was so lethal in those years of the late nineteenth century. In 1870, Colorado awaited her future.

In that year, Denver was connected with the Union Pacific by a line down from Cheyenne. Two months later the Kansas

[2] U.S. Census Office, [*Census Reports*] *Compiled from the Original Returns of the Ninth Census*, I, 16.

[3] *Colorado:A Guide to the Highest State*, 265.

[4] For a good analysis of population trends in Colorado in the 1870's, see Mock, "The Effects of the 'Boom Decade,' 1870–1880, Upon Colorado Population," *Colorado Magazine*, Vol. XI, No. 1 (January, 1934), 30.

Pacific reached Denver, giving the mile-high city a direct connection with Kansas City and St. Louis.[5] The first toot of a locomotive whistle had set off a real estate boom in Denver that did not halt for nearly a decade, and a far-sighted railroad promoter, General William A. Palmer, obtained a charter for his Denver and Rio Grande Railroad and boldly announced plans to enter the sparsely settled mountains with narrow-gauge equipment.[6]

As for the Indians, only the Utes, living in the mountains, still constituted a menace. In 1868, the government had confirmed their claim to a large tract of land in southwestern Colorado, but five years later, by the San Juan Cession of 1873, they were removed from much of the area where mining was being promoted. After the Meeker Massacre in 1879 they were removed from all but a very small strip of land in southwestern Colorado. By the end of the decade the Indian menace was over.[7]

Here, then, was a land about to feel the exploitive touches of American civilization. Yet little was known, in a scientific way, of Colorado's geology, or of her flora and fauna. Maps were essential for proper railroad and mineral development, and no reliable maps of the rugged Central Rockies had ever been drawn. Without some scientific knowledge, without good maps, the exploitation would be wasteful and costly. Colorado was in dire need of a good scientific survey.

It was primarily to fill this need that Hayden decided to abandon the Yellowstone-Teton country and come down to Colorado. There was no portion of the continent, he pointed out, which promised to "yield more useful results, both of a practical and scientific character. . . . The prospect of its rapid development within the next five years, by some of the most important railroads in the West, renders it very desirable that its resources be made known to the world at as early a date as possible."[8]

[5] Percy Stanley Fritz, *Colorado, the Centennial State*, 215.

[6] Frank Hall, *History of the State of Colorado*, I, 498.

[7] Fritz, *Colorado, the Centennial State*, 51, 286–90.

[8] F. V. Hayden, "Letter to the Secretary," [*Seventh*] *Annual Report of the United States Geological and Geographical Survey of the Territories, Embracing Colorado, Being a Report of Progress of the Exploration for the Year 1873*, (hereafter cited as *Seventh Annual Report*), 1. This was the first year *Geographical* appeared in the official title.

Who knew what secrets were locked up in Colorado's mountains? There were all kinds of rumors—of ancient Aztec ruins, of a mountain with a holy cross facing the rising sun, of veins of gold and silver in fantastic abundance. The ruggedness of the territory was generally known although not yet corroborated statistically. Today we know that Colorado has 1,143 peaks rising to over 10,000 feet, 830 over 11,000 feet, and 52 over 14,000 feet.[9] It offered all the challenge the Hayden men could desire.

In this land Hayden proposed his most ambitious project: a long-term, comprehensive survey. Geologists would examine the Rockies and give aid to future mining developments, and natural scientists would do the collecting and classifying that would constitute the basis of all the future knowledge of Colorado's plants and animals. And Jackson would take pictures to show the true grandeur of the Rockies, in contrast to the Currier and Ives distortions. Hayden envisioned a three- to four-year task, and Congress came through with from $65,000 to $95,000 each year to expedite survey operations.[10]

Hayden was especially anxious that the Rockies be mapped so that at the end of the survey an atlas could be issued, beautiful and accurate, as precise as the topographical methods of the 1870's could make it. Such an atlas would give the ruggedest territory a map more settled states of the Union would envy.

Hayden had delved into topography before, but his luck had run against him. Although some maps had been produced of the Yellowstone-Teton country, they had not come up to his expectations, and some of his topographers had not been very reliable. In 1872, however, Gustavus Bechler, Henry Gannett, and William Henry Holmes had joined the survey. They remained on and became stalwarts of Hayden's slowly expanding topographical corps. Then in 1873 he enticed James Terry Gardner to join his staff. Gardner, who had formerly been with King's Fortieth Parallel Survey, became the chief topographer for the Hayden

---

[9] *Year Book of the State of Colorado, 1948–1950,* 155.

[10] *Geological and Geographical Surveys,* 45 Cong., 2 sess., *House Exec. Doc.* 81, 5.

Survey and the guiding spirit behind the atlas of Colorado.[11] Later A. D. Wilson, who had also been with King, joined the survey, and over the years other topographers joined, the most useful being Franklin Rhoda and George B. Chittenden.

Hayden had little interest in the plains east of the Rockies, and his atlas was to begin along a north-south line running approximately through the Colorado towns of Greeley, Pueblo, and Trinidad (104° 30″) and extending westward to the Utah line. The northern boundary would be the southern line of King's Fortieth Parallel Survey (which extended a few miles into Colorado). The southern limits were originally to embrace all the land to the Mexican border, but actually Hayden never advanced far into New Mexico.[12]

The mapping itself was accomplished by painstaking mathematical work which demanded uncompromising honesty from the men. That is why some of them became topographers—because the art (for it was an art, as well as a science)—became a physical, realistic search for truth. And the topographer, transmitting terrain onto a piece of paper with the greatest accuracy of which he was capable, held truth in the strokes of his pencil. Here, then, was a magnificent challenge, and men like Gardner, Wilson, Bechler, Rhoda, and Holmes became topographers par excellence.

For a topographer's job is to interpret correctly the face of nature, to be able to transmit what the eye sees to a sheet of paper so that a person may look at the resultant map and gain a reasonably clear conception of the features of the country portrayed. In order to have distances, latitudes, longitudes, and elevations accurately fixed, Gardner and his men made use of the customary surveying methods. Having established a base line, they developed a system of triangles from the base line to mountain peaks within a half-circle swung from north to west to south. In turn, from these peaks the topographers fixed with

[11] For more details about Gardner, see Chapter 5.

[12] *Geological and Geographical Surveys*, 45 Cong., 2 sess., *House Exec. Doc. 81*, 4–5. National Archives, R.G. 48, Office of the Secretary of the Interior, Patents and Miscellaneous Division, Box 72, Hayden to Delano, January 27, 1873.

their transits more great triangles, so that by the end of three seasons work all of western Colorado, from the Front Range to the Utah border, had been submitted to a "primary triangulation." Within these great triangles they created a system of "secondary triangulation" in which distances between points were fixed at an average of six to eight miles. When both the primary and the secondary triangulation had been carefully finished, all of the principal geographic points in Colorado were represented in very close proximity to their real positions in nature. On the map they would then appear in the right latitude and longitude, and Pikes Peak would not be near Longs Peak, nor would the headwaters of the South Platte River mingle with the flow of the Big Thompson. In addition, altitudes were checked with base points of the railroads, and barometric observations were constantly being taken, checked, and rechecked so that elevations and contours on the map would be as accurate as possible.

All of this work was technical, scientific, and mathematical. But the tracing on the map of the drainage system of an entire region demanded more than triangles and mathematical calculation. Somehow the elevations had to appear as the peaks, craters, cones, knobs, hills, knolls, mounds, dunes, promontories, or headlands that they were, and so, once the triangulation had been done, the topographers sat down on the windy mountain tops and sketched with their lead pencils the drainage system, or the mountains, that met their eyes.

The acknowledged expert in this category was William Henry Holmes, whose magnificent sketches and cutaway drawings of the earth, showing the age and contours of the formations beneath the surface, have become classics of the art. But whether by Holmes or others, the resultant profile sketches, showing all the significant angles, bends, spurs, saddles, and changes in the slope of the land, were fixed on the spot, so that at a time in the future, from an office in far off Washington, D. C., a map would emerge—the end product of transforming the various formations into contours and platting them within the triangles where they belonged. It would be a product of scientific and artistic skill which, to the extent that its makers were seekers of truth, was a true picture of what was really there.[13]

The atlas became the obsession of the Hayden Survey, and in the four seasons spent in Colorado (1873–1876) all other activities revolved about the topographical work. Geology, paleontology, and all the natural sciences received their due attention, but the first considerations invariably went to the topographers. At the start of each season a sort of routine was established which varied but slightly from year to year. The situation in the first year, 1873, was thus quite typical.

In the late spring, James Stevenson established headquarters in a cottonwood grove at Meiers Fisher's ranch along Clear Creek, about four miles from Denver. Because of Hayden's Civil War training the camp was arranged neatly, military fashion, with tents on either side of a wide, clean street, the kitchen, stables, and other sanitary facilities being placed in such a way as to avoid, as much as possible, any contamination, for Hayden valued the health of his men.[14]

Here Stevenson assembled personnel, livestock, and equipment. The camp men drifted in from everywhere, with a few old stand-bys like Potato John, Shep Madera, and Tom Cooper always reappearing like magic from a winter spent in parts unknown. The scientists, rather slow in meeting their deadlines, trickled into the headquarters camp. Once they were all there, the men still had to grow accustomed to each other, packers had to get acquainted with their mules, and preparations for several months in the field had to be pushed along with all haste. The season was always well along, and there was much to be done before the first snowfall.

When the survey was all assembled, Stevenson's task was to divide it into several divisions or parties (Hayden used the terms interchangeably) and disperse them to regions as far removed as the Yampa River in the northwest part of the territory and

[13] Richard A. Bartlett, "The Hayden Survey in Colorado," *Colorado Quarterly,* Vol. IV, No. 1 (Summer, 1955), 77–78.

[14] Clarence S. Jackson and Lawrence W. Marshall, *Quest of the Snowy Cross,* 38–39.

the Mesa Verde in the southwest corner. During these years the survey was never a single unit tramping the mountains; it was always six or more groups working widely apart, but always according to plan. Thus in 1873 the personnel was divided into three divisions of from eight to twelve men each. Although the members of each division could change over to another, a geologist, a topographer, two packers and a cook were common to each one. There were often two or three other men along—naturalists, journalists, or guests. Usually a mongrel dog tagged along as a mascot.

These divisions worked up the topography, geology, and natural history of fixed geographical areas. In addition, a primary triangulation party and Hayden's own supervisory party roamed the entire region being surveyed while the photographic party, led by William Henry Jackson, made its way through the areas assigned to the other three divisions in the search for good photographs. A quartermaster's party under Stevenson's direction likewise roamed the Rockies, trying to keep all groups supplied with food. Including both the geographical divisions and the several parties under Hayden's general direction, the survey each summer put into the field six to eight groups of men.

Gardner, with his years of topographical experience to aid him, grasped the enormity of the project and dissected the territory into logical parts. On the east was the Front Range, with Longs Peak, Mount Evans, and Pikes Peak among its "fourteeners"—peaks over 14,000 feet high. Westward lay the North, Middle and South Parks, separated from each other by low cross-ridges; across the Sangre de Cristo Mountains from South Park lay the San Luis Park. Thirty to forty miles across the parks the mountains rose again. On the north was the Park Range and south of this group the Gore Range (called by Gardner the Blue River group). Still southward, across South Park, the Sawatch Mountains (called the National Range by Gardner) set in, the highest of all. West and southwest of the Sawatch Mountains were the remote Elk Mountains, resembling the Canadian Rockies with their strata of dark-red sandstone, and, south of them, the northwest-southeast-running San Juan Mountains. North of these two ranges the territory was cut up into high plateaus, deep river valleys, and occasional mountain ranges. Thus the best way of envisioning Colorado's mountains is to picture them as lying in an inverted L.[15]

Gardner pitched into the work with zeal. Since he first had to establish the primary triangulation over the entire area, upon which the divisional topographers would base their secondary triangulation, he could ill afford to waste time. The first few weeks were spent in and about Denver, where he established his six-mile-long base line from which the entire triangulation of Colorado was to be determined. Every means of insuring accuracy was followed in establishing this base line: the length was twice measured with steel tape, kept under twenty pounds strain, with temperature observations being taken every five minutes. For if the base line was a true six miles in length and if it was placed accurately with regard to latitude and longitude, then all subsequent triangulations, even to the Utah border, would be just as accurate. When the length had been established, triangular pyramids thirty feet high were erected at each end, by means of which readings were expanded to conspicuous mountain peaks on whose summits rough stone monuments had been built.[16]

The correct elevations of the base line and all the peaks which figured in the triangulation were essential, and this constituted a problem, since the determination of high points with the mercurial barometer were liable to errors varying from 150 to 300 feet. In order to achieve greater accuracy, Gardner arranged to have permanent meteorological observations made during the field season of 1873 from four stations: Denver (5,000 feet), Canon City (6,000 feet), Fairplay (10,000 feet), and Mount

15 James T. Gardner, "Hayden and Gardner's Survey of the Territories, Under the Direction of the Department of the Interior," *American Journal of Science and Arts,* Third Series, Vol. VI, No. 34 (October, 1873), 297–98. Roger W. Toll, "The Hayden Survey in Colorado in 1873 and 1874," *Colorado Magazine,* Vol. VI, No. 4 (July, 1929), 152–54. The names of the peaks have been checked in Robert M. Ormes, *Guide to the Colorado Mountains.* Ormes suggests the inverted L to describe Colorado's mountains.

16 James T. Gardner, "Sketch of the Methods of Survey in the Geographical Department," *Seventh Annual Report,* 627.

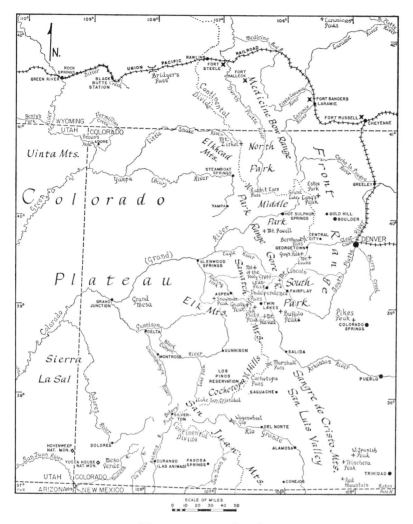

Mountainous Colorado

Lincoln (14,000 feet). Readings were to be taken at 7:00 A.M., 2:00 P.M., and 9:00 P.M. The observations taken by the field parties were then classified according to elevation, and each class was referred to the base station which was nearest in elevation.[17]

[17] James T. Gardner, "On the Hypsometric Work of U.S. Geological and Geographical Survey of the Territories, F. V. Hayden, U.S. Geologist in Charge," *American Journal of Science and Arts,* Third Series, Vol. VI, No. 35 (November, 1873), 373.

With the base line laid and the initial triangulation points spotted, Gardner was next ready to send the divisions into the field. He had selected about 20,000 square miles, roughly bounded on the east by a line from Longs Peak to Pikes Peak and then stretching westward about 130 miles. He divided the area into three districts, each about 58 miles broad and 130 miles deep. To each of these he entrusted a division of geologists and topographers, with orders to cover the district topographically before the first snow fell in autumn.[18]

Gardner's task was to accomplish the primary triangulation, season after season, until the territory was covered, while at the same time supervising the entire topographical phase of the Hayden Survey. In 1873, he found it convenient to accompany one of the three divisions for a few weeks. This was the First, or Middle Park, Division. Its leader was Archibald Marvine, a mild-mannered geologist with a wild, untended, dark-brown beard, who had previously been with the Michigan Survey and with Lieutenant Wheeler. The chief topographer was Gustavus Bechler. Altogether, the beginning party, including Gardner, Holmes, and another topographer, George B. Chittenden, numbered nine persons. Besides their riding animals, the outfit took along seven pack mules. Thus prepared, Marvine set out late in May and stayed in the mountains until mid-October, when snow drove him back to the Denver camp.

During this period the Marvine party made seventy stations at high points about eight miles apart. From these commanding stations the secondary triangles were plotted, and drainage sketches expressed in contours and profile sketches were made. All significant angles, crooks, bends, spurs, saddles, and changes in slope were fixed so that, as Hayden said, by the end of the season the topographers had recorded "thousands of points . . . with an exceedingly close approximation of absolute truth." From these a map could later be drawn.

[18] Gardner, "Hayden and Gardner's Survey of the Territories, Under the Direction of the Department of the Interior," *American Journal of Science and Arts*, Third Series, Vol. VI, No. 34 (October, 1873), 297.

It should be noted that in all this topographical work there was a close association with geology. While the topographer was busy with his transit, gradienter, or sketch pad, the geologist was making his own detailed and special studies, generalizing "from the higher stations made by the topographer, obtaining extensive views from them, from which he can trace his formations across the country, and . . . secure data by which he can readily color a general geological map upon his return." The topographer also profited, for the geologist's understanding of the anatomy of the country gave perspective and depth to the work of the topographer who merely understood the surface.[19]

Within a few weeks Gardner took leave of the Marvine party, for his primary triangulation was to take him southward and westward into the areas being worked up by other divisions. For three seasons, 1873, 1874, and 1875, he extended his work westward until the boundaries of Colorado were reached. The highest peaks in every area had to be climbed—Mounts Lincoln and Harvard, Italia Mountain, Red Mountain, Teocalli Mountain, La Plata Mountain, Grays Peak, Pikes Peak, and Longs Peak, to name but a very few. Many of these were climbed for the first time by the men of the Hayden Survey, and were christened by the topographers with names which they still carry.

Obviously something more was needed than scientific skill and artistic sketching ability. Climbing two or three mountain peaks above 10,000 feet in altitude each day was hard physical labor. The atmosphere was clearest in the early hours after sunrise, so as often as possible camp was pitched at timberline, with the distance to the summit providing a short, brisk climb for an early morning constitutional. Gardner's party often arose between three and four o'clock, built a fire, and sat shivering in the frosty air with a few coals under their tin cups and plates to keep the food and drink from freezing. The peak, their target for the day, loomed high above them, as often as not newly dusted with snow. It was not unusual for the topographers to spend six to eight hours at work on a mountain peak, and, if the

19 Hayden, "Letter to the Secretary," *Seventh Annual Report*, 3.

85

weather closed in on them, to return to the summit the next day. In August, 1874, Gardner spent two days and a night on top of Pikes Peak. "It snowed and blew bitterly cold," he wrote to his wife, "but there were hours of wonderful clearness when I saw points 150 miles off."[20]

What Gardner described as the most difficult and dangerous climb he ever made occurred on August 20, 1873, when he tackled Snowmass Peak, a "fourteener" in the Elk Mountains just southwest of the town of Aspen. Three times his assistant prevented Gardner from falling backward by placing the transit tripod against his back. Incidentally, these transits, which had to be carried by the climbers, weighed more than forty pounds each.

Yet it was not all such trying work. Gardner was taken with the grassy meadows, bright with the thousands of flowers—wild flax, purple-blue lupia, and scarlet trumpet-shaped little flowers, probably scarlet gilia—that grew at the high altitudes. From the Elk Mountains he wrote Hayden of the beauties of that remote area:

> Constantly as we wound through the darker forest, our trail would wind out into these luxuriant meadows, and then pass again into the cool shade of the aspen trees whose straight silvery stems and crown of shivering leaves soften the light without excluding it, and make not a gloom as do the dark conifers of the high altitudes; but cheerful woods where grass grows, and flowers bloom, and the atmosphere has the softened tone of great solitude.[21]

Sometimes things went wrong, jealousies arose, and animosities smoldered. Topographers were men of strong character and many idiosyncrasies, and it was well that they had to separate and go out in little parties, for otherwise violent antagonisms would have erupted. Hard-working Gus Bechler complained in 1875 that, having arrived at the rendezvous camp in Denver

---

[20] Toll, "The Hayden Survey in Colorado in 1873 and 1874," *Colorado Magazine*, Vol. VI, No. 4 (July, 1929), 152–54.

[21] National Archives, R.G. 48, Office of the Secretary of the Interior, Patents and Miscellaneous Division, Box 72, Gardner to Hayden, August 5, 1875.

twenty-four hours later than the others, he had fallen heir to the broken-down animals that nobody else wanted: mules "with numerous scars on their sides and backs, ready to break open at the first days march." Therefore, he had no alternative but to use his "own bones harder than any of the animals." As if this was not sufficient adversity, he looked down from the top of the second peak he climbed (one close to Lost Park in Park County, near South Park) to see his camp on fire. With commendable self-control he remained on the summit until his observations were finished. Once back in camp he discovered that the fire had destroyed his tent and everything in it—all his bedding, a good coat, two pairs of saddle blankets, and a pack saddle.[22]

Forest fires were a nuisance as well as a hazard, and they were very common in the 1870's and 1880's. The smoke obstructed the view and hindered the topographical work, and on occasion an unpredictable inferno, swept by mountain winds, might threaten to engulf an entire party of men. The topographer Franklin Rhoda described such a fire, as well as other irritating conditions, that troubled his group in 1874:

> Leaving Del Norte [in southwest Colorado] we commenced work in the mountains to the south of that town and found a good deal of snow still on the ground but it was melting fast, at the same time giving rise to millions of mosquitoes and bogs everywhere. In this region the new "Summit District" mines are situated. They are building a new road to them which for 15 miles is nowhere below 12,000 feet in elevation and at one point crosses a mountain nearly 13,000 feet high. For the first week in this part of the country we were troubled by the smoke from several great fires. One in particular was raging down in a deep canyon as we passed along the highway above mentioned. The smoke extended clear across San Luis Valley. . . . As we came along the smoke came out in awful volumes almost thick enough to cut. Now and then a break in the great clouds would give us a glimpse into the great furnace and reminded us muchly of the warm place that all good topographers go

[22] National Archives, R.G. 57, Hayden Survey, General Letters Received, Bechler to Hayden, July 8, 1875.

to when they die. Every moment I expected to see the little devils, with the typical wings of flame playing leap frog from the fiery furnace.[23]

Electrical storms were another hazard. Rhoda and his companion, A. D. Wilson, had a near-tragic, though not uncommon, experience. Having reached the summit of a peak, they had barely set to work sketching when they both began to feel "a peculiar tickling sensation" along the roots of their hair. It was accompanied by "a peculiar sound almost exactly like that produced by frying bacon." As the thunderheads swept closer, the electrical tension increased, while the topographers, as if themselves charged with high voltage, made increasing efforts to complete their work. The transit began to click like a telegraph, faster and faster, and even their lead pencils hummed. Their hair stood on end. Then, "there was a sudden and instantaneous release," for lightning had struck somewhere, discharging the electricity, and a peal of thunder struck their ears. Then the ticking began again, the hair stood up straighter and straighter from their heads, until another stroke of lightning brought relief. "By this time," Rhoda remarked, ". . . we were electrified, and our notes were taken and recorded with lightning speed. . . . When we raised our hats our hair stood on end, the sharp points of the hundreds of stones about us emitted a continuous sound, while the instrument outsang everything else, and even at this high altitude could be heard distinctly at the distance of fifty yards."

Both men finally ran to safety among the rocks below. The next time lightning struck the adjoining peak, Wilson scrambled back up to the summit to get the transit. He grabbed the tripod, hastily threw it over his shoulder, and dashed back. Even so, he received a strong shock "accompanied by a pain as if a sharp-pointed instrument had pierced his shoulder." Hardly had they climbed more than thirty feet below the summit when it was struck by lightning.[24]

[23] National Archives, R.G. 57, Hayden Survey, General Letters Received, Rhoda to Hayden, July 13, 1875.

[24] Franklin Rhoda, "Report on the Topography of the San Juan Country," [*Eighth*] *Annual Report of the United States Geological and Geographical Sur-*

When they started on a season's campaign, the bell mare tinkling her musical pendant in the soft mountain stillness, the men riding leisurely astride their walking mules, and the pack mules trudging along, their eyes half closed, fuzzy ears twitching off the flies, one might have thought that a summer vacation lay ahead. But by noon, after the mules had cavorted and spilled out their packs a couple of times, and tender human posteriors had begun to get stiff and sore from the hard saddles, and the noses and backs of the necks began to feel tender from the Colorado sun, any thoughts of vacation were soon lost. If they could average twenty miles a day, they were doing well. The trail, such as it was, might lead through glorious mountain country, or across an alkali desert. The weather might be delightful, or rainy, or a wind might be blowing up a dust storm or a blizzard. At noon a sandwich munched on the march allayed the pangs of hunger. And always there were the great indeterminables, the mules.

These animals, "so long of ear and quick of heel," commanded three times the cost of a pack horse in Denver. The western pack mules were small, sinewy, tough, and devilishly sly. Most of them had been bred from Indian ponies and were born on the open plains. When they were three years old, they were corralled and sold as broncos, and breaking a mule made a horse bronco seem as gentle as a lamb by comparison. Hell had no fury like a mule when the crupper was placed under his tail for the first time. And the blacksmith who could shoe a mule could be a volunteer for straddling a thunderbolt![25]

Whenever men of the survey congregated around a campfire, the yarns about the mules began. The Hayden Survey had about 120 of the beasts, and every one of them had some part of the devil lodging in his head. "Nine mules out of ten seem to have all the stubborn perversity of the ass, with the spirit of the horse," commented Cuthbert Mills, correspondent for the New York *Times*. "Very little consideration is shown them, a kick in

vey of the Territories, Embracing Colorado and Parts of Adjacent Territories; Being a Report of Progress of the Exploration for the Year 1874 (hereafter cited as *Eighth Annual Report*), 457–59.

[25] Ernest Ingersoll, "Rocky Mountain Mules," *Scribner's Monthly*, Vol. XIX, No. 6 (April, 1880), 929–36.

the ribs being the most common method of starting." And from its initial separation from the herd in the spring until its release to pasture in the fall, the mule was a problem.[26]

Once the mule was separated from the herd (a major task in itself), the packing began. From each side a packer approached, one with a blanket and the other with the aparejo. The mule braced for a buck, sprang high into the air, and landed on his four feet, holding his legs perfectly stiff. He kicked in every direction. On occasion a mule had even been known to chase a man around the tree to which it was tied, "with open mouth and glaring eyes." And if he got the chance, he would bite. If the mule persisted in kicking, one of his front legs would be tied up close to his breast. Even then he might kick and buck and rear over backwards, but in the end the human masters always succeeded in loading the packs.

The lash rope, thrown around his dusty body, was looped and fashioned into an expert diamond hitch. Now the pack saddle, looking like a small saw horse, was fastened securely on his back, four horns, one at each corner, sticking up from it. With professional skill the packers, old-timers like Tom Cooper and Shep Madera, attached bed rolls, tents, cooking utensils, engineering instruments, bottles of whisky, and everything else used by the expedition. Flashing pie pans, gadgets that tinkled, and instruments that might stick out and catch on a tree or a bush were carefully eliminated or enclosed deep within the pack, which was loaded with such finesse that not a square inch of space was left over. Finally a covering, attached to the lash rope, was thrown over the whole.

Then came the moment of truth. On each side of the mule a packer held an end of the rope, and at a signal each man placed a booted foot on his side. Then both men pulled in the cinch with all the strength at their command. The poor mule brayed for mercy as the rope tightened around his belly like a corset on a plump girl. The mule twitched his dusty tail, flipped his ears, brayed in anguish, but it was all over. He was packed and cinched and ready for a full day's journeying. (Unless of course

[26] New York *Times*, June 13, 1875, p. 7.

he had held his breath so that when he exhaled, the pack would slip. Then the air would turn blue with profanity.)

When they hit the trail, the mules always filed along one behind the other. Travel with a pack train was possible only because mules would invariably follow a horse. Turn a herd loose where there was a horse, and they would follow him wherever he went. The solution of this horse fetish was the use of the bell mare which, by tradition, was always ridden by the cook. "When the cook leads off in the morning," wrote Mills, "and the bell begins to jingle, every mule follows." Of course at first there was a fight for the first place behind her, but after this matter was settled, they all followed at a steady gait, for trotting loosened the packs and rubbed sores onto their backs and bellies. Good packers like Shep Madera and his partner Clarence Kelsey kept the packs balanced and readjusted them or tightened them while the rest of the train moved on.

Mules would scare at the flash of a pie pan or the sight of an Indian. They would spook when a geologist's pick appeared, or at the sight of a bright shirt. They would rub their riders against every rock and tree alongside a wide trail. They could get just plain tired of difficult terrain and all jump into a river to drown —as happened with Jackson's mules in the Yellowstone—that is, unless someone pulled them out. They could lose their footing and fall a hundred feet, stand up and bray, and then start grazing. They could kick like greased lightning and break a man's leg in an instant if contact was made. "And it is my honest opinion," Ingersoll concluded, "founded upon much observation, that so long as any considerable numbers of mules are employed there, it is utterly useless for missionaries to go to the Rocky Mountains." Yet the surefootedness of the mule made him indispensable to the survey.[27]

If the surveyor was not riding with the pack train, then his lot was toiling up a mountain through snow and loose rocks, in a rarefied atmosphere, "observing" and perhaps building a pyra-

[27] New York *Times,* November 22, 1874, p. 1, June 13, 1875, p. 7, June 23, 1875, p. 4. Ingersoll, "Rocky Mountain Mules," *Scribner's Monthly,* Vol. XIX, No. 6 (April, 1880), 931, 936.

mid of rocks, shivering through a mountain squall, and then descending to camp. Or it was searching along precarious ledges, swinging his hammer, breaking up rocks in the search for fossils. Gradually, as the naturalist-writer Ingersoll said, "your 'glory of existence' oozes away, while the most dismal reflections arise to keep company with your strained muscles."[28]

But there was always the scenery, the sight of new terrain, and the glimpses of game—antelope, elk, deer, bear, mountain lion, as well as rabbit and beaver, woodchuck and skunk. Of all the animals, the bear proved the most thrilling. There was something about a bear that roused the sporting blood. Standing up seven to eight feet tall on its hind legs, weighing three hundred to one thousand pounds, with its great, beautiful, shaggy coat rippling in the wind, its nose sniffing the air, and its little eyes searching the landscape, bruin was a greater challenge than any deer or elk. The sight of a male looming up like a lord of the landscape, or of a female ambling along the base of a snowbank with a couple of cubs trailing behind, was the only valid excuse for breaking the plodding rhythm of the pack train or deviating from the conquest of a mountain. Bear was *the* game, and everyone wanted to "git a b'ar!"

Jackson shot his giant silvertip grizzly in 1878 in the Yellowstone, the cartridge entering the great beast's nostrils and killing him immediately.[29] Archibald Marvine's party, west of Middle Park until late November, 1874, lived for two weeks on flour and the game brought in by their hunter, Harry Yount. He shot a huge grizzly four times as it came smashing toward him, hatred in its eyes. One of the bullets smashed the front of its skull, two hit it in the flanks, and one penetrated its heart before it died, too close to Harry for comfort.[30] William Henry Holmes, "an independent cuss," was returning alone to camp near the Roaring Fork River one day in 1873 when he discovered a bear on the other side of a high log, with its head down, rooting for food.

[28] Ernest Ingersoll, "Rocky Mountain Nights," *Scribner's Monthly*, Vol. XX, No. 2 (June, 1880), 218.

[29] Jackson, *Time Exposure*, 249–50.

[30] New York *Times*, January 18, 1875, p. 5, August 29, 1875, p. 5. Yount became the first ranger of Yellowstone National Park.

Holmes shouted, "Boo-hoo," the bear reared up, and momentarily Holmes and the bear were face to face; but just one bullet from his trusty Springfield dispensed the beast.[31]

Occasionally, the monotony of hard work was broken by the presence of Indians lurking in the neighborhood. They were usually Utes, Paiutes, or renegades from several tribes.

In 1874, Jackson hoped to obtain fine pictures of the Utes at the Los Pinos Reservation, just west of Cochetopa Pass in south-central Colorado. Arriving there late in August, he found seventy occupied tepees and the plain dotted with Indian ponies. But although he met with Chiefs Ouray and Piah, most of the Indians refused to let him take pictures, and after four days of haggling, Jackson had to give up and continue on his way to the San Juan Mountains.[32]

The *Times* correspondent, visiting the agency the next year, was disappointed with what he saw. The Indians, he said, looked best from a distance. "As they came galloping over the hill, with their bright scarlet blankets loosely hung around them, and their feathers and beaded trappings flying in the wind, they looked picturesque enough," he wrote, "but nearer acquaintance disenchanted us." Furthermore, they paid little attention to the Sabbath, gambling the whole day through on their horse races.[33]

William Henry Holmes nearly ran into trouble with the Indians in 1875. The district assigned to him was in the Four Corners area of southwestern Colorado. Parts of three Indian reservations were included in his assigned field, Ute, Apache, and Navaho. Of these the Wiminuche, or Southern Utes, were the

[31] Holmes, Random Records, Vol. VI, 64. There is an interesting sidelight to this story. George B. Chittenden, a newcomer in 1873, ran down from the camp to help skin the bear. In his excitement, he laid his nickel-plated Smith and Wesson, a gift from his friends of the Coastal Survey, on which he had worked, on a nearby log. He forgot about it until he was miles away and, disheartened, gave it up for lost. In 1928, Jackson packed in to Snowmass Lake, and one of the guides, Henry Hutchins, prodding him about old times, discovered that a rusted Smith and Wesson pistol inscribed to Chittenden, which he had found in 1912, belonged to a topographer then living in Washington. In a fitting ceremony in February, 1929, the pistol was returned to "Chitty" while his two fellow topographers, Holmes and Story B. Ladd, who shared an apartment with him, looked on.

[32] Jackson, *Time Exposure,* 227–28.

[33] New York *Times,* July 27, 1875, p. 1.

most formidable, for they had been forced to sell a part of the San Juan mining area and had been driven from that excellent hunting ground. Disgruntled and brooding over their treatment, they threatened to prevent surveyors employed by the General Land Office from laying their new boundary lines. Knowing that the Indians would confuse his men with the hated men of the G.L.O., Holmes arranged for a messenger to go to their village and inform them that his party was not laying the line. The Indians heeded this intelligence and gave Holmes no real trouble.[34]

Still, Indians were lurking in the general neighborhood, and they gave the party some uneasy moments. On the night of August 28, when Holmes's party was camped close to the Utah border, the chief packer, Tom Cooper, was awakened about midnight by the sound of the stock moving down the canyon. Believing there was a bear, a mountain lion, or some other marauding animal, he grabbed his rifle and chased after the stock. Coming up to one of the tethered animals, he was startled momentarily by the sight of an Indian crouching only a few feet away from him. The Indian was also frightened, and Cooper, the first to compose his thoughts, soon had the marauder and his companions running away to the sound of his rifle fire.[35]

The most serious Indian trouble occurred in the Sierra La Sal Mountains on the border of Colorado and Utah in 1875. In order to join the Hayden Survey with the Powell Survey in Utah, Gardner had to run the risk of trouble with a renegade band of Utes and Paiutes who were known to occupy the area. He had asked Powell about it, but Powell predicted no trouble. Chief Ouray, however, had warned Gardner to stay out of the Sierra La Sal, where, he said, a dark and grizzled old Indian led several lodges.

Early in August, 1875, Gardner joined forces with the division led by Henry Gannett, meeting him on the Gunnison River near

[34] William Henry Holmes, "Report of William H. Holmes, Geologist of the San Juan Division, 1875, on the San Juan District," *Ninth Annual Report of the United States Geological and Geographical Survey of the Territories, Embracing Colorado and Parts of Adjacent Territories; Being a Report of Progress of the Exploration for the Year 1875* (hereafter cited as *Ninth Annual Report*), 238.

[35] Holmes, "Episodes and Adventures," Random Records, Vol. II, Chap. 2.

its junction with the Grand River (the Colorado), close to the present site of Grand Junction. The combined party, consisting of seven scientists and eight camp men and packers, started south down the Dolores River, leaving two young men, Holman and Dallas, to look after a base camp on the way. The thirteen remaining men cautiously marched southward, maintaining guard day and night. The heat was intense, and man and beast alike suffered from thirst as they followed an old Indian trail into narrow canyons and among steep bluffs.

All day they had seen Indian sign—recently irrigated little corn fields, an old Indian and a boy. Then late in the afternoon nine Indians mounted on swift ponies suddenly surrounded Henry Gannett, who was far to the rear. They made signs of friendship, and he returned them, at the same time pushing his tired mule ahead to catch up with the main party. The Indians wanted to trade, but the Hayden men, themselves low on powder and tobacco, refused. Then the Indians urged them to make camp at some mud holes close by, but since neither the men nor the beasts could drink the "nasty fluid" (as Gardner described it), they refused the invitation and moved on. No sooner had the rear guard passed over the brow of a hill than the Indians began firing. Bullets threw up small clouds of dust at the feet of Kelsey and Adams, two camp men who were in the rear.

Gardner ordered the men to lead the tired mules ahead at a trot, while several members of the party scattered to the flanks to protect the main train. When the narrow canyon opened up at one point into a wide sagebrush plain, Gardner brought his men to the center, and there established camp as far as possible from the hills from which the Indians could fire down upon them. A ravine about three hundred yards away offered the Indians some closer protection, however, and from this they exchanged volleys with the topographers. Meanwhile a circular barricade of the aparejos and baggage had been erected.

At sunset, the Indians began crawling through the sagebrush toward the camp, and with the rising of the full moon, they increased their attack, firing often. About midnight the Indians withdrew, but, as the old-timers well knew, only until sunup.

No one had yet been hit, but one mule had been wounded, and men and animals alike were suffering from thirst. As Gardner later described it, their situation was critical:

> We had reached the edge of the great plateau [the Colorado Plateau] and were in an irregular valley running up into it, the surrounding cliffs 1000 feet high. Southward the valley narrowed gradually to a canyon, up which the trail went to a spring. The Indians would undoubtedly be reinforced in the night by the remainder of the band, and while a part would take up the best positions for ambush in the canyon, the remainder, mounted on their swift ponies, would fight us from every knoll as the slow moving train passed on. We had eighteen pack animals. Could they but keep us in this valley a day longer, we would become frantic with thirst and rush to certain death up the canyon.

Gardner saw but one chance, and that was to get out of the canyon and onto the plateau where an ambush would be nearly impossible. At 2:00 A.M., he ordered the mules saddled and packed, and at dawn the party headed toward a point to the southwest that seemed to offer escape from the canyon—a route to the plateau, one thousand feet above. Quickly the Indians renewed their attack, and they dashed along on their ponies, just out of rifle range, trying to reach high points along the path from which they could shoot. Gardner's men at the same time raced for these points, sometimes getting there first, sometimes not, in which case they made a mad run to get out of range of the Indians' fire. In this way the party hurried on down the valley, thirsty, tired, and under fire for five hot hours. One man had a mule shot out from under him, three other mules were lost, and three more were wounded, but a deer trail was finally discovered which led to the plateau, from which the party escaped to safety.[36]

Meanwhile Holman and Dallas, back on the Dolores, had also

---

[36] *Rocky Mountain News*, September 5, 1875, p. 2. New York *Times*, September 5, 1875, p. 4, September 9, 1875, p. 2. Gardner's quotation is from the *Rocky Mountain News*.

been honored by the presence of Indians. Twenty or more Utes, with a certificate of good character from their agent, had come into camp from the White River Agency. They threatened to kill the boys, and they did set fire to the high grass around the tents. But the flames were extinguished, and the Indians finally rode off southward, hurling dire threats as they left. Probably they had spared the lives of the two young men because Holman, who had spent some time at the White River Agency the year before, recognized some of them and called them by name.[37]

The Indians who disrupted Gardner's party were close neighbors of a band which gave Jackson's photographic party a scare several weeks later in a region west of the Mesa Verde, about twenty-five miles east of the Gardner attack. Eighteen to twenty young bucks suddenly appeared, shouting and swinging their rifles over their heads. They had barely greeted Jackson when they struck all of his mules and horses with quirts. "Immediately," wrote Jackson, "we were in a wild stampede down the canyon, driven by howling savages." Jackson soon met the chief, an old Indian named Pogonobogwint, with whom he traded some silver for some corn, and his party got out safely.[38]

There were bears, and there were Indians, but most of the time there was just plain hard work and lots of discomfort. After a rainy day the men tried to dry out their clothing but it took time to dry woolen trousers, foxed in seat and knees with tanned buckskin, or heavy woolen or cotton flannel shirts. Dinner was at six, or later, or not at all. Their mainstay was coffee, which was "water, and milk, and whisky, and medicine combined." The cook ground and roasted it right in camp and brewed a generous pot over the campfire, settling it with a dash of cold water. It was "a cup of condensed vigor, the true *elixir vitae*, a perpetual source of comfort and strength." Of butter there was none, nor milk, nor potatoes, nor vegetables, except rice and hominy, but

[37] *Rocky Mountain News,* September 17, 1875, p. 4. New York *Times,* September 25, 1875, p. 1. The party that picked up Holman and Dallas destroyed all the supplies at the camp, save for what could be packed on one mule, in order to keep them from falling into the hands of the Indians.

[38] Jackson, *Time Exposure,* 240–41.

there was plenty of fruit sauce—apricots, peaches, and prunes which, when dried, were easily portable.

Beans have always been a mainstay of outdoorsmen, and the Hayden Survey used them in abundance. Dried beans were easily carried and, cooked, they contained all the protein that active men needed. But at ten or twelve thousand feet the softening up process was long and tedious. The typical cook therefore usually kept a pail of beans on hand for days at a time, pouring off water and packing them for the trail, taking them out, adding water, and cooking them in the evening all over again. By the end of a week the beans were soft enough to be served as food.

Regardless of how plain the fare, the added spice of the outdoors made it taste good. "Under how many varying circumstances, then, this evening meal is eaten," Ingersoll reminisced. "Sometimes . . . in a pleasant bower; next, out on the dry plains, where an illimitable landscape of sere grass stretches away to where the delectable mountains lie on the snow-silvered rim of the world; again . . . at high timberline in Colorado, where sleet and snow contest the passage down your throat with rapidly cooling coffee and chilly bacon; or beside the Yellowstone in August, with its millions of ravenous flies and hordes of thirsty mosquitoes; or it is anywhere and everywhere, with the royal vigor of appetite that comes of this outdoor life, and the marvelous grandeur of the Rocky Mountains as garniture for your dining hall."

After the meal, with the animals tethered and the utensils cleaned, the men spun yarns until complete darkness set in. They enjoyed a last fragrant pipeful of tobacco, pipes being nearly as common then as cigarettes are today. Then they laid out their beds. Sometimes a man's bed was no more than a buffalo robe and a blanket. More often it was a heavy canvas folded over and under two "California" blankets, "thick as a board and soft and pliable as wool." Ingersoll declared that he had "thus slept at timberline, right between snowbanks and on the borders of an icy lake . . . night after night, with perfect comfort."[39]

[39] Ernest Ingersoll, "Rocky Mountain Cooking," *Scribner's Monthly*, Vol. XX, No. 1 (May, 1880), 125–31.

Some of the divisions made use of pup tents, but the contribution to comfort of these flimsy shelters was questionable. Rhoda told of spending a rainy night in a narrow, low, little tent, "with the water running under at the edges, and leaking through at the top." It was a dismal and restless night, and he was glad to see their big Negro cook finally arise and begin gathering what dry firewood he could find. Next, the two packers emerged from their tents, one going after the mules while the other began the preparations for packing. The cook baked sour dough biscuits with a Dutch oven and opened the mess boxes in such a way as to make a table. Soon he yelled "Grub pile!" and the other occupants stumbled out of their tents, washed in the icy stream, and ate in silence. By seven o'clock the entire outfit was in the saddle and on the trail.[40]

Rain was unpleasant, but as each season neared its end, the snowstorms and near-zero temperatures reduced much of the work to the basic problem of survival. More often than not the parties were behind schedule, and they manifested a natural reluctance to come in from the field without having achieved their goals.

When, on September 27, 1875, Franklin Rhoda and Frederick Endlich set out to climb Trinchera Peak in south-central Colorado, they found the snow above timberline to be two feet deep, with the banks much deeper. But when they reached a razor-edged divide at an altitude of about 13,000 feet, they discovered the fresh tracks of a large grizzly bear who had recently climbed to the top of the mountain. The climbers stepped carefully in the bear tracks and thus avoided breaking through the steep snow banks and plunging head over heels down the mountainside. "Thus too," commented Rhoda, "we were able to put to good use the unerring instinct of the bear in selecting the best route to travel by."[41]

When each season ended, the mules were put out to pasture, and the equipment was stored at convenient places such as at

[40] Franklin Rhoda, "Report on the Topography of the San Juan Country," *Eighth Annual Report*, 459–60.

[41] Franklin Rhoda, "Topographical Report on the Southeastern District," *Ninth Annual Report*, 331.

Denver or Cheyenne. Packers, cooks, and camp men were released to make their way as best they could until the survey re-
assembled for the field the next spring. As for the professional
men, they headed for Washington, D. C., and the permanent
offices of the survey there. During most of its existence the headquarters were in a building on the northwest corner of 11th street
and Pennsylvania Avenue.[42]

Hayden's offices soon became a meeting place for scientists,
interested congressmen, and other V.I.P.'s. On any given afternoon, Major Powell, geologist Arnold Guyot, Leo Lesquereux,
Edward Drinker Cope, or Fielding Bradford Meek might be
found there. James A. Garfield might show up, or Senator Logan,
of Illinois, or Abram Hewitt. Besides political matters to discuss
with Hayden, they always found plenty of stimulating conversation with the other Hayden men, as well as interesting things
to look at.

Several of the rooms were equipped with drafting tables, over
which Gardner, Rhoda, Bechler, or Holmes might be observed,
meticulously working up geologic, contour, or drainage maps for
the forthcoming atlas. Jackson had his own laboratories there,
and the odor of chemicals identified his allotted space. Great al-
bums of his photographs filled the shelves on the walls, and parts
of his camera equipment were scattered here and there.[43]

When the maps were completed in Hayden's offices, they were
sent to the lithographing firm of Julius Bien and Company in
New York City. German-born Bien was a lithographer's son who
had attended the Academy of Fine Arts at Cassel and the Stadel
Art Institute at Frankfurt to train for his father's profession. But
as an energetic young Jew he found himself deeply embroiled
in the Revolution of 1848, and when it failed, Julius found it
healthful to leave the country. That explains why, as one of the
"forty-eighters," he arrived in New York City, just twenty-two
years old, and boldly set himself up in business as a lithographer.
While looking for business, he saw the need in this country for

[42] The Washington *Star* was until recently on this spot, and a plaque in the
lobby commemorated the old Hayden Survey.
[43] New York *Times,* April 27, 1875, p. 1.

improved techniques in map publishing. Convinced of his own ability, he got himself called to the attention of Secretary of War Jefferson Davis, and from this contact he was soon put to work lithographing maps from the Pacific Railroad Surveys. Probably Bien's outstanding major work prior to the Civil War was Lieutenant G. K. Warren's wonderful map of the territories between the Mississippi and the Pacific. By the time of the Civil War, then, the lithographing firm of Julius Bien and Company was the outstanding one for map work.[44]

Lithography was a painstaking process. When Hayden or King referred to maps being "put on stone," they were referring to the technique of literally drawing the map, tiny line for tiny line, into the smooth, prepared surface of a stone that was ninety-seven per cent carbonate of lime and that had probably been quarried at Solenhofen, Bavaria. Greasy black chalk or ink was used to make the lines. Since carbonate of lime is sensitive to grease, in time, and after several intermediate steps, the grease remained and formed the design. The ink then adheres to the lines but not to the other surface; paper run over the stone "took" the ink, and a map emerged.[45]

Washington, D. C., was a long way from the Rockies, but year after year, when the breeze turned warm and spring-like, the Hayden men got dreamy looks in their eyes, and they tarried longer than necessary over their gear, or spent overlong noon hours at the supply stores, buying blankets or clothing for use in the Rockies. Yet the end was coming into view, and by 1876, with heavy hearts, the topographers realized that the Great Survey of Colorado was about to end.

For men who had worked primarily in the high mountains it was a depressing change to come down off the Grand Mesa—a high, piñon-covered wonderland of lakes and forests and game—and find themselves at the end of the great chains of broken and twisted rock that are the Colorado Rockies. Working conditions in the desert areas in the Colorado–New Mexico–Utah border

[44] *Dictionary of American Biography,* II, 249–50. Carl Wittke, *Refugees of Revolution: The German Forty-eighters in America,* 323–24.
[45] Louis A. Holman, *The Graphic Processes: Intaglio, Relief and Planographic.*

regions were as difficult as those in the mountains and did not offer the compensating scenic effects. Holmes's outfit, on the La Plata River southwest of Durango, suffered from thirst and nearly lost everything in a flash flood that roared down at high noon and washed away their noon meal and some of their packs. Later on, when the men discovered a centipede, a large spider, and a scorpion, they knew that they were indeed out of the Rockies. Holmes wrote to the *Rocky Mountain News:*

> This is the third year of the survey in Colorado; its belt of 200 miles of mountains have kept us busy up to this time. Range after range has been climbed and studied and passed by, and still it seemed there would always be another; but now we are absolutely sure that to the west are only the broad, barren, canyoned tablelands, through which the Rio Colorado of the West cuts its way.[46]

Yet Holmes went on to make some of his finest sketches in the desert country of western Colorado. In winding up the topographical work in 1876, he climbed Abajo Peak and became almost poetic in describing the view. Much of what he sketched from the top of the peak he had never seen before. Eastward the view was not interrupted until the La Plata and San Juan Mountains arose a hundred miles away; to the south was the Sierra Cariso range; in the west the Henry Mountains; and to the north the Sierra La Sal, "all in plain view," he said, "yet outlining a circle nearly 150 miles in diameter, and including an area of 20,000 square miles. The vast area lies beneath us as a silent desert, a plateau land cut by innumerable waterless canyons, and dotted with a thousand fancifully carved and brilliantly colored rocks."[47]

With the completion of the survey to the Utah line, and in a few instances even a short distance beyond, the field work of the

[46] *Rocky Mountain News,* August 10, 1875, p. 4.

[47] William Henry Holmes, "Report of William H. Holmes, on the Geology of the Sierra Abajo and West San Miguel Mountains," *Tenth Annual Report of the United States Geological and Geographical Survey of the Territories, Embracing Colorado and Parts of Adjacent Territories, Being a Report of Progress of the Exploration for the Year 1876* (hereafter cited as *Tenth Annual Report*), 189. Some of his finest profiles accompany this report.

Hayden topographers in Colorado came to an end. James T. Gardner had resigned at the end of the 1875 season, partly because he was offered a better position as director of the State Survey of New York, and partly because of criticism of the way he handled his division during the Indian attack.[48] But A. D. Wilson took over for the remaining work to be done, and in 1877 the Hayden atlas was issued. Officially called the *Geological and Geographical Atlas of Colorado and Portions of Adjacent Territory*, it contained four maps of the state on a scale of 12 miles to the inch. A drainage map, a triangulation map, an economic map, and a general geological map were followed by six topographic and six geologic maps, each covering one-sixth of the state, with a scale of four miles to the inch. Two cutaway drawings of mountains showing their geologic make-up and two panoramic views—all the work of W. H. Holmes—completed the atlas.

After it appeared, the Hayden atlas became immediately valuable to Colorado, which was barely through her first year of statehood. The maps proved highly useful to such railroad builders as R. L. Berthoud, of the Colorado Central, and General William J. Palmer, of the Denver and Rio Grande, and to such capitalists as Baron Rothschild and the well-known Colorado booster and first territorial governor, William Gilpin. The successful completion of the atlas endeared the Hayden Survey to the people of Colorado, and even today it serves as an indispensable tool for geologists working in certain remote parts of the state where more modern methods of mapping have not yet been applied.

Ten maps, two cutaways, and two profiles—the results of four seasons in the Rockies, climbing a thousand high points, packing mules, eating beans, and shivering through rains. What visions the atlas must have conjured up for Holmes and Jackson and Ingersoll as they approached their octogenarian years! Probably, they remembered most vividly the pack train winding up a Rocky Mountain canyon, single file, the bell mare in the lead, the

[48] National Archives, R.G. 57, Hayden Survey, General Letters Received, Adams to Hayden, October 15, 1875; Gannett to Hayden, October 15, 1875; Jackson to Hayden, October 19, 1875.

bell jingling, and the cook astride her singing as he rode along:

> *Hokey pokey winky dang*
> *Linkum lankum mussodang*
> *The Injun swore that he would hang*
> *The man that couldn't keep warm.*[49]

[49] Ingersoll, "Rocky Mountain Mules," *Scribner's Monthly,* Vol. XIX, No. 6 (April, 1880), 935.

4

The Mount of the Holy Cross and the Cliff Dwellings

THE HAYDEN SURVEY fulfilled its basic function of mapping the West and laying the foundations for much of the knowledge we possess of its natural history, but its accomplishments did not stop there. It also served another valuable purpose. Through the journalists and photographers who accompanied its expeditions, it popularized the wonders of the West and gave to the rest of the world a new and more accurate image of western scenic wonders. And it gave the first accurate information about the Mount of the Holy Cross and the Cliff Dwellings of southwestern Colorado.

In the 1870's, articles about the West were good newspaper material. Robert Adams, Jr., wrote for the New York *Herald* and for the Philadelphia *Inquirer,* Cuthbert Mills wrote for the New York *Times,* and Ernest Ingersoll for the New York *Tribune.* William N. Byers wrote for his own *Rocky Mountain News.* Mills and Adams did not turn out very good material, but Ingersoll and Byers were journalists of far better quality, and something more should be said about them.

Ingersoll was a product of the Michigan countryside, and the fields and woods always fascinated him. He went on to attend Oberlin, became curator of the museum there, and then attended

Harvard, working with Louis Agassiz until that great scientist died. It was at this juncture that he armed himself with strong recommendations, including one from Spencer Baird, and applied for work with the survey.[1]

Hayden offered him a job, and although Ingersoll was only twenty-two at the time, he proved to be a good collector, especially in the field of conchology. He used his experiences with the survey as part of the material for two of his most successful books, *Knocking Round the Rockies,* and *Crest of the Continent,*[2] and he wrote articles for *Scribner's Monthly, Harper's Magazine, St. Nicholas,* and others. Yet in spite of the quantity of words that he produced, there was always a charm and an accuracy about Ingersoll's writing that makes it pleasant reading even today.

In later years he found his niche in life as the director of the department of educational natural history in the Montreal *Family Herald* and *Weekly Star,* although he lived during these years —from the 1890's until 1938—in New York City. Ingersoll died in 1946 at the age of ninety-four, several years after the deaths of his close friends Jackson and Holmes.[3]

William N. Byers was never more than a guest of the survey, but since he was owner and editor of the *Rocky Mountain News,* his interest in scientific exploration bore more than ordinary importance. Born in Ohio in 1831, he had learned surveying, and at the time of the Pikes Peak rush was making his living in Omaha as a surveyor and politician. But he was also interested in printing, and the news of the diggings led him to load his press and type into a wagon and head for Cherry Creek. His *News* was the first newspaper published in the region, and it soon became the greatest booster of Denver and Colorado. Byers loved the country and grew up with it, defending his policies with pistols when necessary.[4]

[1] National Archives, R.G. 57, Hayden Survey, Applications, Vol. II, Box 1, Letter of Hawley to Hayden; see also General Letters Received, Ingersoll to Hayden, 1874.

[2] See Bibliography.

[3] New York *Times,* November 14, 1946, p. 29.

[4] Fritz, *Colorado, the Centennial State,* 40–41. *National Cyclopaedia of American Biography,* XIII, 514–15.

When Hayden and Powell began exploring in Colorado, Byers left his paper in the hands of subordinates and headed into the hills with the scientists, climbing peaks with them, eating their food, and suffering through inclement weather just as if he were a regular member of their surveys. Then he wrote lengthy travelogues of his experiences and sent them to the *News* for publication. These articles were well written and concise, for Byers was hardly paying himself by the word. Many of them were lifted *in toto* and republished again and again in the Eastern newspapers.

For those people who did not bother to read, photographs and stereopticon slides served the purpose of informing them of the wonders of the West. The period following the Civil War was the great age of the stereoscope. Rare was the parlor with its marble-topped table, chiming mantel clock, horsehair chair, and velveteen settee that did not also contain a stereoscope and several bundles of slides. Many young lovers must have secretly squeezed hands, exchanged long glances, and stolen quick kisses while fitting the slides or pretending to look into the instruments. And as for ordinary photographs, some of them, big 11x14 prints, sold by the thousands.

Whether they purchased big prints or stereo slides, the flatlanders back east could thank William Henry Jackson for the best ones. His real ability with a camera can only be appreciated when the difficulties of early day photography are understood. At first he hauled most of the three hundred pounds of equipment in an ambulance wagon, but in later years he carried all of it on mules. On fat, trustworthy, little Hypo he mounted a smaller kit that would enable him to take pictures anywhere man or beast could go. This meant that the poor little mule had to carry a dark box with bath holder, camera, glass plates, chemicals, tripod, and, resting on top of the pack between two brightly colored parfleches, a small keg of water.[5]

Later on, Jackson abandoned the dark box and substituted a small tent in which he prepared his large glass plates by cover-

[5] Robert Taft, *Photography and the American Scene*, 309. Driggs, *The Pioneer Photographer*, 77–78.

ing them with a sensitizing chemical. Then he ran to his camera, inserted the plate, uncapped the lens, and exposed the plate for five, ten, or fifteen seconds, recapped the lens, removed the plate, and hastily ran back to the dark tent where he covered the exposed glass with the fixing solution. Only then was the picture "taken." When hard pressed, he could make a negative in fifteen minutes from the time the first rope was thrown from the pack to the final repacking. Ordinarily the process took half an hour, however, and the whims of the clouds cut down even more on the number of photographs he could take in a day.[6]

The hardships of the work would have taxed the patience of Job. Glass plates broke then as easily as they do today. Enlargements were unheard of, and if an 11x14 print was desired, then an 11x14 plate had to be used—a plate packed on a mule. In 1875, Jackson ventured even more boldly, taking along a camera made to his own specifications to take pictures on plates 20x24 inches. "It is a wonder to me even now," he wrote years later, "that I had the temerity to undertake it."[7]

In all his years with the survey only one major calamity befell Jackson's plates. It was early August in 1873, and he had just come through some of the grandest mountain scenery in central Colorado when "an evil mule named Gimlet" slipped his pack and broke many of the exposed plates. Most of the photographer's fine 11x14 plates were lost. "I think I have never been so distressed in my life—my finest negatives lost before anyone had even seen a print," Jackson reminisced more than sixty-five years later. But Hayden, who was along at the time, reassured him that the loss was not beyond repair; he could retrace his steps and take the views over again—which he did.[8]

Through the photographic work of Jackson and the news stories of Mills, Adams, Byers, and Ingersoll, the Hayden Survey attained world-wide fame. It was also helped along the way by

[6] Taft, *Photography and the American Scene,* 309.
[7] Driggs, *The Pioneer Photographer,* 217. See pages 217–225 for much interesting material on adventures with the 20x24 camera.
[8] Jackson, *Time Exposure,* 215.

the "discoveries" of the Mount of the Holy Cross in 1873 and the cliff dwellings of southwestern Colorado in 1874.

The official discovery of the Mount of the Holy Cross was the culmination of six weeks of hard work by the Jackson, Hayden, Gardner, Marvine, and Gannett groups who, by previous arrangement, met at Fairplay, in South Park, in the first week of July, 1873. William Byers was along during most of the month, and William D. Whitney, the well-known Yale philologist, spent both July and August as a guest of the survey. Those weeks were filled with explorations into the depths of the Central Rockies and with ascents of high and magnificent peaks. It would not do justice to the 1873 survey to entirely ignore their work that preceded the discovery of the Holy Cross.

The first high point of the exploration was Mount Lincoln, where Henry Gannett established a barometric station. It was 14,284 feet high, the northernmost of three mountains in the Northern Mosquito Range. It was not a hard climb, and in 1873 men were actually working the Montezuma mine within a hundred feet of the summit.[9]

William Byers described the sunrise he watched from its crest:

We spent the night at the Montezuma mine, nearly three miles above the sea, and this morning enjoyed a scene that comes to but few people, and to hardly any more than once in a lifetime. Daylight revealed the park [South Park] filled with clouds, but the highest were a thousand feet below us. Above and around the sky was absolutely clear. The sun rose over the sea, boundless to the south and east, fleecy and luminous. Buffalo Mountain, Pike's Peak, Silver Heels, and one or two other lofty summits, appeared as islands. The clouds were moving very slowly from the south, but as they crowded into the passes, or rolled up the slopes of the range, they were met by a breeze from the north which forced them up and backward into the seething sea below.[10]

[9] Ormes, *Guide to the Colorado Mountains*, 81–82. National Archives, R.G. 48, Office of the Secretary of the Interior, Patents and Miscellaneous Division, Box 72, Hayden to Delano, July 18, 1873.
[10] *Rocky Mountain News*, July 22, 1873, p. 4.

From Mount Lincoln the party headed southwest toward the Twin Lakes, south of present-day Leadville. Much of the time they were separated into various groups, the topographers following along the crests while the geologists and natural scientists worked their way along the valleys and canyons.[11]

Byers found the Central Rockies a high-country Garden of Eden. From sunrise, when the vegetation was stiff and sparkling with frost, until the darkness of evening, when the valley party used their blazing pine-knot fire to exchange signals with Gardner's topographers four miles away and several thousand feet above, he enjoyed his days with the survey. And as he puffed up that one last mile, he still noticed the strawberry vines and raspberry bushes in bloom at 12,000 feet, wild celery and parsnips even closer to the summit, and at the very limits of vegetation the sky-blue forget-me-nots and other tiny flowering plants. From the summit of La Plata Peak, fifth highest in Colorado, he absorbed the view. "The world," he wrote, "seems made of mountains; a chaotic mass of rocky ridges, peaks, and spurs."[12]

He left the scientific men at work on the summit and returned to camp. While he kept warm by the fire with a steaming cup of coffee in his hands, the men on the summit withstood a snow squall and only reached their temporary camp at timberline after dark. "They go everywhere and at all hours of daylight, each seeming ambitious to do the most work," Byers said of them. "They have caught the spirit of Dr. Hayden, who never tires and never rests."[13]

The frontier editor's travelogue continued throughout most of August. Working westward over the Sawatch Range via Lake Creek Pass they named Grizzly Peak and conquered the multi-hued, jagged North Italian Mountain and Teocalli Mountain and gave them their names. They were particularly intrigued by the Elk Mountains in the vicinity of what is now the resort town of Aspen. Hayden described their geology as "the grandest and

[11] National Archives, R.G. 48, Office of the Secretary of the Interior, Patents and Miscellaneous Division, Box 72, Hayden to Delano, July 18, 1873.

[12] *Rocky Mountain News*, July 29, 1873, p. 4; August 3, 1873, p. 3. La Plata Peak, 14,377 feet high, is in the Sawatch Range south of Independence Pass.

[13] *Rocky Mountain News*, August 3, 1873, p. 3.

most varied" he had seen in his lifetime of experience, and the party was exhilarated by their Canadian Rocky type of grandeur. They conquered peak after peak and christened each one: Snowmass, Capitol, Treasury, Whitehouse, and others. Most of the names have remained.

From the top of Snowmass, Byers was fascinated by the little snow-water lakelets far below in the great moraine amphitheatre on the southwest side of the mountain. Ice floes drifted out on them before the cool wind, and "the effects of varying light, sunshine and cloud shadow upon them, and the diamond-like sparkle of their ripplings, "and their vivid sea-green color created a total beauty beyond description. On one of the snowbanks was a grizzly bear, now sauntering about, now rolling over in the snow, now scooping a bunch of snow-frozen grasshoppers in his great paws and licking them down his throat, and then sitting up on his haunches to watch the strange party of human beings on the mountain above him.[14]

This was as far west as the party went. Byers returned to Denver (although he rejoined them later on), and Jackson, his broken negatives replaced, joined the main group again which then advanced up the Arkansas, crossed Tennessee Pass, and camped on the Eagle River, a tributary of the Grand, or, since 1929, the Colorado, River. Their immediate goal was the Mount of the Holy Cross.

There was no doubt in 1873 that the Holy Cross existed, and attempts to surround its existence with an aura of mystery were wrong. But it had not been seen by many people because Notch Mountain obstructs it from the east. Furthermore, its exact location had not been established, and Hayden maintained that until his topographers had mapped it, the mountain had appeared on all maps some thirty miles out of its true position.[15] So there was a challenge in placing the mountain exactly where it belonged

[14] *Rocky Mountain News*, August 7, 1873, p. 2; August 14, 1873, p. 2; August 17, 1873, p. 2; August 20, 1873, p. 2. Lake Creek Pass is south of Independence Pass and does not have a road over it. Ralph H. Brown, "Colorado Mountain Passes," *Colorado Magazine*, Vol. VI, No. 6 (November, 1929), 235.

[15] *Geographical and Geological Surveys West of the Mississippi River*, 43 Cong., 1 sess., *House Report 612*, 34.

on the map, and if it was as strikingly beautiful as it was claimed to be, photographs of it would be of great value.

Gardner and Jackson, from their camp on the Eagle River, determined the exact location of the mountain. Whether they were going to climb it or take pictures of it, they had to approach the mountain up a canyon leading southwestward directly toward it, though separated from it by great ridges on either side. Slowly they picked their way up this canyon (now Cross Creek Canyon), which was filled with great, smooth-rounded rocks of glacial origin—*roches moutonées,* or "sheep-backed rocks," as the Hayden men called them. By evening of the first day the entire party was bogged down amidst fallen timber and was camped barely two hours' distance from the Eagle River. The next morning they broke into two groups, Gardner, Hayden, Whitney and Holmes intending to climb the mountain, while Jackson's party, still carrying over one hundred pounds of equipment, hacked its way up the other side of the canyon to the top of Notch Mountain. Tom Cooper carried the camera, Coulter, another packer, the plate boxes, and Jackson, the chemicals. The photographer's account of what followed cannot be improved upon:

> On this day, as usual, I pushed on ahead, and thus it was that I became the first member of the Survey to sight the Cross. Near the top of the ridge I emerged above timberline and the clouds, and suddenly, as I clambered over a vast mass of jagged rocks, I discovered the great shining cross before me, tilted against the mountainside.[16]

The weather closed in before pictures could be taken, so Jackson and his aides retreated to the timber, shivered throughout the night, and climbed the mountain again at the crack of dawn. The day was clear although the horizon was much obscured by "flying storms" (as Whitney called them), but Gardner com-

[16] Jackson, *Time Exposure,* 217. See also Driggs, *The Pioneer Photographer,* 177–87, and Whitney's letters to the *Rocky Mountain News,* August 31, 1873, p. 2. A microfilm copy of Jackson's 1873 diary, in the custody of the State Historical Society of Colorado, has also been studied, but the writing is so small and the ink so faded that it proved of little use. Pages 38–42 of this diary pertain to the Holy Cross.

pleted his topographic work, and Jackson took one 11x14 and seven 6x8 photographs, "the finest pictures," he later wrote, "I have ever made of the Holy Cross."[17]

As the two parties, the one on the Holy Cross mountain and the other on Notch Mountain, began their descent in a drizzle, they both witnessed a rare phenomenon. Deep down in the valley the sun broke through and formed a magnificent rainbow of many colors. But it was not in the traditional arc of a rainbow. This one was circular, "a spectral ring," Holmes wrote, "magnificent in its bright and pure and vivid colors."[18]

The American people were thrilled at the news of the "discovery" of the Holy Cross, and Jackson's most popular pictures, the ones in greatest demand, were those of the mountain with the shining cross. With its great upright of snow, 1500 feet in length, its arms extending 750 feet on each side, and the peak rising 13,996 feet, it was indeed a beautiful sight. Thomas Moran was so excited by the "discovery" that he made a special trip to Colorado in August, 1874, journeyed with Stevenson and a party of easterners to the mountain, filled his book with sketches, and returned to his studio.[19] His subsequent painting, "The Mount of the Holy Cross," was awarded a medal at the Centennial Exposition in 1876. Thousands of lithographs of this indescribably beautiful painting were sold all over the world.[20]

One day in 1879, the poet Henry Wadsworth Longfellow was looking through an illustrated book of western scenery. Eighteen years before, his wife had died as the result of a flash fire, and the deep sorrow of this personal tragedy remained in his heart, denying him happiness for the rest of his life. Suddenly his eyes fell upon the Mount of the Holy Cross, and his creative ability

[17] Jackson, *Time Exposure*, 218. For a charming narration based on Jackson's diary and the recollections of his son, Clarence, see Clarence S. Jackson and Lawrence W. Marshall, *Quest of the Snowy Cross.*

[18] Holmes, Random Records, Vol. II, 54. Jackson, Diary, 40. Holmes sketched the position of the rainbow to accompany his description.

[19] *Rocky Mountain News*, September 1, 1874, p. 4. Four miles west of the Holy Cross is Mount Jackson, 13,687 feet high, named in honor of the photographer.

[20] In 1952, the original was hanging at Pendell Court, Bletchingly, Surrey, England. For how it got there, see *Quest of the Snowy Cross*, 11.

swelled up within him. That night, as he gazed at his dead wife's portrait, the great, white, rugged cross came to his mind, and he penned two verses about his departed wife, his deep sorrow, and "The Cross of Snow."

> *There is a mountain in the distant west*
> *That, sun-defying, in its deep ravines*
> *Displays a cross of snow upon its side.*
> *Such is the cross I bear upon my breast*
> *These eighteen years, through all the changing scenes*
> *And seasons, changeless since the day she died.*

He placed the poem in his portfolio, where it remained until after his death.[21]

The publicity gained from the "discovery" of the Holy Cross was followed the next year by Jackson's "discovery" of the cliff dwellings of southwestern Colorado. This is called a "discovery," yet actually the ruins of the ancient culture had been seen by many a prospector, and in the saloons and around the assay offices from Denver southwest to the mining camps in the San Juan Mountains the stories were told of these strange ruins. Indeed it was a rare sight that had not already been seen by some lone prospector. Many a time a Hayden surveyor reached a summit with the exhilarating feeling of being the first white man there, only to find an empty whisky bottle lying beside a rock, the aroma still there, mute evidence that someone white, human, and contemporary had been there before him.

Most of the prospectors who had seen the ruins had come from the San Juan Mountains, a rugged, isolated range in the southwest with known deposits of gold and silver. As early as 1860 a gold rush had started there, but it had petered out. In anger, the miners had created their own court, so it was reported, and had placed the perpetrator of the false rumors, one Captain Baker, on trial. In his own defense Baker had insisted that on the very spot where the miners were sitting in judgment upon him they could "pass out" gold better than he had ever claimed. Immedi-

[21] Samuel Longfellow (ed.), *Life of Henry Wadsworth Longfellow*, II, 425–26.

ately a miner's pan was called for, a scoop of earth thrown into it was washed with that gentle, swirling motion that only long practice can master, and lo, a trace of color worth half a dollar lay at the bottom of the pan. It saved Baker's life.[22]

In 1874, Jackson's party, which that season included Ernest Ingersoll, headed for Baker's Park in the heart of the San Juan Mountains. It was a landscape photographer's paradise, and Jackson had no instructions nor intentions to advance beyond there. But when he met John Moss, the high-muck-a-muck of the La Plata mining region (southwest of the mountains and close to the mesa country), who offered to guide him to the cliff dwellings, the pioneer photographer accepted the proposal. He would find out for himself if the stories were true.[23]

The party set out early in September, and they were soon in a beautiful valley with fine groves of cottonwood scattered about. Running through it was the Mancos River, about a rod wide and a foot deep, clear and limpid until it struck a series of beaver dams lower down the valley. Five to six miles below Merritt's ranch they noticed "little grass-covered knolls" which Captain Moss said were ruins, and such they turned out to be, with broken pieces of pottery about the size of a half-dollar scattered in abundance. Still there was nothing really worth photographing, so they continued down the canyon following a trail recently made by about one hundred Indians with lodge poles and herds of goats. Some stone ruins were found, so far reduced to rubble as to be worthless for Jackson's purposes.

> As evening approached [Jackson recorded in his diary] we made our camp under a little bunch of cedars beneath the highest walls of the canyon. Had found nothing that really came up to my idea of the grand and picturesque for photos and began to feel a little doubtful and discouraged. . . . After disposing of what sowbelly and bread we had [we began joking with] Steve [Hovey, a packer] upon the prospect of having to assist in carrying the boxes to the top

[22] New York *Times*, October 25, 1873, p. 2.

[23] William H. Jackson, "First Official Visit to the Cliff Dwellings," *Colorado Magazine*, Vol. I, No. 4 (May, 1924), 153. Jackson, *Time Exposure*, 230. Driggs, *The Pioneer Photographer*, 228–38.

of the mesa to photo some houses, not dreaming . . . that any were really there. He asked us to point out the spot. The Captain pointed at random. "Yes," said he, "I see it." And behold upon my close observation there was something that appeared very like a house. The doors and windows could be seen. We all started at once to investigate. The sides of the canyon were formed of successive tables or benches of sandstone rising perpendicularly one above the other to a total of 800 feet. Our house was upon the last one and below it the precipice was fully 100 feet from the narrow bench at its foot. Half way up the others with the exceptions of Ingersoll and myself were satisfied . . . not to go any further as they were afraid of darkness overtaking them before they could get back. We determined to see all that was to be seen that night so as to know how to approach it on the morrow. Found a tree and a series of crevices by which . . . we reached the plateau upon which the house stood. There perched away in the crevice like a swallow's or a bat's nest it was, a marvel and a puzzle.[24]

The next morning they raised the photographic equipment to the little house, and there took pictures. It was a remarkably well-preserved dwelling, even retaining a mortised cistern which could have held two to three hundred gallons of rain water. "The entire construction of this little human eyrie," wrote Jackson, "displays wonderful perseverance, ingenuity, and some taste."[25]

Thrilled by their discovery, and with good photographs as proof, the party continued down the Mancos, "a street a thousand feet deep," as Ingersoll called it because of the many ruins on the adjoining cliffs. Then, veering westward, they made a 350 mile circle of the Mesa Verde, ending up once again in Baker's Park. Ironically they never saw the spectacular cliff palace at Mesa Verde or the ruins included in the present-day Yucca House and Hovenweep National Monuments. Had Jackson's party explored up some of the narrow canyons opening into the Mancos Valley, they would have discovered some of the great apartment houses. That honor fell in 1888 to a couple

24 Jackson, Diary, 106–114.
25 William H. Jackson, "Report of W. H. Jackson on Ancient Ruins in Southwestern Colorado," *Eighth Annual Report*, 373.

of cowboys who were searching for cattle. But what Jackson had discovered was sufficient in 1874, and his forty negatives of the ruins gave to the world its first accurate concept of the lost cities of the Southwest.[26]

This was the last great discovery of the Hayden Survey. In later years, Jackson photographed the Moqui towns in northwestern Arizona, and in 1878 he returned to Yellowstone and the Tetons, but these were second visits and they ranked accordingly. In 1876, Hayden assigned him to the survey's exhibit at the Centennial Exhibition in Philadelphia, where the models that Jackson and Holmes had so painstakingly and artistically constructed of the cliff dwellings and the Elk Mountains attracted considerable attention.[27]

In 1877 and 1878, Hayden returned to Wyoming, Montana, and Idaho, working on topographic maps of these regions and carrying on a more detailed study of the Yellowstone and the Tetons. Yet the survey was never quite the same after Gardner's Indian fight in 1875, and opposition from other scientists brought on its demise with the creation of the United States Geological Survey in 1879.[28]

Thus for eleven years, from 1867 through 1878, Ferdinand Vandeveer Hayden and his men explored, classified, collected, conjectured. At a cost to the American taxpayer of $690,000[29] the Hayden Survey—the United States Geological and Geographical Survey of the Territories—laid the principal foundations for much of our knowledge of the geology, paleontology, paleobotany, zoology, botany, entomology, and ornithology of the Rocky Mountain West. Hayden and his men are forgotten now, and the massive octavo and quarto volumes issued under

[26] *Ibid.*, 373–77. Jackson, "First Official Visit to the Cliff Dwellings," *Colorado Magazine*, Vol. I, No. 4 (May, 1929), 159.

[27] Driggs, *The Pioneer Photographer*, 273.

[28] Henry Nash Smith, "Clarence King, John Wesley Powell, and the Establishment of the United States Geological Survey," *Mississippi Valley Historical Review*, Vol. XXXIV, No. 1 (June, 1947), 55. This essay is Powell oriented and is unfair to Hayden.

[29] *Geological and Geographical Surveys*, 45 Cong., 2 sess., *House Exec. Doc.* 81, 5. U.S. *Statutes at Large*, Vol. 20, 230.

the survey seal gather dust in our libraries. But it is only because others have used the knowledge contained within those dusty pages to build an even larger edifice of knowledge.

Theirs had been the great days of adventure, the great days of discovery. Back in the 1870's every new mountain was a challenge and a mystery. What was its geologic history? What of its botany? What kinds of birds lived there? What new insects climbed over its surface? And so they went to work to find out: in geology, F. V. Hayden, Frank Bradley, William Henry Holmes, Archibald Marvine, Frederick Endlich, A. C. Peale, C. A. White, Orestes St. John, and others; in topography, Henry Gannett, A. D. Wilson, Story B. Ladd, James T. Gardner, George B. Chittenden, Gustavus Bechler, Franklin Rhoda, and others; in botany, John Merle Coulter; in entomology, W. L. Carpenter; in ornithology, C. Hart Merriam. From offices in the East or in the field Leo Lesquereux, Fielding Bradford Meek, Edward Drinker Cope, and Joseph Leidy added their talents. A. S. Packard, A. E. Verrill, and Elliott Coues classified mammals from collections sent to them by the survey and later published their descriptions in survey publications. And the list goes on and on. Not the least of Hayden's achievements was his selection of personnel: it was consistently good.[30]

Hayden always pursued his scientific activities in a pragmatic way, publishing rapidly and attempting to aid the settlement of the country with easily accessible scientific information. Sometimes he published too quickly for his own good, and inaccuracies crept in that were pounced upon by his opponents as proof that he was a charlatan and an incompetent. But the land was being settled by a great inundating wave, and even a little scientific information made available then was, to Hayden's way of thinking, better than volumes of pure and correct analysis published later.

Surely there is no doubt of the popularity of his survey among the men of the West. Businessmen, agriculturalists, railroad promoters, and miners made use of his reports and maps and praised

[30] No attempt is made here to list all of the contributors to the publications of the Hayden Survey. See Schmeckebier, *Catalogue and Index of the Hayden, King, Powell, and Wheeler Surveys.*

his work. As R. O. Thompson, geologist for the Union Pacific Railroad, said, "I am with you in the practical work of development over the great West. I regard your work as the most beneficial to science, and adaptable to the wants of the miner and explorer, as well as to the capitalist who seeks investment, of any yet presented to the American people."[31]

In many scholarly circles his contributions were enthusiastically received. A physics professor at Princeton who had accompanied a party of students to Colorado said that the survey had "done much to arouse and stimulate a love for investigation in all branches of the Natural Sciences. . . . The Survey is no doubt unsurpassed, by any which has ever been organized, in all that should serve to make its results valuable, whether to the people or the scientist."[32]

As for Hayden himself, there was no letup in his activities until 1886, when the disease that killed him, locomotor ataxia, compelled him to resign from the new United States Geological Survey, with which he was to be associated until the completion of his investigations in Montana and Idaho.

As he sat ill in his study in Philadelphia, the aging, practical man of science surely relived those days of long ago when he was a young man exploring the wild young country of the upper Missouri. He must have seen himself once more with a little party of ten men, using army "seconds" for mounts, clambering, observing, contemplating, speculating, as they made their slow way southward along the Front Range of the Rockies in 1867. Again he must have relived the historic exploration of the Yellowstone, with its geysers, mud-pots, hot springs, and canyons, and, closing his eyes, dreamed the long dreams of his youth anew: challenging the majestic Tetons, exploring the North, Middle, and South Parks of Colorado, riding over the San Luis Valley, examining the geology of the Elk Mountains, riding a trotting mule into

[31] National Archives, R.G. 57, Hayden Survey, General Letters Received, Thompson to Hayden, December 14, 1875; see also Berthoud to Hayden, June 10, 1878, and Palmer to Hayden, May 30, 1878.

[32] National Archives, R.G. 48, Office of the Secretary of the Interior, Patents and Miscellaneous Division, Box 72, C. F. Brackett to Hayden, September 27, 1877.

the enchanted mesa country, searching for more cliff dwellings, examining the bluffs of the Roaring Fork and the Frying Pan and the Yampa and the North Platte.

He had made his dreams come true: all this he had done. And people were grateful for his contributions.

Among his mementos was a resolution, engrossed upon parchment, from the state legislature of Colorado:

> Whereas the geological and geographical survey of the Territories of the United States made under the general government has been completed for the area embracing the State of Colorado.
>
> And Whereas, the publication of the Reports, views and maps of this survey form a collection invaluable alike for the advancement of science and the development of the mining and agricultural interests of this State.
>
> Resolved that the thanks of this Assembly are hereby tendered to Dr. F. V. Hayden, United States geologist in charge of this survey and his assistants for the merit of their contributions to the successful achievement of this great work.
>
> Resolved that a copy of this resolution engrossed on parchment shall be presented to Dr. F. V. Hayden.[33]

The University of Rochester, in 1876, and the University of Pennsylvania, in 1886, granted him honorary LL.D. degrees. The impressive group of scientists who made up the pro-Hayden group all spoke highly of his achievements: Edward Drinker Cope, Leo Lesquereux, Spencer Baird, Josiah Whitney. The well-known British geologist Archibald Geikie felt that "among the names of those who have pioneered in the marvellous geology of Western North America, that of F. V. Hayden will always hold a high and honored place."[34] But perhaps C. D. Walcott, a well-known geologist with the new United States Geological Survey, best summarized Hayden's approach: "His work for the government and science was a labor of love."[35]

[33] National Archives, R.G. 48, Office of the Secretary of the Interior, Patents and Miscellaneous Division, Box 72, January 14, 1879.

[34] "Ferdinand Vandeveer Hayden," *Nature,* Vol. XXXVII, No. 953 (February 2, 1888), 326.

[35] Walcott, "Ferdinand Vandeveer Hayden," U.S. Geological Survey, *Ninth Annual Report, 1887–1889,* 36.

PART TWO

*Clarence King's
Fortieth Parallel Survey*

5

King's Formative Years

THE SECOND of the Great Surveys was the United States Geological Exploration of the Fortieth Parallel, with Clarence King as geologist in charge. It was the result of careful planning on the part of a twenty-five-year-old New Englander who guided his ambitious plan through the high offices of Washington and then led the organization which carried the idea to completion. The Fortieth Parallel Survey and Clarence King are indissolubly linked, and it is impossible to consider the one without the other.

"If there were any graceful and inoffensive way of doing it," "Clare" King once wrote to his geologist friend James D. Hague, "I wish it could be intimated in my life and engraved on my tombstone that I am to the last fibre aristocratic in belief, that I think that the only fine thing to do with the masses is to govern and educate them into some semblance of their social superiors." Then, to soften his harsh words, he added a literary twinkle: "This is ticklish ground and you may not like to impair my presidential chances by frivolities of this kind."[1]

Although the twinkle was facetious, the first statement was

[1] King Collection, Box 1, James D. Hague, "C. K.'s Notes for My Biographical Notice of Him for Appleton's Encyclopaedia."

not. Clarence King, friend of the wealthy, the powerful, the very cream of the American intelligentsia of the late nineteenth century, meant every word of it. Charming, affable, artistic, lover of good conversation, liver of the busy life, man of affairs always on the go, Clarence King was himself an aristocrat, and he believed in aristocracy as a class. Yet when he died, he was deeply in debt —among others, he owed John Hay, secretary of state, $44,800[2] —and the summation of his life equaled tragedy. Clarence King was a failure.

But why? Henry Adams, King's friend, often asked himself this question. For to lonely, thoughtful little Henry, King was everything a man should be in order to face the new age of man. He was of medium size, robust, cheerful, a scintillating conversationalist; and more than that, King was a man who had faced up to the challenge of a giant task which he had conceived and personally nourished into a reality. His very title had implied success: Clarence King, geologist in charge of the United States Geological Survey of the Fortieth Parallel. To cosmopolitan, dilettante Henry, King had been a true man among men. Yet today men read Henry Adams because he was a giant of intellect, but they read about King only because he was a close friend of Adams.[3]

It could be that Adams' adulation of this man was compounded in part from the circumstances of his first long visit with King. From the Quincy-raised geologist Samuel Franklin Emmons, who was one of the Fortieth Parallel men, Adams had accepted an invitation to go west and be a guest of the survey during the season of 1871. In the course of his ramblings with at least two different groups of scientists, Adams ended up in Colorado's Estes Park.

It was nearing autumn, and there was a haze in the air, a stillness and a cool comfort in the atmosphere that acted upon both man and beast like an opiate, preparing them for the snows of

[2] Samuel Franklin Emmons Papers, Box 28.

[3] Thurman Wilkins, *Clarence King*. Harry Crosby, "So Deep a Trail: A Biography of Clarence King." See also David H. Dickason, "Henry Adams and Clarence King, the Record of a Friendship," *New England Quarterly*, Vol. XVII, No. 2 (June, 1944), 229–54.

winter. "The Park," said Adams nostalgically, "stretched its English beauties off to the base of its bordering mountains in natural landscape and archaic peace; the stream was just fishy enough to tempt lingering along its banks." The opiate did its work. Sunset came on before Adams turned his back to the rippling stream, tucked his gear away, and cinched his mule. Before he could find his trail, darkness had enshrouded him. So, using a frontiersman's common sense, Adams let the mule go where she wished, and two hours later the warm yellow light of a cabin window appeared. Three men came out of the cabin, and one of them was Clarence King.

So here the wealthy Adams, who was never quite certain what he should do with himself, became the lifelong friend of a New Englander who in his life anticipated the attitudes of the twentieth century. King was everything Adams was not. King possessed the exuberance of success, the optimism of the dedicated man, the preparation for a scientific career in a world becoming a slave to science. King, twenty-nine at the time, had achieved recognition, and respect, and he had done it without the aid of a powerful family. Conversely, Adams, thirty-three, possessed everything King did not: powerful family connections, inherited wealth, a liberal arts education, and the ripening experience of long periods in England and on the Continent. Small wonder that the two men, sharing the single guest bed in that little cabin in Estes Park, talked till the sky over the eastern hills blushed pink with the approach of a new day. Adams thought King was a little like the Greeks had been, like Alcibiades or Alexander, and he said that men worshiped King "as the ideal American they all wanted to be."[4]

Their friendship lasted until death, and King was always welcome at the Adams home in Washington where Henry and his wife contributed a gathering place for a coterie of the most valuable political and business contacts. To the Adams residence on "H" street came the powerful men, the "right" men of the coming age of honesty: Rutherford B. Hayes, Carl Schurz, John Wesley Powell, John Hay, John La Farge, Othniel C. Marsh,

[4] Henry Adams, *The Education of Henry Adams*, 309-13.

James Garfield, and Abram S. Hewitt. From them the lines of authority led straight to the press, to Congress, to the executive branches of the government, and to the White House. And these men opened doors for King.

Quite a fellow he was, this Clarence King. Yet just twenty years after Adams first met him in Estes Park, King was wiped out just as fortune seemed within his grasp and was in an insane asylum. Adams was puzzled and felt that the lesson of King's lost fortune held a valid moral, if he could only understand it. But Adams never really tried to understand it, or possibly he had an unpleasant feeling that the real answer lay very close to himself. So he passed off the question superficially, concluding that lack of money had ruined King.[5]

In recent years, scholars have uncovered much about King's life, including his attraction to supple, brown-skinned women (he married a negress) and the remote possibility that Henry Adams' wife found herself secretly, passionately, and hopelessly in love with him.[6] Scholars have taken King as he was, which makes interesting enough reading, and have either left the question of his failure unanswered or have unquestioningly accepted Adams' pat conclusion.

But King's failure was not lack of money, it was lack of judgment. His judgment was faulty, just vaguely so, something like the way the view on a Nevada desert is distorted ever so slightly by heat waves in the atmosphere. A shade of poor judgment reduced the significance of the Fortieth Parallel Survey, yet it was never noticed at the time. Slight failures in judgment caused King's mining operations to fail when other men's succeeded and made them rich. King could have been an outstanding literary man or a long-remembered government administrator, but instead he viewed himself as a rich man enjoying a life of leisure. Perhaps he was a bit like Alcibiades or Alexander, as Adams thought, but he could have done well to have taken Socrates' famous admonition about self-knowledge.

[5] *Ibid.*, 346.
[6] Wilkins, *King*, 312–22.

Clarence King was born at Newport, Rhode Island, on January 6, 1842, the newest addition to a long line of transplanted Englishmen. Tradition had it that his great grandfather, Samuel King, of Newport, had been an artist of some ability and a friend of Benjamin Franklin's, even helping the good doctor with some of his electrical experiments. And throughout the American part of their history, the Kings had enjoyed a generous sprinkling of gentlemen, scholars, and men of wealth.

In the King family there was a strain of the imaginative, the curious, and the adventurous. In the early days of the nineteenth century, Yankees went to sea to make their fortunes, and among them had been Clarence's grandfather, Samuel King. He went all the way to China and eventually became senior partner in the East Indian firm of King and Talbot. From Samuel King, Clarence's father inherited a love of the sea and far-off places, and the time came when he left his young wife and precocious little son Clarence behind and in the best tradition of family and fortune sailed for China as a member of the firm of Talbot, Oliphant and Company. In China, at the port of Amoy, he died, June 2, 1848. He left his fortune, what there was of it, invested in the trading firm, and when it went bankrupt in 1857, the widow King and her young son were left nearly penniless.[7]

But the widowed Mrs. King was a remarkably intelligent young woman who was determined to help her little son in every way possible. In the pre-Darwinian era, fossils and pretty rocks were strange things indeed for a small boy to collect, but it is related that she shared his enthusiasms. Once, when Clare was just seven, she let him take her by the hand and lead her over a mile of snow to show her what was perhaps his first geological discovery, a fossil fern in a stone wall. This so aroused the boy's interests that from then on the room he and his mother inhabited became "a veritable museum."[8] The close mother-son relationship was to last throughout King's life. In manhood, he found in his mother his closest intellectual companion, and even on

[7] King Collection, Folder A–3, Rossiter W. Raymond, "Biographical Notice," Box 1, Rufus King, "Pedigree of King."

[8] Samuel Franklin Emmons, "Biographical Memoir of Clarence King," National Academy of Sciences, *Biographical Memoirs*, VI, 27.

his death bed his closest thoughts were of her.[9] This relationship is doubly extraordinary since she remarried in 1860, becoming Mrs. Howland. She bore Howland two children and upon his death in 1866 was burdened not only with Clarence and her two children by Howland, but also with a crippled child of Howland's by his first marriage.[10]

Come what might, Mrs. Howland was determined that Clare should receive a good education. He was fitted for college in the Endowed Grammar School at Hartford, Connecticut, after which he went up to New Haven and enrolled in the Sheffield Scientific School of Yale University.

Yale by this time had accumulated a small group of dedicated scientists, and the stimulating influence of these men spurred young King's imagination. Science then was on the threshold of its coming-of-age, Darwin published his great work while King was still a student, and Sheffield's young men sensed something of the increased interest in things scientific.

The noted scientist and geologist James Dwight Dana was there, founder with Benjamin Silliman of the *American Journal of Science and Arts,* and George J. Brush, a leading mineralogist, contributed his knowledge. Of use to King in later years were the practical astronomy taught him by Chester S. Lyman, who introduced his students to the art of making observations in the field, and the course in surveying taught by William A. Norton. King probably took courses in French and German from William D. Whitney, whose brother Josiah was head of the California Survey. All in all, it was a good faculty, professionally capable and intellectually alert.[11]

Young Clarence studied books and nature with equal enthusiasm, displayed a vivid memory for natural objects, and wrote readily with "delicate literary judgment and skill."[12] He

[9] Samuel Franklin Emmons Papers, Box 28, G. W. Middleton to S. F. Emmons, April 5, 1902.

[10] King Collection, Folder A–3, Raymond, "Biographical Notice."

[11] Daniel Coit Gilman, "Clarence King's School Days," *Clarence King Memoirs,* 298–99.

[12] Emmons, "Biographical Memoir of Clarence King," *Biographical Memoirs,* VI, 30.

did well in his studies and was "alert, independent, quick to receive impressions, ready to act on his own impulses, fond of literature and science, with that token of genius which is said to
be 'the art of lighting one's own fires.' "[13] He possessed a robust
physique, excelled in rowing, and was a natural leader of his
fellow students.[14] "Don't think that I never *lead men*," he wrote
to his friend James Terry Gardner, "for in my own humble way
I do. I can see my influence in college plainly enough. I am
happy here. I am loved by some people and that is happiness."[15]

In the summer of 1862, King was graduated with the first class
to receive bachelor of science degrees from the Sheffield Scientific School.[16] For a summer vacation he rowed up Lake
Champlain and down the St. Lawrence to Quebec, accompanied
by three friends including Gardner. That winter of 1862–63
found him studying glacial geology with Alexander Agassiz and
even dabbling in the study of the Pre-Raphaelite school of art.[17]
Not until the spring of 1863 did the emergency arise that determined the course of his life.

It concerned the health of a rather frail little fellow, of considerably smaller stature than King, who was nevertheless his
best friend. James Terry Gardner had known King since they
were both lads of fourteen, and, as Gardner once testified before
a congressional committee, he and King had lived together "on
terms of intimacy closer than those of most brothers."[18] During
their summers together they had learned the joys of hunting
and fishing and botanizing, and when the time came for them
to choose their professions, both had chosen science. Gardner
had attended the Polytechnic School (Rensselaer) at Troy and
then had gone on to the Sheffield School, where he and King had

---

[13] Gilman, "Clarence King's School Days," *Clarence King Memoirs*, 299.

[14] Emmons, "Biographical Memoir of Clarence King," *Biographical Memoirs*,
VI, 30.

[15] Farquhar Collection, King to Gardner, March 18, 1862.

[16] Gilman, "Clarence King's School Days," *Clarence King Memoirs*, 298.

[17] Emmons, "Biographical Memoir of Clarence King," *Biographical Memoirs*,
VI, 30–31.

[18] *Geographical and Geological Surveys West of the Mississippi River*, 43
Cong., 1 sess., *House Report 612*, 70.

renewed their friendship.[19] But the cold climate and the hard work had taxed Gardner's constitution, and the two close friends, King, handsome and robust, and Gardner, haggard and exhausted, decided to head for California.[20]

California! What visions of high adventure that storied land conjured up in the minds of two young men of twenty-one! It meant a train trip into Kansas, and then a journey of more than two months up the sides of the shallow Platte, over a sea of rolling grassland, past Fort Laramie, an island in that sea, up to where the wind smelled of sagebrush and pine, through South Pass, then downward toward the Great Salt Lake, across the hot, dry deserts of Nevada, into Virginia City and the lands of the Washoe, over the high Sierras, past the Mother Lode country, and finally down into Sacramento. Here, for King and Gardner, was the real beginning of their adult lives. Here, somehow, they would find the careers for which Sheffield had prepared them.

One wonders at the sad partings from home. What did Mrs. Howland have to say about her favorite child leaving for the Far West? What did Jamie's parents say when their frail son, harboring an insistent cough, proudly announced that California was the place for *him?* But it was 1863. That summer witnessed Gettysburg and the fall of Vicksburg. The argument that going to California was safer than enlisting in the Union Army had a telling effect. The young men won out, and, with a third companion named Jim Hyde, they hit the road for Kansas, the great jumping-off place for the long trek to the land of the setting sun.

At St. Joseph, Missouri, they met a man named Speers who was leading a wagon train to California, and they joined up with him. They bought horses, gathered their frontiersman's gear together, and set out. Hardly had they hit the trail before their adventures began.

They had just reached the little settlement of Troy, thirteen miles west of St. Joseph, when a gang of "big raw-boned Kansans" halted the train, accused King, Gardner, and Hyde of kid-

---

[19] James Terry Gardner Papers, in the William Croswell Doane Papers, "Obituary of James Terry Gardner."

[20] Emmons, "Biographical Memoir of Clarence King," *Biographical Memoirs,* VI, 31.

napping some Negroes and running them back to Missouri, and summarily brought them into court. These were rough times, and Kansans were noticeably quick to accuse and fast to sentence. Fortunately, Spears convinced the judge of their innocence, and the party proceeded on its way.[21]

Slowly, they moved up the Platte Valley, the livestock searching for green grass along an immigrant trail that was sometimes a sprawling mile or more in width. They spied the slinking coyote, a scraggly, sneaking, little yellowish cur with its tail between its legs, a symbol of perpetual guilt. Again and again they watched as the prairie hare, better known as the jack rabbit, leaped aside from its feeding place and, ears perked toward the sun, bounded away over the prairie. They heard the shrill "pip" of the prairie dog, watched the little animals in their dirt-mound villages, and made sure that the horses did not step in the holes and pitch them to the bumpy earth. They watched the hawk circling, circling, lazily circling—then swooping earthward fast as a rattler's strike to climb skyward again with a limp rodent clasped in its long, pointed talons. Later on they saw antelope flicking their white tails in the prairie semaphore language. Occasionally a sound like dried grass rustling in the breeze, when there was no breeze, warned of a rattler's lair. Indians appeared occasionally: Cheyennes, Arapahoes, Shoshones, Sioux, and Crows—dirty, most of them sullen, not to be trusted. And great herds of buffalo covered the prairie.

On June 1, they reached Fort Laramie, close to where the Platte loops southeastward, and where the Laramie River joins it. There the young men witnessed a panorama of frontier life: Indians, a few soldiers, immigrants, fur traders, a few dirty mountain men. There was a busy blacksmith's shop, the anvil ringing, the hearth glowing from the forced air from the bellows. There was the odor of stacked up hay, the pungent smell of saddle leather, of horses, of unwashed humanity, and of rotgut whisky. But outside, there was the ever-present breeze, blowing

---

[21] J. T. Redman, "Reminiscences and Experiences on My Trip Across the Plains to California Sixty-one Years Ago When I Drove Four Mules to a Covered Wagon." Redman was a member of Speers' party.

from the West, calling, reminding, urging men onward, ever westward.

Then the climb started toward the Great Divide. On June 12, they reached Devil's Gate, a remarkable, narrow chasm of the Sweetwater River. The great herds of buffalo gave King itchy fingers. First he traded his horse for a buffalo pony. Then, when an enormous herd came into view—King estimated it at 10,000 head—he impetuously dashed into the midst and searched out an enormous male. He fired, and the great beast, maddened with pain, pawed the earth, lowered his great shaggy head, and charged into King's pony, caving in its side. The horse fell, painfully wounded, pinning one of King's legs underneath it. Luckily, the fall only lamed the young hunter, but the buffalo pony, poor beast, had to be shot. King wisely laid over a day, catching up with the wagon train via the Overland Stage.

And one day, still in June, the wagon train came to a place among the hills where the earth had been grooved by thousands of wagon wheels, and as they coasted through it, they realized that they had just crossed South Pass. It was quite a letdown, for they were not in mountains, and there was not a pine tree in sight. Southward lay high bluffs, however, and far to the northwest, rising abruptly in the summer haze, lay the ominous hulks of the Wind River Mountains. Straight west lay the cool, shallow waters of the Green River. The divide was crossed, and the true West lay beyond: Mormons, the desert, the Comstock Lode at Virginia City, the high Sierras, and California. With renewed energy they clattered on.

For a time, King was mighty worried about Gardner. He may have been a little fellow not in the best of health, but he had an eye for pretty girls, and there were two very attractive young ladies with the train. Daringly bloomered, the younger sister, Amanda, turned Gardner's head. For hours on end, he and Amanda rode together, arousing in King a noticeable envy, jealousy, or perhaps just a concern over young Gardner's moral life. King was glad indeed on the day Amanda's party, no longer fearing Indians, left the wagon train and went their own way.[22]

[22] *Ibid.* The dates used are from Redman's manuscript.

Westward they traveled, to Fort Bridger, crowded with nine hundred Indians held prisoners; to Echo Canyon and the Weber Valley; and finally to Salt Lake City, where they encamped on a square in the center of the city and feasted on lettuce and green onions.[23]

But California still called. The wagon train worked its way around the northern shores of the Great Salt Lake, then westward across the parched sagebrush and alkali flats to the Humboldt River in Nevada. In this valley the three young men turned away from the main party and toward Virginia City. Until then, they had followed the approximate route of the future railroad and had included in their journey much of the area which would later be studied by the Fortieth Parallel Survey. The trip so far had taken them three months, and each of the three thought of himself a completely different man than he had been just three months before back in New York.

Virginia City! Chaste name for a riproaring bonanza town that knew no day or night, fed red-gaitered, tobacco chewing, whisky drinking hard-rock miners and lightened them of the burdens of gold and silver coin that jingled in their pockets. Here was sweating, hard-working, hard-playing, teeming American humanity. For each and every man there was still a great day coming, and if a man weren't rich today, tomorrow his luck was sure to turn. Hot, dry, barren, a very hell of a place to live in for long, Virginia City was going full blast in 1863, exploiting the Comstock Lode.

Somewhere along the way, Jim Hyde disappears from the few narrations we have about the young New Yorkers, but Clare and Jamie made it to Virginia City, took rooms in a lodging house, and set out to investigate the Comstock Lode. Almost immediately their adventures began. The very first night, their lodging house burned down, destroying all their belongings and nearly costing King his life. But fires in that tinderbox of a town were commonplace. The miners slapped the boys on the back, offered them nips from high-smelling bottles, and generously outfitted

---

[23] *Ibid.* Farquhar Collection, Anne T. Gardner (James's mother) to her sister, Mrs. Clarke, of Buffalo, New York.

them in rough miner's clothing. Next, the two young men found work in one of the quartz mills in the town, and there they worked until they had saved enough money to continue their journey.[24]

As they tramped up into the Sierras (they had sold their horses), they paused occasionally for breath and turned their eyes eastward, surveying the land over which they had passed. It was hot and dry out there, but a few clouds shaded the hills, and the delicate blues of the distant mountains would have defied the painting abilities of a great artist. Both King and Gardner had fallen in love with the Great Basin, and when Jamie wrote home to his mother, he told her so. "But seriously," he said, "before we left the plains we had become so fascinated with the life and so interested in the vast loneliness in those deserts . . . that I would gladly have turned around and traveled right back over the same road."[25]

They trekked across the divide and down through the Mother Lode country, analyzing the lay of the land as they went. Soon they were at Sacramento, where they took passage on a river steamer for San Francisco. And here again fate intervened, this time fortuitously. The steamer was filled with men from the mines, rough, sunburned men in flannel shirts and high boots, wearing belts and revolvers. But one of them, though dressed much the same way, had a different face. Gardner walked past him, then sat down opposite him and pretended to be reading a newspaper. "An old felt hat, a quick eye, a sunburned face with different lines from the other mountaineers, a long weather-beaten neck protruding from a coarse gray flannel shirt and a rough coat, a heavy revolver belt and long legs made up the man," Gardner recalled. "And yet," he felt, "he is an intellectual man: I know it."[26] The "intellectual" turned out to be William H. Brewer, assistant to Josiah Whitney on the California Geological Survey. Brewer had worn down his exploring party to a single packer, and he eagerly hired King to go northward with him to

[24] Emmons, "Biographical Memoir of Clarence King," *Biographical Memoirs,* VI, 32.

[25] Farquhar Collection, Gardner to Anne T. Gardner, September 11, 1863.

[26] Farquhar Collection, Gardner to Anne T. Gardner, March 10, 1864.

Lassen Peak and Mount Shasta.[27] While Gardner went on to San Francisco and took work with the U. S. Topographical Engineers,[28] King got in his first large-scale geological work and had an opportunity for a first-hand study of volcanism—a branch of geology in which he later became the foremost authority in the United States.[29]

For the next four years, King's and Gardner's stars were hitched to the California Geological Survey. Once during this period, King took time off to help in a geological survey of the huge Mariposa estate, once owned by John C. Frémont. On another occasion, he and Gardner accompanied General Mc-Dowell on a reconnaissance of the desert regions of southern California and part of Arizona. Gardner had joined the survey in April, 1864. The bracing San Francisco climate had not improved his health, and he had resigned his job rather than work on the Sabbath. He had about decided to return home when Professor Whitney invited him to go into the southern Sierras with King, Brewer, and Charles F. Hoffman, the survey topographer. Gardner was to be an "assistant," furnishing his own horse and blankets, for a trip of about four months. As the party progressed, Gardner helped Hoffman and thus learned the secrets of the good topographical methodology which he put to such good use during his service with the Fortieth Parallel Survey and with Hayden.[30]

The importance of the association of King and Gardner with the California Geological Survey cannot be overestimated. Josiah Whitney was one of the most respected geologists then at work in the United States, and his appointment as head of the survey had been urged by such eminent scientists as the Sillimans, Dana, Marsh, Leidy, and Meek. His associate, Professor Brewer, like King and Gardner, was a product of the Sheffield Scientific

[27] Edward Tenney Brewster, *Life and Letters of Josiah Dwight Whitney*, 236.
[28] Farquhar Collection, Gardner to Anne T. Gardner, September 17, 1863.
[29] Emmons, "Biographical Memoir of Clarence King," *Biographical Memoirs*, VI, 33.
[30] Farquhar Collection, Gardner to Anne T. Gardner, November 25, 1863, March 26, 1864, April 7, 1864. King Collection, Folder A–3, Raymond, "Biographical Notice."

School. Charles F. Hoffman, the topographer, was a well-trained young German who became one of the most valuable men on the survey.[31]

The California Survey had been created by an act of the state legislature in 1860, and Whitney was appointed state geologist. He was supposed to make a complete geological survey of the state and furnish a complete scientific report. From the first, however, he failed to placate the state legislature, and that old bogey appropriations—or lack of them—brought the Survey to an end in 1872, although Whitney continued as state geologist until 1874.[32]

Whitney was a scholar and a scientist, and he never understood the necessity of coming down from the clouds of scientific speculation and doing some earthly lobbying. American legislators tend to be pragmatic, and California legislators in the 1860's were no exception. They had to have an idea of a practical, industrial application for the results of a geological survey, or else they would reject the survey entirely. Whitney's overall plan embraced a preliminary topographical and geological survey as preparation for more specialized studies which ultimately would have practical significance. But the legislature could neither understand this nor wait for the transformation from lofty speculation to concrete and applicable data. When a lawmaker brought one of the survey publications, a fossil-like tome on paleontology, onto the floor of the legislature and proceeded to read from it, the California Geological Survey was as doomed as the dinosaur.[33]

King learned both good and bad things from his experiences with the California Survey. To his benefit were nearly four years with some of the nation's leading geologists, four years of working with scientific field expeditions, and four years of roughing it in the unexplored mountains of the Sierras. Then there was Whitney's idealism. His men, wrote Brewster, "were about the only persons in California who were concerned with the earth, and

[31] Brewster, *Josiah Dwight Whitney*, 186–205.
[32] Merrill, *American Geology*, 407.
[33] *Ibid.*, 410.

Mount of the Holy Cross, 1873, probably Jackson's
greatest picture (Hayden Survey).

A. D. Wilson and Franklin Rhoda at the summit of Sultan Mountain,
San Juan County, Colorado (Hayden Survey).

John Moss and Ernest Ingersoll at the first cliff dwelling
discovered by the Hayden party (1874).

National Archives

Panoramic views by W. H. Holmes in the Hayden *Atlas.*
Top: The Teton Range from upper Grosventre Butte.
Below: Southwestern border of the Mesa Verde, showing the
Sierra El Late in the distance.

Sketch by Holmes of Twin Lakes, Colorado, 1873.
William D. Whitney, Dr. Hayden, and Holmes are shown.

Holmes' party at camp at Parrott City, near present town of
Mancos, Colorado. Left to right: Tom Cooper, unidentified
packer, W. H. Holmes, Townsend S. Brandegee, George B.
Chittenden, and "Potato John" Raymond.

Harry Yount, hunter for the Hayden Survey and later the
first Ranger in Yellowstone Park. Here he is at Berthoud Pass,
Colorado Territory, in 1874.

The odometer recorded the distance and was run by Mr. Goodfellow, assistant (Hayden Survey, 1872).

were not trying to make money out of it." Nor could any member of the survey make a penny for himself.[34]

Such insistence upon personal integrity was of course good. But the personal aspect embraced the policy of the survey as a whole: *it* reflected no interest in the mining industry. It was engaged in pure science, something very close to a scientist's heart. But its appropriations came from a less intellectual body, and so the survey failed for lack of funds. King's concept of a survey of the fortieth parallel reflected in some degree this impracticality, this interest in pure science, which was a product of his years with Whitney.

These were the formative years for Clarence King, and happy ones, and he left more reminiscences of his work with the California Survey than he did for all his years on the fortieth parallel project. Most of his stories are gathered in a single volume, *Mountaineering in the Sierra Nevada,* which is for the most part a compilation of sketches which had previously appeared in the *Atlantic Monthly.*[35] The book is filled with striking word pictures of the western country. Take, for example, King's description of the desert as seen from far up on its western rim:

> Spread out below us lay the desert, stark and glaring, its rigid hill-chains lying in disordered grouping, in attitudes of the dead. The bare hills are cut out with sharp gorges, and over their stone skeletons scanty earth clings in folds, like shrunken flesh; they are emaciated corpses of once noble ranges now lifeless, outstretched as in a long sleep. Ghastly colors define them from the ashen plain in which their feet are buried. Far in the south were a procession of whirlwind columns slowly moving across the desert in spectral dimness. A white light beat down, dispelling the last trace of shadow, and above hung the burnished shield of hard, pitiless sky.[36]

[34] Brewster, *Josiah Dwight Whitney,* 238–39.

[35] Edward Cary, "King's 'Mountaineering,'" *Clarence King Memoirs,* 239. Four editions of *Mountaineering in the Sierra Nevada* came out before 1874, and in 1947, Francis P. Farquhar, acting as editor, brought another edition, published in London. I have used the edition published by James R. Osgood and Company in Boston in 1872.

[36] King, *Mountaineering,* 21.

King also had a remarkable ability to impart just the right shade of meaning to his statements, with a dash of humor thrown in. Concerning Indians, "the Quakers," he said, "will have to work a really great reformation in the Indian before he is really fit to be exterminated." His thoughts on mules were brought on specifically by a one-eyed beast that used her blindness as a pretext "to commit excesses, such as crowding me against trees and refusing to follow trails. . . . Realizing how terrible under reinforcement of hereditary transmission the peculiarly mulish traits would have become," he added, "one is more than thankful to Nature for depriving this singular hybrid of the capacity of handing them down." And what a dismal picture he drew of himself and Gardner in the desert, for Gardner's mule had "developed a singular apathy for my mule, and utterly refused to march within a quarter of a mile of me; so that over a wearying route of three hundred miles we were obliged to travel just beyond the reach of a shout. Hour after hour, plodding along at a dog-trot, we pursued our solitary way without the spice of companionship, and altogether deprived of the melodramatic satisfaction of loneliness."[37]

The leading American critic of the time, William Dean Howells, expressed the greatest admiration for King's literary accomplishment. "He has brilliantly fixed forever a place of the Great West already vanished from actuality," Howells said. "In one glowing picture he has portrayed a sublime mood of nature, with all those varying moods of human nature which best give it relief."[38]

To appreciate his storytelling abilities, one should read "The Newtys of Pike."[39] It concerns a long and lanky family of Missouri hog farmers who pioneered the West but who instead of pulling themselves up by the bootstraps, started there and worked down. King reveals his understanding of human nature, his love of people, even his compassion when he probes Susan

[37] *Ibid.*, 13, 14, 40, 148.
[38] William Dean Howells, "Meeting with King," *Clarence King Memoirs*, 155–56.
[39] King, *Mountaineering*, 94–111.

Newtys' character. There he finds, even in her, poor child, "the presence of undeveloped seed in the human mind."[40]

Most of King's known experiences during these years appear in *Mountaineering*, but one episode about which he did not write occurred in the winter of 1865–66 when he and Gardner were with General McDowell in Arizona. It had not been a pleasant reconnaissance. Their mules were in such terrible condition that they had begun eating cotton rags and buckskin on cabin doors, and one poor beast had died within a mile after they had started out from Prescott. Indians—cruel Apaches—were around too, and the charred ruins of settlers' cabins reminded them to be on guard. But suddenly one day the two young men were surrounded by Apaches who began preparations for a fandango with King and Gardner as honored guests, to be staked out on the sand and slowly burned to death. Only King's cool appraisal of the situation saved them. He and Gardner interested the Indians in a cistern barometer, retarding preparations until a cavalry unit came on the scene and saved the young scientists.[41]

During the years with the California Survey, King was in wonderful physical condition. "King," Professor Brewer recorded in his journal in 1864, "is enthusiastic, is wonderfully tough, has the greatest endurance I have ever seen, and is withal very muscular. He is a most perfect specimen of health."[42] *Mountaineering* is sufficient evidence of his mental capacities, for nine of the fourteen sketches in the book bear dates prior to 1866, which means that they were written when King was under twenty-five years of age.[43]

Yet King rightfully looked upon these pleasant years in the Sierras as a period of preparation for more serious duties, as perhaps a last golden experience in the happy days of youth and a prelude to the more profound professional work of adulthood. "There are turning-points in all men's lives which must give them both pause and retrospect," he wrote.

[40] *Ibid.*, 109.

[41] King Collection, Folders A–3, B–5, and B–11.

[42] Francis P. Farquhar (ed.), *Up and Down California in 1860–1864; the Journal of William H. Brewer*, 525.

[43] Cary, "King's 'Mountaineering,'" *Clarence King Memoirs*, 239.

In long Sierra journeys the mountaineer looks forward eagerly, gladly, till pass or ridge-crest is gained, and then, turning with a fonder interest, surveys the scene of his march, letting the eye wander over each crag and valley, every blue hollow or pine-land or sunlit gem of alpine meadow. . . . With a lingering look he starts forward, and the closing pass-gate with its granite walls shuts away the retrospect, yet the delightful picture forever after hangs on the gallery wall of his memory. It is thus with me about mountaineering; the pass which divides youth from manhood is traversed, and the serious service of science must hereafter claim me.[44]

For Clarence King, the year 1866 marked his crossing of the pass from youth to manhood.

[44] Clarence King, "Introduction," *Mountaineering in the Sierra Nevada* (New York, Charles Scribner's Sons, 1902), x. This introduction does not appear in earlier editions.

6

The Birth of the Survey

ONE CLEAR AND PLEASANT DAY in the late summer of 1866, King
and Gardner found themselves in the region east of Yosemite,
perched on the summit of one of the high peaks of the Sierras.
Eastward as far as their eyes could see were the deserts and
ranges of Nevada. Their conversation wandered: they talked of
problems of geology and about their future careers. Their previous activities in Arizona and California had made it clear that
a true comprehension of the geology of the West could be mastered only through studying "the structure, topographical and
geological, of the whole mountain system of western America
from the Plains to the Pacific." And as the cool west wind tore
at their clothing and the sun beat down its ultra-violet rays upon
them in that rarefied atmosphere, the two young scientists developed an exhilarating idea: why not make a scientific continental cross section of the fortieth parallel?[1]

King was jubilant over the idea. He needed money and he
needed challenge, and the idea of a survey of the fortieth parallel
offered both. The money was needed because the sudden death
of his stepfather had left him the sole support of his mother and
three small children, and his salary with the California Survey

[1] King Collection, Folder A-3, Raymond, "Biographical Notice," 332-35.

141

was not sufficient to meet such obligations. The fortieth parallel idea could mean a good salary, and the challenge it offered was obvious.[2]

This is what prompted King to go to Washington in the winter of 1866–67 and make the proposals which launched the Fortieth Parallel Survey. From this time until he resigned his post in a letter to his chief, General A. A. Humphreys, in 1879, King devoted much of his time and energy to this great work. It occupied the very prime of his life and was also his most successful undertaking, brought to fruition in seven beautiful volumes and a very useful atlas.

When young King arrived in Washington in the winter of 1867, the Civil War had been over for nearly two years. Lincoln was dead. Andrew Johnson had fought a losing battle with the acrimonious radicals; Thaddeus Stephens and Charles Sumner controlled Congress, and Congress controlled the nation. Radical reconstruction was being forced upon the prostrate South. Yet everywhere in the North there was bustling activity, optimism, and political immorality. Bribery and fraud were prevalent throughout the land, and in the competition to strike claims and exploit the virgin land, the nation's resources—both human and natural—were going to suffer. Nowhere was the uncouth face of the reckless promoter more evident than in Washington. And the cold winter sleet fell upon the thoughtful, determined faces of Union veterans who, with government help, were trying to re-establish civilian lives for themselves, trying to find ways, now that the war was over, to earn respectable livings in a time of peace.

What chance, then, did King have? He was not a veteran, but he was young—approaching twenty-five at the time—and possessed of the charm of a salesman, the education of a scientist, and the culture of a literary man. And he had a remarkable idea. Who could say, he argued, that the right of way of the new transcontinental railroad contained only sagebrush and greasewood, rattlers, kangaroo rats, and jackrabbits? Was it not possible that

[2] Emmons, "Biographical Memoir of Clarence King," *Biographical Memoirs,* VI, 35.

coal or iron or precious metals lay out there? A trained geologist, he insisted, should be employed by the government to find the answers. Then King boldly revealed his plan: a survey across the entire West from the crest of the Sierra Nevadas to the western slope of the Rockies which would dispel the mysteries of geology and natural history in the region traversed by the transcontinental railroad.

He was not a veteran seeking an appointment, a get-rich-quick schemer, or an influence peddler. But he could offer a degree from the Sheffield Scientific School at Yale, four years in the Sierras with Whitney and Brewer, and the determination of his heart and soul. And that purposefulness was reflected in every action, every stance of his robust figure. Clarence King was a thinker and a doer. And he did have quite an idea.

When King arrived in Washington, he had already prepared his campaign. Professor Whitney had written to California's Senator John Conness in his behalf, describing King as being "well qualified to make geological and geographical exploration." Whitney added, "I believe that the cause of science will be subserved and the material interests of the country advanced by such exploration . . . and I therefore have not hesitated to ask you to favor his plan, if you find it in your power to do so."[3]

King also carried a recommendation to Professor Baird of the Smithsonian from Yale's eminent scientist, James D. Dana. This letter, which described King as "an excellent geologist, a most trustworthy observer, companionable, and every way reliable," also described his aim—a survey embracing both geology and natural history, to last three to four years. Dana's letter and one from R. S. Williamson, who had employed King in California as an engineering assistant, suggested that steps be taken to

[3] National Archives, R.G. 77, Office of the Chief of Engineers, Letters Received, Third and Fifth Divisions, File Number Secretary of War 245, Whitney to Conness, November 9, 1866. Rossiter W. Raymond insists that Whitney refused to write a recommendation because King's idea was impractical. After his own experiences with the California legislature, Whitney must indeed have sensed the weakness of the plan, but the letter cited above is an original and must be accepted as proof of Whitney's support. See King Collection, Folder A–3, Raymond, "Statements of Rossiter W. Raymond."

introduce him to General A. A. Humphreys, chief of the Army Engineers. Three more letters, including one from Agassiz, were addressed to Secretary of War Edwin Stanton. Perhaps King's naïveté is best reflected in Williamson's letter: "King has an idea that it would be easy to make a successful application to Congress for a small appropriation. Of this I know very little, but should think it no easy thing to get."[4]

In spite of all, King got his survey, with himself as geologist in charge, subject only to the administrative supervision of the Engineer Department of the U.S. Army. Henry Adams, commenting on King's appointment, only heightened the mystery of how he got it and in no way suggested the answer. "It is not necessary," Adams wrote in the *North American Review*, "to investigate by what 'happy accident' it was brought about that a work of such importance should be inaugurated, or how it came to be placed in charge of a competent person, and carried on uninterruptedly until important results had been obtained."[5] The citation in the *U.S. Statutes at Large* merely provided for "a geological and topographical exploration of the territory between the Rocky Mountains and the Sierra Nevada mountains, including the route or routes of the Pacific railroad; Provided, That the same can be done out of existing appropriations."[6]

When King took over the survey, the Secretary of War handed him his commission as geologist in charge and gave him some sage advice: "Now, Mr. King, the sooner you get out of Washington, the better—you are too young a man to be seen about town with this appointment in your pocket—there are four major-generals who want your place."[7] Before leaving, however, he had to call on General A. A. Humphreys.

If the confident Mr. King approached any of his interviews in Washington with misgivings, surely it was the one with General

[4] National Archives, R.G. 77, Office of the Chief of Engineers, Letters Received, Dana to Baird, December 13, 1866; Williamson to General H. L. Abbott, November 3, 1866.

[5] Henry Adams, Editorial comments on the King Survey, *North American Review*, Vol. CXIII, No. 233 (July, 1871), 204.

[6] *U.S. Statutes at Large*, Vol. 14, 457.

[7] James D. Hague, "Memorabilia," *Clarence King Memoirs*, 385.

Humphreys. In 1867, Andrew Atkinson Humphreys was fifty-six years old and a full brigadier general. The product of an outstanding family (a grandfather was known proudly as "the Father of the American Navy"), young Andrew had been educated at private schools, had entered West Point at seventeen, and four years later, in 1831, had graduated thirteenth in a class of thirty-three. He had then seen service in the Seminole War, after which he had temporarily resigned and had worked for the Topographical Engineers in a civilian capacity. In 1838, he had rejoined the army and was attached again to the Topographical Engineers. Before the Civil War interrupted his engineering career, Humphreys had made a topographic and hydrographic survey of the Mississippi delta, a work that had established his professional reputation both in America and abroad. He had traveled extensively in Europe, had been placed in charge of the overall administration of the Pacific Railroad Surveys, and seemed well on the way to the top of his particular branch of the army. Then came the war, during which he saw action and displayed great courage and ability in the Peninsular Campaign, at Antietam, Fredericksburg, Chancellorsville, and Gettysburg. After the war, he was appointed chief of the Corps of Engineers with the rank of brigadier general.[8]

Humphreys was a man widely respected in military and scientific circles throughout the United States and Europe. He was "brave in action and wise in council . . . a man of truth, integrity, and honor."[9] What this man, an honored veteran of a long and vicious war, thought about the appointment of a young civilian who had spent the war years in California, we do not know. But in his military way he set King right on matters of bookkeeping. There was an army way of doing things, and King must adhere to it, even if he was a civilian commanding civilians. King walked away from that interview knowing that he was not a free agent.

[8] *Dictionary of American Biography,* IX, 371–72. *Proceedings of the American Philosophical Society,* Vol. XXII, No. 117 (January, 1885), 48–71.

[9] *Proceedings of the American Philosophical Society,* Vol. XXII, No. 117 (January, 1885), 48.

Perhaps the General handed him a copy of his orders. They were succinct and thorough:

> The object of the exploration is to examine and describe the geological structure, geographical condition and natural resources of a belt of country extending from the 120th meridian eastward to the 105th meridian, along the 40th parallel of latitude with sufficient expansion north and south to include the line of the "Central" and "Union Pacific" railroads, and as much more as may be consistent with accuracy and a proper progress, which would be not less than five degrees of longitude yearly. The exploration will be commenced at the 120th meridian where it will connect with the geological survey of California, and should, if practicable, be completed in two years.... It should examine all rock formations, mountain ranges, detrital plains, coal deposits, soils, minerals, ores, saline and alkaline deposits . . . collect . . . material for a topographical map of the regions traversed, ... conduct . . . barometric and thermometric observations [and] make collections in botany and zoology with the view to a memoir on these subjects, illustrating the occurrence and distribution of plants and animals.[10]

King set to work at once, for it was already well into March. He had to muster a scientific corps, make all preparations, sail to California via the Panama route, and be in the high Sierras before the summer season was well advanced. There was no time to be lost. Yet King knew how critical his appointments would be to the success of his survey. Not only would his men have to possess outstanding ability in their chosen professions, but they would also have to be dedicated to a project which would last at least three years. Health, even robust health, would be necessary, so that they could stand the rigors of outdoor life in the Great Basin, and they would have to be well enough adjusted and sufficiently adaptable to get along well with a few other men under all kinds of conditions and hardships. Adherence to some measure of discipline and respect for their leader (who was acutely aware of his youthful appearance) would be essential. It is to King's credit that he chose his men well—so well, indeed, that

[10] National Archives, R.G. 57, "Letters to King," Vol. I, Humphreys to King, March 21, 1867.

some of them came to dominate their fields of specialization for a generation after the fortieth parallel work was completed. It happened that some of his choices were also personal friends. But King always had friends of great ability, so a practice that could have been disastrous proved in his case to be beneficial.

He wrote to all those he wanted to hire, and the first man to reply favorably was his old friend James Terry Gardner. An expert on topographic methods, thanks to his work with Hoffman on the California Geological Survey, Gardner became the first topographic assistant on the new survey. It may have been a difficult decision for Gardner, for he had also been offered the chair of geodesy at the Lawrence School at Harvard under the supervision of Whitney. A second topographer, a Swiss named H. Custer, was appointed on the recommendation of General Gouverneur K. Warren, and a few days later a third assistant, F. A. Clark, was added. A. D. Wilson, later to see service with Hayden and with the U.S. Geological Survey, also joined the Fortieth Parallel Survey. The combined endeavors of these topographers eventually resulted in the publication of an atlas of the Fortieth Parallel Survey, a beautiful job of great value to collectors today.[11]

For his aides in the field of geology, King chose the Hague brothers, James Duncan and Arnold. Both of these young men were Boston-born sons of a Baptist minister and grandsons of a Yankee sea captain. Both, like King, had attended private schools. Then James, the older of the two and six years the senior of King, had attended the Lawrence School at Harvard, the University of Göttingen, and the Royal School of Mines in Germany. In 1859–60, he had been employed as a chemist with a South Seas exploring expedition. James also served with the navy in the Civil War, and when King's offer came through, he was associated with the Institute of Technology at Boston. King had known him and liked him since 1862, when the two had met at Sheffield. "He has been a wide traveler, a superintendent of ex-

---

[11] National Archives, R.G. 57, "Copy Book of Letters Sent by Clarence King to General A. A. Humphreys, 1867–1879," King to Humphreys, April 3, 1867, April 6, 1867, May 6, 1867. All of the letters from King to Humphreys are contained in the above source.

tensive mining operations, and is considered by Dana and other eminent men as very able," King wrote General Humphreys. James D. Hague was also a Bostonian through and through, dignified, gentlemanly, and kind. He and King were kindred spirits.[12]

His brother Arnold was four and one-half years younger, and although he outlived James by nine years, he was always considered the weaker of the two physically. He had also received private school instruction and had then attended the Sheffield School, where he was a year behind King. Following in his brother's path, his educational trail then led to Germany, where he studied at Göttingen, then at Heidelberg, and finally at the Royal School of Mines at Freiberg. Fortunately, Arnold returned to the states just in time to be offered the appointment with King, which he happily accepted. Thus, King had for the survey two brothers, both good friends of his, both well educated, and both men of the same cultural pattern as his own.[13]

Then Arnold put in a word for a close friend of *his*. This young Bostonian, a friend of Henry Adams, was Samuel Franklin Emmons. He, too, had been educated at private schools, then at Harvard, where he graduated in 1861 at the age of twenty. His education had taken him to the Ecole des Mines in France and then to the Royal School of Mines—the *Bergakademie*—at Freiberg, where he had met Arnold and the two had immediately struck up a close friendship. It was a coincidence that he arrived back in America just when the survey was being assembled, and he was forced to accept employment temporarily without pay. But his education, his quiet and kindly disposition, and the similarity of his background with that of the Hagues led King to take him along.[14]

[12] *Dictionary of American Biography*, IV, 87. National Archives, R.G. 57, "Copy Book of Letters," April 6, 1867. Hague, "Memorabilia," *Clarence King Memoirs*, 377.

[13] *Dictionary of American Biography*, IV, 85–86. *American Journal of Science*, Vol. XLIV, Fourth Series, No. 259 (July, 1917), 73.

[14] *Dictionary of American Biography*, VI, 151–52. National Archives, R.G. 57, "Copy Book of Letters," May 8, 1867.

The geological branch of the Fortieth Parallel Survey, then, consisted of four young men, all New Englanders, all educated in private schools and at Harvard or Yale, and all but one having done further study in Europe. In 1867, the oldest of the four, James Hague, was thirty-one, his brother Arnold was twenty-six, Emmons was the same, and King was twenty-five. Their youth compounds the impressiveness of their achievements, for King's *Systematic Geology,* Arnold Hague's and Emmons' *Descriptive Geology,* and James D. Hague's *Mining Industry*—Volumes I, II, and III of the final reports of the survey—were each outstanding contributions.[15]

The flora and fauna of the fortieth parallel region were also to be studied and, in keeping with his policy of obtaining young, well-trained men from good families, King (with an eye for good public relations) gave the botanist's position to William Whitman Bailey, son of a former West Point professor. Bailey was twenty-four years old at the time, a nervous lad who had never quite recovered from a disaster on a Hudson river boat which, when he was just nine, had killed his mother and sister and had nearly cost him his own life. He had graduated from Brown University, and in 1867, he was working at the Massachusetts Institute of Technology. But Bailey, although he was a competent botanist who later became a full professor of the subject at Brown, proved to be physically incapable of the rigors of camp life in the Far West. After nine months with the survey, he retired because of poor health.[16]

Fortunately, another man was present to fill Bailey's place. At first he seemed a most unlikely candidate. His name was Sereno Watson, and in the course of his forty-two years the shy, reticent New England bachelor, a graduate of Yale, had tried teaching, medicine, banking, insurance, editorial work, and farming. At the age of forty, he had entered the Sheffield Scientific School with the aim of preparing himself for a life in Cali-

---

[15] For a list of all seven volumes and the atlas, see Bibliography.

[16] National Archives, R.G. 57, "Copy Book of Letters," April 6, 1867. *National Cyclopaedia of American Biography*, XXIX, 371.

fornia, where he arrived in 1867. There he heard about King's survey, and he set out to find the young geologist and get a job. From the eastern terminus of the uncompleted Central Pacific, Sereno began walking, and finally one July night he arrived tired and dusty at the camp of the Fortieth Parallel Survey along the Truckee River. He asked for a job. King had his troubles with applicants, and he was none too happy about the appearance of this middle-aged man, but, more out of pity than anything else, he let Watson stay on as a volunteer worker without pay. The man knew how to do so many things that his usefulness was immediately apparent, and within a month King placed him on a salary, at the rate of a camp man instead of a topographical assistant, though most of his work was in the latter classification. Early in 1868, he increased Watson's salary, but it was not until March of that year, when Bailey resigned, that Watson finally achieved professional status.[17]

Watson's interest in botany was first aroused when he was in Alabama as secretary of an insurance firm, but it remained a hobby until Bailey's resignation gave him the opportunity to turn it into a profession. As early as December, 1867, Bailey had written to Harvard's great botanist, Asa Gray, that Watson, who had not been ill, had already collected twice the number of specimens that he had. "I cannot speak in terms of too high praise of this gentleman—always genial and kind—and ever persevering," Bailey wrote. "He works early and late, and seems never tired or ruffled."[18] Watson's work, embraced in Volume V of King's final reports, was of the highest merit. It established his professional reputation and contributed to his appointment as curator of the Gray Herbarium at Harvard, where he remained, quiet and studious, for the rest of his life.

Bailey and, later, Watson took care of the flora, but King still needed a man to study the fauna along the fortieth parallel. This

[17] *Dictionary of American Biography,* XIX, 547–48. *Cyclopaedia of National Biography,* VI, 112. National Archives, R.G. 57, "Copy Book of Letters," January 8, 1868. *Scientific American,* Vol. LXVI, No. 15 (April 9, 1892), 233.

[18] Andrew Denny Rodgers III, *American Botany: 1873–1892,* 24. Quoted from a letter in the Gray Herbarium.

assignment fell to young Robert Ridgway, who did not come from a New England family and had never been to college, but was nevertheless an excellent choice.

Ridgway was born in Mount Carmel, in southern Illinois, in 1850, the son of a village pharmacist. In those days much of the magnificent virgin forest still lay close by, as yet unmolested by the woodsman's ax. From his very earliest childhood, Robert and his father took trips into the forest. Although their motivation for most of these excursions was hunting, the wonders of bird and animal life intrigued father and son alike, so that their woodsmanship included the knowledge of the forest creatures, their names, and their habits. Encouragement was offered by a kindly mother who, in spite of the demands of ten children, shared their interest in the outdoors.

But Robert's interest in birds soon became much more than passing. A doting uncle kept bird drawings by his precocious nephew which had been done at the tender ages of four and five, and before Robert was ten he was mixing his own colors for use in painting his birds. Then, when he was fourteen, an incident occurred that determined the future course of his life. He and two other boys had watched a beautifully plumaged bird which they could not identify. The other boys' mother suggested that Robert write to the commissioner of patents in Washington, D.C., describing the bird, in the hope that the commissioner could identify it for him. Of course, the patent officer did not know birds from beans, but in the tradition of a good bureaucrat he sent the letter along to someone in Washington who did—Spencer Baird of the Smithsonian Institution.

Baird replied, identifying the bird as *Carpodacus purpureus,* or Purple Finch. But more than that, he encouraged young Ridgway in ornithology, welcomed his letters and paintings and boxes of birds' nests and birds' eggs, and always replied with advice, information, and encouragement. One afternoon early in March, 1867, when Robert was just sixteen, he brought home two redtailed hawk eggs and found another of Professor Baird's letters awaiting him. "What are you engaged in at present?" asked the

Professor. Then he offered two possibilities to Robert: one was several months of work at the Smithsonian, with expenses paid. "Or," the letter continued, "how would you like to go to the Rocky Mts. and California for a year or two as collector of specimens . . . There would probably be a salary of about $50.00 per month and all expenses necessary."

How would he like to go? How would any healthy, dreamily-inclined lad of sixteen like to go to the Great West? The offer subsequently came through from King, and, after parental consent had been obtained, Robert said goodby to his parents, his infant brother John, and a sister, boarded a train for the first time in his life, and—may we suppose—biting his lips and trying to ignore a certain mistiness in his eyes, watched the familiar countryside become unfamiliar as the train clicked off the miles to Washington.

Ridgway and Baird got along well from the very first, and for two weeks the Professor taught his young protege how to skin birds and collect, classify, and otherwise preserve specimens. Then, early in May, Robert proceeded alone to New York City, where he joined the first party of the survey to depart for California. For more than two years thereafter—from June, 1867, until August, 1869—the youth stayed in the field collecting and preserving some 1,522 specimens of birds (including nests and eggs) and devoting "almost equal attention to the other branches of zoology, particularly to reptiles and fishes." In later years this shy, dedicated man became the respected curator of birds in the United States National Museum and the author of more than 500 scholarly papers. Clarence King had once again made a good choice.[19]

King also saw the potentialities in new innovations, and among these in the 1870's was the camera. Why not take along a photographer? One was available, and his appointment was made. His name was Timothy H. O'Sullivan, and he had learned

[19] Harry Harris, "Robert Ridgway," *The Condor*, Vol. XXX. No. 1 (January–February, 1928), 7–21. *Dictionary of American Biography*, XV, 598–99. Robert Ridgway, "Ornithology," *Professional Papers of the Engineer Department. No. 18. Report of the Geological Exploration of the Fortieth Parallel*, Vol. IV, Part III, 307.

his trade from Mathew Brady, who had known him from boy-hood and spoke most highly of his qualifications.[20] O'Sullivan had been with Brady at Gettysburg and Richmond, and a well-known photograph of Gettysburg the day after, "Harvest of Death," has been attributed to him. Yet very little more is known about this man's early life, or of his personality. When he died of tuberculosis in 1882, even his exact age was not known, al-though he was believed to have been about forty-two years old.[21] This would have made him about twenty-seven in 1867, another young man for a young man's expedition. For three years, O'Sul-livan remained with King, doing outstanding work. King had made another wise choice.

King was naturally in a hurry to get started, but thoroughness was important too. A thousand and one details had to be cleared up before he left the East. He learned that checks and paper money were nearly useless in the Far West and had to request General Humphreys to make an exception to the usual army rule concerning the disbursement of funds by placing five to six thou-sand dollars in gold coin at his disposal.[22] Humphreys went to the secretary of war and the secretary of the treasury to get this money for King, which was thereafter accounted for in a "coin account." Major General H. W. Halleck, commanding the Mili-tary Division of the Pacific, received orders to furnish King with twenty mounted men and provisions, and the quartermaster general's office received orders to sell King supplies "whenever it may be found necessary during the progress of the exploration, provided the same can be spared."[23]

Scientific instruments probably not available in California had to be purchased, packed, and shipped from the East. The list of

[20] For a facsimile of a letter of recommendation from Brady to the Treasury Department, see James D. Horan, *Mathew Brady: Historian with a Camera*, 78.

[21] *Ibid.*, 53. Peter Pollack, *The Picture History of Photography*, 204.

[22] National Archives, R.G. 57, "Copy Book of Letters," April 6, 1867, April 22, 1867.

[23] National Archives, R.G. 57, Letters to King," Vol. I, McCulloch to Stanton, April 25, 1867; Adjutant General to Halleck, April 25, 1867; Adjutant General to Quartermaster General, April 15, 1867.

these instruments, which King compiled in consultation with his men, readily identifies the nature of the survey. Among the items were a six-inch theodolite "with vertical limb and compass," three "new style gradienters," one pocket and two box chronometers, six small compasses "of which two are to be made with ball and socket joint," one small box of drawing instruments, one 100-foot tapeline, three pair of field glasses, seven sets of wet- and dry-bulb thermometers, five sets of "maximum and minimum self-registering thermometers from minus 20 F. min. to 190 F. max.," and "one box blowpipe apparatus." In addition, O'Sullivan selected a complete photographic outfit.[24]

Finally preparations were completed, the personnel was organized, and the survey was ready to take ship. Then King fell ill and was laid up for more than a week. From then on, for the rest of his life, he was subject to occasions of sickness and complete exhaustion which curtailed his activities. Once he felt so weak after a season in the saddle that he went to Hawaii to lie on the beaches and recuperate. But this time, however, his sickness did not make much difference. On May 1, he sent Gardner, the Hagues, Emmons, and the topographic assistant F. A. Clark on ahead. Eleven days later, recovered from his illness, King followed, accompanied by H. Custer (the other topographic assistant), Robert Ridgway, William W. Bailey, and Timothy O'Sullivan. Reacting typically and consistently to the nuisance that he always found paper work to be (to the intense disturbance of the red-tape specialists in the army), he failed to get his receipts for supplies made out before sailing time, but promised to send them from Aspinwall (Colón), in Panama.[25]

Their departure took place with barely a ripple of notice. The New York *Times* chose to run an inconspicuous little item on page eight, but save for that the world little knew about the group of young scientists who were beginning a project that, from beginning to end, would last twelve years.[26]

The Pacific Mail steamer *Henry Chauncy*, a great side-wheel-

[24] National Archives, R.G. 57, "Copy Book of Letters," April 6, 1867; April 22, 1867.

[25] *Ibid.*, May 6, 1867; May 10, 1867; February 2, 1872.

[26] New York *Times*, May 2, 1867, p. 8.

er, got them safely to Aspinwall. From there, they crossed the Isthmus, boarded another side-wheeler, the *Constitution,* at Panama City, and proceeded to San Francisco, where they arrived early in June.[27]

By river steamer the reunited party pushed on to Sacramento, where no less a personage than Ben Crocker, buyer and outfitter for the Central Pacific Railroad, found them a "convenient and pleasant camp ground," lent them horses and teams until they had their own, and helped them choose their stock and wagons.[28] After traveling over two hundred miles with the equipment, King judged Crocker's advice to have been the very best, and was pleased with the quality of the stock and wagons and the prices he had paid for them. Meanwhile, preparations were completed, and by July 3, 1867, the United States Geological Exploration of the Fortieth Parallel, Clarence King, geologist in charge, was ready to take to the trail.[29]

[27] Harris, "Robert Ridgway," *The Condor,* Vol. XXX, No. 1 (January–February, 1928), 21.

[28] Farquhar Collection, Gardner to Anne T. Gardner, June 7, 1867.

[29] National Archives, R.G. 57, "Copy Book of Letters," July 20, 1867; August 3, 1867.

7

The Great Basin

KING AND GARDNER KNEW what lay ahead of them, for they had crossed the Great Basin in 1863 and again in 1866, but most of the party had never been there, and their eyes were still starry with happy, adventurous dreams. The alkali dust had not yet dimmed the sparkle of those eyes, nor made them sting and water. Most of the young men had not yet slept on the hard ground, felt the pinching sting of a hairy tarantula big as a saucer or the excruciating pain of a scorpion's needle-pointed tail. They only knew from hearsay that blood-curdling sound of rustling grass and the hiss of a coiled rattler. They had not lived for days at a time on poor rations and small quantities of rancid, alkaline water, nor had they tried to handle livestock that was jittery and cranky from poor forage and water. They had never had to live and work together with tempers short from living under such hardships.

In Nevada, the fortieth parallel lies a full degree north of where the state's western border begins its southeastward slant. Running eastward into Utah, the parallel lies forty to fifty miles south of the Great Salt Lake, while the transcontinental railroad was to pass north of it. When, after 1869, his survey advanced

156

eastward to the approximate site of Cheyenne, Wyoming, King had to veer north from the parallel in order to touch the railroad.

In 1867, the strip of land from the crest of the Sierras to Cheyenne was a wild and uninviting—not to say forbidding—expanse of country. Even today, most Americans know surprisingly little about it. They often see Utah and Nevada only from the windows of an airliner thousands of feet in the air. A few people still see it by train, more by bus, and many take automobiles. But their thoughts are mostly on getting across the "desert," not on the history of that barren country. Certainly, few ever stop to consider its beauty. And yet, if they would only pause and contemplate the changing desert scene, they would admit that it is beautiful.

True, it has its sinister aspect. When Mark Twain crossed it in 1861, he was permanently impressed—or depressed—by its dismal appearance. In *Roughing It*, he described the trip across the alkali desert: "Imagine team, driver, coach and passengers so deeply coated with ashes that they were all one colorless color; imagine ash-drifts roosting above mustaches and eyebrows like snow accumulations on boughs and bushes. This is the reality of it . . . there is not a sound—not a sigh—not a whisper—not a buzz, or a whir of wings, or a distant pipe of a bird—not even a sob from the lost souls that doubtless people that dead air."[1]

One hundred and fifty miles east of Carson City, Mark and his brother crossed another desert area, so dry and dusty that "the coach wheels sunk from six inches to a foot."

> We worked our passage most of the way across. That is to say, we got out and walked. It was a dreary pull and a long and thirsty one, for we had no water. From one extremity of this desert to the other, the road was white with the bones of oxen and horses. It would hardly be an exaggeration to say that we could have walked the forty miles and set our feet on a bone at every step! The desert was one prodigious graveyard. And the log-chains, wagon tires, and rotting wrecks of vehicles were almost as thick as the bones. I think we saw log-chains enough rusting there in the desert to reach across

[1] Mark Twain, *Roughing It*, I, 151.

any State in the Union. Do not these relics suggest something of an idea of the fearful suffering and privation the early emigrants to California endured?[2]

Even today, that Godforsaken land has not changed much. Civilization has progressed, however, and people no longer have to bother with mules and oxen and stage coaches. Four-wheel Jeeps make a difference! But the average rainfall of Nevada remains at about nine inches, which is hardly a fair statement because that includes twenty inches in the Sierras and four to five inches near the Great Salt Lake—most of which falls as winter snow. The mountains are still there, the salt flats are still there, though worn a little by racing cars. The acrid alkali still lies useless and all-pervading. But if the modern traveler will erase from his mind the strip of black-top that is the highway, and the advertising signs, then it is all like it was in 1867. And perhaps the best description comes from Sereno Watson's "General Report" which introduces Volume V of the final reports.

According to Watson, the area explored was bounded on the west by the high Sierras and a high flanking spur, called the Washoe Mountains, which crossed the border into Nevada. Eastward, the original survey was carried to the Wasatch Mountains. The total intervening distance was about 450 miles at 42° but, due to the convergence of opposing mountains, only about 200 miles at 37°. Between these two elevations, at intervals of about twenty miles, were "numerous short and somewhat isolated minor ranges, having a general north and south trend." These mountains, rising sharply from broad valleys, were narrow at the base, barely ten miles wide from east to west. In Nevada, the areas of mountains and valleys were very nearly equal. The highest mountains, the East Humboldts, rise to over 10,000 feet and stretched north and south between 115° and 116°, somewhat west of the Utah line.

(Never think of the Great Basin—so-called because once it was covered with two great inland seas—as a flat desert. The mountains rise all the way across, in pale blues and deep purples, a

---

[2] *Ibid.*, I, 159–60.

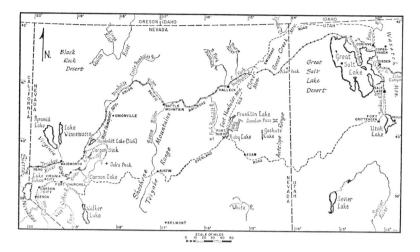

The Fortieth Parallel Country

constantly changing study in color tones. This is what gives the
desert much of its beauty.)

This region between the Sierra and Wasatch ranges had two
main depressions. One was at the base of the Sierras at about
3,850 feet above sea level; the other was the Great Salt Lake Basin. The western depression contained some geographic phenomena unknown elsewhere in North America. Into this low basin
flowed the Truckee, Carson, Quinn, and Humboldt rivers. (Modern irrigation projects have changed several tens of thousands of
acres, yet in the total acreage they hardly constitute more than an
oasis.) The Truckee was a clear, cold stream which flowed from
Lake Tahoe through the Virginia Mountains and then, turning
north, emptied into the deep, moderately saline Pyramid and
Winnemucca lakes. The Carson River rose farther south in the
Sierras, forming a shallow lake on the border of the Carson Desert, then issuing "in a number of devious channels . . . finally
spent in an extensive 'sink' or alkaline mud plain of some twenty
or thirty miles in diameter."

Working eastward from the sinks and the lakes in the depression, the general level rose until the valleys were about 6,000 feet
high. In northeastern Nevada, the Humboldt River had its
source. It was the longest and most important river in the Great

Basin, for it was the Humboldt that provided a logical route for some 300 miles of the Central Pacific, through mountain ranges "that would otherwise have provided a serious obstruction." Finally, it emptied into Humboldt Lake, "shallow and sub-alkaline." From eastern Nevada, the land soon turned into an alkali desert and sharply descended some 2,000 feet into the Salt Lake Valley.

East of the Great Salt Lake lay the Wasatch Range, some fifty miles wide at the base, rising to 10,000 to 12,000 feet, blessed with considerable moisture, and proudly presenting a covering of timber. Beyond lay the Uintas, extending 150 miles east and connecting with the Colorado Rockies.[3]

But most of the Great Basin was desolate and barren. The lowest portion of every valley contained an oyster-white, cracked, evil-smelling alkali flat; even the springs and wells were usually saline. Kangaroo rats, tarantulas, scorpions, some rabbits, some coyotes, and too many rattlesnakes constituted most of the wild life. The Paiute Indians, a branch of the Shoshonean group, lurked in some areas of the fortieth parallel country. Smaller tribes were at the bottom of human culture. Descriptions of these wretched folk are many, but none seems so in keeping with the truth as Mark Twain's description of one tribe, the Goshoots: ". . . small, lean, 'scrawny' creatures; in complexion a dull black like the ordinary American negro; their faces and hands bearing dirt which they had been hoarding and accumulating for months, years, and even generations, according to the age of the proprietor; a silent, sneaking, treacherous-looking race . . . always hungry, and yet never refusing anything that a hog would eat, though often eating what a hog would decline; hunters, but having no higher ambition than to kill and eat jackass rabbits, crickets, and grasshoppers, and embezzle carrion from the buzzards and coyotes."[4] They lived in brush huts called "wickiups," somehow withstood winter, summer, starvation, and thirst, but to what end God only knew.

[3] Sereno Watson, *Botany*, Vol. IV in the *Report of the Geological Exploration of the Fortieth Parallel*, xiii–xix.
[4] Twain, *Roughing It*, I, 155.

Yet white men too, besides the Mormons of Salt Lake, lived in parts of the Great Basin in 1867. Some of them were miners, whose rickety, lonely structures dotted the mountains, as one homesick New Englander put it, as the "red barns [dotted] the rugged hillsides of the old Granite State." And wherever wild hay could be raised, or some timber cut, squatters—forty-niners who never quite made it to California—had established themselves in spite of the Indian danger and existed by selling hay, timber, and garden vegetables to the nearby mining communities. Even then, in the lonely Great Basin, the empty whisky bottle reminded the explorer that someone white and human had been there before him.[5]

When the survey left its Sacramento camp on July 3, King, Gardner, and certainly a few of the packers and cooks knew what lay ahead of them. It would be rough going, especially the first season in the western depression, among the sinks and alkali expanses. But it would not be a superhuman task, and it could be accomplished. The total personnel, all young and eager, numbered fifteen to twenty persons. Later on, on July 17, Sergeant W. A. Martin with nineteen "well mounted and well armed men" joined the survey for purposes of protection, bringing the total number in the party up to about forty.[6]

For several days, the party worked upward through the California foothills, getting the mules well broken in and allowing the men to become sufficiently familiar with each other "to realize the fact that to know a man well you must campaign with him."[7] Eleven men were mounted, and the rest rode on one of the two freight wagons or the single thorough-brace wagon which, because of its gentler ride, housed the delicate instruments. Four

[5] John Samson, "Photographs from the High Rockies," *Harper's New Monthly Magazine*, Vol. XXXIX, No. 232 (September, 1869), 469–70. This article is about Timothy H. O'Sullivan. His photographs illustrate it, and the descriptions given fit no one else. Whether "Jonn Samson" was a pen name used by O'Sullivan or referred to some itinerant journalist, I have not been able to determine.

[6] National Archives, R.G. 57, "Copy Book of Letters," August 3, 1867. The size of the survey team varied, but John Samson, in his *Harper's* article, set the number at seventeen, which seems realistic.

[7] Samson, "Photographs from the High Rockies," *Harper's New Monthly Magazine*, Vol. XXXIX, No. 232 (September, 1869), 466.

mules pulled each wagon. At the summit of Donner Pass, they fought through eight feet of snow, and the intensity of the previous winter might have given the old-timers cause for concern.[8]

While on the eastern slope of the Sierras, or possibly the Virginia Range, Clarence King grew pensive one lovely day: "The sky over the desert plain is peculiarly soft and beautiful and the large bodies of still water in the sinks reflect its delicate color most perfectly, he wrote. "The clouds are unusually fine over these flat deserts. Grand piles of cumulous heap up over the ranges." "Dotted over the desert" were white alkaline mud flats and, here and there, like veins, were stream beds, never entirely dry, never full, their "snowy lines meandering through gray plains." A picture of barren, sterile peacefulness—a land without a pulse.[9]

When they got down into the Truckee meadows, where they camped among the willows beside the stream, active operations began. The cavalry had joined them, and the survey personnel was complete. King occupied his time "in initiating a good system of field work and planning work for the parties," and a work pattern materialized which was followed throughout the life of the survey.[10]

The usual procedure was to choose a good camp site, then erect the tents either in two parallel lines or in the shape of a square. Often a flagpole was raised, carrying the American and Fortieth Parallel flags.

These camp sites were used for any period from several weeks to three months, and they had the virtue of giving the physical scientists—Bailey, later Watson and Ridgway—ample time to study, collect, preserve, and classify the flora and the fauna of the area.[11] Meanwhile, the geologists and topographers worked out from the base camp, covering large areas, sometimes meeting at pre-arranged places and times somewhere in the dry

[8] National Archives, R.G. 57, "Copy Book of Letters," August 3, 1867.

[9] King Collection, Folder D–10, Clarence King, "1867 Descriptive and Geologic Notes."

[10] National Archives, R.G. 57, "Copy Book of Letters," August 3, 1867.

[11] Harris, "Robert Ridgway," *The Condor*, Vol. XXX, No. 1 (January–February, 1928), 21.

wastes, then returning to base camp.[12] But whether in camp or in the field, everyone had assigned work to do, and there is every reason to believe that King's executive ability and the respect that he commanded of his men resulted in unusual harmony and the growth of a very useful *esprit de corps*. Men were proud to be a part of Clarence King's Fortieth Parallel Survey.

Of course such harmony was not immediately gained. Young Gardner, who was occasionally left in command when King was away, wrote from Glendale, Nevada (Camp No. 10), that he got along "pretty well with the party" but that it was "so large and so new that it requires very careful management to reconcile the discordant elements." One day the cooks staged a big flare-up, but after they relieved their minds of grievances, it was not too difficult to arrange matters to their satisfaction. Gardner sounded tired but optimistic. "Fifteen men from all grades of society; from all parts of the Union; of every age and disposition; are not easily made into a homogeneous party at first," he told his mother. "But I think we make a splendid advance."[13]

The military escort caused some trouble too. The actual usefulness of these horse soldiers, whether attached to King, Hayden, or Wheeler, was always debatable, and Robert Ridgway, speaking about the troops with King, said that the escort was used chiefly in looking after the animals of the outfit.[14] But King, who never forgot his narrow escape from the Apaches, always wanted them along. The problem was that after the Civil War the army in the Plains was beset with desertions. The pay was

[12] King mentions such meetings at least twice. National Archives, "Copy Book of Letters," June 4, 1868; August 13, 1868.

[13] Farquhar Collection, Gardner to Anne T. Gardner, July 15, 1867. In this letter, Gardner mentions a new member of the survey whose name never appears in any official correspondence. He was Dick Cotter, and he had been a close and useful friend to King and Gardner on the California Survey. Somewhere, possibly in Alaska, he had taken ill. Out of sympathy King had hired him, sick and mentally deranged as he was, for, wrote Gardner, "his glorious heart is as warm as ever." Cotter recovered and spent most of the rest of his life as a Jack-of-all-trades in York, Montana. See Farquhar, *Up and Down California in 1860–1864*, 516n.

[14] Harris, "Robert Ridgway," *The Condor*, Vol. XXX, No. 1 (January–February, 1928), 22.

poor, and the opportunities for free men in the great, expanding civilian world of the western frontier simply placed army life at a disadvantage. A sergeant and nineteen soldiers might show up in July, but by the end of the field season, one-fourth of them might have gone over the hill. One successful desertion prompted others; if the soldiers could do it, then why couldn't a cook or a packer who hadn't signed his life away? Every time the roster showed a man short, a new morale problem was created. King determined to do something about it.

The poor private who got King on his trail was described as a particularly bad *hombre* who had fitted himself out well with survey party equipment while the camp had been in the field; twelve hours had elapsed before his absence was noticed. "I realized that his successful escape would completely demoralize the little band," wrote King years later, "and I chased him one hundred miles across the desert and through the mountain ranges of northern Nevada accompanied by an old corporal of cavalry, and after a hard ride, trailing him like a bloodhound, I captured him in a hand to hand struggle by which I nearly lost my life and only saved myself by dodging his shot and cramming my pistol in his ear in the nick of time. I lodged him in the Austin jail, and the fact of his capture forever reduced the soldiers and the working men of the survey to obedience."[15]

That first season, the men went to work with a vengeance. Their everyday lives consisted of climbing buttes and mountains, making observations, measuring angles and distances, drawing sketches, examining rocks and fossils, and collecting birds, animals, plants, and reptiles. In parties consisting of two or three scientists, a cook, and a packer, they ranged far and wide over the wastes of the western half of Nevada. Gradually a pattern of accomplishment developed, and the geologic and topographic map of the fortieth parallel began to emerge. Clues to the great geologic mysteries began to fit into place like the pieces of a jigsaw puzzle.

[15] Raymond, "Biographical Notice," *Clarence King Memoirs*, 338. King Collection, Box 1, Hague, "C. K.'s Notes for My Biographical Notice of Him for Appleton's Encyclopaedia."

O'Sullivan, using magnesium light, made photographs inside the Comstock mines. Then a small party consisting of at least O'Sullivan and Ridgway, with their camp men, got hold of a small bateau called the *Nettie*. It had been built by a transplanted Yankee from the rock-bound coast of New England, was trim and serviceable, and was pressed into service by the survey men on the Truckee River. They proposed to sail her down the river to Pyramid Lake, which would make a distance of about twenty-five miles.

At first it was great fun. The rapids were manageable, and in between them were stretches of deep, still water over which the boat glided as in a pleasant dream. But as they approached the lake, the river widened and the rapids grew more treacherous. Hidden rocks threatened the *Nettie's* hull. Then, suddenly, she jammed between two great rocks, the oars were swept away, and she began to fill with water. O'Sullivan dived overboard and swam for shore, forty yards away, but by the time he reached it, he had been swept one hundred yards downstream. He ran back up the shore until he was opposite the floundering vessel and tried to catch a line from the crew. The first time they threw the line, which they had weighted with O'Sullivan's pocketbook, it fell short, and $300 in twenty-dollar gold pieces were swept back to the earth from which they had come while their owner watched with dejected fascination. A second attempt with the line was more successful. O'Sullivan tied it fast to a rock and then hauled the *Nettie* and her crew ashore. Next day, using ropes, she was carefully let down through the remaining rapids, and she finally sailed peacefully out onto Pyramid Lake.[16]

They found the lake a strange body of clear, sparkling, slightly brackish water, almost a throwback to an earlier geologic period. It and its neighbor to the east, Winnemucca Lake, actually were remnants of a primeval lake which King named Lake Lahontan in honor of the Baron de Lahontan, an early French explorer of the West.[17] Pyramid Lake contains several peculiar

[16] Samson, "Photographs from the High Rockies," *Harper's New Monthly Magazine*, Vol. XXXIX, No. 232 (September, 1869), 467. Harris, "Robert Ridgway," *The Condor*, Vol. XXX, No. 1 (January–February, 1928), 24.

[17] Clarence King, *Systematic Geology*, Vol. I in the *Report of the Geological*

rock formations, volcanic in origin, which add to the prehistoric atmosphere one feels so strongly when out on its stormy surface on a cloudy day. Among these formations is a huge, nearly perfect pyramid about 500 feet high. Its sides are covered by a strange calcareous tufa, the deposit of the mineral waters, which O'Sullivan or "Samson" described as resembling "a vegetable growth of vast size."

When the party landed on the pyramid, they met with an emphatic protest from inhabitants who had already pre-empted it. From every crevice there came a hiss, and then a sharp and continual rattling. The pyramid seethed with rattlers, and even the members of the party who liked to kill them—and in every party there are always one or two snake hunters—finally gave up the task.[18]

Today, Pyramid Lake, which has been within the boundaries of a Paiute Indian reservation since 1867, is a bird paradise and the breeding place of the white pelican. The lake is now lower by twenty to thirty feet than it was in 1867, the water is getting saltier, and the fish are dying. This is due primarily to irrigation projects which have cut off most of its supply of fresh water. But even so, the lake is still worth visiting. A beefsteak fry along the shores on a moonlit evening is a never-to-be-forgotten experience. Those strange tufa pyramids in the lake, the dry, eroded rock formations along the banks, and the change of color from rich dark red to vivid purple starts the imagination on a tour of other planets.[19]

But beefsteak frys were not a part of survey activities back in 1867, and the men, having made a preliminary survey, considered themselves through with the lake, at least for a while. They had taken the *Nettie* downstream, but the crew had little desire

---

Exploration of the Fortieth Parallel, 13. The eastern of the two great primeval lakes in the Great Basin, of which only the Great Salt Lake remains, was named Lake Bonneville by Grove Karl Gilbert, a geologist with Powell. For more about Lahontan, see Baron de Lahontan, *New Voyages to North America* (ed. by Reuben Gold Thwaites).

[18] Samson, "Photographs from the High Rockies," *Harper's New Monthly Magazine,* Vol. XXXIX, No. 232 (September, 1869), 467–68.

[19] *Nevada: A Guide to the Silver State,* 143.

to bring her back up, and horses and mules were obtained at the nearby Indian reservation. Then portents of trouble began to appear. Ridgway complained of his mule, so big that he felt as if he were straddling a high-peaked roof. Then the mules stampeded, and the big mule nearly bucked him off. The next morning Robert mounted a different one, and this time the individualism of the mule probably saved his life.

The party was bound for the Humboldt Sink, across the most forbidding kind of country imaginable. And to add to the torment, Ridgway's mule disdained all other mules while on the march and insisted on forging ahead of the rest of the party. It was approaching high noon; the sun blazed down on the desert wastes, and the air shimmered slightly, distorting things, as if the earth was going into a dangerous coma. Suddenly, Ridgway "felt sick and queer." He dismounted, tied his mule to some sagebrush, and lay down in the beast's shadow. "I never knew when they picked me up and placed me in the ambulance, nor was I conscious at all until camp was reached," he later wrote. He was down with malaria—what the few residents of the territory called "the mountain ail"—unable to conduct any activity.[20]

The Humboldt Sink is never a very pleasant place, for its approaches are of volcanic rock, much of which is stacked vertically like great lava matchsticks, making it treacherous to get through with a mule train and undependable for footholds. In a wet year, the sink becomes one great, putrid marsh—the situation in 1867. An uncommonly wet winter, followed by a wet spring and a more humid than normal summer left more moisture in the depression area of western Nevada than any white man could remember. And even when writing his report years later, the horrors of the place came vividly to Ridgway's mind:

The marshes were miles in extent and almost entirely covered by a dense growth of tule [a large bulrush of the American southwest], except where the river meandered through, now and then expand-

[20] Harris, "Robert Ridgway," *The Condor*, Vol. XXX, No. 1 (January–February, 1928), 24–25. Samson, "Photographs from the High Rockies," *Harper's New Monthly Magazine*, Vol. XXXIX, No. 232 (September, 1869), 471. The ambulance was used by O'Sullivan to carry his photographic equipment.

ing into a small lake. These marshes were surrounded by a bare plain, consisting in the winter season of mud, but at this time baked perfectly dry and hard by the heat of the sun, except in the more depressed portions, which were covered by a deep deposit of snow-white "alkali." From these extensive flats, desert plains lead away to the barren mountains on either side, whose summits are bare and rugged eruptive rocks, of weird forms and strange colors. Upon the whole, the entire region was one of the most desolate and forbidding that could be imagined, and in these respects is probably not surpassed by any other portion of the land of "alkali" and the "everlasting sage-brush." The effluvium from the putrid water and decaying vegetation of the marshes was at times sickening, while at night the torments of millions of the most voracious mosquitoes added to the horrors of the place.[21]

The mosquitoes and other insects sometimes came in such swarms about the candles in the camp that they actually extinguished them. The water used for drinking and cooking was so sulphurous that it smelled like rotten eggs, "and the air was redolent of the stench of rotting tules." Understandably, young Ridgway considered this the most uncomfortable camp in all his experience.[22]

Ridgway was not the only one struck down. Nearly all of the expedition fell ill. By early September, conditions had become so bad that King moved his base camp eastward from Wright's Canyon to Unionville, Nevada, "in order to place sick men, who at this time numbered about three-fourths of our whole party, under shelter, for the barometer had indicated the approach of a great storm." King later told Humphreys that "at one time we had out of fifty but three available men."[23]

Yet there was a schedule to be maintained, and King (who for once was not stricken), the topographer Clark, one soldier, and

[21] Ridgway, "Ornithology," *Report of the Geological Exploration of the Fortieth Parallel*, Vol. IV, Part III, 353.

[22] *Ibid.*, 353n. Harris, "Robert Ridgway," *The Condor*, Vol. XXX, No. 1 (January–February, 1928), 25.

[23] National Archives, R.G. 57, "Copy Book of Letters," December 18, 1867, February 14, 1871. King points out that even mining operations in some areas had to be curtailed. The outbreak of malaria was blamed on the vast amount of stagnant water left by a spring flood.

"Son," chief of the Humboldt Paiutes, headed for a mountain range west of the Reese River, almost in the heart of central Nevada. On September 22, they climbed "Job's Peak," reaching the summit just as a great thunder cloud drifted toward the mountain top. They hastily made preparations for their work. "After adjusting my theodolite," King recalled, "I set the cross hair on the initial signal, and as I was about to observe angles, a sudden electrical flash came (apparently) through the instrument, striking my right arm and side. I was staggered and my brain nerves severely shocked." The theodolite was thrown, and Clark, Son, and the soldier helped King back to camp. "In the course of a week," he recalled, "the effects of the stroke wore off." But for some time he suffered from occasional circulation stoppage in his right side."[24]

Nevertheless, King and Clark kept up their work, and as soon as the others were well enough it was understood that they should be up and about their duties. From central Nevada westward to the Sierras they continued their work, now in the sinks, feeling as if they were at the very center of the gravitational drainage of the continent, now in sparsely timbered pine forests in the higher mountains. Sometimes they would come upon groups of Paiutes there, collecting the cones from pine-nut trees for food. These trees look much like any other pine, but when the cones are thrown into the fire they loosen and the little pine-nuts can be shaken out. Some of the cones can release nearly a cupful of nuts, which have a pleasant but just about indescribable taste—something like the smell of a sweet, pungent pine tree. The Indians ate the nuts raw, or dried them, ground them into meal, and baked them as little cakes in the hot ashes of their fires.[25]

Save for the occasional Indians, the wastes were frightfully desolate. A solitary raven, croaking hoarsely, might be seen winging its way across the sky; the desert lark might appear in the sparse sagebrush, and in the mountains Woodhouse's jay and

---

[24] National Archives, R.G. 57, "Copy Book of Letters," December 18, 1867.
[25] Samson, "Photographs from the High Rockies," *Harper's New Monthly Magazine,* Vol. XXXIX, No. 232 (September, 1869), 473.

the little titmouse would announce their presence with squawk or song. Along the banks of the mountain streams were clumps of wild roses, a few green willows, and sometimes chokecherry bushes, whose fruit could pucker a man's mouth until he could barely speak. On the mountainsides there might be some aromatic cedar and, if moisture was sufficient, a few small groves of cheerful aspens.[26]

Sometimes, along the great human migratory trails to California, the surveyors came upon signs of tragedy: wagon wheels so dry in the summer sun that no one would have been surprised to see them crack in two or go up in flames, white, bleached bones of animals that died of thirst, and family heirlooms—heavy lowboys or oaken bedsteads—abandoned by the trail. Now and then they spied weathering wooden crosses atop mounds of earth: "John Hardy b. Pike County Mo. 1835 d. July 5, 1863"; "Matilda Deering beloved wife devoted mother b. June 2, 1838 Alton Illinois d. August 3, 1861." Most pathetic of all were the small graves of departed children. Eventually, the markers would disappear to Indians, marauding beasts, or other whites in need of fire wood. Then the winds would blow the grave mounds back to the level of the adjoining earth, and the human remains would be lost to all save God.

As soon as they recovered, the surveyors tramped back into the miasmic sinks of the Humboldt, Quinn, and Carson Rivers. When Custer suffered a relapse, Gardner stepped in to continue his work. And by "tremendous effort," King reported, the survey "completed the proposed areas for the year by remaining in the field until the middle of December, the last parties coming into . . . winter quarters at Virginia City through two feet of snow on the day before Christmas."

Thus ended the first season of the work of the Fortieth Parallel Survey. What had King accomplished? The survey had covered a block of country from the boundary of California (120° W.) as far east as the second Humboldt Range (about 117°30′ W.) and from the southern boundary at 39°30′ N. to the northern bound-

---

[26] Ridgway, "Ornithology," *Report of the Geological Exploration of the Fortieth Parallel,* Vol. 1, Part III, 354–55.

ary at 41° N. "This," King emphasized, "is in every way the most difficult and dangerous country to campaign in I know of on the continent."

In spite of the hardships, the entire block had been covered with a series of triangles, and the angles had been observed at least eight times. For signals, monuments of rocks had been built on the summits of many stations. Then, within the primary points, secondary points had been carefully located, and between the interior points the topography had been "well fitted in" by gradienters and by the careful sketches of the surveyors. In the realm of geology, a collection of two thousand specimens, illustrating every rock formation in the section surveyed, had been gathered. About three hundred barometrical readings had been observed, and over two thousand meteorological observations made. "The party," King concluded, "are all well and united by a healthy esprit de corps."

The winter of 1867–68 was spent in quarters at Virginia City and at Carson City, thirteen miles away. These two frontier cities were a far cry from the comforts of New Haven, New York, or Washington, but an existence in wooden buildings with real roofs over them was a welcome change from the field work of the preceding six months. Virginia City was an especially exotic mushroom of a town nurtured by a fantastic lode of silver ore. Ignorant and unskilled men had made millions there, and the only explanation for this within human understanding involved the influence of Lady Luck, for it defied all the laws of stern New England Calvinism.

The geologists stayed at the higher-priced Virginia City, where they studied the Comstock Lode, while the rest of the scientific personnel were lodged at Carson City. But wherever they were, time did not lay heavy on their hands. All members were kept busy plotting their field notes or classifying and writing up their collections. But as the winter waned, the men began to look for the first signs of spring, and every time they killed a cockroach, they wished a little more for the winter to end and the field work to begin again.[27]

[27] National Archives, R.G. 57, "Copy Book of Letters," December 18, 1867; February 14, 1871.

8

The Great Salt Lake and the Rockies

SPRING CAME, pleasant, warm, and sunny, and by mid-April of 1868, King had divided his expedition into three divisions and had ordered them into the field. The parties usually separated for weeks at a time, then met at a pre-arranged time and place, only to leave again. In a general way, they resumed work where they had left off in central Nevada the previous December, although a constant characteristic of King's survey methods was the careful re-examination of areas which had been done before. But the place names which predominate in his official reports are those of central and eastern Nevada and western Utah; New Pass, Shoshone Mountains, Reese River, Toyabe Range, Carico Lake, Fort Ruby, White River mining district, Overland Road, Reddings Springs, Salt Lake Desert, Don Don Pass, Antelope Pass, and Clear Valley. All these were explored and surveyed. "I am pushing forward as rapidly as possible," King declared. "We are in the saddle generally by six A.M. and work until sunset."[1]

The year 1868 witnessed no recurrence of malaria, but King had other troubles. He had to learn the hard way that the lonely

---

[1] National Archives, R.G. 57, "Copy Book of Letters," July 10, 1868; August 13, 1868; February 14, 1871.

westerner, whose eyes gazed upon good cash about as often as they gazed upon a beautiful woman, would use almost any "legitimate" means to get money. Thus the picture of a lonely and lazy rancher suing a government surveyor for not paying fantastic prices for camping and grazing privileges on the rancher's land (unposted and unfenced) may have been ludicrous, but it was a procedure by no means uncommon. King's accusers demanded $260.00 for grass the mules had eaten and driftwood that had been gathered and burned. When King refused to pay, he was sued at Virginia City for the charges.[2]

Indians still gave the surveyors some scares. Every member of the expedition retained a group of tall "Injun" stories, and most of them had a kernel of fact in them. Young Ridgway was left at the Indian reservation at Pyramid Lake early in the 1868 season and was looking for birds along the Truckee River when a group of friendly Indians, almost too frightened to speak coherently, galloped up and warned him of a band of hostiles who were going to kill everyone along the river. Ridgway and everyone else except the agent holed up in the heavy log reservation house. There they remained in grave danger for three days until the agent, who had ridden for help sixty miles away, returned with reinforcements. No blood had been spilled, but the threat had been real. An outlaw band made up of the renegades of many tribes had made a foray on the reservation and had taken almost all the stock. But for the alarm spread by a reservation Indian who had escaped from their clutches, Ridgway and all the others, both peaceful Indians and whites, would probably have been massacred.

Another time, in northwestern Nevada, Ridgway's group was surrounded by fifty to sixty yelling Shoshones, and gunshots would have been exchanged (with dire results, since there were only five whites) except that "Captain Frank," the Shoshone chief, pulled a white paper from his shirt, signifying friendship.

[2] National Archives, R.G. 57, "Copy Book of Letters," June 4, 1867. A search of the records of the County Court at Virginia City has failed to reveal such a case. Letter from Ursula MacHenry, county clerk and treasurer, Virginia City, Nevada, November 5, 1960.

That night he and his band camped with Ridgway's group, and the ornithologist even traded an old muzzle loader for a beautiful buffalo robe.[3]

As they worked eastward, the surveyors ran up against several ranges of mountains whose peaks reached to 11,000 feet or more and whose slopes had considerable timber and quantities of perpetual snow in great niches where the summer sun could not reach. The Toyabe Mountains, south of Austin, and the Ruby, East Humboldt, and Clover Mountains, all in northeastern Nevada, posed problems in geology and in topography. They also posed a problem of transportation—how to get mules across the snow-filled divides. Some of the snowdrifts were thirty to forty feet deep, and in daylight the summer warmth so softened the snow that the mules' sharp hoofs broke through. "Men and animals," remarked Samson, "were frequently lost from sight." The only answer to the problem was to travel by night. The party would reach the snow line at sunset, camp until midnight, when, it was hoped, the snow would have crusted stiff enough to support the mules, and then, in the darkness, make their way. Even so, the mules and men often fell through, even at two and three in the morning. "In one instance," Samson wrote, "not less than thirteen hours were consumed in crossing a divide, and the whole distance traveled did not exceed 2½ miles."[4]

But the mountains were beautiful. In their upper reaches they were dotted with little snow-water lakes; at many points cold, fresh, sweet water bubbled out of springs in the earth. The canyons were picturesquely narrow with nearly perpendicular walls. From the camp at the lower levels of the Ruby Mountains, where they spent nearly two months, Ridgway could look down at the depressed center of Ruby Valley, where a marsh lake full of tule provided haven for thousands of birds. The streams feeding the lake could only be observed from above, so thick was the vegetation, but from where he stood they appeared "as silver bands in the dark-green rush-meadows." And when he climbed upward,

[3] Harris, "Robert Ridgway," *The Condor*, Vol. XXX, No. 1 (January–February, 1928), 22–23.

[4] Samson, "Photographs from the High Rockies," *Harper's New Monthly Magazine*, Vol. XXXIX, No. 232 (September, 1869), 471.

great gardens of scarlet castillejas and gilias and blue pentste-
mons and delphiniums stretched all the way to the snow line.
These mountain oases were doubly beautiful because they were
so small in proportion to the deserts of the Great Basin.[5]

By mid-October of 1868, the season's endeavors were ended
and the Great Salt Lake had been reached. In the realm of practical geology, one so-called "desert coal field" had been demol-
ished as a figment of someone's imagination, and a survey had
demonstrated that the Goose Creek coal region in extreme northwestern Nevada was also a humbug. The men of the survey had
carried their topographical and geological work over a belt one
hundred miles wide and five hundred miles long from the Sierras
to the western shores of Great Salt Lake. "Summing up the year's
campaign," King reported, "I may conscientiously say that it has
been an entire success." An enormous task had been completed.[6]

Camp men were discharged, equipment was stored at Camp
Douglas near Salt Lake City, and, after eighteen months, the
men left the West for the civilized East, where they could enjoy
a thirty-day furlough before reporting to King in Washington,
D.C. There he established winter quarters in a brick building
at 294 "H" Street, and the results of the previous season's work
were plotted, classified, and written up according to plan.[7]

But winter, although important, was just an interval before
the advent of what was thought to be the final field season of the
survey. By May 15, when King arrived at Salt Lake City, the military escort was waiting, and the material, much of which had
been stolen during the winter, had been replaced, assembled,
and put in shape for the field. Ten days later he had divided the
party into three groups and had sent them on their way. King's
group was to work the north end of the Great Salt Lake and
Emmons' group the south end; then both were to proceed eastward. A third group, consisting of two topographers, Clark and
Davis, plus the naturalists Watson and Ridgway, with camp
men, was to survey the lake itself. The first two groups conducted

[5] Ridgway, "Ornithology," *Report of the Geological Exploration of the
Fortieth Parallel*, Vol. I, Part III, 358.
[6] National Archives, R.G. 57, "Copy Book of Letters," November 14, 1868.
[7] National Archives, R.G. 57, "Copy Book of Letters," December 1, 1868.

routine work, but the Salt Lake group was confronted with some unusual difficulties.[8]

The first really thorough survey of the lake had been made in the years 1849–50 by Captain Howard Stansbury of the Topographical Engineers. Stansbury had made a study of the past explorations of the Great Salt Lake, and he quoted at length in his own narrative from the writings of the Baron Lahontan, who first claimed to have heard of the lake in 1703.[9] Later, Captain Bonneville claimed to have visited the lake, but he never actually saw it. Then had come John Charles Frémont, who first gazed upon the lake on September 6, 1843, and conducted a brief week's exploration of its salty and barren environs.[10]

Then Captain Stansbury arrived, operating in the best traditions of the United States Topographical Engineers. He established a six-mile base line, set up twenty-four principal triangulation stations, and explored the shores of the islands and the lake.[11]

By the time the Fortieth Parallel men reached its shores, however, they had learned much more about the Great Basin than Stansbury could have known. King knew about the two primeval inland seas, for example. And he had also made the disturbing discovery that Great Salt Lake had risen nine to eleven feet since Stansbury's survey, increasing the area of the lake from about 1,700 square miles to 2,360 square miles, an increase in nineteen years of over 600 square miles.[12]

King's survey of the lake took nearly two months and was not without its dangers. Twice, their little boat, the *Eureka*, was cap-

[8] National Archives, R.G. 57, "Copy Book of Letters," June 17, 1869.

[9] Howard Stansbury, *Exploration and Survey of the Valley of the Great Salt Lake of Utah*, 32 Cong., spec. sess., *Sen. Exec. Doc. 3*, 151. Lahontan, *New Voyages to North America*, I, xxiv, 194.

[10] Dale L. Morgan, *The Great Salt Lake*, [9–11], 140–44.

[11] Stansbury, *Exploration and Survey of the Valley of the Great Salt Lake of Utah*, 32 Cong., spec. sess., *Sen. Exec. Doc. 3*, 216.

[12] National Archives, R.G. 57, "Copy Book of Letters," June 17, 1869. In his report, King stated that the lake had risen nine feet, but in *Systematic Geology* (page 497), he indicated a rise of eleven feet, and his calculations of its size were based on this figure. It is now known that the lake varies considerably in size because of variations in rainfall.

sized, and the men very nearly drowned. The water they swallowed choked and strangled them, and as they held on to the hull of the capsized boat, the thirst that arose in their throats became maddening. Flies "about half the size of a house fly" plagued them from time to time, and sometimes they mistook for the land great bunches of decomposing grasshoppers, covered with alkali dust so that they blended with the shore line. They would step into it thinking it was land, sink to their knees in the horrible mass, and the resulting stench would almost asphyxiate them. But toward the end of July, work on the lake was completed and they, along with the other two parties, worked eastward toward a point about thirty miles west of the Green River.[13]

It was pleasant work for the men, that late summer of 1869, ending what they believed to be the last of three field seasons. Northeastern Utah was rugged and beautiful, canyons were prettier, timber was more plentiful, and there was more water. By late August, the surveyors and the geologists had been in Echo Canyon, in the Uinta Mountains, at Kamas Prairie, in the valley of the Provo (or Timpanogos), and at the headwaters of the Weber River.[14]

Later, King described this last large block of work of the 1869 season as a sort of triangle, with the Uintas, running east and west, forming the south side, the Wasatch Mountains, running north and south, the west side, and the Green River roughly delineating the third side. Within the enclosure was a desert every bit as barren as the deserts of the Great Basin and containing several badland areas.

He was especially fascinated by the Uinta Mountains, an "immense single mountain block about 150 miles long" with an elevation of from 10,000 to 11,000 feet. Unlike any other range in North America it quickly rose to a horizontal plateau summit thirty to forty miles wide, covered with ponderosa pine, Engleman spruce, Douglas fir, juniper, and aspen. Glacial action had carried "a network of immense amphitheatres opening down-

[13] National Archives, R.G. 57, "Copy Book of Letters," July 15, 1869; February 14, 1871. King Collection, Folder B-7, N. W. Davis, "Report." Davis was one of the topographers.

[14] National Archives, R.G. 57, "Copy Book of Letters," August 26, 1869.

ward into a series of ice-worn canyons. . . . The view from one of the upper summits," King reported, "is varied by open, green Alpine pastures, varied by innumerable lakes of transparent water which occupy erosion-hollows of the old glacier beds." It was in the Uintas that King found "the geological evidence of synchronism with the great European Mountain chains"—that is, evidence that both had arisen, though half a world apart, in the same geologic age.[15]

Season's end finally arrived, and on September 1, Watson and Ridgway and several assistants entrained for the East. King, Gardner, Emmons, the Hagues, and a number of the camp men then began a general review of the ground they had covered in the preceding three years, bringing maps and notes up to date with regard to recent changes in mining communities. It was a cold recapitulation out there along the line of the Central Pacific, with the usual sunrise temperature a bitter cold zero and the animals and men suffering alike from bad water. But eventually an end came to their tasks. Their equipment and half of their live-stock—the poorest half—was sold at auctions in Salt Lake City and Virginia City, and the way was cleared for the return East.[16]

What a relief it must have been that day in late autumn when King finally clambered aboard the eastbound train and went clicking off the miles of the Great Basin toward Washington. And how things had changed in just three short years! In 1867, when the Fortieth Parallel Survey began, the Central Pacific was still battling the Sierras and the Union Pacific was creeping across western Wyoming. In 1867, the Great Basin had never yet reverberated to the toot of a railroad whistle, nor had one of its jack rabbits yet been hypnotized by the yellow eye of a speeding locomotive.

King watched the sagebrush wastes pass by in a blur. He propped his booted feet on the seat opposite and in relaxed contemplation pondered his future. He was twenty-eight years old

---

[15] King, *Systematic Geology*, 8–11. National Archives, R.G. 57, "Copy Book of Letters," August 26, 1869.

[16] National Archives, R.G. 57, "Copy Book of Letters," October 1, 1869, November 2, 1869.

and well established. His first job was to complete the survey reports; then he planned to earn some money.

Once in Washington, he immediately set to work on the reports. Offices were established at 252 "G" Street, and by mid-April of 1870, Volume III, *Mining Industry*, by James D. Hague, and Volume V, *Botany*, by Sereno Watson, were ready to be submitted to General Humphreys for criticism and suggestions. On June 1, 1870, the survey moved its offices to New Haven, where there was an excellent geology library.[17]

The original plan had called for three seasons in the field, with office work in the winter and after the final season until the great project was completed. But King always wanted to be positive of his evidence, and questions arose again and again which, in his view, required re-examination of the fortieth parallel country. Thus, he was happy to receive a telegram from General Humphreys notifying him that more money was available for field work, but he was unhappy at being ordered west at the late date of July 27. King pleaded for permission to stay on in New Haven, where work was progressing so satisfactorily on the reports, especially on James D. Hague's *Mining Industry*. He reasoned that the season was so advanced that he could accomplish little before winter set in. But it was all to no avail. He was ordered into the field.[18]

Under these circumstances, King selected a small party made up of Arnold Hague, Samuel Franklin Emmons, and a few aides, and set out upon a short campaign to study the problem "of the sources of the lava flows which have poured eastward from the Sierra Nevada and the Cascade Ranges into the Great Basin." King hoped to enjoy himself pursuing his old love, volcanism.[19]

By early September, King was in northern California, working on Lassen Peak, then concentrating on Mount Shasta. This imposing, lonely sentinel, rising out of a black forest, was obviously

[17] National Archives, R.G. 57, "Copy Book of Letters," December 28, 1869; April 22, 1870; May 11, 1870.

[18] National Archives, R.G. 57, "Copy Book of Letters," July 25, 1870; July 27, 1870; "Letters to King," Vol. I, July 27, 1870.

[19] National Archives, R.G. 57, "Copy Book of Letters," September 2, 1870.

of volcanic origin and therefore demanded investigation. Following the capable guidance of J. H. Sisson, a local postmaster and hotelkeeper at what is today Mount Shasta City, King and his party headed for the summit of the smaller western cone, today known as Shastina. Early in the afternoon of September 11, 1870, they reached the rim. With the cold western wind tearing at their coats, the men all peered down "into a deep gorge lying between the secondary crater and the main mass of Shasta." There they saw something that so thrilled King that he temporarily forgot his interest in volcanism. Directly beneath them, as King described it, was "a fine glacier, which started almost at the very crest of the main mountain, flowing toward us, and curving around the circular base of our cone. Its entire length in view was not less than three miles, its width opposite our station about four thousand feet, the surface here and there broken in 'cascades' and presenting all the characteristic features of glaciers everywhere."

They spent the night on the sharp edge of the rim and the next morning climbed to the extreme summit of Mount Shasta, 14,162 feet high (King estimated it at 14,440). From there King walked out to the edge of a prominent spur and looked down upon a system of three considerable glaciers. Their descent was down the south side, the side from which all climbers to that time had approached this summit, and as they descended, King and his men saw less and less snow and no sign of any glaciers whatsoever. For six weeks thereafter, the party worked around Shasta, camping at the snow line on the east side, discovering still other glaciers there and on the northeast side. One of the glaciers on this last side was very interesting, with chasms, great snow bridges, and a thickness of 1,800 to 2,500 feet, lending, King later wrote, "a spice of danger to the whole examination."[20]

King later described the discovery of the glaciers as "somewhat startling . . . when we consider that Whitney, Brewer,

[20] Clarence King, "On the Discovery of Actual Glaciers on the Mountains of the Pacific Slope," *American Journal of Science and Arts,* Third Series, Vol. I, No. 3 (March, 1871), 158–60.

Dana, and Frémont, all visited the Peak without observing them; and that Whitney, Dana, and Agassiz have all published statements that no true glaciers exist in the United States."[21] And so Clarence King deserves the credit for first discovering living, true glaciers in the continental limits of this country.

Meanwhile, Arnold Hague and A. D. Wilson, the topographer, had been doing similar work and making similar discoveries at Mount Hood, in Oregon, and later Samuel Franklin Emmons, with Wilson again doing the topography, pushed through the great forest to Mount Ranier, in Washington, and laid the foundation for a similar survey of that volcanic cone. By the end of the campaign (about November 2), when the Oregon party had joined him on the eastern slope of the Sierras in Nevada, King happily reported that the brief season's field work had "been an entire success, and for scientific interest of results is decidedly the most profitable of the three years."[22]

King was getting tired of staying within the one-hundred-mile strip along the railroad. He pleaded with General Humphreys to let him go off on this new tangent and pursue his new interests and his new discoveries with all the facilities at the command of the Fortieth Parallel Survey. He envisioned a series of monographic surveys which would result in a "complete series of maps and studies of all the great isolated volcanic cones of the Western United States." Professors Dana, Agassiz, and Whitney all urged him to pursue his study further, and as the winter of 1871 wore on, King's plans became even more ambitious: he wanted to examine extinct volcanoes from Mount St. Elias, in Alaska, to San Francisco Peak, in Arizona.[23]

To these proposals, Humphreys was adamant in his refusal,

---

[21] National Archives, R.G. 57, "Copy Book of Letters," October 10, 1870.

[22] King, "On the Discovery of Actual Glaciers on the Mountains of the Pacific Slope," *American Journal of Science and Arts,* Third Series, Vol. I, No. 3 (March, 1871), 164–67. National Archives, "Copy Book of Letters," November 2, 1870.

[23] King, "On the Discovery of Actual Glaciers on the Mountains of the Pacific Slope," *American Journal of Science and Arts,* Third Series, Vol. I, No. 3 (March, 1871), 167. National Archives, "Copy Book of Letters," January 23, 1871, March 21, 1871.

and when the survey again left its New Haven offices in the spring of 1871, it was headed for western Wyoming. There it was to pick up where it had left off in the autumn of 1869, thirty miles west of the Green River divide, ending at about the longitude of Cheyenne, with the southern boundary of the work to be the fortieth parallel, the northern boundary one hundred miles north of it.[24]

By the middle of May, King was at Fort Bridger, in Wyoming Territory, material was being assembled, cavalry was arriving for escort services, and the fifth field season of the Fortieth Parallel Survey was about to get under way. He had already split the personnel into two divisions, one under Gardner, with headquarters at Cheyenne, and the other under Samuel Franklin Emmons, to work out of Fort Bridger. King had no party of his own, but was to co-ordinate their efforts after winding up some affairs in California.[25]

All the work was in rough terrain, but the Rockies were pleasant indeed after the hot, dusty work in the Great Basin. "Over this area is a sky of liquid but cold blue, singularly vaporless for many weeks of the year," King wrote in *Systematic Geology*. "Clouds, when they come, gather around the mountain summits or drift over the plain at low elevations, sailing against the hillslopes to break up and dissolve in the dry air." He found the Rockies "a region of heavy ranges, well forest-covered in the elevated regions, and dominated by fine peaks which bear perpetual snow." He liked the coloring of the Rockies—"light golden green in summer, russet in autumn, and white in winter; the deep blue-green of the forest-covered heights always in view, looming over a plain; and, perhaps most characteristic of all, the cool but dazzling brilliance of the sunlight."[26]

Range upon range of mountains challenged the geologists, and the topographers had to use their finest skills. In 1871 and 1872, they worked over the Front Range on the east, then the Park Range, the Medicine Bow Range, the Black Hills of Wyoming,

---

[24] National Archives, R.G. 57, "Copy Book of Letters," April 6, 1871.
[25] National Archives, R.G. 57, "Copy Book of Letters," May 27, 1871.
[26] King, *Systematic Geology*, 7–9.

But before they got there, King had a hunting experience which in spite of his fatigue and approaching illness—all caused by the hardships of the campaign—was of such a nature that he was forever proud of it. He followed a grizzly into its lair and shot it dead! Whether this kind of brazenness constitutes bravery or damned foolishness depends upon who wins, the bear or the man. In this instance, the man won.

The party, fatigued and run down, was marching through the barren badland country, horses' heads down to the omnipresent wind, men hunched over in their saddles, mufflers flapping. Suddenly, along an open plain, they spied a grizzly which, seeing them, hastened into an area of sand dunes and rough canyons. After some hours of trailing, King, A. D. Wilson, and Emmons, with a couple of soldiers, ran the trail into a network of ravines. They tied the horses together, no bush or tree being present, and trailed the grizzly's huge paw marks to a small cave opening—so small that some of his fur remained at the top of the entrance.

There he was: they could hear him breathing inside, and by crawling into the opening a little ways, King could even see his two eyes. But they had to get him out. An attempt to smoke him out failed. Time was passing. Finally King cocked his rifle, crawled into the cave, waited for his eyes to adjust to the darkness, aimed at the gleaming two eyes, and fired. The shot brought the big soldier posted behind King into action: excitedly he pulled him out of the cave by the ankles, scratching King's face badly in the sand. But the big grizzly was dead, shot through the brain.[33]

On November 2, the party reached Fort Bridger, got in touch with the other party (which was now under Arnold Hague's supervision), and found that it was safe at Laramie, driven out of the mountains by the snow. The entire survey then went into winter quarters at San Francisco. During the winter King became ill and, to help restore his health, indulged in a six weeks'

[33] Raymond, "Biographical Notice," *Clarence King Memoirs,* 340–43. King Collection, Box 1, Hague, "C. K.'s Notes for My Biographical Notice of Him for Appleton's Encyclopaedia."

sojourn in the Hawaiian Islands, which greatly invigorated him for the final year of field work.[34]

But now he had a new idea. He hoped to go down the Green River by boat, in order "not to be outdone by Powell," but once again Humphreys kept him to the fortieth parallel, wanting 1872, the sixth year of operations, to be the last year of field work.[35]

King pitched into a vigorous last campaign. Between May 1 and November 15, the entire region covered by the exploration, from 105 degrees to 120 degrees, on a belt 100 miles wide and always including the Pacific Railroad, was completely re-examined by King, Hague, and Emmons. Additional new work was done north of the Humboldt River, and King did extensive work on problems of glaciation and volcanism in the high Sierras. The artist Albert Bierstadt accompanied him in this work. Gardner, working in Colorado, meanwhile tackled the Rabbit Ears Range (whose two great "rabbit ears" the traveler can see from U.S. Highway 40) and the Medicine Bow Range and had gone down the Cache la Poudre Canyon onto the plains to the eastern limits of the survey.[36]

The field work of the Fortieth Parallel Survey was about finished. But something new had arisen. There was a rumor about, a rumor that had spread like the wind all over the West. Diamonds, it was said, diamonds had been discovered! The Fortieth Parallel men arched their eyebrows. Diamonds? In six years of geologic exploration in the area they had not seen any diamonds! Diamonds? Where?

[34] National Archives, R.G. 57, "Copy Book of Letters," December 16, 1871; April 3, 1872.

[35] National Archives, R.G. 57, "Copy Book of Letters," December 18, 1871.

[36] National Archives, R.G. 57, S. F. Emmons to J. G. Foster (Emmons writing for King) February 10, 1873; "Copy Book of Letters," August 14, 1872.

9

The Diamond Hoax

THE YEARS of the Great Surveys were also the peak years for the thousands of free men who tramped the virgin lands of the West and searched mightily for quick riches. The country was not yet settled. It was still full of mysteries, still pregnant with possibilities. And government regulations and restrictions, and law and order, had not yet caught up with the turbulent society. It was anyone's field, anyone's game. Make a fortune by hook or by crook and try not to be swindled in turn.

This resulted in a fascinating society, for where men were so free, every manner of get-rich-quick scheme, every kind of a rumor imaginable, every will-o'-the-wisp promotion found its takers. In hotel lobbies, at assay offices, and most especially in saloons, grizzled men in cowhide boots, woolen pantaloons, and heavy greatcoats drank together and exchanged gossip. Rare was the westerner who had not been taken at least once.

And it was in the nature of things that someone would eventually perpetrate a gigantic hoax that would be looked on as the greatest fraud to come out of the West. That someone turned out to be two drifting prospectors who possessed far more than their share of shrewdness, boldness, and dishonesty. Their names were Philip Arnold and John Slack. They appeared one foggy morning early in 1872 in the city of San Francisco. When the first employee arrived at the doors of one of the prominent banks there, these two prospectors, dirty, bearded, and disheveled, just as prospectors should be, emerged from the mists and requested the nervous bank employee to allow them inside. And what business did they have with the bank? Cautiously the two men looked up and down the street, peering into the fog, wary of thieves who might be about. Then Arnold produced a small leather pouch, indicating that it contained something of great value. Could they place it in safekeeping in the bank?

The employee bade them enter and, his curiosity aroused, casually inquired about the contents of the pouch. Nuggets? Arnold and Slack paused, scanned the still vacant lobby, swore the official to secrecy, and then gave him their reply. Not nuggets. Diamonds! And they spilled the contents of the pouch out on the table and let the diamonds dazzle the already excited employee. *Of course* the bank would be pleased to place the diamonds in safekeeping.

Then Philip Arnold and John Slack disappeared into the fog. For several weeks they kept out of sight while they let human nature do their work for them. The clerk, sworn to secrecy, showed the gems to the officers of his bank; they in turn contacted a number of the most prominent wealthy men of San Francisco—among them William M. Lent, George D. Roberts, Milton Latham, William C. Ralston, and Alfred Rubery (an Englishman who lived in San Francisco). They instituted a widespread search for the missing prospectors who then conveniently showed themselves. Arnold and Slack played their parts beautifully. Acting like naïve and ignorant country bumpkins, they reluctantly let themselves be included among the founders of the New York and San Francisco Mining and Commercial Company—after their rich colleagues had paid them a sum in the neighborhood of $600,000. Arnold even consented to take the long railroad trip to New York with a group of the founders, and there the New York jewelry firm of Tiffany and Company assessed the rough diamonds "discovered" by Arnold and Slack as bona fide gems of considerable value. And before the party left for the West, the outstanding corporation lawyer, Samuel Latham Barlow, had been appointed as New York agent for the company, and General Grenville Dodge, General George McClellan, and General Benjamin F. Butler had been drawn into the plans as officers of the company. Even the skeptics—and there were a lot of the "once burned" around in the 1870's—were taking second looks at a company founded by such respectable people.

But the founders of the New York and San Francisco Mining and Commercial Company had one more surprise for the skeptics. They hired as a consultant one of the best-known mining men in California, Henry Janin. His reputation, Samuel Franklin Emmons later remarked, "had been made by condemning most every new scheme he had been called to report upon." They took him out to the so-called diamond fields—the location of which was kept secret—let him investigate at will, and then pridefully announced Janin's conclusion: the diamond fields were real.[1]

The secrecy surrounding the location of the fields gave rise to widespread excitement, and the western newspapers published all rumors as soon as they were heard. Soon it was generally believed that the diamond fields were in northeastern Arizona. Then a man who claimed to be, and probably was, Philip Arnold appeared in Laramie, Wyoming, and gave out to the editor of the Laramie *Sentinel* a fantastic tale of diamond fields. He even

[1] A scholarly, thorough, and highly readable account of the diamond hoax is Bruce Woodard, *Diamonds in the Salt.* I have consulted at length with Mr. Woodard on the subject. The early history of the hoax is treated in Asbury Harpending, *The Great Diamond Hoax and Other Stirring Incidents in the Life of Asbury Harpending* (ed. by James H. Wilkins), 202–208. This is an unreliable account, Harpending having been connected with the hoax. See also A. J. Liebling, "The American Golconda," *New Yorker*, Vol. XVI (November 16, 1940), 40–48; New York *Times*, November 27, 1872, p. 1; December 5, 1872, p. 1; December 6, 1872, pp. 1, 4; December 7, 1872, p. 1; December 8, 1872, p. 1; National Archives, R.G. 57, Emmons' Field Notes, "The Diamond Discovery of 1872." (A copy of this manuscript is in the Emmons Papers, Manuscripts Division, Library of Congress, along with the partly burned and water-soaked diary he kept while hunting for the diamonds). Unless otherwise indicated, Emmons' description has been my principal source.

brought in the name of the New York and San Francisco Mining and Commercial Company, and he implied that the diamond fields were on Flax Creek in the San Luis Valley of Colorado.[2]

From May until November of 1872, the diamond frenzy mounted. Conflicting stories only added to the mystery. Hoaxers appeared in Denver and Salt Lake, often with a precious stone or two, told fantastic stories, and thus continued the speculation. Published accounts were picked up by other newspapers and re-published. There was no end to the rumors.[3]

The mystery, however, was soon settled. Arnold and Slack had never counted on the intervention—they would have called it meddling—of a group of government geologists. Neither had the San Francisco financiers who were investing heavily in the dia-mond fields given any thought to the possibility of having trained government geologists investigating their claims. Nevertheless it was from this unexpected direction that the exposure came.

If the diamond fields were in Arizona or New Mexico or in the San Luis Valley of Colorado, then they would have been of no concern to King, and he would have left them alone. But what if they turned out to be somewhere within the one-hundred-mile strip of land that had been explored by the Fortieth Parallel Survey? Such a find within territory supposedly covered by gov-ernment geologists would place the professional reputations of the Fortieth Parallel men in jeopardy. For the unpleasant fact was that in all their geological investigations of that one-hun-dred-mile strip along the lines of the Union Pacific and the Cen-tral Pacific, King and his assistants had never found a diamond or a ruby, nor had they seen the type of geologic formation in which such gems were likely to occur. But what if they *had* slipped up? They realized that they could take no chances. Be-fore any final report on the geology of their survey could be pub-lished, any *real* diamond fields, if they lay anywhere within the fortieth parallel country, must be visited and their genuineness established. And the King men were more than a little curious

[2] Frank Hall, *History of the State of Colorado*, II, 126–28. In pages 126–45, Hall traces the course of the diamond frenzy admirably.

[3] The *Rocky Mountain News* was full of such news items; see September 8, 1872, p. 4; September 15, 1872, p. 4; October 2, 1872, p. 2.

too. It would be an enjoyable end to six long seasons of field work to go out and find the mysterious diamond fields.[4]

As the Fortieth Parallel men worked the remote lands from Cheyenne to the Sierras that summer of 1872, they heard the diamond rumors on all sides. When their chief dropped into camp to check on progress, they pleaded with him to let them search for the diamonds. King forestalled them by promising a search when the season's work was over. With their leader thus committed, the men went back to their lonely chores, elated at the prospects of high adventure when their assignments were completed. And meanwhile they kept their eyes and ears open for any intelligence about the location of the mysterious diamonds.[5]

The man who finally started his colleagues on a serious search for the source of the gems was the geologist Samuel Franklin Emmons. He had put in a busy season working first north of the Humboldt River in Nevada, then in the region south of Fort Fred Steele in Wyoming, then about the Green River and the Uinta Mountains with T. H. O'Sullivan and finally west of the Reese River in Nevada. He had had little time, he related, to hear or read much about the discoveries, although his interest quickened when he learned that Henry Janin had pronounced the discoveries genuine. Then he gave little attention to the matter again until a series of circumstances aroused his curiosity and maintained it until the answers were found.

"It was on the 5th of October," Emmons wrote, "when I took the westward bound train at Battle Mountain, Nevada, congratulating myself upon the final completion of a work which had lasted six long years, and upon the unusually early season at which I was able to go into winter quarters, as the Fall season promised to be an unusually severe one." At first he paid little notice to the other passengers on the train, "but the following morning while breakfasting at the Summit of the Sierras with James T. Gardner . . . we both remarked upon a rather suspi-

---

[4] Hayden was busy in the Yellowstone area that summer, and Powell was on the Colorado River, which explains why they did not investigate the rumors. Wheeler was not yet involved in geological exploration.

[5] National Archives, R.G. 57, "Copy Book of Letters," November 27, 1872.

cious looking set of men whose rough clothes, top boots, and bronzed faces seemed somewhat at variance with a certain citified air, and decided they must be returning diamond hunters." By sheer coincidence, Gardner and Emmons had boarded a train that was returning some surveyors from the diamond fields.

Emmons and Gardner sat in their seats and quietly watched. At Alta Station, Henry Janin appeared and immediately closeted himself with the diamond party. When he appeared again, the Fortieth Parallel men got up and approached him, for they knew him to be a fellow geologist. Janin was not embarrassed to talk to them. Yes, the men had been to the diamond fields. Janin had wanted to go, but he had been so closely followed that he had finally given up. In his place, he had sent along a surveyor from Sacramento named King—no relation to Clarence King—who had managed to shake the pursuers off the trail. To accomplish this, the party had taken such a roundabout route that they had themselves lost the way, but finally, after much wandering, they had found the diamond fields. Before they left the area, they had all been allowed one hour in which to look for jewels using only their pocket knives. Ten men had collected together 280 diamonds and rubies "too common to count." Some of the stones were shown, ranging in size from "a grain of wheat to a small pea."

Emmons' professional curiosity was aroused. For if the discovery was genuine, it might result in the solution of the great problem of the origin and manner of formation of the diamond. And the fact that Janin would not divulge the location of the fields made Emmons and Gardner more determined than ever to find them on their own. For a start, Gardner "proceeded to ingratiate himself with the surveyor King, who was all the more easily approached as it seemed he was desirous of getting some information from us with regard to the boundary lines of Colorado, Utah, and Wyoming."[6]

When the train pulled in to San Francisco, Emmons and Gardner got in touch with James D. Hague to discuss the mystery.

[6] National Archives, R.G. 57, Emmons' Field Notes, "The Diamond Discovery of 1872."

Then A. D. Wilson arrived from the field, and he was as enthusi-astic about solving the mystery as the others. Earlier in the season he had heard the usual rumors about diamond fields in Arizona, but when he learned that the diamond hunters had departed from and returned to the Union Pacific at various points be-tween Green River and Rawlins, he concluded that the fields must be south of the railroad. In Arizona? Hardly, for the Yampa and the Green were virtually impassable in the late spring and summer. Therefore the fields must have been somewhere in the Yampa–Green River country where Wilson had been hard at work during most of the summer. When his friends informed him that actual diamonds had been found, he was even more sur-prised and more anxious than ever to go back into the field and solve the mystery.[7]

For about a week, the team gathered information, meeting every morning to compare notes. They soon found that Janin's first trip had taken less than three weeks from the time he left the Union Pacific Railroad until he returned to it. This was too short a period for him to have gone to New Mexico or Arizona and returned. Coupled with Wilson's information, this estab-lished the general area in which the diamond fields lay. Then Emmons learned from Janin that the diamond hunters had camped at the foot of a pine-covered mountain which, even in June, still had some snow on its slopes. Gardner had meanwhile wrested the information from the surveyor, King, that the camp had been on the northeast side of a mountain from which no high mountains could be seen to the north or east.

This was a meagre amount of intelligence, but for these ex-perienced men it was sufficient. Gardner, Emmons, Wilson, and Hague fixed the locality at the foot of a peak, which was after-wards named Diamond Peak, lying about ten miles north of Brown's Park and forty miles east of Green River. The surveyor, King, had probably been curious about boundary lines because Colorado, Utah, and Wyoming met about fifteen miles north-

[7] King Collection, Allan D. Wilson, "The Great California Diamond Mines." This manuscript appeared, somewhat revised, as "The Great California Diamond Swindle," *Overland Monthly,* New Series, No. 51 (April, 1904), 291–96.

west of this peak. Impatiently they waited for Clarence King's arrival in San Francisco.[8]

On October 19, tired from arduous work in the southern Sierras, King arrived. "We asked leave to proceed at once," A. D. Wilson remembered, "not thinking he would care to accompany us on such a wild goose chase." But King was interested. He sat down with his men and discussed all the aspects of the mystery, soon discovering that he had independently placed the fields just where Gardner and his colleagues had placed them. And with his usual promptness, King hastily laid the plans for the adventure. On the very next morning, Gardner, Wilson, and Emmons were on the eastbound Overland chugging along toward what they hoped was the solution of a great mystery. Not to arouse suspicion, they had agreed to speak only of "carboniferous fossils," never of diamonds. And although their baggage did include some wire sieves and other instruments for testing the soil and any gems they might find, they were saved the discomfort of many questions because their stock was not along. It was at Fort Bridger, where Wilson had left his animals a few weeks before. And to avoid suspicion, King himself did not leave until the next day.[9]

King was so careful that he did not even indicate the nature of his expedition to General Humphreys until it was all over. In a letter from Fort Bridger dated October 28, he merely informed his superior that he was leaving that day to inspect the Brown's Hole and Uinta Canyon regions, expecting to be back by November 20. Later he explained that "he had the further intention of settling the diamond question, but deemed it unwise to say so. The balance of probabilities," he added "seemed against finding the spot, and I had judged it quite as well to say nothing of a subject upon which I could not speak assuredly."[10]

[8] National Archives, R.G. 57, Emmons' Field Notes, "The Diamond Discovery of 1872."

[9] King Collection, Wilson, "The Great California Diamond Mines." National Archives, R.G. 57, Emmons' Field Notes, "The Diamond Discovery of 1872"; "Copy Book of Letters," November 27, 1872. In this letter King does not mention the work of Emmons, Wilson, and Hague.

[10] National Archives, R.G. 57, "Copy Book of Letters," November 27, 1872.

There was some delay at Fort Bridger. Hague had to go to Laramie for saddles, and an untrustworthy and highly suspicious camp man was sent with an important letter to Fort Steele. The letter instructed the officer in charge there to keep the camp man "out of the way for a while." Meanwhile the officers and men at Fort Bridger seemed not at all surprised that the group was going after "carboniferous fossils." They only expressed sorrow that the work had to be done so late in the season. The two long-handled shovels the party was taking along were explained by reference to their experiences of a year before when they had been snowed in at 10,000 feet, with only a single hand shovel to get them out. But they did not fool everyone. "As we were on the point of starting,"Emmons wrote, "Dr. Carson, the Post surgeon, whispered in my ear, 'Bring me back a couple of solitaires, will you?' but as he was a confirmed wag it did not occur to me at the time that he suspected our object."

The start from Fort Bridger was made on October 29, after a slight snow the day before and a bitterly cold night. The temperature was below zero, and a stiff breeze was blowing over the sage-covered plains and high mesas, tearing at their clothing as if in anger at their intrusion into the treeless waste. And it was 150 miles to their destination. King had given each man a bright, big woolen muffler, and Emmons recalled that in order to save space on the pack mules he had worn four flannel shirts and two pairs of socks. It was "a bitterly cold journey," he said, "on tired and worn-out animals, whose legs from crossing the frequent thinly frozen mountain streams became encased in balls of ice, which rattled as they went like crude castinets."

On the fourth day out, they forded Green River successfully and then began ascending the mountains, the farther side of which was their destination. It was cold and lonely country, and yet civilization was about. Halfway up the mountains they passed the deserted camp of some hunters. A forlorn white horse, left in camp to rest while his owners and the other mounts were out hunting, whinnied with joy at their arrival and insisted upon following the party. "Lest in searching for him they should discover us and our object we camped early," Emmons continued, "and the following morning started before daylight in a drifting snow storm, hoping the fresh snow would effectually cover our tracks." They skirted around the north side of the mountains, struck the edge of the mesas where they suspected the diamond fields to be, and at about noon stopped "at a clear spring in a deep narrow gulch, sunk some 600 feet below the uniform level of the surrounding mesas." Since the place afforded both protection from the elements and concealment, camp was made there.

Emmons, Wilson, and King then left the packers at camp and rode down the gulch to find some way of climbing the walls to the mesa above. Hardly 500 yards from the camp, they came across "a small fresh blaze on one of the cottonwoods." At the foot of the tree they found a piece of paper which contained a written claim to the water privileges of the gulch, dated Golconda City, June 15, and signed by Henry Janin. This quickly led to the discovery of mining notices, and within two hours, by circling around the gulch, they had found tracks leading up to the table rock where the gems were salted. Emmons' description is worth quoting:

> . . . after a ride of about a mile and a half [we] came upon a bare iron-stained bit of coarse sandstone rock about a hundred feet long, just jutting out above the level of the mesa, to which all the various tracks converged. Throwing down our bridle reins we began examining the rock on our hands and knees, and in another instant I had found a small ruby. This was indeed the spot. The diamond fever had now attacked us with vigor, and while daylight lasted we continued in this position picking up precious stones. We were perhaps a little disappointed at finding but one diamond each, but attributed our slight success to want of training our eyes, since the stones we found were all about the same size and shape as the quartz grains of which the rock was composed, and could only be distinguished from them by the difference of lustre, which in the rough diamond is of a steely tinge. The work was rendered slow also by the intense cold, for there was not protection from the fierce wind which swept scarcely broken for hundreds of miles over these barren mesas, and when a diamond was found it was quite a time before our benumbed fingers could succeed in grasping the tiny stone. That night we were full-believers in the verity of Janin's reports, and dreamed of the untold wealth that might be gathered.

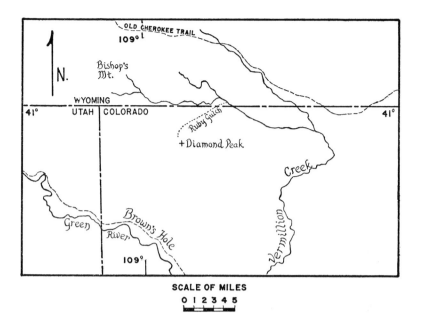

Site of the Diamond Hoax

The following morning they sent their two camp men out hunting, which seemed logical enough since they were out of meat. Then the party traced out the claim, looking for diamonds at all times, especially in the ant hills. It did not take them long to discover that the number of diamonds and rubies dwindled rapidly as they worked away from the wind-swept table rock that constituted the heart of the claim. When afternoon came, they decided to study more intensely the manner of occurrence of the gems on the table rock, since there they were most abundant. King soon announced the discovery of an interesting mathematical fact: where there were a dozen rubies there was sure to be one diamond. Nature certainly didn't work like that, so they brought out their sieves and tried the earth that surrounded the table rock. They soon discovered that they could only find gems in places where the earth had already been disturbed. Patches of soil that had not been touched in years, if ever, failed to yield anything more than quartz grains. Then they examined the ant hills, carefully removing the crusty exterior, then sifting the in-

197

terior. In several cases they found rubies—"a decided point in favor of the natural occurrence of the stones," Emmons declared —but upon further investigation they found that the ant hills gave them their first sure signs of fraud:

> Examining the other ant-hills with the greatest care we found some with only a single footstep on the ground near, and beside the top hole by which the ants made their exit, there was visible in the side another small break in the crust. From the centre of these the sieve would yield us a small ruby or two, but when we found one with no footsteps near, no holes but at the top, no ruby rewarded our search, and our explanation was that some one must have pushed in a ruby or two on the end of a stick. We dug in the gulch again, and found the rubies decreased as we left the rock, until at a certain distance, sift the sand as we would we got none at all.

The evidence of fraud seemed conclusive, but King was not yet satisfied. He was aware of the power and prestige of the founders of the New York and San Francisco Mining and Commercial Company. If he shouted fraud when there was no fraud, then the Fortieth Parallel Survey would be discredited and his career ruined. Then there was the matter of Henry Janin. That man was just about the most respected geologist in California; his reputation was without a blemish. Yet he had pronounced the claim genuine. King shivered as the frigid wind tore at him, but finally nodded his head affirmatively. They had better stay and conduct a few more tests.

According to Emmons' narration (which is most accurate), all of the third day was employed in sifting the gravel, and on the fourth day the camp men were told of the nature of the investigation and were put to work digging a hole three feet wide and ten feet deep. The site chosen was at a point in the gulch where the gems, if they really did occur in nature, would be sure to be found. All the gravel thus dug up was saved, and later in the day it was panned in the stream—the specific gravity of diamonds would cause them to be left in the pan.

Just as they were completing the first part of their experiment, a lone horseman, "a stout party, city dressed, and looking very much out of keeping with his surroundings," appeared coming toward them. The stranger dismounted and asked, "Have you found any carats around here?" The Fortieth Parallel men frankly replied in the negative, explaining that the whole thing was a fraud. The man whistled softly. "What a chance to sell short on the stock," he mused. Then he explained that he was a New York diamond dealer who, for the past year, had been interested in mines in Utah. When he had heard of the diamond fields, he had determined to find their location at any cost and had employed men all summer long to watch for Janin and King along the Union Pacific Railroad.

His name was J. F. Berry, and his interests were shady, if not actually dark and sinister. Emmons said that Berry had combined with George Hearst, later a senator, to employ Janin for a $1,000 fee to come out and give them his opinion on a mine. They wined and dined him in an effort to find out the location of the diamond fields. They did not succeed, but he did tell them that a man named King had surveyed the fields. The diamond dealer knew nothing about King the surveyor, of course, but he had heard of Clarence King the geologist, and that is whom he assumed he was looking for. At Salt Lake City the local newspaper commented on King's passage through the city, so Berry immediately picked up his trail, found that King had got off at Fort Bridger, and began trailing him. For three days, from the top of a nearby mountain, he had watched the Fortieth Parallel men through a spyglass, and when he saw them lying down on their bellies and digging for some hours at the same spot, he was convinced that it was diamonds and not fossils that they were after.

Huddled around their campfire that night, King and his men discussed the turn of events. Not far off they could see the fire of the Berry camp, and Berry meant trouble. The wind blew ceaselessly through the camp, and the sounds of canvas flapping and coyotes howling reminded them of how far they were from the gas-lighted luxuries of San Francisco. But they had discovered a great hoax, and Berry knew about it and hoped to profit by it. The comfortable capitalists in San Francisco had to be publicly chastised, or at least warned. Finally, King turned to Emmons and Wilson. "How can we reach the railroad in the quickest way from here?" he asked. Emmons replied that the logical way was by the road from Green River City to Brown's Park—a two-day ride. But if one really was in a hurry, he might head out through the badland country directly to Black Buttes Station, a trip of some forty to forty-five miles.

King determined to start that way immediately, taking Wilson, the topographer, along to guide him. Emmons and the rest of the party were to return by the usual route. But King felt that he must get to the company officials and force them to expose the fraud immediately. Unless they could make the public believe the hoax, now that the locality was known, he reasoned, "thousands of poor devils will be rushing in here from every quarter, utterly unprepared, and perish by hundreds in this bleak winter, without water or fuel." And Berry would sell short if he reached civilization before King had exposed the hoax. King and Wilson had to start at once.

Before dawn tinted the eastern sky, King and Wilson started for Black Butte Station. "We had a long day's ride, Wilson later wrote, "without track or trail, over sage-covered hills and plateaus. We crossed ridges, gulleys, washouts, and late at night with only the stars as guides during the latter part of the trip, we arrived at the station. Arousing the agent, we procured for our two mules a box car, which the agent kindly attached to a west-found freight train. Just after daylight we boarded a westbound passenger train and proceeded west."

In his letter of explanation to Humphreys, dated November 27, King continued his narration:

> At that time [arrival at the station] I would have telegraphed to you a full statement, but the operators all along the line, are on a *qui vive*, and *no dispatch is safe in their hands.*
>
> I arrived at San Francisco on the night of Nov. 10th not knowing what capitalists had controlled nor what stockholders made up the Company. I however knew Mr. Janin the mining expert of the Company, and I at once sought him. Through nearly all the night I detailed to him the discovery, and at last convinced him of its correctness.

On the morning of November 11, King met the directors of the company, who had been hastily assembled, and presented to them a lengthy letter in which he detailed in clear and concise fashion all the evidence that he had collected which proved the hoax.[11] Said King, "They were astonished and thrown into utter confusion." Nevertheless he convinced them with but one reservation—they insisted on being taken to the fields and actually shown proof of the fraud.

Reluctantly, King gave in. The next morning, tired though he was, he left for the diamond fields in the company of Henry Janin, General David Colton, manager of the company, John W. Bost, former surveyor general of California, and E. M. Fry, who had been to the fields with a previous party. Within three hours' ride south of Black Buttes, the pine-clad mountain appeared, and the men were relieved to see their goal so soon, for the temperature was twenty below zero and even the whisky froze in the bottle. Arrived at the site, they made fifty-six separate tests, without a diamond or a ruby appearing. Then Colton found some rubies on a bare rock overlooking the field where, he said in his report, "in my opinion, it would have been as impossible for nature to have deposited them as for a person in San Francisco to toss a marble in the air and have it fall on Bunker Hill Monument."[12] After two days of exhaustive tests the party was convinced. They rode back to Black Buttes and with heavy hearts prepared for the onslaught of public wrath that was sure to come when they announced the fraud in San Francisco.

King may have been duped in being persuaded to lead the group back to the diamond fields. Emmons is the authority for the fact that one of the officials suggested to King that the letter and the facts be kept quiet for a few days—that it might be to his interest to acquiesce in this. King replied, "There is not enough money in the Bank of California to make me delay the publication a single hour. If you do not [publish] I will, but it will come

[11] This letter is a remarkable example of King's literary ability. It appears in the *Annual Report of the Chief of Engineers*, 43 Cong., 1 sess., *House Exec. Doc. 1 (II)*, 1208–10.

[12] New York *Times*, December 5, 1872, p. 1. This article summarizes Colton's report.

with much better grace from you. Stop all transfers of stock."
Yet, in granting the directors this additional time, King was in
fact forestalling the publication of the letter for a few days, in
which time some stockholders may have been able to sell and
prepare for the storm of abuse that followed the exposure of the
hoax.[13]

In any event, when they arrived back at San Francisco, the
board of directors met, received General Colton's report, passed
a resolution to publish King's letter plus all their own information, and then washed their hands of the whole affair.

The company was none too soon in announcing the fraud.
Berry, the diamond merchant, had been up to mischief just as
King had suspected. When Berry reached Fort Bridger, he distributed diamonds and raised the excitement to a higher pitch
than before. He then went to Salt Lake City, where he exhibited
twenty-six diamonds, one of which weighed three carats, and
declared his readiness to pilot a party to the fields at once. He
accurately placed the locality in western Colorado and allowed a
number of Salt Lake capitalists to put up money for an expedition. The departure of the company party from San Francisco
was also noted, and the arrival of the same group at Black Buttes
Station and their departure into the unknown areas south of
there was headlined in the newspapers. The final announcement
of the exposure of the hoax was big news, but it was not entirely
unexpected.[14]

From the exposure there grew a libel suit by the Englishman
Alfred Rubery against the London *Times* and a grand jury investigation in San Francisco. Arnold fled to his home in Eliza-
bethtown, Harlan County, Kentucky, with the sum of money
paid him by the company, estimated at from $300,000 to as much
as $600,000. All attempts of the Yankees to sue him are said to
have been futile—possibly one man collected $150,000 from him
—and he eventually died in 1879.[15]

---

[13] Hall, *History of the State of Colorado, II,* 141.

[14] *Rocky Mountain News,* November 16, 1872, p. 4; November 23, 1872, p. 4.
New York *Times,* November 17, 1872, p. 1.

[15] Hall, *History of the State of Colorado, II,* 142–44.

The greatest abuse fell not upon Arnold and Slack, but upon the original promoters of the company. Though the San Francisco financier William Lent was said to have lost $100,000 and his friend William Ralston $250,000, the public would not forgive them. High financiers were supposed to know better. "It is most astonishing that leading citizens of recognized shrewdness in all money matters should have been so duped, and that the engineer who was employed to investigate the alleged diamond fields should also have fallen into the trap set for him by the most adroit and unconscionable villains," editorialized the San Francisco *Bulletin*.[16]

Were Arnold and Slack the guilty parties, taking in the richest and shrewdest men of San Francisco? Or were these men in the know all along, deeply embroiled in a fantastic get-rich-quick scheme as utterly dishonest as Jim Fisk's manipulation of the Erie Railroad? Whatever the answer, Clarence King upset their plans and saved thousands of small investors from losing their capital.

One of the pleasanter aspects of the whole case was the praise heaped upon a public servant, Clarence King. The San Francisco *Bulletin* thanked King for the exposure, calling him a "cool-headed man of scientific education who esteemed it a duty to investigate the matter in the only right way, and who proceeded about his task with a degree of spirit and strong common sense as striking as his success." The newspaper even praised the Fortieth Parallel Survey, pointing out that the diamond exposure sharply emphasized the practical value "in the ordinary business of society, of scientific education and research. . . . Mr. King . . . has done the public a memorable service, the mere statement of which carries with it all the praise a man like him can desire, as it is the only reward he will receive."[17] The *Chronicle* said, "We have escaped, thanks to God and Clarence King, a great financial calamity."[18] And the Georgetown, Colorado, *Mining Re-*

---

[16] November 26, 1872. This clipping is in the National Archives, R.G. 77, Records of the Office of the Chief of Engineers, Letters Received, 2442, 1872.

[17] November 26, 1872.

[18] November 28, 1872.

view, commented, "Let it not be said that geological surveys are useless. . . . This one act has certainly paid for the survey of the 40th Parallel and has brought deserved credit to Mr. King and his assistants."[19]

Unfortunately, the man who could have best written the story of the part played by the Fortieth Parallel men in exposing the diamond hoax was forbidden to do so. King's request to publish his story in the *Overland Monthly* was refused. Humphreys wired him that it was "not a matter in which the Engineer Department has any right under the law to take action."[20] The best sources are Emmons' "The Diamond Discovery of 1872," Wilson's "The Great California Diamond Mines," and King's letter to Humphreys of November 27. These three accounts, however, differ on many points, and a fourth, Harpending's, differs greatly from them.

King's letter to Humphreys is obviously controlled by a desire to avoid censure. King knew Humphreys from six long years of administrative dealings, and he knew the ways of the army. He could just hear Humphreys asking, "What right did you have to spend government funds to investigate a hoax?" So King emphasized that he was making a last geological exploration of the country around the Uintas and down the Green River. That is why he failed to mention some of the men who were with him, never mentioned the diamond dealer Berry, and never said a word about all the detective work Gardner, Wilson and Hague had conducted in San Francisco.

Asbury Harpending's account of the hoax, though interesting reading, is of whole cloth. He was a successful, shady capitalist in a robber baron era, and his story reflects his pique at King for having exposed a fraud that he, Harpending, knew a great deal about.

The diamond hoax was the greatest fraud ever perpetrated in the West, and it was an omen of the changing times that gullible investors were saved by salaried government officials who had

[19] Vol. I, No. 4 (December, 1872), 5.

[20] National Archives, R.G. 77, Office of the Chief of Engineers, Humphreys to King, December 7, 1872.

no monetary stake in the matter whatsoever. Well educated, honest, and dedicated, the Fortieth Parallel men were in the vanguard of the many government men who later conducted their investigations with dispassionate efficiency, protecting the people and their natural resources alike for their own generation and for generations yet to come.

In their dedication, in their curiosity, and in their objectivity, Clarence King and his Fortieth Parallel men established a great precedent.

IO

Scientific Publications

By 1872, six years of King's life had gone into the Fortieth Parallel Survey, but his own volume, *Systematic Geology*, Emmons' and Arnold Hague's work, *Descriptive Geology*, the atlas, and several monographs were still to be written. They would demand hard and exacting work, take much time, and try the patience of men who still had their future careers to think about. But the work had to be done, so offices were rented in New York City, and for the next six years—until early in 1879—King spent at least a part of his time in working up the *final reports*.

It is to his everlasting credit that King possessed a sound scholarly concept of how the results of his great exploration should be presented. The idea jelled in his mind during the years of field work—years in which the vigorous twenty-five-year-old New Englander put on weight, lost much of his hair, and changed into a middle-aged, professional, respected scientist. "The day has passed in geological science," he wrote to General Humphreys, "when it is either decent or tolerable to rush into print with undigested field operations, ignoring the methods and appliances in use among advanced investigators. It is my intention to give to this work a finish which will place it on an equal footing with the best European productions, and those few which have redeemed the wavering reputation of our American investigators."[1] In direct contrast to the policies of Hayden, who felt that discoveries should be made immediately available to the world, King sensed the dawn of a new day when much meticulous research would precede cautiously delivered announcements of scientific advances. There was to be nothing haphazard about his final reports. They were to be a distillation of six years of field work and of re-examinations of doubtful points over a period of another six years. They were to appear in a physical package representing the finest achievements of modern printing and lithography.

The Fortieth Parallel Survey published its final reports in seven volumes and an atlas. The dates of publication extended from 1870, when James D. Hague's monograph, *Mining Industry*, appeared, until 1880, when Marsh published his work, *Odontornithes: A Monograph on the Extinct Toothed Birds of North America*. There was no co-ordination between the volume numbers and the dates of publication.

Thus, Volume I, *Systematic Geology*, was not issued until 1878. Yet it embraced King's own brilliant investigations as well as those of his staff, and in a sense covered the very heart of the purpose in the whole Fortieth Parallel Survey idea. In the 800-page monograph, King traced the geologic history of the "Middle Cordilleras"—104° 30' W. to 102° W., a distance of 800 miles—from the ancient deposits of the Archean era on through the Paleozoic, the Mesozoic, and the most recent, the Cenozoic, with breakdowns into the various geologic periods including the recent Quaternary. He hoped, he said in his letter of transmittal, that the report would have "value either as a permanent contribution to knowledge or as a stepping-stone worthy to be built into the great stairway of science." For in essence it constituted the study "of a continuous geological section across the widest expansion of the great Cordillera Mountain System."[2]

King felt that his scientific conclusions were safe, and for the

[1] National Archives, R.G. 57, "Copy Book of Letters," February 25, 1874.
[2] King, *Systematic Geology*, xi.

most part they have withstood the test of time. The one-hundred-mile-wide belt (from 39° 30′ N. to 42° N.—actually 107 miles) was, he believed, sufficiently wide to avoid the errors that would have appeared in a study of a belt five miles wide. Furthermore, he was able to link his work with Whitney's in the Sierras and Hayden's on the eastern High Plains and south of the fortieth parallel. King's boundaries were, then, ample enough to prevent error yet sufficiently restricted to be workable by a group of men such as King had at his disposal. Moreover, those sixteen degrees of longitude from Cheyenne to the Sierras were the very least known within the boundaries of the continental limits of the nation. The challenge had been there, and King and his men had faced up to it. They had traced a section of the earth's crust through 125,000 feet, "taking in," King wrote, "all the broader divisions of geological time—a section which has been subjected to a great sequence of mechanical violence, and can hardly fail to become classic for its display of the products of eruption—this Exploration has actually covered an epitome of geological history."[3]

King's *Systematic Geology* remains to this day a classic in the field of historical geology. In 1878, it represented the greatest, broadest monograph yet written about the total geologic history of so great an area, and along with Dana's text, two generations of geology students were expected to read excerpts from King. Its chapters point up its logical arrangement: "Area of Exploration of the Fortieth Parallel," separate chapters on Archean, Paleozoic, Mesozoic, and Cenozoic formations, a "Resume of Stratigraphical Geology," a chapter on "Tertiary and Volcanic Rocks," and a chapter on orography. Twenty-six chromolithographs, many of them still remarkably handsome in the great volume after more than a century, are generously sprinkled throughout, as are twelve maps of the fortieth parallel country showing exposures of various geologic periods, glaciers in the ice age, and the ancient Lakes Lahontan and Bonneville, with the outlines of the present Great Salt Lake and Winnemucca and Pyramid lakes clearly defined. And the book made an im-

[3] *Ibid.*, 3.

pression. "Mr. King's graceful pen never showed itself to better advantage," commented the *American Journal of Science*,[4] and it was clear that whatever turn his career took, his reputation was well established.

In January, 1877, King submitted Volume II, *Descriptive Geology*. This 853-page monograph was the product of the untiring efforts of Samuel Franklin Emmons and Arnold Hague. It differed from King's volume in that while King traced the geology of the fortieth parallel historically, Emmons and Hague traced it geographically. They worked from east to west in five great chapters that coincided with the five logical breakdowns of the belt, each of which constituted a separate map in the atlas. Twenty-five chromolithographs added interest to the volume.

Volume III, James Hague's *Mining Industry,* was issued in 1870, and it met with immediate approval from the mining industry and the geology profession It was the single best source of information on gold and silver mines, concentration mills, smelters, furnaces, hoists, pumps—in short, on everything involved in getting precious metal from the earth, refining it, and taking it to the mints. Thirty-seven plates showed with great clarity how it was all done. The volume contained the best description of the great complex of the Comstock and of the whole Washoe Mining District; the two Hagues, Emmons, and King all combined their knowledge to describe everything from the tunnels to the treatment of the ores. Arranged by districts west to east, the volume ended with essays on the silver mining areas of Colorado. In it lay perhaps the only scholarly survey of the technological problems of western mining available in 1870.

Volume IV, *Palaeontology and Ornithology,* appeared in 1877 and was in three parts. Part I, "Palaeontology," by Fielding Bradford Meek, dealt with fossils from the Lower Silurian to the Tertiary; Part II, "Palaeontology," by James Hall and R. P. Whitfield, dealt with certain fossils from the Eureka and White Pine mining districts of Nevada. Twenty-four plates accompanied these highly technical reports.

Part III, "Ornithology," represented the work of Robert Ridg-

[4] New Series, Vol. XVII, No. 97 (January, 1879), 67.

way. After the complex studies of Meek and Hall, his essay is as welcome as the Nevada streams he describes, havens in the desert where "the refreshing breeze brings to the ear the rippling of cooling waters and the glad voices of the birds! The merry little Wood-Wrens . . . gabble and chatter among the trunks and massive branches of the old cotton-wood trees; the black-and-orange orioles . . . and crimson-headed linnets . . . whistle plaintively or chant a cheerful ditty as they sport among the leafy branches, while from the willows or the more open thickets is heard the mellow flute-like song of the Black-headed Grosbeak."[5]

Ridgway's report is over 300 pages long, and in it he presents an excellent word picture of the survey area, lists the camps of the survey, and happily describes the birds of the Great Basin.

Volume V, *Botany,* was Sereno Watson's great work. It appeared in 1871 immediately following Hague's *Mining Industry.* In over 500 pages, with a map and forty plates, this monumental work established a precedent of accuracy and thoroughness and laid the foundation of our knowledge of the flora of the Great Basin.

Volume VI was the result of an idea that had originated in 1874. In that year King had sent Emmons to Germany "to examine the collections of the Surveys of Germany, France, and England, and to establish a connection and a common nomenclature between European and American rocks." Emmons was also to purchase books necessary for the completion of the work, and he was to bring back with him Ferdinand Zirkel, "the great German authority on rocks who is to enrich our report with a short memoir."[6]

Zirkel's memoir was issued in 1876 and bore the title *Microscopical Petrography.* The volume demonstrated King's feeling for scholarliness and scientific advance. Before 1870, the microscope had been little used in geological research, but King sensed its value and obtained, in Zirkel, the world's leading authority on what has since become the science of microscopic

[5] Page 323.
[6] National Archives, R.G. 57, "Copy Book of Letters," April 22, 1874.

petrology.[7] To Zirkel, there were made available the hundreds of rock specimens collected by the survey. He talked with King for long hours over a period of many weeks about the links between American and European rocks and about the related problems of nomenclature. He came up with a 275-page monograph, accompanied by twelve remarkably good color plates, which "sold" petrography to American scientists.[8] In Zirkel's honor, King named a 12,220-foot peak in the Park Range of northwestern Colorado.

Volume VII was not published until 1880. It was Marsh's *Odontornithes: A Monograph on the Extinct Toothed Birds of North America*, with thirty-four plates and forty woodcuts. Marsh hoped this would be but the first of several monographs on the extinct vertebrate life of North America, and although he was never able to realize his hope, the volume attests to the soundness of the idea.

As a necessary accompaniment to the seven reports, James Terry Gardner's great atlas of the fortieth parallel was added. It was completed in 1878, and it consisted of one map embracing the entire fortieth parallel area and five topographic and five geologic maps, each of which embraced one of the five great areas into which the area had been divided. The scale was four miles to the inch with grade curves of 300-foot vertical interval, with the various formations appearing in appropriate colors. Two final atlas sheets carried continuous geologic sections from east to west from 104° W. to 120° W.

The first of the five great section maps embraced the Rockies from the eastern slope westward to the Park Range; the second map was of the Green River Basin and the Uinta Mountains; the third covered the highlands to the east of the Wasatch Range, the range itself, and the Great Salt Lake; the fourth was of the arid plateau of central Nevada; and the fifth was of the basin of Nevada to the Sierras and the California line.[9]

The trigonometric methods which Gardner later employed

[7] Merrill, *American Geology*, 643–47.

[8] Ferdinand Zirkel, *Microscopical Petrography*, Vol. VI in *Report of the Geological Exploration of the Fortieth Parallel*, xv.

[9] King, *Systematic Geology*, 4–13.

with the Hayden Survey were first practiced in the arid lands of the fortieth parallel country, and if the Hayden atlas of Colorado is a better technical job, it is because its two leading topographers, Gardner and A. D. Wilson, perfected their techniques while on the Fortieth Parallel Survey. Julius Bien did the lithographic work, and the maps are collectors' items today.

Thus, save for Marsh's monograph on extinct birds, King's scientific package was all wrapped up and the survey was ended by 1878. And what of the achievements of the survey as a whole? Was it worth the $600,000 that it cost the government?[10]

The published reports raised the reputation of American science in Europe. King's own contribution served as a model for geological investigation and reporting for years to come. Moreover, of the four Great Surveys, the King Survey was the one imitated in scope by Hayden and Wheeler and partly by Powell. King planned a geographical and topographical atlas; Hayden copied King's idea even to similarities in format and organization in his own atlas of Colorado. Both Wheeler and Hayden were inspired in their presentation of materials by King's masterful plan of seven volumes covering the natural sciences and geology. Wheeler's final reports are strikingly similar in design to those of the Fortieth Parallel Survey. And it was not until several years of topographical work had been accomplished by King that Powell conceived the plan of mapping the Great Plateau. Since King began large-scale operations several years before any of the others entered the field extensively (for Hayden was limited to expenses of only $5,000 in 1867, only $10,000 in 1868 and 1869), it becomes apparent that King led the way, and the others followed.

Yet the Fortieth Parallel Survey may have had one great failing. However grand and logical the idea of a survey of a one-hundred-mile-wide strip of land always including the Pacific Railroad may have been, the fact remains that actual settlement did not always occur along that strip. Where deserts

---

[10] National Archives, R.G. 57, "Copy Book of Letters," March 20, 1878. King here gave $523,851.90 as the total cost, but he did not include 1867 or 1878. The amounts spent in those two years brought the total close to $600,000.

lay, men stayed away. Settlement went elsewhere, and much of the work done along the fortieth parallel by the King Survey was quite scientific, but unfortunately, in a practical sense it was quite useless.

When the United States Geological Exploration of the Fortieth Parallel came to an end, Clarence King was thirty-six years old. Despite a flaw or two, the survey had been a brilliant idea, and King had pushed it through to a brilliant completion. His reputation was firmly established, he was in his prime, was in good health, and was trained in a profession that was earning its followers sizable fortunes. With all this in his favor, what became of Clarence King?

In 1879 he became the first director of the new United States Geological Survey. Yet he quit the post after just one year and set out to earn money. He had profited from investments in western ranching while still in charge of the Fortieth Parallel Survey, and in 1880, he invested heavily in Mexican mining operations. He traveled extensively—from New York across the continent, back again to Colorado or Arizona or Utah, then down into old Mexico. Then he sailed to Europe and had a delightful time as a *bon vivant* and a collector of bric-a-brac, occasionally promoting mining stock to increase his income.[11]

By the mid-1880's his coterie of friends included Henry Adams, John Hay, Baron Rothschild, William Dean Howells, W. C. Ralston, J. Pierpont Morgan, Carl Schurz, Henry Holt, Edward H. Harriman, and many others.[12] They stuck by him when he married a Negress. They lent him large sums of money and watched his investments from both a friendly and a financial point of view, and they were genuinely sorry when he failed. In 1893, a bad financial situation contributed to a nervous breakdown; recovered, he went at it again, investing in mines, charging high fees as a consultant for capitalists and mining interests. He lived well, knew all the right people, and traveled, traveled,

[11] Thurman Wilkins, *Clarence King*, chapters 13, 16, 17.

[12] At least, these men were subscribers to the *Clarence King Memoirs;* see King Collection, File 1, *Memoirs*.

traveled. But as for a fortune—that was a will-o'-the-wisp that he never grasped.

Finally, one day in the early months of the twentieth century, he dropped in to see his old friend Henry Adams. It was a sad meeting. Wrote Adams, "He stopped an hour in Washington to bid good-bye, cheerily and simply telling how his doctors had condemned him to Arizona for his lungs."[13]

The end of a busy life was approaching. But King had not realized the great monetary fortune for which he had searched. The one flaw in this gem of a man—the flaw of poor judgment—had denied him success. He had overestimated the wealth of his mines and underestimated the cost of extracting the ores. Other geologists had grown wealthy, but King had grown more deeply in debt.

With better judgment, he might have remained an administrator, a leader of professional men. He had the verve and youthful eagerness to inspire men, to innovate, to test new theories. With better judgment, and with his wide field of experience to use for material, he might have done something with his graceful pen, for *Mountaineering in the Sierra Nevada* was the work of a man with real writing ability.

A complicated, capable, cheerful, tragic personality—that was Clarence King. And his greatest work by far was his leadership of the Fortieth Parallel Survey.

He came to realize this in the last months of his life. "If I succeeded in anything," he wrote to James D. Hague, "it was in personally impressing the whole corps and making it uniformly harmonious and patient; and I think I did that as much as anything else by a sort of natural spirit of command and personal sympathy with all hands and conditions, from geologists to mules. 'Tis but a step from the sublime to the ridiculous. As I look back I wonder that at my age, taking command as early as I did, that I should have carried through all the necessary steps to thoroughly control the organization."[14]

---

[13] Adams, *The Education of Henry Adams,* 395.

[14] King Collection, Box 1, Hague, "C. K.'s Notes for My Biographical Notice of Him for Appleton's Encyclopaedia."

As he lay alone and mortally ill in 1901, his thoughts wandered back to the 1870's, back to the deserts and the mountains, the acrid alkali and the pungent pine along the fortieth parallel. "Most of the time," he wrote his close friend S. F. Emmons, "the fever keeps me in a half dreamy condition, quite conscious of my extreme discomfort and then like the lifting of a veil my faculties come back and I pass intervals of repose. In these enforced spaces of rest I find myself going back on the past, resuming the 40th Parallel [work], climbing the peaks and pushing in a little into the future with curiosity and deep interest." And then he asked Emmons about his work, adding, "Mine is already done and my hammer hung up forever. But I am fuller of geological ideas than ever and I shall mass and publish them if I get a reprieve."[15]

But Clarence King got no reprieve. He pleaded with Emmons to intercede in his behalf in an effort to get him an honorary degree from Yale during its bicentennial celebration, and the attempt was made, but all the powers of his many friends failed to obtain this honor for him.[16]

He died at Phoenix, Arizona, on December 24, 1901. Subsequently, his friends gathered a group of essays together and published them as the *Clarence King Memoirs*. When Adams received his copy, he wrote his old friend Emmons a letter which contained one sentence that, in or out of context, expressed the great mystery of the life of the geologist Clarence King. "It makes me wonder at geology," wrote Adams, "when I think that this is all that remains of the most remarkable man of our time."[17]

[15] Emmons Papers, Box 28, King to Emmons, August 29, 1901.

[16] *Ibid.;* see also Charles Walcott to Emmons, October 3, 1901.

[17] Emmons Papers, Box 30, Adams to Emmons, March 17, 1902.

PART THREE

❧

*Powell's Survey
of the Plateaus and Canyons*

II

Powell as Schoolteacher and Soldier

ON THE BASIS of tangible assets, John Wesley Powell did not seem destined for success. He came from humble agrarian origins. He did not have money. He did not possess an earned degree. He did not have a right arm.

But Powell had some intangible assets that made up for the tangibles he lacked. He had a brilliant mind and possessed drive, verve, shrewdness, and intellectual curiosity. Endowed with a forceful personality, he attracted faithful friends and made bitter enemies. He could write and speak well, and there was a clear purposefulness in all his actions.

These assets were sufficient to insure his success. "The Major," as he was fondly called, emerged as the scientific leader of the period 1875–1900. He led the United States Geographical and Geological Survey of the Rocky Mountain Region, and he braved the canyons of the Colorado River. He became the spokesman of the nation's scientists in the government. He was the second director of the United States Geological Survey and the founder and first director of the Bureau of American Ethnology.

Major John Wesley Powell was a man who accomplished a

great deal, and his entire career centered about his activities as
leader of one of the Great Surveys.

This great explorer-scientist-administrator sprang from restless English stock, from a family endowed with the pioneer
spirit, constantly on the move from place to place. The pattern
that emerged from its travels was a consistent direction: West.

When John began life on March 24, 1834 (he was nearly five
years younger than Hayden, about eight years older than King
and Wheeler), the family was living at Mount Morris, New
York, in the fertile Genessee Valley. His father, Joseph Powell,
had been a Wesleyan preacher in England, and he was then
living by preaching, farming, and doing a little tailoring. When
John was seven, the family moved to Jackson, Ohio; five years
later the elder Powell sold his Ohio properties, loaded the house-
hold goods on an emigrant wagon, put his family in two car-
riages, and headed westward. Across northern Indiana, through
bustling Chicago, and on up through the green timberland into
Walworth County, in southern Wisconsin, the Powell clan made
its way. There Joseph Powell settled his family on a partly improved farm, and there Wes—as John came to be called—settled
into the backbreaking, dreary routine of a nineteenth-century
American farm.[1]

And there—or somewhere in the farm country—Wes might
have spent the rest of his life had it not been for a few chance
meetings with the world of the intellect. Back in Ohio, he had
studied under the private tutelage of a devout Calvinist and
successful farmer, George Crookham. Intelligent and literate,
Crookham, who was a student of natural history, took a special
interest in Wes Powell and gave the boy his first real taste of
learning.[2]

From then on, Powell nourished an ambition, fuzzy in its
ultimate aim but clear in its immediate goals, to get an education
and leave the farm. And sometimes, as he plowed a straight

[1] Grove Karl Gilbert (ed.), *John Wesley Powell*, 1-4.
[2] *Ibid.*, 3. William Culp Darrah, *Powell of the Colorado*, 11.

furrow, milked the cows, threw slop to the hogs, or pitched hay onto a wagon, he must have thought that it was no use to try to break away from his stern, religious father and go his own way. But as he neared the age of eighteen, when neighboring farm boys were already marrying, raising families, and settling down to farming, just as their fathers had done before them, Wes thought he saw a way out. It was not very romantic, or easy, but it was a workable way, even in the farming country. Wes Powell proposed to teach school.

To be qualified even in those days it was necessary to know *something*, and Wes "studied almost day and night" for six weeks in the garret of the family house in order to qualify. Then, one day late in November, he walked the twenty miles to the superintendent's house, the wind blowing in his face. The school official turned out to be a sympathetic, cultured man, who urged Wes to spend the night there. During the evening, as the wind whistled mournfully outside and the countryside turned into a white wonderland, the family and Wes sat at the supper table, the dim lamp flickering in the occasional drafts. Superintendent and candidate conversed at length about the academic world, the problems of teaching, the material that was being taught. Just before they all retired, the superintendent filled out the certificate, signed it, and handed it to Wes. Without being aware that he had been tested, the young man had passed his examination. The next day, Wes trudged back to his school, where he had been allowed to teach until then without official approval.[3]

Now he could stand in front of his students with his head a little more erect, for his certificate carried with it some small element of prestige. It was, after all, a sort of public recognition of his ability. Yet the young man must have felt that his career was beginning very humbly.

The country school over which Powell presided was located on the north side of the Jefferson County prairie in southern Wisconsin, some thirty miles from his home. It was a one-room, stone schoolhouse, with split-log seats, eight inches in diameter

[3] Gilbert, *John Wesley Powell*, 7.

and about fifteen feet long; around three of the walls, boards set up on pins served as desks. Pupils faced the wall unless called upon. About half of them were older than he, and many were just as advanced in their studies.

Powell met the challenge of keeping ahead of his students by studying more than they did. While the students worked out of one arithmetic, he pored over several; while they used one grammar, he studied three or four. He was fortunate to board at the home of a Mr. Little, whose wife had been a New England school teacher and whose home possessed what Powell considered a marvelous library. Mrs. Little even aided the young man in organizing the geography lectures which he gave to his advanced students and other interested persons one evening a week. For his teaching and lectures, Powell received the fabulous sum of $14.00 a month.[4]

From 1852 until 1861, when he went off to war, Wes Powell's life consisted of teaching, attending various colleges, and, as his interests developed, making natural history excursions. He taught school at Decatur, Clinton, and Hennepin in Illinois;[5] he attended Wheaton College (of which his father was a trustee), Illinois College at Jacksonville, and was registered for a short time at Oberlin, but he never attended any of these colleges for more than a year.[6] And he traversed much of Wisconsin, Illinois, Iowa, and the Iron Mountain region of Missouri collecting shells, minerals, and plants. He probably floated down the Mississippi, possibly from St. Paul to New Orleans, and he also explored along the Ohio and the Decatur rivers.[7] By 1859 he had earned a sufficiently wide reputation to be elected secretary

[4] *Ibid.*, 7–8. Darrah, *Powell of the Colorado*, 27. "John Wesley Powell," *National Cyclopaedia of American Biography*, 340.

[5] "John Wesley Powell," *National Cyclopaedia of American Biography*, 340. Gilbert, *John Wesley Powell*, 10–11.

[6] Darrah, *Powell of the Colorado*, 37, 40.

[7] "John Wesley Powell," *National Cyclopaedia of American Biography*, 340. W. M. Davis, "Biographical Memoir of John Wesley Powell, 1832–1902," National Academy of Sciences, *Biographical Memoirs*, VIII, 13. This is a useful memoir even though Powell's birth date is wrong. Darrah, in *Powell of the Colorado*, 38n., comments, "It is unfortunate so little is known of the river trips of John Wesley Powell."

of the Illinois Natural History Society, of which he had been a member since 1854.[8]

Then came the nation's traumatic experience. The Civil War reached into the quiet farm regions of Illinois and beckoned the boys of the Union to rally to freedom's standard. And Powell, still single (although in love with a cousin in Detroit), twenty-seven years of age, healthy, and convinced of the justice of the Union cause, joined up early in May, 1861, becoming a private in Company H of the Twentieth Illinois.[9]

It would not have been in character for Wes Powell to have remained a private. His comrades soon elected him sergeant major of the regiment, and at the end of the month, when the Twentieth Illinois was mustered into the United States service, he was commissioned second lieutenant. Nor would it have been like him to have pursued the career of soldier with only such training as was given by the army. Even before he was commissioned, he had obtained leave to go to Chicago, some sixty miles away, ostensibly to buy a uniform, but actually to purchase some books on military matters. There he obtained Vauban's book on military engineering, which, with a small volume of tactics and the army regulations, gave him the basis for an above-average knowledge of warfare.[10]

Subsequently, the regiment was ordered to Cape Girardeau, Missouri, where Powell planned the fortifications and directed their construction. He took a brief leave to go to Detroit where he married Emma Dean on November 28, 1861, then returned to duty and promotion to captain of artillery in command of Battery F, Second Illinois Light Artillery. On March 11, 1862, Powell, with his battery consisting of 156 men with full equipment, arrived at Pittsburg Landing. On April 6, the Battle of Shiloh began, one of the bloodiest battles of a bloody, tragic war. On that day, Powell, cognizant of the general situation, soon had his artillery in a peach orchard near a sunken road, where it caused such havoc in the enemy lines that it was dubbed the

[8] "John Wesley Powell," *National Cyclopaedia of American Biography,* 340. "John Wesley Powell," *Dictionary of American Biography,* XV, 146.
[9] Darrah, *Powell of the Colorado,* 47.
[10] Gilbert, *John Wesley Powell,* 13.

"hornet's nest." Shortly after four o'clock, as he raised his right arm to signify "Fire," a half-spent Minié ball struck Powell's wrist, glanced toward the elbow, and buried itself in his flesh. On April 8, the arm was amputated.[11]

The loss of his right arm did not deter this indomitable man. He subsequently saw service in Louisiana, constructing bridges and corduroy roads over bayous and through deep mud, and during the siege of Vicksburg he labored day and night to be ready to open fire at daybreak on July 4, only to have the surrender make his preparations—which he later described as consuming the forty hardest days of his life—useless. Until January, 1865, Powell was on active duty, being attached to the Department of the Tennessee and later taking part in the operations around Atlanta.[12] The military title of major which he had earned in 1864 so suited his personality that he was called "Major" by his friends for the rest of his life.

When he returned to civilian life, Powell was approaching thirty-one. He had a wife to support and a career to get started upon. The question that always confronts the discharged soldier confronted him: what to do? Strictly speaking, he had been a sort of drifter before the war. He had attended several colleges but had failed to earn a degree; he had established a reputation as a naturalist and school teacher, but he had never remained in one place for very long. After four years and many battles, the war had earned him a reputation which he hoped would help him get started again. After all, not every Illinois volunteer who joined as a private returned as a major with an arm shot off to prove his bravery. And the crucible of conflict, while it had deprived him of an arm, had contributed to the development of his character. It taught him lessons of discipline and leadership which proved useful when he became an expedition leader and a high-level administrator.

That his stature had increased was apparent from the offer he then accepted. Instead of returning to public school teaching, he accepted the position of professor of geology at Illinois

[11] *Ibid.* Darrah, *Powell of the Colorado,* 51–60.
[12] "John Wesley Powell," *National Cyclopaedia of American Biography,* 340.

Wesleyan University at a salary of $1,000 per year. Aside from his love of science and teaching, Powell was aware that not far away was Illinois State Normal where the headquarters of the Illionis Natural History Society, of which he was still the secretary, were maintained. In the winter of 1866–67, Powell went to Springfield and obtained from the legislature a small endowment for a museum at Normal. On his return he was elected to the curatorship, although he still remained professor at Illinois Wesleyan.[13]

Such activities were a portent of Powell's future life. He was active in many things, he had many interests, and he was a "doer." When he was in charge, things got done. And with his persuasive manner and articulate presentation of the problems at hand, he confidently appeared before legislators and, later, congressmen and walked off with his plans approved, his aims achieved. John Wesley Powell understood the politics of the new age, and he used them to good advantage. His trip to the state legislature at Springfield was only a modest beginning.

He was also an innovator in the realm of teaching. He believed in the value of field work as an adjunct to the textbook. In mineralogy, he soon started his students on blowpipe analysis, and his students of botany were quickly introduced to the actual world of plants. In zoology, the woods and streams became Powell's laboratory, and field trips introduced his geology students to rocks and fossils.[14]

But Powell was not content with the career that was developing for him in Illinois. He was thirty-three, and his future as a professor and respected scientist in a regional sense was assured. But some of his old wanderlust remained. He wanted to see new places, investigate new and different kinds of flora and fauna. As the summer of 1867 approached, he determined upon a course of action.

[13] Gilbert, *John Wesley Powell*, 23.
[14] *Ibid.*, 24.

12

Preliminary Explorations in Colorado

In the spring of 1867, Ferdinand Vandeveer Hayden went to Washington and applied for the position of geologist in charge of a geological survey of Nebraska. He won the appointment. Clarence King arrived fresh from the high Sierras and succeeded in bringing about the creation of the Fortieth Parallel Survey, with himself as geologist in charge. And a third man, standing militarily erect, possessing a long, dark beard and keen, perceptive eyes, whose empty, pinned-up right sleeve marked his sacrifice for the Union, also walked the streets of Washington and made the calls. He too was seeking government aid—funds for a natural history exploration of Colorado. Yet, in spite of his military background, the one-armed man who introduced himself as Mr. Powell received no money. All he managed to get was the promise of some wagons, livestock, camp equipment, and surveying gadgets from the War Department and the Smithsonian Insitution.[1]

[1] Darrah, *Powell of the Colorado*, 80–82. Powell may have met Hayden at this time. Among Powell's letters there is a note from Meek to Hayden stating that "The bearer, Prof. Powell . . . will call on you to get any suggestions you may be able to give." This does not prove however that a meeting actually took place. See National Archives, R.G. 57, Powell Survey, Letters Received, Vol. I, April 25, 1867.

This set-back did not, however, deter the Major. He raised a sufficiently large sum from various Illinois colleges, gathered together a party of eleven, including his wife Emma, and headed west. Two of the members, Frank Bishop and Almon Harris Thompson, served as loyal co-workers for years to come, and before the Major left Denver he also made the acquaintance of William Byers of the *News* and met Jack Sumner and Oramel G. Howland, both of whom helped him in his later explorations.[2]

By mid-July of 1867, the party was pushing southwestward into the mountains and parks north and northwest of Pikes Peak. It had passed through its shakedown period and was functioning smoothly. The first great achievement was the conquest of Pikes Peak, which was climbed by eight members of the party including Mrs. Powell.[3]

Then they moved northwestward, went over Berthoud Pass (which thousands now cross on U. S. Highway 40) and slowly came down into Middle Park. Like all the high mountain parks of Colorado, it enchanted the visitors, giving them a feeling of dreamy listlessness, of otherworldliness, as if some powerful drug had taken an effect upon them. Situated at a high altitude and relatively flat and treeless, with fresh-water streams tracing green serpentine lines of willow and cottonwood here and there, the park lay peaceful in the midsummer sun. Mountains loomed on all sides, constituting walls of a great natural fortress. Deer, elk, and bear abounded, and trout were plentiful in the streams.

In the evenings, Powell drank his hot, black coffee from a tin cup and strolled around the camp. He leaned against the wagons, or checked on the stock, and as he breathed deeply of the brisk, sage-scented air, his keen eyes scanned the mountains that loomed in all directions. To the southwest from their camp at Hot Sulphur Springs (known to Powell as Middle Park Hot Springs) lay the rugged crests of the Gore Range, with one particularly menacing 13,000-foot peak, later named after him,

[2] Darrah, *Powell of the Colorado*, 84–88.

[3] *Ibid.* However, Mrs. Powell was not, as Darrah points out (page 88), the first woman to climb the peak. That honor belongs to Julia Holmes, a Kansas "Bloomer Girl," who made the climb in 1858. See Bruce Woodard, *The Garden of the Gods Story*, 24–25.

that Powell was to climb in the next year. Due east lay the Continental Divide and Berthoud Pass, and to the northeast Longs Peak loomed, a rugged 14,000-footer with Grand Lake lying at its western base, pouring out the beginnings of the Grand River, later named the Colorado. North and northwest lay more of the rugged peaks of the divide, which follows a twisting course in this region.

But due west lay an area of mystery. Men knew most of what there was to know about the great drainage system of the Missouri, the Ohio, and the Mississippi, but they knew next to nothing about the drainage pattern of the western slope of the Rockies and the Great Basin. Millions of tons of snow and rain water had to be carried off. The Grand, the Gunnison, the Blue, the Eagle, the White, the Snake, the Yampa, and the Green rivers, and their dozens of tributaries, eventually, inexorably came together and formed the mighty Colorado River of the West. Churning up millions of tons of earth, it ground its way juggernaut fashion through the milleniums of time, through any mountains that might rise in its path, down more than 7,000 feet to the level of the sea, where it spilled its silt-saturated water into the Gulf of California. And of these rivers the Green, the Yampa, and the Grand were the most interesting.

Because Powell was curious about the western country and its drainage, he had already asked questions and pieced together a vague picture of the terrain. Most of it lay dry and sterile with deep canyons and gorges formed by rivers slashing their way towards the sea. To the southwest, he had been told, lay the mesas—great tablelands like the Grand Mesa, flat at 10,000 feet, over fifty square miles in area, abundant with wild life. Aspen, piñon, and Engelmann spruce trees grew there, and gemlike little lakes flashed in the sun, yet a few miles away the sagebrush, scorpions, road runners, and rattlers of the desert flourished. On hot days the mesas were distorted by the rising heat waves from the sterile soil. They loomed silent, mysterious, beckoning yet warning away, their great bluffs revealing nakedly their private geologic lives.

Occasionally, valleys opened up, rather than chasms, and spread wide for man's civilized hands to plant them with lettuce and celery and melons, or to establish peach orchards here and there, or to let the hay grow thick and tall, to be harvested and fed to the livestock in winter. The valleys challenged men to consider the potentialities of every oasis in the sterile land and put it to use.

Going westward, the adventure, Powell knew, would be progressive, for the farther a man went, the deeper the canyons became, the drier the land, the more exotic the geologic formations. At the Utah line the terrain was as different, as wild, as lonely, as the heart of darkest Africa.

Powell realized that here, in this great domain of the unrestricted functions of the earth, lay the great challenge for which he had been searching. And years later he said as much in his preface to the *Exploration of the Colorado River of the West.* "While in Middle Park," he wrote, "I explored a little canyon, through which the Grand River runs, immediately below the well-known watering place, Middle Park Hot Springs. Later in the Fall I passed through Cedar Canyon, the gorge by which the Grand leaves the park. The result of this summer's study was to kindle a desire to explore the canyons of the Grand, Green, and Colorado Rivers, and the next summer I organized an expedition with the intention of penetrating still further into the canyon country."[4]

As autumn came on, and the first Powell expedition came down out of the Rockies and headed east, the Major let it be known that he was returning the next year. He was already planning his trip down the Colorado, but he felt that he needed one more season of preliminary investigation in the canyon and plateau country of western Colorado, much farther west than he had penetrated in 1867. So, back again in Illinois, he immediately began preparations for the next field season. Powell obtained aid from the Chicago Academy of Sciences, the Illinois Industrial University at Champaign, the Normal and Wesleyan

[4] 47 Cong., 1 sess., *House Misc. Doc. 6.*

universities at Bloomington, the government, and the railroads.[5] When he set out in late June of 1868 with about twenty friends and students and his wife, rumors were already being circulated that he was going to descend either the Green or the Grand.[6] The rumors were substantially correct save that they were a year premature.

Powell's first major accomplishment in 1868 was his successful ascent of Longs Peak which, so far as is known, had never yet been conquered by a white man.[7] Accompanying him on this climb was William Byers of the *Rocky Mountain News*. He joined Powell's group in mid-August, finding them encamped near the summit of Berthoud Pass, collecting plants, animals, birds, insects, and geologic specimens and making careful barometric observations. Upon his arrival the expedition made its way down through the timber and the high country bogs, through myriads of black gnats and mosquitoes, to the base camp at Hot Sulphur Springs. As soon as preparations were completed, they set out, going up the Grand past the mouth of the Fraser River, pausing now and then to nibble on the gooseberries which were abundant and delectably ripe.[8]

The first night on the trail was interrupted by the human-like wails of a mountain lion. When dawn came, the sleepy campers found the grass white and crisp with frost. A storm, preceded by enshrouding clouds over the peaks, brought with it rain, sleet and actual snow. But undaunted, they pushed on and that night camped at Grand Lake, whose beauty called forth Byers' best writing skill:

> Imagine a great mirror, a mile wide and two miles long, bordered all round with thick timber, and beyond that with stupendous mountains, flecked with patches and great fields of snow, except one narrow, scarce noticeable notch through which the river escapes, and you have Grand Lake. Inside the timber is a beach of

[5] *Rocky Mountain News*, June 28, 1868, p. 1. Reprinted from the Chicago *Republican*.
[6] *Ibid.*
[7] Ormes, *Guide to the Colorado Mountains*, 71.
[8] *Rocky Mountain News*, August 20, 1868, p. 1; August 24, 1868, p. 1.

white sand upon which the waves beat when the mountain gales find their way down so low.[9]

Powell also thought it beautiful, but Grand Lake held more than aesthetic significance for him. Here, he knew, lay the source of the Grand River that flowed on to become the mighty Colorado of the West. Having seen it, he could visualize the whole drainage system of this inland world.

Due east, rising up from the shores of the lake, ridge above ridge, loomed Longs Peak, cresting at 14,255 feet. On its east side was a precipitous cliff which would later offer the rope-and-crampon expert 1,700 feet of danger. On the north side lay a tremendous field of great boulders above which more conservative climbers would later scramble up towards the summit, skirting the east face. On the south and west sides were great masses of loose granite and sheer surfaces of hard rock at an angle steep enough to make progress difficult, and cliffs and shelves here and there challenged any explorer looking for a route up.[10]

Longs Peak represented challenge, but if conquered it would offer more than the exhilaration of victory. Powell knew that the view from the summit must be superb. Probably all the mountain peaks from the Wyoming line on the north to Pikes Peak on the south could be seen. And since Longs was in the Front Range, east of the divide, and higher than most of the mountains in view, he guessed it would offer a panorama of range upon range of mountains to the west. North and Middle parks would appear spread out below, and their river systems might be traced into the rugged canyons that led to junctions with the Colorado or one of its larger tributaries. So, there was scientific reason as well as sporting challenge in the conquest of Longs, and John Wesley Powell proposed to climb the peak in spite of the nerve-sensitive stump of his right arm. From the summit of Longs Peak he could gain a better idea of the drainage system of western Colorado.

[9] *Ibid.*, August 24, 1868, p. 1.
[10] Ormes, *Guide to the Colorado Mountains*, 176–77. Today a steel cable aids climbers on the north side.

On August 20, the party of seven men set out. The group included Powell and his brother Walter, Byers, and a man named Keplinger, who later published his description of the trip.[11] They were all mounted and were accompanied by a single pack mule to lighten their burdens. That mule carried ten days' rations, although the trip was not expected to take that long. In addition, each man carried his own bedding under or behind his saddle, a pistol at his belt, and those not burdened with scientific instruments carried their rifles.

They crossed the Grand River at its outlet and then circled the lake, stumbling and thumping, crackling and cursing, "through a dense mass of fallen brush and timber," until they reached a point on the eastern shore straight across from their camp. Then, swinging their mounts at right angles to the lake, they started up a narrow, steep, rocky ridge, nearly impassable because of fallen timber. It took three hours to make the first four miles, but then the green, virgin timber of the upper mountain was reached, and then the way became much easier. Within another three miles they reached timber line and soon thereafter found themslves on the crest of a sharp, rocky ridge. When they looked down on either side, they saw chains of little lakes, thousands of feet below, "dark and solitary looking in their inaccessibility." As evening came on and the setting sun cast great shadows of the ridges across the chasms to west-facing cliffs, the party returned to timber line and camped for the night at an altitude, according to their barometer, of 11,150 feet.

As they discovered the next day, they were to suffer the setbacks of all true explorers. After much clambering over rocks, or climbing up and down to get around projecting ledges, or slipping and sliding over huge snow banks, they came to a steep, impassable precipice. "We spent the day in searching for a place to get down or around it, but without success," Byers reported, "and were compelled to go into camp, like the night before, at the timber line." Horses and mules could go no farther, so they barricaded the descending route with a few loose stones

[11] L. W. Keplinger, "First Ascent of Long's Peak," *The Trail*, Vol. VII, No. 8 (January, 1914), 13-15.

T. H. O'Sullivan photograph
Bancroft Library

Clarence King in the act of climbing a mountain (King Survey).

T. H. O'Sullivan photograph
Bancroft Library

The Fortieth Parallel (King) Survey en route.

T. H. O'Sullivan photograph
Library of Congress

Salt Lake City and the Wasatch Mountains (King Survey).

T. H. O'Sullivan photograph
Bancroft Library

Expedition camp of the King Survey at Salt Lake. The Fortieth
Parallel flag—showing a geologist's pick and hammer—
is barely discernible at the right.

T. H. O'Sullivan photograph
Bancroft Library

King, wearing a derby hat, in camp.

T. H. O'Sullivan photograph
National Archives

Ambulance wagon and buggy and a portable dark room
amid the desolation of Nevada (King Survey).

The *Nettie* on the Truckee River, Nevada (King Survey).

John Wesley Powell, leader of the U. S. Geographical and
Geological Survey of the Rocky Mountain Region.

and poles and left the animals to graze at will. Escape in any other direction was impossible.

On August 22, 1868, the seven men set out on foot, each man with enough biscuit and bacon for two days, and only "one or two of them" bothered to take along their blankets. It was a hard day, and when it ended, they realized that the rarefied atmosphere of the Rockies had tricked them. Distances had fooled them, and ridges had blended into more distant ridges so well that, from down at Grand Lake, what were in reality several great ridges separated by deep, precipitous valleys and glacial moraines had appeared as one solid mountain. They were as far from the summit of Longs Peak then as they had been the night before. "The night," wrote Byers, "was a cheerless one, with gusts of wind and sprinkles of rain; our only shelter under the sides of an immense boulder, where we shivered the long hours through."[12]

About an hour after dark, Keplinger returned to camp after conducting his own brief reconnaissance. He claimed to have discovered a way to the summit, saying he would have gone on but for the approaching darkness. His guiding the next day saved much time that might have been lost in trying to scale the peak where it was inaccessible.[13]

On August 23, the thermometer dropped as dawn approached, but the day promised to be gloriously fair. By 6:00 A.M., the seven climbers were on their way, kneading their stiff limbs to get the circulation started. Optimism bolstered their reluctant bodies, for they were convinced that on this day white men, for the first time, were going to conquer Longs Peak.[14]

Their final approach was from the south. The mountaineers worked their way up a great rock slide, then scrambled up the steep, narrow gorge down which the river of loose rock had come. Hands as well as feet were needed, and at that altitude every step was a laborious achievement. About seven to eight

[12] *Rocky Mountain News*, September 1, 1868, p. 1.

[13] Keplinger, "First Ascent of Long's Peak," *The Trail*, Vol. VII, No. 8 (January, 1914), 13–14.

[14] Indians may have climbed the peak earlier, perhaps keeping eagle traps there. Ormes, *Guide to the Colorado Rockies*, 71.

hundred feet from the top, the mountain assumed the appearance of a great block of solid granite, a capstone to its great height. At close range, however, faults and passageways appeared and, using caution, coolness, and infinite labor (as Byers described it), with "life depending upon a grasp of the fingers in a crevice that would hardly admit them," the seven men made it to the summit. By 10:00 A.M., they stood as conquerors where no white man had ever stood before.

Powell, loyal to the interests of science, saw to it that barometric and thermometric observations were taken. He had a stone cairn constructed to protect a tin case containing data about their ascent, and a small flagstaff was stuck in the top of the pyramid and a flag unfurled to flutter in the constant wind until it ravelled away. If they were like most climbers who reach the summit of Longs Peak, they probably crouched in the shelter of the rocks for protection from the constant west wind while they counted over thirty alpine lakes and noted many other landmarks.

For three hours they exhilarated in their achievement, enjoyed the view, registered the terrain to the west well in their minds, and outlined their plan of descent. Then they started down. Within two hours they were at the headwaters of the east-flowing St. Vrain, which rises in the glacial valleys south of Longs Peak. They had skirted beautiful little lakes and had crossed great snow fields impregnated with millions of dead grasshoppers, upon which fat bears were seen feasting. That night was an unpleasant one, however, for they had no blankets and little food. But early the next morning they were on their way again, and before noon they were at the base camp luxuriating in a rich breakfast, congratulating themselves upon their successful conquest of a mountain previously considered inaccessible.[15]

The ascent of Longs Peak was indeed an important achievement, and the people back in Illinois could be satisfied that their money was being wisely used. But to the Major it was only incidental to his real purpose. He wanted to go farther west, on into Middle Park, to the larger tributaries and their canyons.

[15] *Rocky Mountain News*, September 1, 1868, p. 1.

And so he continued west exploring in a great north-south arc, pushing ever deeper into the Colorado River drainage system. When Powell came to a new mountain range, he paused to explore it and then went on. The rugged, narrow Gore Range, through which the Grand River cuts its way, challenged his climbing ability, and he and Ned Farrell, one of the Longs Peak climbers, assaulted the highest pinnacles, which by their barometer were just slightly lower than Longs. Oramel G. Howland, another member of the expedition (although he was not one of the climbers) named that peak in the Gorge Range "Powell's Mountain."[16]

As autumn came on, Powell searched for a winter camp. He wanted it to be far enough west for him to be able to reach the Bear River (now known as the Yampa), which flowed westward to a junction with the Green. Although he was never afraid of Indians, he knew that he would be camping in Ute lands, and the feelings of these mountain people also had to be taken into consideration. The Major finally decided upon a small, protected little park just west of the White River Indian Agency. It was a pleasant site, with plenty of good grass for the stock and an abundance of game amidst great spreading cottonwoods. The Indians knew he was there, but Powell was far enough away from their agency to avoid antagonizing them by his presence. What was most important was the strategic location of this little park as a base camp for his winter explorations. Powell was within hiking distance of the Bear and the Green, and northward 175 miles was Green River City—hardly a city, but still a settlement on the Union Pacific Railroad. He knew that it was the logical point to unload boats and supplies from a freight car, launch them on the Green, and begin a long journey of exploration.[17]

The expedition members who remained with the Major set to work constructing three cabins to house the Powells, the two

[16] *Ibid.*, October 14, 1868, p. 4. The peak, now called Mount Powell, is 13,534 feet high, 721 feet lower than Longs Peak. Ormes, *Guide to the Colorado Rockies*, 79.

[17] *Rocky Mountain News*, November 19, 1868, p. 2.

Howland brothers, and the mountaineers Bill Dunn and William Hawkins. A few others may have also stayed with Powell during the winter.[18]

The winter proved favorable for carrying out of further investigations in preparation for the greater adventure to come. There were never more than two to three inches of snow on the ground, the stock thrived, there was excellent hunting, and the Indians behaved themselves.[19] In March, 1869, when the first green leaves were sprouting through the snow, Powell and his party set out for Fort Bridger and the Green River Station on the Union Pacific. Their route lay across rugged, wild, and barren country, northwest through an open valley for some forty-five miles to the Yampa River, then on in the same direction to the Elk River until they reached the confluence of the Vermilion with the Green, at the lower end of Browns Park.[20]

There they camped for a few days, enjoying the protection of this nook among the wastes, surrounded on all sides by high bluffs and mountains. They reviewed their earlier geological studies and then proceeded over still more rugged, dry land to the Green River, camping at Flaming Gorge for a few days. From there they went up to Henry's Fork in Utah, studying the region along the way, then crossed the divide to Fort Bridger in Wyoming Territory.[21] This ended their winter exploration. Powell and his wife Emma went up to the railroad and entrained for the East. But the Major knew he would soon return with boats and supplies. He was going down the river.

[18] Darrah, *Powell of the Colorado,* 104–105.
[19] *Rocky Mountain News,* March 2, 1869, p. 4.
[20] *Rocky Mountain News,* May 14, 1869, p. 2.
[21] J. W. Powell, *Report on the Geology of the Eastern Portion of the Uinta Mountains and a Region of Country Adjacent Thereto,* iv.

13

The Men and the River

As THE POWELLS had trekked northwestward out of their winter camp in the spring of 1869, they had paused occasionally on the brinks of canyons, and sometimes the Major had sat on a rock and gazed for long moments down at the dark ribbon that was the Green River. The one-armed man had some doubts, but he truly felt that the feat of navigating it could be accomplished.

For one thing, the Major had talked to enough Indians, Mormons, and mountain men to piece together a scanty composite knowledge of much of the stream. He knew about the Green, the Grand, and the great tributaries—the Yampa, the White, the San Juan, the Rio Virgin. He had heard no stories possessing the ring of authenticity about any waterfalls comparable to Niagara, nor tales of the river being swallowed up by the mountains. So, as he gazed down at the river, he theorized that men could go down it. There would be rapids—the white water that he could see from the canyon rims told him that, and he also knew that the river had to fall from six to seven thousand feet before reaching tidewater. Still, he was convinced that the river could be navigated.

And his judgment was, after all, based upon some actual experience. Powell knew something about boats and rivers from paddling on the Mississippi and the Ohio and their tributaries, and he had occasionally managed a boat on white water. He knew something about canyons too, especially that the cliffs rarely came right down to the water's edge. Usually there was a space of one foot, a few feet, maybe even one hundred yards between river and cliff. If the rapids proved too dangerous along the way, the men could wade ashore and plan their next moves from the safety of land. The scientist also knew that river men could tell by the looks of the water, by the sounds coming up the canyon, by the geology of the cliffs, what kind of water lay ahead. An unusual roar, the sight of vigorous white foam, or a change in the character of the cliffs were read as warnings. The signal could be given to pitch in to shore while a member of the crew scampered ahead along the banks to see what lay below. Then a decision could be made to run the rapids, lower the boats with ropes, or portage them.

Powell surmised that it could be done. But there were other problems, such as obtaining the money to finance the expedition, getting the boats and the supplies, and finding some men who were willing to make the trip. His brilliant mind had tackled these problems even before he and Emma had boarded the east-bound Union Pacific train at Green River Station, and some of the groundwork had already been laid. He had enlisted for the trip several of the men who had stayed with him through the winter in Middle Park, and when the train pulled into Chicago, he immediately contracted for the boats, which he had already designed. Sending Emma off to her parents in Detroit, he then entrained for the college towns of Illinois and finally for Washington, D.C., where he hoped to raise money and get supplies and scientific equipment.

During the last weeks of April he collected over $1,100 from Illinois Normal and Illinois Industrial University, and he put up over $2,000 of his own money. The Union Pacific and the Burlington agreed to carry his men and supplies to Green River, Joseph Henry of the Smithsonian furnished him with instruments, and the War Department provided supplies. When

Powell got back to Chicago, the boats were ready, and they met with his approval. Three of them "were 21 feet long, 4 feet wide, and 22 inches deep, double ribbed, and with double stem and stern posts." A fourth boat was similar in design but was constructed of white pine instead of oak and was only 16 feet long. The design provided for bulkheads at each end which the Major and the crew called "cabins." These were to buoy up the craft and serve as storage places for the supplies. Unfortunately the cabins were not suitably waterproofed—perhaps that was impossible to do in 1869—and as a result supplies were wet again and again, resulting in widespread spoilage.[1]

In these preparatory activities the Major was so successful that within less than six weeks he had his boats, his money, his supplies, and his crew, and was on his way back to Green River to begin the great adventure.[2]

When he arrived at that desolate little frontier town, his men were already drifting in. First came the "hunters" (as the Major called them) who had been with him in Middle Park.[3] There was Oramel G. Howland, thirty-six years old in 1869, a native of Vermont whose line of work was editing and printing. He had been associated for several years with William N. Byers of the *Rocky Mountain News* and had become prominent in Denver business and social circles. Howland loved the mountains. He

[1] William Culp Darrah (ed.), "The Colorado River Expedition of 1869," *Utah Historical Quarterly*, Vol. XV (1947), 11, 73. Powell's activities between 1867 and 1875 have been adequately researched, and Mr. Darrah has very competently compiled and edited the known journals and letters of the 1869, 1870, and 1871 expeditions (material on 1870 and 1871 appears in *Utah Historical Quarterly*, Vol. XVI). This chapter is based on these journals and letters and some material from Powell's *Exploration of the Colorado River of the West*, which purports to be the story of the 1869 expedition but actually embraces many incidents that occurred in 1871. (Powell does not mention the 1871 party, nor does he credit its loyal and dedicated members.) Unless otherwise noted, I have not relied on Powell's description except where it is borne out by the other sources.

[2] The *Rocky Mountain News*, April 15, 1869, p. 1, mentions that Powell left Green River on April 6. He returned, according to Darrah (*Powell of the Colorado*, 115), on May 11.

[3] Darrah, "The Colorado River Expedition of 1869," *Utah Historical Quarterly*, Vol. XV (1947), 72. Powell's referring to these men as "hunters" indicates that he did not consider them as equals or colleagues on the expedition.

had accompanied Byers into Middle Park in 1868 and had continued on west with the Major, staying with him through the winter of 1869. His brother Seneca Howland was ten years younger—a Union veteran who had been wounded at Gettysburg. Bill Dunn, a third member of the group, had joined Powell in Middle Park the year before, but almost nothing is known about him.[4]

The fourth member of this group was John C. (Jack) Sumner. He was a twenty-nine-year-old Hoosier who had made his living before the Civil War by hunting game birds commercially. During the war he saw considerable action but remained a private for nearly two years before being promoted to corporal. Afterward, he drifted west, called on his sister who was married to William Byers, headed into the hills, and in the spring of 1866 established a trading post in Middle Park. The Major had met Sumner there in 1867, and a letter of introduction from Byers had smoothed the way for pleasant relations which culminated the next year in Sumner's closing his store and accompanying the Major. Jack Sumner was indeed a hunter, a proud, restless man whose forebears had been of the Massachusetts Sumners and whose grandfather had been a governor of both Ohio and Iowa. Many such men roamed the West.[5]

The fifth hunter was William Rhodes Hawkins, who preferred to be known as "Billy Rhodes," or "Missouri," for his home state. Twenty-eight years old in 1869, he had met Powell the year before at Sumner's store and had stayed with him through the winter. He had fought in the war, had been under civilian arrest at one time, and was suspected by the other members of the expedition of being a fugitive from justice. He always got nervous when a sheriff was around.[6]

---

[4] William Culp Darrah, "The Howland Brothers and Bill Dunn," *Utah Historical Quarterly*, Vol. XV (1947), 93. Oramel Howland wrote several letters to the *Rocky Mountain News*: November 19, 1868, p. 2; March 2, 1869, p. 4; May 14, 1869, p. 2.

[5] William Culp Darrah, "John C. Sumner," *Utah Historical Quarterly*, Vol. XV (1947), 109–10.

[6] William Culp Darrah, "Hawkins, Hall, and Goodman," *Utah Historical Quarterly*, Vol. XV (1947), 105–107.

All of these men had stayed with Major Powell and Emma through the winter of 1868–69. After agreeing to serve with Powell, they put their affairs in order and met at Green River Station. Not until many years later did Jack Sumner insist that there had been a verbal monetary agreement. No conclusion can be drawn as to the validity of his claim.[7]

The sixth member was a twenty-one-year-old, Andrew Hall, better known to his friends as "Dare-devil Dick." Born in Scotland, Andy Hall had settled with his mother near Kewanee, Illinois. When he was rejected because of his youth for service in the war, he had joined a wagon train, experienced all manner of adventures, and by 1868 was hauling wood for the railroad near Green River City. Sometime in 1868, the young bullwhacker met Powell. The two got along well, and Hall agreed to trade his bull whip for a pair of oars and try the Colorado. He was one of the two men to paddle all the way down to tidewater (the other was Billy Rhodes Hawkins).[8]

The seventh adventurer was an Englishman, Frank Goodman. Virtually nothing is known of him except that he appeared at Green River City and pleaded to be taken on. He was the first of the crew to abandon the project.[9]

The eighth member was George Young Bradley. Thirty-three years old in 1869, Bradley had seen active service in the Second Massachusetts Infantry and had been injured at Fredericksburg. He was discharged in 1864, but after drifting about re-enlisted in 1867. The Major met Bradley somewhere south of the Union Pacific in 1868 and offered to use his influence to get him out of the army if he would join the Colorado River expedition. Bradley had had his fill of the peacetime army, and when discharged at Fort Bridger by order of the secretary of war, he kept his word. Of medium build, with a dark complexion and brown hair, Bradley was healthy, reasonably cheerful, and intelligent.[10]

[7] See the discussion in Robert Brewster Stanton, *Colorado River Controversies*.

[8] Andrew Hall, "Three Letters by Andrew Hall," *Utah Historical Quarterly*, Vol. XVI (1948), 505–507.

[9] Darrah, "Hawkins, Hall, and Goodman," *Utah Historical Quarterly*, Vol. XV (1947), 108.

[10] William Culp Darrah, "George Young Bradley," *Utah Historical Quarterly*, Vol. XV (1947), 29–30.

The ninth man was Walter Henry Powell, the Major's brother. He was twenty-seven years old in 1869, the victim of terrible experiences as a Confederate prisoner during the war, having undergone a period of insanity while in prison and finally having been exchanged. He had recovered to a degree, but never enough to be able to hold steady employment. After the Colorado River experience his mind failed rapidly, and he spent his final years in a military hospital.[11] One wonders at the Major's judgment in taking his brother along on such a dangerous journey.

And finally there was Major John Wesley Powell, thirty-five years old, in good health, brilliant of mind, and fired with ambition. To the nine men going with him the Colorado meant adventure, but to Powell the accomplishment of the feat meant a leap to success. It could earn him notoriety, open doors, overcome the handicaps of his humble midwestern background and his lack of a college degree. It could establish him as a leader among America's men of science.

With this motley crew of nine, ranging in ages from twenty-one to thirty-six, the one-armed Powell proposed to conquer 800 to 1,000 miles of the mighty Colorado in four little boats, down through mountains and deserts from an altitude of over 6,000 feet to sea level.

From the time the boats were unloaded from the freight cars at Green River, Powell knew that other men would ridicule his feat and discount his accomplishments. Some critics would certainly point out that a substantial part of the lower river had already been explored. Lieutenant Ives, in 1857, had advanced up the Colorado from the mouth to Black Canyon, about twenty miles south of the site of Hoover Dam, in an iron steamer.[12] The public would be reminded that Captain J. N. Macomb had explored from the junction of the Grand and the Green southward to the San Juan, which he then followed for some distance

---

[11] William Culp Darrah, "Walter Henry Powell," *Utah Historical Quarterly*, Vol. XV (1947), 89.

[12] Joseph C. Ives, *Report upon the Colorado River of the West*, 36 Cong., 1 sess., *House Exec. Doc. 90.*

before directing his path southeastward toward Santa Fe.[13] And both of these men had been accompanied by Professor John S. Newberry, who was so incensed by news of Powell's expedition "into the unknown" that he issued a statement to the press setting the record straight. He reminded readers of the Ives and Macomb expeditions and emphasized that only that length of the river between the San Juan and the Little Colorado, a distance of about 200 miles (actually closer to 150), remained virtual *terra incognita* and that a man named White claimed to have descended even that span of the Colorado on a raft.[14]

But many years later, Robert Brewster Stanton, an engineer who had himself descended the Colorado in a boat, investigated White's claim—even interviewed the old man—and completely refuted it. Old James White may have been a horse thief, or a murderer, or a refugee from an Indian scalping knife, but he was not a conqueror of the Colorado.[15]

The Major also knew that there were some "characters" on the frontier who took fiendish delight in publicizing all kinds of absurdities about the river. In the spring of 1867, "Captain" Samuel Adams, for example, had tried to obtain money from Congress for an exploration, emphasizing that the stream was navigable to Callville, Utah, 630 miles above the mouth, and that steamers could probably go up the Colorado all the way to the junction of the Grand and the Green.[16] Adams even turned up at Green River and, in Powell's absence, tried to convince the men that he should be their leader. He showed them letters from Secretary of War Stanton, Thad Stevens, and General Butler, but the men were not convinced, and "Captain" Adams later was reported to be in Denver, trying to organize his own expedition.[17]

[13] U. S. Engineer Department, *Report of Exploring Expedition from Santa Fe, N. Mexico, to Junction of Grand and Green Rivers of Great Colorado of the West in 1859 under Command of J. N. Macomb.*

[14] *Rocky Mountain News*, June 23, 1869, p. 1.

[15] Stanton, *Colorado River Controversies*, 3–93.

[16] New York *Times*, April 12, 1867, p. 5.

[17] Darrah, *Powell of the Colorado*, 116. *Rocky Mountain News*, May 27, 1869,

And the profit that could be derived, the fame that could be gained by the first person to successfully navigate the Colorado River was understood by many an ambitious, wandering frontiersman. Powell knew that the descent of the Colorado in boats was something that was going to be accomplished by someone, and it would be done before many years had elapsed. Powell wanted to get under way as soon as possible.

For nearly two weeks, the Major trained his men and completed his preparations. The crew practiced rowing the boats and learned the idiosyncrasies of each one. They learned the Major's flag signals and were impressed with the importance of watching for such signals at all times and heeding the instructions instantly. The sixteen-foot boat, the one intended to take the lead, was christened the *Emma Dean*. It was to carry scientific instruments, three guns, and three small bundles of clothing. The three twenty-four-foot boats were dubbed the *Maid of the Canyon,* the *No-Name,* and *Kitty Clyde's Sister.* Bacon, beans, flour, sugar, coffee, and some tea were divided more or less equally among the big boats, each of which held about 2,000 pounds—enough, the Major hoped, to keep the expedition going for ten months.

At a little after one o'clock on the afternoon of May 24, the party shoved off from Green River City. The Major had chosen Jack Sumner and Bill Dunn, both acquaintances from Middle Park days, as the boatmen for his little flagship. The moody Walter Powell and George Bradley followed in *Kitty Clyde's Sister;* the two Howlands and Frank Goodman were in the *No-Name,* and the last of the four boats, the *Maid of the Canyon,* was manned by Billy Rhodes Hawkins with the help of young Andy Hall. Four boats and ten men: ahead lay mystery, danger, and, for three of the men, death. But on that spring day in 1869, they were just anxious to get started.

The four boats glided quietly with the flow of the stream while the cottonwood groves and the barren, buff-colored cliffs, silent

p. 4. Later, Adams claimed to have made a trip down the Grand from the town of Breckenridge on the Blue River, a tributary of the Grand (*Rocky Mountain News,* July 7, 1869, p. 4). See also Louis R. Freeman, *The Colorado River: Yesterday, Today and Tomorrow,* 201–22.

and desolate as they had been through geologic time, slipped past. When the Major spoke, it was usually concerning the scientific aspects of the expedition. He mentioned his plans to make astronomic stations every fifty miles, including a determination of latitude and longitude, and barometric observations three times a day. Oramel G. Howland was to draw maps and sections whenever the geology revealed by the canyons warranted such additional work. Bradley understood that he was to show interest in geology and help in the collection of fossils and rocks. And at a more mundane level, Powell reminded Billy Rhodes that he was to be the cook, with Andy Hall occasionally helping. And finally the Major checked to make sure his rubber life belt was in a readily accessible place.[18]

After floating downriver for about seven to ten miles, the expedition put up for the first night in a pleasant grove. The Major, exhilarated and relieved at being on the way, estimated that two more hours of daylight remained, so he climbed the cliffs. From the top he scanned the "barren desolation" that stretched before him, "fantastic carving . . . suggesting rude but weird statuary . . . to make a scene such as the dweller in verdure-clad hill can scarcely appreciate." Then he continued:

> Standing on a high rock, I can look off in every direction over a vast landscape, with salient rocks and cliffs glittering in the evening sun. Dark shadows are settling in the valleys and gulches, and the heights are made higher and the depths deeper by the glamour and witchery of light and shade.
>
> Away to the south, the Uinta Mountains stretch in a long line; high peaks thrust into the sky, and snow-fields glittering like lakes of molten silver; and pine-forests in somber green; and rosy clouds playing around the borders of huge, black masses; and heights and clouds, and mountains and snow-fields, and forests and rock-lands, are blended into one grand view.

And his vision certainly went beyond what he could actually see. He must have thought back to the camp at Grand Lake in

[18] The life belt is mentioned in Stanton, *Colorado River Controversies*, 132–137; a picture of it faces page 224.

1868, passed back in memory to what he had read or heard about the sources of the Green River, up in the Wind River Mountains. There, he knew, among those high boundary ridges of the drainage system, the story of the Colorado of the West really began. Powell later wrote:

> All winter long snow falls, filling the gorges, half burying the forests, and covering the crags and peaks with a mantle woven by the winds from the waves of the sea—a mantle of snow. When the summer sun comes, this snow melts, and tumbles down the mountain-sides in millions of cascades. Ten million cascade brooks unite to form ten thousand torrent creeks, ten thousand torrent creeks unite to form a hundred rivers beset with cataracts; a hundred roaring rivers unite to form the Colorado, which rolls, a mad, turbid stream, into the Gulf of California.[19]

The setting of the sun and the sound of the men gathering firewood reminded the Major that supper was being prepared and that it was time to return to camp.

The next day they got their first dousing. About 9:30 A.M., the lead boat struck a sand bar, and before the signal was noticed two of the other boats ran aground. No damage was done, but some of the men got wet, and since it was raining anyway, they pulled into a cottonwood grove and built a big fire, prepared a pot of coffee, and dried their wet clothes. Bill Rhodes took the opportunity to stalk some mountain sheep and shot a fat lamb that gave the entire crew an excellent dinner. They continued downstream again, camping for an uncomfortable night under rainy skies. So far the Green River had been pleasantly navigable, there had been no serious incidents of any kind, and Bill Rhodes' lamb, as well as a duck and a goose, helped the food situation. The country was broken, with gaunt cliffs and *mauvaises terres* predominating. Deer occasionally leaped out of sight among the cottonwoods and willows, and occasionally mountain

---

[19] Powell, *Exploration of the Colorado River of the West*, 4–10. As I have mentioned, this description is difficult to use because Powell included incidents from the 1871 expedition without indicating such.

goats or mountain sheep, standing like statues in the most precarious spots, watched the strange procession of four boats gliding downriver.

But the weather could have been better, and when they stopped to pick up some supplies that Powell had cached the previous spring, a cold, brisk wind was blowing down from the mountains. Fortunately, the cache, in a cave at the foot of the cliffs, was still intact. Neither wild animals nor Indians had got at it—"chronometer wheels," wrote Powell, "were not taken for Ute hair ornaments, barometer tubes for beads, nor the sextant thrown into the river as 'bad medicine.' "

They coasted on downriver, past the mouth of Henry's Fork, which spilled its waters into the Green from the regions to the west. The terrain became more interesting. When they established camp in another grove below Henry's Fork, they had already entered a deep canyon with "bluffs 1200 feet high and on one side nearly perpendicular," Bradley recorded in his diary. "It is the grandest scenery I have found in the mountains, and I am delighted with it. The river winds like a serpent . . . but instead of rapids it is deep and calm as a lake."

The Major knew that they were about to enter the first of several canyons that would carry them through the east-west running Uinta Mountains, a rather spectacular range with several peaks rising to 12,000 to 13,000 feet.[20] Southward down the river lay "a flaming, brilliant red gorge" cut through "bright vermilion rocks . . . surmounted by broad bands of mottled buff and gray," some of which curved gently down to the water's edge. Because of his explorations in the previous year, Powell knew that the canyon cut southward nearly halfway across the range, then turned eastward almost at the central line, or axis, of the Uintas and continued in that direction for fifty miles, then turned again taking a *southwesterly* bent, cutting diagonally through the south half of the range. Only nature could have been so illogical. Here and there deep lateral canyons carried

---

[20] Interestingly enough, the principal peaks in the Uintas are Hayden Peak, Kings Peak, Marsh Peak, Gilbert Peak, and Mt. Emmons.

tributaries to the Green. Powell knew about them because he had explored along the banks of some of them in the previous year. And he was also aware that along the eastern half of the east-west course, the Green had spread the mountains apart and created a broad valley, protected from the cold winds of winter, a haven for Texas cattle and, at a later date, for outlaws. This was Brown's Hole, so named for an old trapper who had once lived there. For Powell, then, much of the mystery of the next hundred miles or more was gone, and only the question of whether the boats and the men could take the river remained.

But Frank Bradley and the other members of the crew did not experience quite so analytical a feeling. Flaming Gorge was dazzling and beautiful, but as the river sank out of sight deep within the cliffs, they felt that anxiety that even the Major later described—"the shadow of a pang of dread ever present to the mind."

After laying over near the mouth of Henry's Fork for a few days, the expedition broke camp and passed down through Flaming Gorge, then veered left with the river and, with the Major first analyzing the foaming rapids and then flagging his directions from his perch on the *Dean,* shot down the roiling water successfully. Again the river turned, this time to the right, and then, having made a great elongated U, turned eastward.[21] There they camped for the rest of the day, having run in one hour three canyons, which they named Flaming Gorge, Canyon of the Rapids, and Kingfisher Canyon.

For most of the men their lack of skill at the oars made those first few days unforgettable. Actually, they knew nothing about boating, and yet they were on a stream where even the most expert old salt would have his hands full. To the young bull-whacker Andy Hall the physical problem was real enough, but what did one do when he couldn't express himself? He swore "that his boat would 'neither gee nor haw nor whoa worth a damn'—in fact, it 'wasn't *broke* at all!' "[22]

21 Powell mentioned that U only in the account written in 1875.
22 Stanton, *Colorado River Controversies,* 175.

They named their campsite "Beehive Point" for a dome-shaped mountain just across the river. It was full of cells, like a great beehive, and each cell contained nests of the swallows that swarmed about the area. Rhodes killed and dressed some geese, and others regretted the loss in the swirling river of a beaver they had shot.

The next day, May 31, they began the run down Red Canyon, so named for the brilliant sandstone, made even more beautiful by strips of green vegetation that banded it. But the time for sight-seeing had passed. The canyon narrowed, the rate of descent increased, and great rocks cluttered the channel and threatened any imposters with calamity. "In the canyon we would run a bend in the river and prospect ahead with our light boat," Oramel Howland explained in one of his letters to the *News*, "and signal the large boats to come on if all was all right." After the boats cleared the rapids, they were halted in quiet water to be bailed out.

Several times that day the men had to let the craft down slowly with the aid of ropes. First, they tied a length of rope to the bow of a boat and another to the stern. The boat was let down from the stern until the pull became too great, then that rope was released and the rope on the bow was quickly pulled in from a point on the shore downstream. It was tedious work, but it usually got the boats down safely.

The next day the explorers ran some of the finest water of the entire trip—free of rocks but fast as a railroad train. "We ran with the speed of the wind," Howland wrote. They covered one distance of three-quarters of a mile in two minutes, and the Major estimated that they ran one twelve-mile length in an hour, including stoppages. Rest stages of a sort usually came at the end of a series of rapids in a calm, or nearly calm, cove, where the boats were turned in, the water bailed out, and the decision made whether to ride the next rapids, lower the boats by rope, or make a portage. On this day the work ended with the boats being lowered by rope over some falls while all the supplies were carried down. It was on the pleasant prospect of this kind of work for the next day that the men went to sleep that night. This, and the question of the name *ASHLEY* inscribed on the rocks nearby, with the date 1825.[23]

Some fifteen miles were run the next day, and by three o'clock the water had calmed and the walls had opened up—they had reached Brown's Park. There they pitched camp on a grassy spot between two imposing pines and prepared for a day's lay-over. They got out their dampened provisions and spread them out to dry along with their clothes. Meanwhile, the Major went for a walk, climbing a mountain to better comprehend the country. He found the grass "bedecked with crimson velvet flowers, set in groups on the stems of a cactus that was like a huge pear; groups of painted cups were seen here and there, with yellow blossoms protruding through scarlet bracts . . . and the air was fragrant with a white flower of the family 'Rosacae.'" He shot two fat grouse to add to the evening's bill of fare.

Some of the other men had gone hunting, but Bradley, at least, was losing confidence in the nimrod abilities of his friends. "If they have their usual luck," he wrote, *"we shall have bacon for breakfast."* True to his predictions, they returned empty handed. If the crew had to depend on *them*, Bradley added, they would all be "as fat as 'Job's turkey' in a few weeks." For his own contribution, Bradley went fishing and caught twelve white-fish, some of them weighing as much as four pounds.

On June 4, their exploration was resumed. They ran through Swallow Canyon midway through the park, named by them for the presence of the birds there. Then the river calmed again, and camp was established under a giant cottonwood tree. They moored their craft next to a boat belonging to prospectors who had left Green River a few days before them. (Since no other comment appears, it must be presumed that the prospectors were off in the side canyons and were not seen by the Powell party.) Some wild ducks and geese were shot, more fish were caught, and the crew was contented.

[23] This referred to the attempt of General William Ashley to go down the river in 1825. See Harrison Clifford Dale, *The Ashley-Smith Explorations and the Discovery of a Central Route to the Pacific, 1822–1829.*

They laid over another day while the Major took more observations, then resumed their trip. At daybreak the cook, probably Andy Hall, used bullwhacker's phrases to rouse the men. "Roll out! Roll out! Bulls in the corral. Chain up the gap. Roll out! Roll out!" The men did roll out, stretched, yawned, shivered, scratched their beards, drank coffee and ate bacon and biscuits, and started off again, rowing down the limpid stream to the end of Brown's Park. Life grew dull. "Would rather have rapids than still water," Bradley griped, "but think I shall be accommodated." He was looking down the canyon at the end of Brown's Hole. "It looks like a rough one," he added dryly, for the walls were of sandstone, which meant boulders in the stream, rapids, and danger.

Powell scanned the canyon opening, the Gateway to the Canyon of Lodore, as they named it, and felt much the way Bradley felt, but he described his feelings with more of a flair. At noon, he said, the canyon had "opened like a beautiful portal to a region of glory." But as the sun was setting that evening, and the shadows were lengthening, "the vermilion gleams and rosy hues, the green and gray tints are changing to sombre brown above, and black shadows below. Now," Powell wrote with his love of the romantic, "'tis a black portal to a region of gloom."

Whatever lay ahead of them, morning arrived and it was time to travel again. The gateway lay ahead—to gloom, doom, or glory. On June 8, two weeks out of Green River City, they started down the Canyon of Lodore and experienced their worst rapids so far. But the men felt that they understood their watery highway. The waves, for example, were unlike the waves of the sea. On the river, the Major explained, "the water of the wave passes on, while the form remains. The waters plunge down ten or twenty feet, to the foot of a fall, spring up again in a great wave; then down and up, in a series of billows, that gradually disappear in the more quiet waters below; but these waves are always there, and you can stand above and count them." He went on to show how a boat riding the waves "leaps and plunges along with great velocity." If a boat hit just as the wave was breaking back, the breaker could throw spray all over it and wash the men overboard if they did not hold on tightly. If the boat was caught in a cross current it usually capsized, but its compartments would buoy it up and the men could cling to it until they reached shore."

Possibly the men had become overconfident, or perhaps it could not have been helped, but shortly after noon, the Howlands and Frank Goodman failed to catch the Major's signal, and the *No-Name*, perhaps too swamped to be managed, raced on down through the foam, over the brink, and into dangerous rapids and rocks, where her sides were soon stove in. The men clung to her, twice having been thrown out, but eventually it was clear that the craft was completely wrecked. The two Howlands swam to temporary safety on a sandy shoal while Goodman clung for his life to a boulder "as big as a barrel." He had taken on a good deal of water, Howland later wrote, but the two brothers finally got him to the shoal. Then the shoal began to disappear as the water rose (as it always does as the day wears on), and the danger was renewed. Then, Jack Sumner ventured forth in the *Dean* and in a masterful use of the oars steered to the shoal, took the men on board, and returned safely to shore. "We were as glad to shake hands with them," wrote Powell, "as if they had been on a voyage 'round the world and wrecked on a distant coast."

The loss of the *No-Name* was serious, for 2,000 pounds of provisions had been stored in her compartments, besides bedding and clothing for three men. Three guns, ammunition, pistols, knives, belts, scabbards, and half the mess kit had been swept down the Green. Oramel Howland's notes were lost, and worst of all, the barometers, so very essential for hypsometric work, had been inadvertently placed in the *No-Name*. And there she lay, her hulk hung up on an island downriver, white foam and angry rapids all about. Spirits were low that night, not only for the loss but because the white water that had cost one boat still lay ahead, to be conquered on the morrow. Bradley was philosophical: "All's well that ends well," he wrote, "but the end is not yet."

That night, the Major could not sleep for the problems which

the wreck had created. For his scientific work he needed the
barometers. When morning came, he hiked down the shore after
breakfast until he was opposite the island and the bashed-in
hulk of the little boat. Strange how things looked better in the
morning. The night before he had pronounced the danger too
great to send anyone out to the *No-Name*. But in the light of
morning, he decided that it would be worth a try. Jack Sumner
and Andy Hall volunteered to make the trip down to the island in
the *Dean*. While the rest of the crew watched from shore with
what seemed to the Major unusual interest, the two men reached
the *No-Name*, retrieved the barometers and some thermometers,
and then came up with a two-gallon keg of whisky. The mystery
of the men's enthusiasm was solved. Powell had not known of its
presence, but all the others had. Spirits rose perceptibly.

The portage around the rapids took four long, tedious days.
The crew carried the sacks of flour and bacon in stages of about
500 yards, then began all over again. The work was very tiring.
"Have been working like galley slaves all day," protested
Bradley in his best discontented-soldier fashion. "The Major as
usual has chosen the worst camping-ground possible. If I had
a dog that would lie where my bed is tonight I would kill him
burn his collar and swear I never owned him. . . . Have been
wet all day. . . . The clothes in my valise are all wet and I have
nothing dry to put on. . . . I fell today while trying to save my
boat from a rock and have a bad cut over the left eye which
I feel will make an ugly scar. But what odds, it can't disfigure
my ugly mug and it may improve it, who knows?" The next day
the eye was black. "If it is not very *useful*," he remarked, "it is
very ornamental."

When they had completed this portage, the Major wisely
suggested a layover, for they had found a pleasant campsite in a
grove of box elders on the left (east) bank, and everything was
wet and needed drying out. Bradley griped about the souring
flour and complained that the hunters acted too much like school
boys on a holiday. If they would only keep quiet they might get
something! But the warm sun, the prospect of dry clothing,
and the blue sky overhead raised even Bradley's spirits. The

second day in camp he was happier. Walter Powell lay on his back and sang "John Anderson, My Joe." Others played cards or made moccasins or caulked their boats. Oramel Howland and the Major worked on the map. The only apprehension shared by all was that they were still in the Canyon of Lodore, with rapids of unknown severity ahead of them.

During the next few days they did meet with more rapids, until the Canyon of Lodore began to seem interminable. Once, the *Maid of the Canyon* broke away, the hemp rope burning fingers and hands that tried to hold it as the line whipped away in the wake of the boat. But fortunately the craft spun into an eddy and was saved. Then the expedition encountered a second disaster nearly as serious as the loss of the *No-Name*. They were camped on a little point close to some pines, for they needed pitch to caulk the boats. A whirlwind danced through the canyon and spread the cook's fire to the dry sagebrush and pines. In a moment the whole point was a sheath of flames. The men ran for the boats with clothing burned and hair singed. Bradley's neckerchief caught fire and burned his ears, his eyebrows, and even his carefully tended mustache. The cook lost his balance rushing to get into the boat and dropped the cooking and eating utensils into the river. In just the nick of time, with a sigh of relief, the men shoved off and ran down the river a little ways and came in to land again.

Again the fire caught up with them, and this time before they got away one man was left shirtless, another hatless, a third without his pants and with a hole burned in his drawers.

Their letters and journals indicate that the men took the loss from the fire with good humor, but actually it was really a disaster. They were already short of clothing, for much of it had been lost on the *No-Name,* and the constant dampness was proving harmful to what extras they still possessed. The situation would have been even more serious if the obvious privacy of the great canyons, as well as the constant wetting and the danger of accidents where the encumbrances of clothing could contribute to a drowning, had not prompted the men to discard all but their shirts and drawers. Furthermore, the water was not cold, and as they advanced southward it became warmer.

Years later, in 1907, Billy Rhodes Hawkins reminisced about the clothing situation. "It was not long," he said, "before we began to lose our hats and clothes. I had a pair of buckskin breeches. They were so wet all the time that they kept stretching and I kept cutting off the lower ends till I had nothing left but the waist band. When this was gone I was left with a pair of pants and two shirts. I took the pants and one shirt and put them in the boat's locker, as I did not know what the law was below as to nakedness. I cut holes in my shirt tail and tied the loose ends around my legs so they would not bother me in the water." And then he added, "Major Powell said he was dressed when he had his life preserver on.[24]

The loss of many of the cooking utensils simply increased the hardships. Some had been lost on the *No-Name* and still more by the cook's accident at the time of the fire. After that, according to Oramel Howland, the mess kit for the ten men consisted of one gold pan, for making bread, a baking oven with a broken lid, a camp kettle, a frying pan, one large spoon and two teaspoons, three tin plates, and five bailing cups.

The long canyon, the continual run of rapids, the fire, had all contributed to low spirits, but the very next day they ran "at almost railroad speed" down to the mouth of the Yampa River. The Canyon of Lodore had been conquered.

From the mouth of the Yampa at Echo Park—so named by them for its remarkable acoustics—to the mouth of the Uinta River was one of the easier links of the trip. Even so, they ran through the rapids of Split Mountain Canyon and Whirlpool Canyon, where the river had boldly challenged the highest mountains that could possibly have been in its path and had ground out its channel with undaunted insolence. The men caught trout, Billy Rhodes shot a fat buck, and where the canyons widened, antelope pranced among the cedars and, less welcome, great clouds of mosquitoes swarmed.

[24] Stanton, *Colorado River Controversies,* 146.

Such were their experiences until, on June 28, a little over a month out of Green River City, the expedition reached the mouth of the Uinta. It flowed in from the west about one mile and a quarter above the mouth of the White, which flowed in from the east. A pleasant valley spread out before them, with a lake that offered fine duck hunting—a good place to lay over for a while.

For several days the crew rested while the Major and several of the others went in to the Uinta Indian Agency, some twenty-five to thirty miles inland. There they sent out many of the letters that have since been reprinted and traded with the agent there, Powell obtaining an additional 300 pounds of flour. Meanwhile, the men left at camp went currant hunting, gathering great handfuls of the luscious little red berries that were just then ripening. They helped strengthen the bodies of men who had worked terribly hard, living on a diet of bacon and biscuits dipped in the drippings. When they tired of eating currants, they lolled around camp, maintaining smoky fires to keep the mosquitoes away, cooking occasionally, sleeping a lot. Bradley underestimated the swelling power of dried beans in water, and the small pan of them that he started with ended up as a big bread pan filled to the brim. News finally reached them that Frank Goodman, the Englishman who had nearly lost his life when the *No-Name* was wrecked, had given up and left the expedition at the Uinta Agency.

There were nine men, and three boats left to face the river. After five weeks and 300 miles on the great artery, Powell could scan the Green, swollen now by the additional waters of the Yampa, the Uinta, and the White, and could appraise the men and the boats. With replenished supplies, he looked forward to the next grim struggle with confidence.

Meanwhile, in the East, totally unknown to Powell, his expedition was receiving notoriety. A man named John Risdon, one of those strange characters of which the West produced more than its share, had appeared in Cheyenne, Omaha, and Springfield, Illinois, with stories for the local press about the tragic deaths of the gallant Major and all his comrades, who had been drowned and swept on down the River.[25]

Although Mrs. Powell quickly refuted the story, and the *Rocky Mountain News* wrote of "man's extreme capacity to be without object or provocation" and scoffed at the whole affair, and although John Risdon was ultimately jailed as a horse thief, the real consequences of the hoax were favorable. People became interested in Major John Wesley Powell and his valiant crew, and the letters mailed out from the Uinta Agency were widely reprinted. As the New York *Times* later editorialized, it had all "been fortunate for the fame of Major Powell . . . that the rascal Risdon propagated the falsehood of the tragical loss of the whole expedition."[26]

Back on the Green, Powell knew that the next major step would take them from the mouth of the Uinta southward to the mouth of the Grand. This would be a long journey covering about 200 miles, and it would take at least two weeks. But when they started, spirits were high in spite of the hardships that the future promised. "Danger is our life," Oramel Howland had written from the Yampa. "Just let a white foam show itself ahead and everything is as jolly as an Irish 'wake.' "

Yet their first troubles upon leaving the mouth of the Uinta were of an entirely different nature from the usual difficulties. At an island below the White River they found a garden that had been planted by an Indian interpreter whom Powell had met. The plants had gone completely untended, and the owner was not there. Temptation won out, the boats put in, a fire was started, and the pot was filled with water, along with all the beets, carrots, turnips, and potatoes they could find. Since the tubers had barely swelled in the untended soil, the hungry men simply threw in the greens, the stems, *and* the undeveloped roots. After a suitable cooking time the conglomeration was dished out, and all the men save Bradley and one of the Howlands ate the mess with fervor. Then the fire was extinguished,

[25] New York *Times,* July 5, 1869, p. 5.
[26] New York *Times,* July 26, 1869, p. 5.

the pot emptied, and the men all shoved off again in high spirits. Within a mile every man except the two who had not eaten came down sick. They all had to land, and for the remainder of the afternoon they retched and rolled on the ground in agony. "We all learned one lesson," Jack Sumner wrote after his recovery, "—never rob gardens."

Several days later, having recovered from this ordeal, the Major was up to his usual scientific work, climbing the escarpment to see the country above and beyond at every opportunity. Too much concerned with science and too little with what he was doing, the Major found himself in a place where he could neither go up nor come down, and the strain of holding on was taking its toll; he began to shake nervously, and his hold became weaker. Bradley, up above, searched frantically for a stick or a pole for the Major to grab, but none was available. In desperation, he pulled off his drawers and lowered them to Powell, who grabbed them and with their aid—and Bradley on the other end of them—pulled himself up to safety.

They continued down the river, entering a long, narrow gorge with high bleak walls broken by numerous lateral canyons. Sometimes the side canyons were so close together that the intervening walls had caved in, making windows between the great crevices. This gorge they named, appropriately, the Canyon of Desolation. On July 9, the third day in the canyon, a gale of hot air swept without warning through their camp, roaring through the great grottoes, caverns, amphitheaters, crags, and lateral canyons, booming weirdly to the accompaniment of the rushing water. The seering blasts warned that it would be sheer folly to try to walk out to civilization, and all the members exerted more than their usual care with the boats. In some places, the canyon proved swift and exhilarating, in other places it was treacherous and tricky. Once, the *Dean* was swamped, and guns, a barometer, and some bed rolls were lost. Time had to be taken to find suitable lumber to carve out new oars to replace those that had been swept away. But spirits were still high in those first two weeks of July, and Andy Hall "would tear out with a voice like a cross-cut saw . . . 'When he put his arm around her she *bustified* like a forty pounder . . . Away, Away, Away down South in Dixie!' "

Quite suddenly, the tumultuous river leveled off, the current slowed, the mountains spread, lowered, and disappeared. The canyon ended, and a bare desert plain presented itself as far as the eyes could see—dazzling, shimmering, the view waving in the heat waves as if one were looking through a sheet of cheap glass. The men complained of the work as they heaved on the oars in order to make progress. It was quiet, desolate. "Hardly a bird save the ill-omened raven or an occasional eagle scream-ing over us," wrote Bradley, "one feels a sense of loneliness as he looks on the little party, only three boats and nine men, hundreds of miles from civilization." Then briefly they entered another canyon, but the heat reflecting off the sandstone cliffs made the chasm a funnel of hot air. Some sour beans the men had eaten made them all feel sick, and when the Grand River appeared on their left at about five-thirty on the evening of July 16, they all set up a loud hurrah for the respite it promised them.

Again, the Major ordered several days spent in camp. All the supplies were spread out for cleaning and drying. The rancid bacon was temporarily replaced with soup made from two fat beavers which had been killed. Bradley spread a blanket under the shade of some willows and slept off the after effects of the big and unusual feed. The desolate region provided few irritants —no mosquitoes, for example—but the big black crickets that infest that part of the country possessed the loudest chirps he had ever heard, and they got on his nerves. Great cliffs, spires, and domes arose in all directions, bereft of foliage and greenery of any kind. Unearthly, unreal, it was like being on the moon. On July 21, the men were glad to get underway again—nearly two months and about 375 miles out of Green River City.

They had hoped that the Colorado (now that the Grand had joined the Green) would prove easier boating, but the rapids proved just as numerous and just as treacherous: the *Dean* got swamped the first day and three oars were lost. Still the men's morale remained high, for they believed that their rate of fall since Green River had been so great that no more serious rapids should be encountered. The end must be near, they felt, or else they would have to row the final miles up hill, and, Bradley added in his diary, this "is not often the case with rivers." Yet day after day the rapids continued, their clothing stayed wet, the food spoiled. The hard work, the rancid bacon, the sour, moldy flour was beginning to take effect.

But if the men were growing tired, the Major remained entranced by this magic land. One evening before supper he and Bradley and Walter Powell worked their way up a side canyon and came upon an earthly paradise away from the oppressive heat, the roar of the river, the glare of the canyon walls:

> We enter through a very narrow passage, having to wade along the course of a little stream until a cascade interrupts our progress. Then we climb to the right, for a hundred feet, until we reach a little shelf, along which we pass, walking with great care, for it is narrow, until we pass around the fall. Here the gorge widens into a spacious, sky roofed chamber. In the farther end is a beautiful grove of cottonwoods, and between us and the cottonwoods the little stream widens out into three clear lakelets, with bottoms of smooth rock. Beyond the cottonwoods, the brook tumbles, in a series of white, shining cascades, from heights that seem immeasurable. Turning around, we can look through the cleft through which we came, and see the river, with towering walls beyond. What a chamber for a resting place is this! hewn from solid rock; the heavens for a ceiling; cascade fountains within; a grove in the conservatory, clear lakelets for a refreshing bath, and an outlook through the doorway on a raging river, with cliffs and mountains beyond.[27]

And so they continued. July 27, 1869: "We were so lucky as to get two sheep today which in the present reduced state of our ration is hailed as the greatest event of the trip," Bradley recorded. July 28: "Row a mile of smooth water. We came to 100 yards portage, made it on the south side, then ran another mile of smooth water and got to a very bad rapid. . . . Camped on

---

[27] Powell, *Exploration of the Colorado River of the West*, 61–62. This is not mentioned in any other journals of the expedition, which suggests that Powell discovered this grotto in 1871.

the north side at the mouth of a stream. . . . The water is about as filthy as the sewers of some large, dirty city, but stinks more than cologne ever did. It has been named 'Dirty [Devil] Creek.'" Thus did Jack Sumner record the experiences of that day.

August 1: "Up early taking obs. Dropped down ¾ mile and went into camp. Took obs. for time, by Lunar. During afternoon I went into "Music Temple," 100 yds. long, 50 yds. wide, cleft of rock above "skylight" 25 feet wide. Tinkling canyon." Thus did the Major, entranced by the beauty, record the day by day happenings in his journal.

He remained all scientist and sight-seer while his men became increasingly concerned over the problem of mere survival. The Major's thoughtlessness about their situation irritated the men. "Another day wasted foolishly," Bradley remarked when Powell made another exploration. And his insistence upon taking barometric readings and figuring latitude and longitude, when the bacon and coffee were fast being consumed and the only alternative lay in getting out of the canyons, became a sore point with the crew. Even the discovery of abandoned Moqui (Pueblo) dwellings failed to revive the men's spirits—only the killing of another sheep on August 3 really made them happy.

But along with the poor rations and their general fatigue the men had to accept the hardest reality of all: the rapids were getting successively worse, worse than anything they had previously encountered. "Am very tired tonight," Bradley wrote on August 5. "Hope a good sleep will do me good but this constant wetting in fresh water and exposure to a parching sun begins to tell on all of us." Difficult portages had to be made nearly every day, and the limestone cliffs hugging the river presented a magnificent beauty which they all but missed, so miserable did they feel. The Paria River, coming in from the northwest, had been passed on August 4, and the Little Colorado, a loathsome stream, was reached on August 10. Three days before, the Major had tried to observe an eclipse, but failed because of clouds. All the while the food grew more sour and moldy, the rapids continued without letup, the men grew more tired.

Bradley's boots were too worn to hike in, and his clothing was nothing but rags. "Thank God," he wrote on August 11, "the trip is nearly over. . . . The men are uneasy and discontented and anxious to move on. If Major does not do something I fear the consequences, but he is contented and seems to think that biscuit made of sour and musty flour and a few dried apples is ample to sustain a laboring man. If he can only study geology he will be happy without food or shelter but the rest of us are not afflicted with it to an alarming extent."

The Major's affliction included an overpowering interest in science and a love of the beautiful. He left the crew and went for his own walks, enjoying the limestone cliffs, naming Marble Canyon, which he found extremely beautiful. "At one place," he wrote, "I have a walk, for more than a mile, on a marble pavement, all polished and fretted with strange devices, and embossed in a thousand fantastic patterns. Through a cleft in the wall the sun shines on this pavement, which gleams in iridescent beauty."

The mouth of the Little Colorado marked the end of Marble Canyon and the beginning of the long last lap of the journey, for now they were in the Grand Canyon. By August 14, their course had swung around to the west and the expedition was deep in the mother earth—and the rapids grew worse! That night, they all slept in crevices among the rocks or along narrow ledges where to turn over meant to fall into the river. The trip had now lasted two and one-half months, and the river still rolled on, the roar greater, the cataracts swifter and more perilous.

On August 16, the box of soda fell in the river, and from then on their bread was unleavened. True, the scenery was superb—but only the Major appreciated it. Occasionally, a storm broke, and the thunder reverberated through the canyons. And then the wispy gray clouds would come down. The Major described them this way:

> Sometimes they roll down in great masses, filling the gorge with gloom; sometimes they hang above, from wall to wall, and cover the canyon with a roof of impending storm; and we can peer long distances up and down the canyon corridor, with its cloud roof

overhead, its walls of black granite, and its river bright with the
sheen of broken waters. Then, a gust of wind sweeps down a side
gulch, and, making a rift in the clouds, reveals the blue heavens,
and a stream of sunlight pours in. Then, the clouds drift away into
the distance, and hang around crags, and peaks, and pinnacles,
and towers, and walls, and cover them with a mantle, that lifts from
time to time, and sets them all in sharp relief. Then, baby clouds
creep out of side canyons, glide around points, and creep back
again, into more distant gorges. Then, clouds, set in strata, [sweep]
across the canyon, with intervening vista views, to cliffs and rocks
beyond. The clouds are children of the heavens, and when they
play among the rocks, they lift them to the region above.[28]

And after a shower, great cascades of fresh water leaped from
the cliffs and turned to vapor before ever reaching the rocks
below. "There are thousands of them," Bradley wrote, "of all
sizes, pure and white as molten silver."

But the men, down deep in the canyon amidst the foaming,
angry torrent, paid little attention to the beauty. On August 25,
they started on their last sack of flour. Their rations could not
last more than five days. On August 26, they appropriated some
squashes and melons from an Indian camp, but the melons were
not yet ripe. On August 27, better than three months out of
Green River City, camp was made overlooking a series of rapids
that seemed to defy conquest. Would the toil, the danger, the
wetness never cease? Did the River go on forever?

The mere hope for quiet water did not bring it. Tired, weakened by poor food, constantly wet, practically naked, the nine
miserable men ran another twelve miles before noon of the next
day. Then they met "the worst rapid yet seen." Bradley added
in his journal, "The water dashes against the left bank and then
is thrown furiously back against the right. The billows are huge
and I fear our boats could not ride them if we could keep them
off the rocks. The spectacle is appalling to us. We have only sub-
sistence for about five days and have been trying for half a day
to get around this one rapid while there are three others in sight
below. . . . There is discontent in camp tonight and I fear some

[28] *Ibid.*, 85–86.

of the party will take to the mountains but hope not. This is decidedly the darkest day of the trip but I don't despair yet. " 'Tis darkest just before the day,' and I trust our day is about to dawn."

On August 28, 1869, Oramel and Seneca Howland and Bill Dunn left the party. Bradley wrote that they refused to go further, "and we had to let them take to the mountains. They left us with good feelings though we deeply regret their loss for they are fine fellows as I ever had the good fortune to meet."

Now there were six men against the river. They tied the *Emma Dean* to the bank, transferred supplies into the other two boats, ran the first rapid, pulled into an eddy, caught their breaths, and bailed out the water "as the boats shipped nearly half full in a perfect hell of foam." At one point Bradley remained in the boat to keep it from smashing into the rocks on shore. But the rope was not long enough, and it allowed the boat to go out into the current, then be smashed back into the rocks. Below him roared the worst foaming cataract of the entire trip. Suddenly the rope snapped, "flew full thirty feet in the air and the loosened boat dashed out like a war-horse eager for the fray." Bradley held on, and the boat shot through the rapids like lightning. It had seemed impossible, but if Bradley could do it, the Major could, and Powell climbed into the other boat and made the trip safely.

On Sunday, August 29, even Bradley, who had never approved of the way the Major broke the Sabbath, felt justified in continuing the journey, for now it was "a race for life." And that afternoon the terrible ordeal ended. "We came to a low rolling desert," Jack Sumner wrote in his simple frontiersman's English, "and [we] saw plainly that our work of danger was done." The next day they pulled along on smooth water, passing an Indian family "wallowing in the hot sand and ashes." The woman wore half a yard of dirty buckskin and a brass ring. "She was," Sumner commented, "as disgusting a hag as ever rode a broomstick."

A little after one o'clock they came to the mouth of the Virgin River, not far from the Mormon settlement of Callville. There they found three Mormon men and a boy fishing. That afternoon they feasted on fish and squash, lolled in the mental luxury of a great task completed, and sent an Indian to the settlement of St. Thomas, twenty-five miles away, for mail. The terrible ordeal was over.

It was too bad the Howlands and Bill Dunn had left. Just two and one-half more days and they could have been enjoying the fresh melons, the succulent squash, the wonderful feeling of victory.

Powell and his men did not know then, but Oramel and Seneca Howland and Bill Dunn lay dead, full of Shivwits arrows. The river was the safest way out after all.

14

Preparations for Another Trip

ALTHOUGH HE HAD but one arm, Powell was blessed with a good stomach and digestion. Spoiled flour, rancid bacon, and dried apples kept him alive and healthy, and neither the dangers of the Colorado nor its discomforts—the heat, the mosquitoes, the constant wettings—bothered him a whit.

When he emerged from the long journey at the mouth of the Virgin, he was more than ever in love with the Colorado River country. Everything about the great wasteland fascinated him: the Indians, from the primitive Paiutes to the highly civilized Hopis, the white Mormons, establishing their outposts of Zion where few Gentiles were likely to bother them, the geologic story waiting to be read in the naked cliffs, and the problems inherent in the white man's settlement of the arid regions of the West. Even as he sat in safety in the Mormon cabin by the Virgin River, letting the squash, melons, and fish renew his physical strength, Powell was formulating his plans for the future.

First, he wrote off the crew of the 1869 expedition. Bradley and Sumner went on down to Fort Yuma, Hall and Hawkins all the way to sea level. Only Jack Sumner remained even temporarily in correspondence with the Major and was invited on the second trip down the Colorado. (Heavy spring snows prevented his arrival at Green River on time.)[1] Otherwise, as far as the Major was concerned, the four men could disappear into the far corners of the West. After all, they had been just "hunters," camp men, and subordinates, so why waste more time with them?[2]

When everyone else had gone on down the river, the Major and his brother Walter trekked overland to Salt Lake City. While they were there, the news came in that Oramel and Seneca Howland and Bill Dunn had been killed by the Shivwits Indians. This increased the interest in the Major's exploits, and before he left Salt Lake City, he had already given a stirring lecture that had met with a most favorable reception when he delivered it in the assembly rooms of the Thirteenth Ward.[3]

From Salt Lake, the Major headed back east on the newly completed Union Pacific. At Illinois Industrial University, he wound up his affairs and resigned. He had deposited all manner of specimens in unopened boxes there, and had failed to sort them, he had failed to stay there and teach, and generally he had not lived up to his obligations to the school. Then he lectured during the winter of 1870 in the Middle West and in the Northeast, enlarging his reputation. Finally, he received a $12,000 appropriation from Congress "for completing the survey of the Colorado of the West and its tributaries."[4]

Thus did Major John Wesley Powell enter into government survey and exploratory work. He realized that he was still on the periphery of this fertile source of funds, for Ferdinand V. Hayden and Clarence King were already strongly entrenched and Lieutenant George M. Wheeler of the Army Engineers was

---

[1] Darrah, "John C. Sumner," *Utah Historical Quarterly*, Vol. XV (1947), 110.

[2] When Robert Brewster Stanton interviewed Powell in 1892, he began by mentioning that he had "seen one of his old friends of long ago—Jack Sumner." To which Powell replied indifferently, "Is he alive yet?" *Colorado River Controversies*, 110.

[3] Quoted from the *Deseret Evening News*, September 8, 1869; September 17, 1869; by Darrah in "The Colorado River Expedition of 1869," *Utah Historical Quarterly*, Vol. XV (1947), 140-45. The death of Oramel Howland eliminated the one man of some education and literary ability who could have given Powell competition in newspaper stories and lectures.

[4] Darrah, *Powell of the Colorado*, 146-53. *U.S. Statutes at Large*, Vol. 16, 242.

getting his surveys west of the one hundredth meridian well under way. Yet, even though he was a late-comer, Powell knew that he had several advantages working for him. First, as an outsider, he could view the situation of government-in-science far more objectively than the other three scientists could, for they were already deeply absorbed in their own work. Powell spotted the fatal weakness in the situation—the presence of several surveys working the West at the same time, virtually unco-ordinated, wasting government funds. He used this weakness to his own advantage later on. Secondly, the Major could be congenial and suave when he wanted to be, and among the powers in Washington he used his best charm and won over such men as James Garfield, Abram Hewitt, and Spencer Baird. Thirdly, he was an excellent public speaker, an ability which served him well not only on the lecture platform but also whenever he appeared before congressional committees.

And finally he realized that his own survey, the concept of which was jelling in his mind, would embrace an area that had not yet been claimed by Hayden, King, or Wheeler. Powell envisioned a general scientific survey of the great canyon and plateau region between 35° N. and 39° N. and 109° W. and 115° W. This would include an area bounded by the Green River and the Uinta Mountains on the north, the Grand Canyon on the south, and extending from western Colorado, including the lower reaches of the Grand and the Yampa, into east-central Utah. It was on this narrow rectangle that Powell's survey finally centered.

He envisioned a second trip down the Colorado, but first he felt that ways should be found from the Mormon settlements down into the deep canyons, at two or three widely separated points at least, where supplies could be cached to replenish the canyon voyagers as they fought their way down the river. He also wanted to find out, if possible, what had actually happened to the Howlands and Bill Dunn. And, since he was going to map the plateau country, he felt he should acquaint himself with the lay of the land so he could establish a sound plan of procedure for the work.

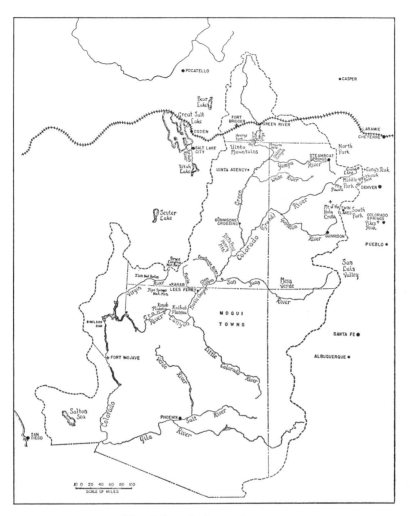

The Colorado River Country

In the autumn of 1870, the Major began his long-range project by making an expedition from Salt Lake City southward and eastward into the tributary river systems of the northern and western side of the Colorado River. It was a hot, arid region in summer, of deserts, piñon and cedar forests, deep canyons, high plateaus, and rugged cliffs. It was inhabited by a few Mormons, and some miserable Indians eked out a desperate

269

existence there. It was not the kind of land for a novice to plunge into blindly, and the one-armed scientist was glad to have the aid of an intelligent, trustworthy Mormon guide named Jacob Hamblin to help him in this colorful but dangerous region.

> We made our way southward to the valley of the Sevier River [Powell later wrote], and then up to the headwaters of that stream. There we were at the summit of a great watershed. The Sevier it-self flows north, and then westward into the lake of the same name. The Rio Virgin, rising near by, flows to the southwest, and enters the Colorado sixty or seventy miles below the Grand Canyon. The Kanab, also rising near by, runs south into the heart of the Grand Canyon. The Paria, which has its source in the same vicinity, runs a little south of east, and enters the river at the head of Marble Canyon. To the north-west of this point other streams, which run into the Colorado, have their sources. Forty or fifty miles away we reach the southern branches of the Dirty Devil River, the mouth of which stream is but a short distance below the junction of the Grand and the Green.[5]

From a point where springs and brooks headed toward larger streams—a central watershed for the area—Powell established a base camp from which his party could carry on southward and eastward to the Colorado. His immediate aim was to find a fairly direct route to the Colorado River, for up until then no such route was known to exist between Gunnison's Crossing, at the Mormon settlement of Green River (not to be confused with Green River City, in Wyoming), and the Crossing of the Fathers, just above the Arizona boundary.[6] This implied that it was impossible to reach the river from the west within a north-south span of roughly 150 miles. Powell thought that there must be a way to the river in this area, and he intended to find it. He

[5] John Wesley Powell, "An Overland Trip to the Grand Canyon," *Scribner's Monthly,* Vol. X, No. 6 (October, 1875), 659. Unless otherwise noted, my account of Powell's 1870 expedition is based on this article and the description in Powell's *Exploration of the Colorado River of the West,* 106–45.

[6] Father Escalante was a Spanish Franciscan who explored the Interior Basin in 1776. See Herbert E. Bolton, "Pageant in the Wilderness: The Story of the Escalante Expedition to the Interior Basin, 1776," *Utah Historical Quarterly,* Vol. XVIII (1950).

also wanted to determine the practicality of the crossing at the mouth of the Paria. Finally, he wanted to find a trail to the Colorado from the north rim of the Grand Canyon. Between September, 1870, and the autumn of 1872, he found satisfactory solutions to all of these problems, which he wrote up in great detail, implying that the work had all been done in 1870.

To help him, Jacob Hamblin, who had done missionary work among the Indians for twenty years, brought a number of the Indians of that area, the Kaibabs, with their chief Chu-ar-ru-um-peak, in to camp with the white men. Quite solemnly, these poor, degraded savages assured Powell that he could not get to the depths of the Colorado Canyon. But they did agree to show him the springs and water pockets without which the men would surely die of thirst.

On September 9, the party set out, and by ten o'clock in the morning the stark contrasts of the desert and canyon country were apparent:

> We made a fair start from the beautiful meadow at the head of the Kanab, and crossed the line of little hills at the head of the Rio Virgin, and passed to the south by a pretty valley, and at ten o'clock came to the brink of a great geographic bench—a line of cliffs. Behind us were cool springs, green meadows, and forest-clad slopes; below us, stretching to the south until the world was lost in blue haze, was a painted desert—not a desert plain, but a desert of rocks cut by deep gorges and relieved by towering cliffs and pinnacled rocks, naked rocks brilliant in the sunlight.[7]

The Powell group picked its way down into this wasteland, this unfinished part of the earth. That night they camped "under an overarching cliff, on the side of a beautiful glen or park," which was enclosed by high rocks on all sides "save up and down the Rio Virgin." When morning came, Powell knew that the logical route to the Grand Canyon was due south, but the Rio Virgin turned west—and its narrow canyon attracted him like flame attracts a moth. So he sent the mules and most of the mem-

[7] Powell, "An Overland Trip to the Grand Canyon," *Scribner's Monthly*, Vol. X, No. 6 (October, 1875), 661.

bers of the party around to a Mormon settlement called Schunesburg, while he and a few others, with a minimum of supplies,
assaulted the canyon.[8]

The Indians called the canyon, which today forms the prin-
ciple part of Zion National Park, *Pa-ru-nu-weap,* or "Roaring
Water Canyon." The party made its way through a "dense
growth of willows, vines, and wild-rose bushes" between the
canyon walls and the stream. They found the Virgin swift though
shallow, most of the time stretching twenty to thirty feet across.
After a few hours along the narrow banks they abandoned all
attempts to keep dry and simply waded downstream, while the
narrow canyon walls became higher and higher, and the men
felt lost in the giant crevice. Sometimes they had to wade in
breast-deep water, occasionally they ran into quicksand, and in
a few places they had to swim, pushing their blankets along on
improvised driftwood rafts. Now and then the canyon widened,
and the river became placid along a flood plain. Beside one of
these, where there "was a huge pile of driftwood and a clump of
box-elders," and where, close by, a great natural spring bubbled
out of the ground, they camped for the night. "Here," Powell
recalled, "we soon had a huge fire; our clothes were spread to
dry; we made a cup of coffee, took out our bread and cheese and
dried beef, and enjoyed a hearty supper." They had wound
down the tortuous, narrow canyon for about eight miles; twelve
hundred feet straight up lay the outside world.

The next day brought them even deeper into the canyon, and
sometimes its course narrowed to twenty feet, at the base, and
occasionally even narrower overhead. "There are places," said
Powell, "where the river, in sweeping by curves, has cut far
under the rocks, but still preserving its narrow channel, so that
there is an overhanging wall on one side and an inclined wall
on the other. In places a few hundred feet above, it becomes
vertical again, and thus the view to the sky is entirely closed.

[8] Schunesburg, or Schoensburg, was one of many little Mormon communities
founded in Mormon "Dixie" in the late 1850's and early 1860's. It was on the
Virgin River, in Washington County. Hubert Howe Bancroft, *History of Utah:
1540–1886,* Vol. XXVI in *Works,* 601n.

Everywhere this deep passage is dark and gloomy, and resounds with the noise of rapid waters." By noon they were at the bottom of a 2,500-foot canyon, but by late afternoon they had come to a little clearing, the Mormon settlement appeared, and their party, supplied with melons and grapes, met them as they emerged, like being born again, from the Canyon of Pa-ru-nu-weap.

Then they succumbed to the temptation of a tributary of the Virgin that came down from the north out of a canyon called Mu-koon-tu-weap, or Straight Canyon. It had smooth walls one thousand feet high, and the stream was fed all along by springs "bursting out at the foot of the walls." But as they passed above the springs in their exploration, the river dwindled into a mere brook, and a diminishing one at that. But to the west, above the walls, were great buttes and pinnacles and towers, which could be seen from seventy miles away. Locally, these great landmarks were called the Temples of the Virgin.

But to the Indians these were the temples of Tu-mu-ur-ru-grait-si-gaip, or Rock Rovers, and this was their land. For years ago (Chief Chu-ar-ru-um-peak of the Kaibabs explained to Powell in camp that evening), a great light was seen somewhere in the region by the Pa-ru-sha-pats, a tribe to the southwest. They thought it was a warning that the dreaded Navahos were approaching, so they lighted signal fires to warn all the other tribes, and this went on from the mountain tops of the whole region. Yet no Navahos appeared. And when the Pa-ru-sha-pats came near, they discovered that the great light was a fire on one of the Temples, "and then they knew that the fire was not kindled by men, for no human being had scaled the rocks. . . . the Rock Rovers had kindled a fire to deceive the people. . . ." Powell was already manifesting an interest in the mythology of these rapidly disappearing people and attempting to set it down before it was lost for all time.[9]

Southward and eastward the party traveled the next day, into an arid land in northern Arizona, and at night they camped

[9] Powell's description of this journey also appears in his *Exploration of the Colorado River of the West*, 108ff., where it is ascribed to 1870. But Frederick L. Dellenbaugh, in *A Canyon Voyage*, 248, points out that the Major made the journey with a Mormon companion and a Paiute in the fall of 1872.

at Pipe Spring, where a nearby cabin attested to the presence of Mormon herders before them.[10] The next day, taking along two Indians as guides, Powell headed into the tremendous Arizona strip—an area between the Utah border and the north rim of the Grand Canyon, hot and desolate, equal in size to Vermont and New Hampshire, but with barely half a dozen springs and water pockets throughout its desert expanse.

> As we started on [Powell wrote], we left behind a long line of cliffs, many hundred feet high, composed of orange and vermilion sandstones. I have named them "Vermilion Cliffs." When we were out a few miles I looked back and saw the morning sun shining in splendor on their painted faces. The salient angles were on fire, and the retreating angles buried in shade. I gazed and gazed until my vision dreamed, and the cliffs appeared on a long bank of purple clouds piled from the horizon high into the heavens. At noon we passed along a ledge of chocolate cliffs, and taking our sandwiches, we made dinner as we rode along.[11]

At nightfall, they camped near a large water pocket, "containing several barrels." This was a relief, for they were traveling with only two kegs of the precious fluid for both men and beasts. The next day, they scrambled over volcanic rock, crossing deep ravines, the heads of canyons opening into the Grand Canyon. Unerringly, the Indians, always carrying their forked canes with which they killed rattlers and picked rodents out of their lairs like a thief picks a lock, led the way, knowing every trail, every landmark, every handhold. That night they camped at *U-nu-pin Pi-ka-vu,* or "Elfin Water Pocket."

On the following day, they made their first contact with the Indians of the region. There were two of them, the male of whom scurried away to carry news to the village, leaving his young, dusky yet comely little wife, Wu-nai-vai, as naked as the day she was born, to pause from her task of picking seeds to meet

---

[10] Pipe Spring National Monument, a forty-acre tract of some historical interest, now occupies this area.

[11] Powell, "An Overland Trip to the Grand Canyon," *Scribner's Monthly,* Vol. X, No. 6 (October, 1875), 662.

with Powell and explain about her master's abrupt departure. The scientist named her Godiva and persuaded the pretty young lady to accept some biscuits. Then he dispatched some of his own Indians to the village to notify them of his peaceful mission. In two more hours they were all at the village, and all was well.

The Major had a remarkable way with Indians. He genuinely trusted these simple people of the arid lands, and he acted accordingly. His attitude told them: "I enjoy being among you and I have no immoral or criminal aims upon you." And his message got through. Their animalistic extrasensory perception told them that the one-armed man was all right. Here was a white man who enjoyed being with them, approached them as equals.

Then, with his acceptance by the Indians achieved, Powell's next step was to cater to their simple whims. By doing this he usually achieved his aims. For example, after grub that first evening the Major asked the chief about their mythology. The chief nodded a negative. Mythology, he explained, was retained for the long nights of winter.

But I had anticipated this [Powell later wrote], and soon some members of the party come with pipes and tobacco, a large kettle of coffee, and a tray of biscuits, and, after sundry ceremonies of pipe lighting and smoking, we all feast, and warmed up by this, to them, unusual good living, it is decided that the night shall be spent in relating mythology. . . . It is long after midnight when the performance is ended. The story itself was interesting, though I had heard it many times before; but never, perhaps, under circumstances more effective. Stretched beneath tall, somber pines; a great camp fire, and by the fire, men, old, wrinkled, and ugly; deformed, blear eyed, wry faced women; lithe, stately young men; pretty but simpering maidens, naked children, all intently listening or laughing and talking by times, their strange faces and dusky forms lit up with the glare of the pine-knot fire. All the circumstances conspired to make it a scene strange and weird.[12]

The next day a grizzled old Indian guide whom Powell called

[12] Powell, *Exploration of the Colorado River of the West,* 122.

"the human pickle" guided the party down through the cliffs to the Colorado River. The trip was not without danger, for night came on, and they had to use torches, made from a tenacious cliff-side bush, to light their way. One group had gone ahead, and their flares gloomily indicated their descent. "Soon," Powell related, "every man of our party had a torch of his own, and the light by the river, and the lights in the opposite gulch, and our own torches, made more manifest the awful darkness which filled the stupendous gorge." But eventually the riverside was reached, where a hot cup of coffee awaited, and a peaceful sleep by the roaring Colorado rejuvenated them.

They needed the rest, for the next morning they had to return to their camp on the mountain side, 6,000 feet above. Powell had achieved his objective, however, for the site on the Colorado could be used as a station for supplies in a future exploration. So, with mission accomplished, they picked their way up to their camp, and did it without incident save for the half-crazed condition of their thirsty horses.

The Major, whose brilliant mind jumped around from geology to land utilization to ethnology and finally to philosophy, was intrigued by the primitive Indians of that arid country. Too poor to attract the trader, and living in a land too arid to attract the settler, these Indians lived out their animal-like existence in stark simplicity. To keep warm they would clear out a "small circular space of ground, . . . bank it around with brush and sand, and wallow in it during the day, and huddle together in a heap at night, men, women, and children, buckskin, rags, and sand." They ate the fruit of the yucca and of cactus plants and the seeds of sunflowers, golden rods, and grasses. Occasionally they caught game, even a mountain sheep or a deer. A Shivwits woman could make as many different dishes from grasshoppers or crickets as an Iowa farm wife could from flour or corn.

His friendliness with the Indians jeopardized the Major's health on at least one occasion during this exploration. The Shivwits Indians had come into camp and, with the aid of Jacob Hamblin, Powell hoped to exact from these reticent people the story of why they had killed the Howlands and Dunn. Prelim-

inaries—for Indians could never be rushed—included a common
smoking of pipes. Powell lit his own pipe, puffed on it a few
times, and handed it on. Then the Indians passed their pipe.

> I can smoke my own pipe in turn [Powell later wrote], but, when
> the Indian pipe comes around, I am nonplussed. It has a large
> stem, which has, at some time, been broken, and now there is a
> buckskin rag wound around it, and tied with sinew, so that the end
> of the stem is a huge mouthful, and looks like the burying ground
> of old dead spittle, venerable for a century. To gain time, I refill it,
> then engage in a very earnest conversation, and, all unawares, I
> pass it to my neighbor unlighted.[13]

From the Indians, Ka-pu-rats (for that was the name the
Shoshones and Utes gave Powell—it meant "one arm") learned
how his men had been killed through mistaken identity. The
Indians had confused them with some miners who had killed
one of their women. And the Indians were sorry:

> When white men kill our people, we kill them. Then they kill
> more of us. It is not good. . . . We do not want their good lands;
> we want our rocks, and the great mountains where our fathers
> lived. We are very poor; we are very ignorant; but we are very
> honest. You have horses and many things. You are very wise; you
> have a good heart. We will be friends.[14]

By this time, the Major had found several trails down to the
Colorado and had cleared up the mystery surrounding the death
of the Howlands and Dunn. He had exacted a promise from the
Indians that they would not harm his men, who would be coming
into their lands for awhile. Thus the ground work was laid for
the next year's trip down the Colorado and for a general survey
of the plateau and canyon wilderness of southern Utah.

He gave the mountains wherein he had talked with the
Shivwits the Indian name of Uinkarets, and he wisely named
the highest point Mount Trumbull in honor of the senator from
Illinois. After climbing it, he returned to civilization by way of

[13] *Ibid.*, 129.
[14] *Ibid.*, 130.

Pipe Spring and Kanab. Later on in the season he went down into the desert area of northeastern Arizona and visited the Hopi villages there.[15] He then worked his way east by way of Fort Defiance, New Mexico, where he offered his good services to help Hamblin conclude a treaty of peace with the Navaho Indians.[16]

And so the preliminary work in the year 1870 came to an end. Back east again, Powell called on his Washington friends and told them what he had done and what he proposed to do. Professor Henry was especially impressed with "the extensive series of specimens" which the Major had added to the collections of the Smithsonian Institution and the National Museum. He also looked with favor upon Powell's plans for systematic work on the flora and fauna and the Indian relics and mythology, the geologic investigation of the area, and the topographical work aimed toward an eventual mapping of the plateau, canyon, and desert country. He recommended a continuation of appropriations for the work.[17]

When the $12,000 became available Powell began preparations for the second descent of the Green and Colorado Rivers, with additional plans for the mapping of the surrounding country. He had taken his cue from Hayden and King, and he now considered his survey to include a general geographical and scientific investigation of the plateau and canyon country of Utah, Arizona, and parts of western Colorado and New Mexico.[18]

[15] John Wesley Powell, "The Ancient Province of Tusayan," *Scribner's Monthly*, Vol. XI, No. 1 (December, 1875), 193–213.

[16] Powell, *Survey of the Colorado River of the West*, 152–53.

[17] *Annual Report of the Smithsonian Institution for 1871*, Departmental edition, 26. Powell worked under the Smithsonian Institution until 1874, when his survey was placed under the jurisdiction of the Department of the Interior. Lawrence F. Schmeckebier's *Catalogue and Index of the Hayden, King, Powell, and Wheeler Surveys* does not list any items for the Powell Survey until the first report under the Interior Department in 1876. But commonly, Powell's western work from 1867 until the consolidation of the Great Surveys into the U.S. Geological Survey in 1879 has been considered as "the Powell Survey," and is so considered here.

[18] John Wesley Powell, *Survey of the Colorado River of the West*, 42 Cong., 2 sess., *House Misc. Doc. 173*, 2. National Academy of Sciences, *A Report on the Surveys of the Territories*, 45 Cong., 3 sess., *House Misc. Doc. 5*, 22.

And from 1871 on, the pattern of the Powell Survey was remarkably similar to the patterns of the other Great Surveys. Every year until 1879, its men set out for the territories, made their triangulations, and climbed the peaks just as the topographers of the other surveys were doing. The Powell geologists, like their brethern with other organizations, scrambled up cliffs and across plateaus hacking at the formations with their picks, examining fragments, and carrying some of them back to camp, there to be studied with greater care and possibly classified, packed, and shipped out by buckboard and railroad to a final depository in the rambling Smithsonian buildings in Washington. Photographers, topographers, geologists, and occasionally journalists and artists accompanied the groups. And despite his love for pure science, Powell followed Hayden's pattern by at least paying lip service to the practical: he searched also for "coal, salt, the metals, and other resources of the country."[19]

[19] Powell, *Report of the Survey of the Colorado River of the West,* Letter of Transmittal of Professor Henry of the Smithsonian Institution, 42 Cong., 3 sess., *House Misc. Doc. 76,* 1.

15

The Second Trip

DESPITE HIS CONTACTS with leading men of science and the fact that he was receiving financial aid from Congress, the Major chose the personnel for his 1871 expedition from among his Illinois friends and relatives. His reasons for doing this are as unknown as they are unforgivable. Surely Spencer Baird and Joseph Henry could have suggested better appointees. But whatever the circumstances, Powell chose three relatives, a fourth man who was a cousin of Oramel Howland, and the rest Illinois veterans of the Civil War. For the most part they were brave and sincere men, but they were not the best men available.

The most important individual hired by the Major was Almon Harris Thompson, who had accompanied him to Colorado in 1867. A New Hampshire–born school teacher, Thompson, thirty-one years old in 1871, had graduated from Wheaton College, served as a first lieutenant in the Civil War, been superintendent of schools at Lacon and Bloomington, Illinois, and in 1869 had been appointed acting curator of the Illinois Natural History Society. Thompson—"Prof" as the men called him—loved mathematics and science, and since he was well acquainted with Powell both professionally and through his marriage to Powell's sister, the logic if not the wisdom of his appointment becomes apparent. Powell placed him in complete charge of the geographical—that is, topographical—work and much of the time left Thompson in Utah as the field supervisor while he was busy elsewhere. Thompson learned the techniques of good map work as he went along and finally emerged as a capable geographer. By 1878 his competence was sufficiently recognized for him to be appointed the chief geographer of the United States Geological Survey, a post which he retained until his death in 1906.[1]

Francis Marion Bishop, also a veteran of the 1867 trip, was hired as a topographer. He was twenty-eight years old in 1871, New York born, and a veteran of the Civil War with the scars of a serious wound in his upper chest, a memento of the Battle of Fredericksburg. After the war he had attended Wesleyan University at Bloomington and graduated from that institution in 1870. One of his professors had been John Wesley Powell, and it was from this contact that he was appointed as topographer of the expedition. (Actually, Thompson was the chief topographer, but he was called the "geographer.") Bishop was a very religious man, resenting the Major's violation of the Sabbath as a day of rest. "Perhaps I miss most the dear privileges of the Christian Church," he wrote at one place in his journal, "thrown as I am among so many who, if not infidels full-grown, are embryotic [*sic*], and I fear are germs of vigorous growth."[2] In addition, he was troubled with pleurisy. Nevertheless, Bishop stuck with the Major until the Colorado River map was completed in 1872, at which time he settled down in Salt Lake, became a Mormon, and lived a long and useful life, dying in 1933.[3]

Particularly important was flame-haired, seventeen-year-old Frederick Samuel Dellenbaugh. He was a relative of Thompson's, and since he was known as a budding young artist, Powell

[1] Herbert E. Gregory (ed.), "Diary of Almon Harris Thompson," *Utah Historical Quarterly*, Vol. VII (1939), 5–10.

[2] Francis Marion Bishop, "Captain Francis Marion Bishop's Journal," *Utah Historical Quarterly*, Vol. XV (1947), 184.

[3] Ralph B. Chamberlain, "Francis Marion Bishop," *Utah Historical Quarterly*, Vol. XV (1947), 155–58.

offered him the position of assistant topographer. Fred was spirited, literate, and agreeable, a lover of the outdoors and an inveterate romanticist. The Colorado River expedition was the key to his entire life, for although he traveled widely through the West, and then studied painting in Europe, his greatest contributions were his many books about the West and exploration. Two of his volumes dealt with the Colorado. *The Romance of the Colorado River* (1902) was a historical elaboration, and *A Canyon Voyage* (1908) was his narrative of the journey down the Colorado. It breathes the excitement, the mystery of the great abyss, and pulsates with the interest of a man who, a generation after the event, still considered it the most thrilling episode of his life. Whether he is relating the thrill of discovering naked footprints, only to be told that they belong to a grizzly, or describing the appearance of the Indian Douglas-Boy with his comely, stolen wife, or recalling the dangerous rapids, with Jack Hillers singing "We will cross to Killiloo, whacky-whay!" Dellenbaugh's book reflects the meeting of eternal youth with a youthful and unexplored land. Fred Dellenbaugh lived to be eighty-two years old, was a member of many societies, and in later years shared honors with William Henry Jackson at the Explorers' Club in New York.[4]

Stephen Vandeveer Jones, assistant topographer, must be mentioned primarily because of the excellence of his journal, which for clarity and good English stands as the best of the group. A Wisconsin-born teacher, thirty-one years old in 1871, he learned of the expedition from Thompson, applied for the job, and was hired. He was an uncomplaining, loyal employee, accepting rheumatism so severe that he could not get out of bed, kicks from horses, and poor food all as part of the job. He remained in the field until the basic topographic work had been accomplished.[5]

John Steward, thirty years old in 1871, was a geologist with

[4] William Culp Darrah, "Frederick Samuel Dellenbaugh," *Utah Historical Quarterly*, Vol. XVI (1948), 497–99. Jackson, *Time Exposure*, 333.

[5] Herbert E. Gregory, "Stephen Vandeveer Jones," *Utah Historical Quarterly*, Vol. XVI (1948), 11–18.

Powell for six months, but the trip down the river broke his health (he had suffered a chest wound and a back injury during the war), and he became somewhat bitter toward the Major.[6] Clem Powell, the Major's first cousin, wrote his journal with some verve and clarity. He was only twenty-one, considered himself "above" the others culturally, and teamed with Bishop most of the time.[7] There was a professional photographer from New York, E. O. Beaman, who took about 350 pictures before he resigned in January, 1872. And the last two members of the expedition (besides the Major) were Frank Richardson, a family friend who left the party at Browns Park, and Andy Hattan, the cook—and a good one.[8]

These, then, were the men Powell chose to make the second descent of the Green and Colorado rivers. He hoped they would successfully carry out their assigned duties—topographical and hypsometric work, sketching, photography—and prove competent, brave river men who could get along well together under conditions of considerable tension. And if all went well, the Major planned to continue scientific work in the plateau and canyon country, west and north of the river, until a map could be drawn.

For purposes of clarity, a statement of how the Major's plans materialized is perhaps acceptable here. From May 22 until October 26, 1871, the men went down the river from Green River, Wyoming, to Lees Ferry, at the mouth of the Paria. Powell left them on July 7 at Island Park just below Whirlpool Canyon, and they were to follow him to the mouth of the Uinta and wait there for his return from the Uinta Agency. As things developed, however, they did not see the Major again until Gunnison's Crossing; on October 10 he left them again at the Crossing of the Fathers, went up to Kanab, geologizing on the

[6] William Culp Darrah, "John F. Steward," *Utah Historical Quarterly*, Vol. XVI (1948), 175–79.

[7] Charles Kelly, "Walter Clement Powell," *Utah Historical Quarterly*, Vol. XVI, (1948), 253–55.

[8] Herbert E. Gregory, "Beaman, Fennemore, Hillers, Dellenbaugh, Johnson and Hattan," *Utah Historical Quarterly*, Vol. XVI (1948), 491–503.

way, and did not see them again until early in December at Kanab. During Powell's absence the river party was under the direction of Professor Thompson.

From November, 1871, until August, 1872, the Powell group— Thompson, Jones, Hillers, Dellenbaugh, Andy Hattan, Clem Powell, and the Major—mapped the great southern expanse of Utah and Arizona north of the Grand Canyon. And from August 17 until September 7, 1872, the exploration was continued in boats from Lees Ferry at the mouth of the Paria to the mouth of the Kanab Canyon. The party could have gone further, but to do so would not have added to their knowledge, so they wisely stopped where they were. Then they made their way back to Kanab, completed the preliminary map, and Fred Dellenbaugh carried it out to Salt Lake City, guarding it in its tin tube (made by a local tinsmith) with his very life. He arrived at Salt Lake on February 25, 1873, and put the map on the eastbound train. Thus ended the first phase of the work of the Powell Survey.[9]

Our first interest, then, is in the boat journey from Green River City to Lees Ferry at the mouth of the Paria. For the Major it was, of course, a repeat of his voyage of two summers before, but this time, building upon experience, he hoped to conduct an expedition more scientific than exploratory.

Powell had contracted for three new boats of essentially the same design as the ones he had used previously, the only substantial difference being that they contained a middle bulkhead. The boats arrived at Green River in time, the freight car was pushed to a siding by the river, and there they were carefully lowered into the water. They were named the *Emma Dean,* the *Nellie Powell,* and the *Cañonita.* Base camp was established among some willows, and Andy Hattan was soon at work turning out the basic grub. Food was boiled, baked, fried, or stewed from a pantry of flour, beans, rice, bacon, dried apples and peaches, sugar, tea, and coffee. Bread and biscuits were baked in a Dutch oven—"a sort of skillet of cast iron, about three inches

[9] Gregory, "Diary of Almon Harris Thompson," *Utah Historical Quarterly,* Vol. VII (1939), 6–7, 25, 30, 63. Frederick Dellenbaugh, *A Canyon Voyage,* 261–67. The John D. Lee who ran Lees Ferry was implicated in the Mountain Meadows Massacre and was brought to justice and executed in 1877.

deep, ten or twelve inches in diameter, with short legs, and a cast iron cover with a turned-up rim that would hold hot coals." Saleratus—baking soda—and cream of tartar were used to make dough rise.[10]

The crew waited at Green River from April 29 until May 22, getting acquainted with one another, caulking and painting the boats. In a day before plastics and zippers, the Major ordered green canvas, which was stretched upon the decks of the cabins and buttoned. It kept the water out of the hatch joints. When this was done, the crew turned to the matter of packing. The Major, fully aware of the wet voyage that lay ahead, also purchased rubber sacks, "each having a soft mouth inside a double lip with a row of eyelets in each lip through which ran a strong cord. When the soft mouth was rolled up," Dellenbaugh explained, "the air was forced out, and the lips could be drawn to a bunch by means of the cord." In addition, each rubber bag was encased in a heavy cotton one. Powell restricted each man to 100 pounds including blankets, and each person was given two rubber bags—one for bedding, the other for personal effects.

On May 22, the period of relative inactivity ended. At ten o'clock the three little boats shoved off into the current. First there was the *Dean*, with the Major sitting in an armchair lashed to the deck of the middle compartment. He was thirty-eight years old, with a bushy beard broken by streaks of gray and a sturdy, well-filled body that spoke of good health. At the steering oar was Stephen Vandeveer Jones; Jack Hillers moved the oars in the after standing room, and seventeen-year-old Fred Dellenbaugh pulled at the bow oars.

Next came the *Nellie Powell*, with Thompson steering, Steward, the geologist, rowing aft, Bishop forward, and Frank Richardson—the family friend who left the expedition at Browns Park—sitting on the middle deck. In the *Cañonita* the photographer, E. O. Beaman, steered, Andy Hattan rowed aft, and Clem Powell rowed forward. By noon an oar had been broken

[10] My description of these twenty-one months is based on Dellenbaugh's *A Canyon Voyage* and the diaries and journals of the various members of the party as contained in Volumes XV–XVII (1947–49) of the *Utah Historical Quarterly*.

and Clem Powell and Frank Richardson were sent back to Green River to get some thermometers that had been left behind. The voyage was well under way, and unforeseen events were already happening.

At lunch the wind came up and Hattan's fire burned hot. Biscuits with sand were served, and the bacon, three inches thick and almost all grease, tasted good. The clear grease poured over the bread made a nourishing meal for active outdoor men. "And how good it was!" Dellenbaugh recalled. "I was ready to call it one of the greatest delicacies I had ever tasted!"

That night, camp was made nine miles out of Green River. They chose the right bank, in a little valley full of cottonwoods with a deserted cabin to remind the men of civilization. It was cold, but the big fire, the bacon and biscuits, the fragrance of pipe tobacco, and the congeniality of eleven men just beginning a long adventure created a wonderful contentment. Soon they grew tired and bunked down together in twos. Dellenbaugh lay awake as the fire burned down and studied the ragged breaks in the flying clouds. Then, overtired, he went to sleep, dreamed that some men were trying to steal the boats, reached over and began strangling Jones, his bunk mate. Jones yelled and reached for his gun. Everyone was awakened, the youngest member of the party suffered terrible humiliation, and then all went off to sleep again until morning.

And so the voyage began. Days followed days on the river, rapids followed rapids. One night, camped in a clump of pines at the head of Ashley Falls, the full moon came out and played on the river foam, creating a lunar rainbow that "danced fairy-like in the mists." Thompson read aloud from *The Song of Hiawatha* to add charm to the romantic scene. On June 8 they arrived at Browns Park, where they were surprised to find wagons, some Texans named Harrell, and a sizable herd of cattle bedded down for the winter before moving on to California. Here Frank Richardson left the expedition, going with the Harrells over a trail back to Green River.

Here, also, in this peaceful setting, the men got their topographical, hypsometrical, and geological notes in order and traded for some beef, which they "jerked" by hanging it in strips over a slow fire for three to four days. Then they glided down the limpid stream while the .Major, from his armchair, read selections to them from *The Lady of the Lake*. Sometimes, when the water was calm, they lashed the boats together so that conversation could be carried on more easily. Soon, however, they came to the Canyon of Lodore, and the roar up ahead warned them that the peaceful time had ended and rapids lay ahead. They stopped a day and examined a beautiful grotto. Through a crack in the canyon wall it opened up into a great amphitheater, about 100 feet in diameter, with the appearance of a domed top, so close did the walls come together some 1500 feet above. Clear, cold water trickled down over the great boulders and dropped in thousands of sparkling globules, and green mosses and ferns softened the walls. Steward named it "Winnie's Grotto" after his small daughter. As they went farther south on the river they learned to approach such grottoes a little more carefully, for they soon discovered that they were the favorite dwelling places of scorpions and hairy tarantulas.

They navigated Disaster Falls, where the *No-Name* had been wrecked two years before, with no mishaps, although the Major had to give Beaman a dressing-down for ignoring signals. The photographer had been a pilot on the Great Lakes and as a result was a bit too cocky about his prowess in navigating a boat. But this unpleasantness was soon passed over, and the journey continued on down to the mouth of the Yampa. From there the Major took a short trip up that tributary while the rest of the crew remained in camp, except for Clem Powell and Steward, who explored back up the river and nearly drowned when they tried to float a small raft back to camp.[11]

The Major soon returned, and the journey continued. At the bottom of Whirlpool Canyon, Powell took the *Dean* with Jones, Hillers, and Bishop and headed for the mouth of the Uinta. The others were instructed to follow at such a rate as their scientific duties allowed. To cheer up the remaining members, Dellen-

[11] See Darrah, "John F. Steward," *Utah Historical Quarterly*, Vol. XVI (1948), 199–202, for a thrilling description of this narrow escape.

baugh concocted a coffee cake of flour, water, cream of tartar, saleratus, sugar, salt, and ground coffee. So occupied was he with this experiment that when the others returned, tired and hungry after a day's work, all he could offer them was a two-inch-thick "brown, sugary solid" full of coffee grounds. The crew grumbled and ate it, but poor Fred never lived down his attempt at baking coffee cake.

Before they reached the mouth of the Uinta they met their first Indians. Douglas-Boy was a Ute, the son of Chief Douglas of the Northern Utes, and he and his pretty bride, stolen from another tribe, were honeymooning along the river, keeping a sharp lookout for members of her tribe who might be unhappy over the theft of one of their prime saleable women. They had first appeared on July 13, and the young man had shown his bride the white man's "water ponies." They then lingered about camp for another three weeks. The young Indian wore leggings made from a red blanket with a "fin" about five inches wide on the outside of each leg, plain moccasins, and a dirty "hickory" shirt. "His hair," Steward recorded, "was braided into 2 long queues with bits of red cloth tied about the ends and left hanging down a few inches. A profusion of paint completed his ward-robe." The comely young girl wore moccasins that came nearly to her knees; her dress, of navy-blue flannel, was covered with beads of various colors, and around her trim waist she wore a leather belt about four inches wide decorated with brass bangles and a brass buckle. Vermilion paint added to her barbaric beauty, going well with her dark complexion and black eyes. Other Indians were also spotted along the banks of the Green, but as often as not they were so frightened by the sight of the white men that all the males scampered off into the bushes leaving their women to accept sugar, tobacco, or massacre, according to the whims of the intruders. With the Powell men, sugar and tobacco sufficed.

From July 15 until August 5, they remained encamped in the Uinta–White River area. The Major failed to meet them as planned, but Jones and Steward did return with the mail. Time was spent in reading letters from home, writing replies which

Thompson could take out when he went up to the agency, and exploring and putting records in order. During this time Bishop, Steward, and Dellenbaugh packed five days' rations and trekked up the White River in search of a weird, eroded place called Goblin City. They found it at the end of a little valley. It was of "small buttes and square rocks, almost in rows and about the size of small buildings, so that there was a striking suggestion of a town." But it was the fourth week of July, and the heat was intolerable. So they collected a number of poles, conveniently cut by beavers, bound them together with straps from their knapsacks and canteens, and rode the White some eighteen miles toward the Green before abandoning the raft and trudging overland to camp, the irksome meanderings of the White making further river travel a waste of time.[12]

On August 5, they weighed anchor and started downstream toward Gunnisons Crossing. The full crew was along except for the Major, who planned to see them at their next destination. They saw deer bounding through the willows and cottonwoods, and Douglas-Boy and his wife begged their last bit of "sug"— sugar—from the crew. Beaver were plentiful, and they often shot them, but the animals immediately sank into the water and were lost. They did get one on the bank, however, and they found the old fellow to be three feet long, tip to tip, and weighing a good fifty pounds. "The habitations of the beavers here are in the banks," Steward wrote in his journal. "A hole enters at about the water line. The homes are usually covered with bunches of willows cut and brought there. As we passed one of their places this morning we could hear them chattering like a group of children. The sounds are as soft as the voice of a child."

When the men put in to shore at night they were usually wet through, and the first thing they did was get out their rubber sacks, remove dry clothing, put it on, and hang up their wet clothing on tree limbs or over bushes. Usually, as Steward pointed out, their camp was "more grotesque than beautiful." On the evening in which he wrote that description, Dellenbaugh

[12] In 1947, Goblin City had not yet been photographed.

was sitting on the sand singing "Put Me in My Little Bed" and keeping time with a stick that he was beating in the sand, kicking some of it up toward Bishop, who protested with "Methodist oaths." Jack Hillers lay spread-eagled on the ground, letting the sun warm his drenched body. Thompson was down looking over the next day's run, and Jones, "always ready with a mouthful of advice," was pointing out *his* plan for the morrow. Hattan had his hands in the dough, waiting for the Dutch oven to heat, and meanwhile denied that he had laughed when Clem Powell had been thrown into the water. At night the men went to sleep to the chirps of katydids and the occasional howls of wolves and coyotes, while bats flitted about in the gloaming and added a sinister aspect to the great canyons.

On August 25, they reached Gunnisons Crossing at the end of the Canyon of Desolation, and on August 29 the Major appeared with provisions—300 pounds of flour, 20 pounds of sugar, and a little meat. While waiting for Powell's arrival, they had fixed barometers, explored, hunted fossils, and brought their sketches and records up to date. The *Cañonita* had sprung one of its boards, and they mended it with several new ribs, caulking it with pitch which they had to cook over a fire while the sun beat down upon them. "If anyone thinks it is fun," Clem Powell wrote in his journal, "just let him try it, that's all." Fred Dellenbaugh tried his luck at fishing and caught three large Colorado River salmon (actually a giant of the minnow family), one of which weighed twenty pounds. They dressed and cooked that one and were amazed that its heart continued to pulsate at the rate of twenty beats per minute for a full half-hour after removal.

On September 1, Jacob Hamblin, who had brought the pack train in with the Major, left for the settlements, carrying with him forty-two letters from the crew to their loved ones. And the next day they started down the river again. They met swollen streams caused by torrential thunderstorms which came up sometimes in the far distance, sometimes right over them, so that they were drenched both from the river and by the skies. When they got to Labyrinth Canyon, the results of the rain on the walls became very apparent. "Hundreds of beautiful cascades," wrote Dellenbaugh, "were plunging into the river. They were of all sizes, all heights, and almost all colors, chocolate, amber, and red predominating."

They were approaching what the Major later called the Plateau Province, the great area south of the Great Basin. When they climbed out of the canyons, they saw a desolate, barren world of great terraces sloping upward to the north. There were buttes and long ridges; far eastward was the Sierra La Sal, the mountains lying "like blue clouds in the horizon." To the south, towerlike buttes marked the course of the Grand River, and to the southwest the Unknown—later named by Powell the Henry— Mountains arose. "Weird and wild, barren and ghost-like, it seemed like an unknown world," Thompson recorded in his diary. "The River had sunk, all was level; there was no sign of the River, so abruptly had it cut its channel."

On September 15, they arrived at the junction of the Grand and the Green, "at the confluence," Bishop wrote in his journal, "of the two great arteries of this great mountain desert. No more," he added poetically, "shall our frail boats dash through thy turbid waters, Old Green, and no more shall we press on to see the dark flood from the peaks and parks of Colorado. Grand and Green here sink to thy rest, and from thy grave the *Colorado de Grande* shall flow on forever, and on thy bosom henceforth will we battle with rock and wave."

Bishop should have been glad to have battled on the bosom of the watery Colorado, for the junction of the Grand and the Green still lies in perhaps the most remote and barren area left within the borders of the United States. Thirty to fifty miles northeast of the junction is the Arches National Monument and the town of Moab, but what elsewhere? Save for a few Jeep roads, there is little more in any direction than there was when the Major climbed to the plateau to take a look around.

Here they remained a few days while the Major, Hillers, Beaman, Clem Powell, and Dellenbaugh rowed back up the Green some distance to where they could climb out of the canyon and take observations. When they reached the plateau, 1200 to 1300 feet above the rivers, they found themselves in the center of a ghostly, weird, and arid land. "Here," said Dellenbaugh, "was revealed a wide cyclorama that was astounding. Nothing was in sight but barren sandstone, red, yellow, brown, gray, carved into an amazing multitude of towers, buttes, spires, pinnacles, some of them several hundred feet high, and all shimmering under a dazzling sun. It was a marvellous mighty desert of bare rock, chiselled by the ages out of the foundations of the globe, fantastic, extraordinary, antediluvian, labyrinthian, and slashed in all directions by crevices; crevices wide, crevices narrow, crevices medium, some shallow, some dropping till a falling stone clanked resounding into the far hollow depths."

The whole area was broken by great cracks in the surface ranging from a few inches to many yards, and their depths were unfathomable. Here, on this gray sandstone plateau, Beaman and Clem put up their "mountain howitzers"—camera boxes and dark tent—and took pictures. At noon the men sat under a cedar, ate lunch, and smoked, and then Dellenbaugh and Hillers went searching for pitch, the Major and Jones geologized over the area, and Beaman and Clem took more pictures. This land, with its surface as barren as the moon, so attracted Powell that Jones said he "seemed like one entranced," and the Major named the place Sin-av-to-weap—"Spirit Land."

Back from the brink of the plateau they found a whole series of little cedar-studded parks, 200 to 300 acres in extent, which would have been luxuriant save for their complete aridity. Indian relics—potsherds, arrowheads, chips of chalcedon—were everywhere abundant, proving that the Hopis or their ancestors, whom they called Shinumos, had lived there long ago. Down by the river, Andy Hattan discovered a cache containing a round stone kettle of four to five gallons capacity covered with a flat rock and containing "several bundles of split willows tied with cord made from the wild flax." For the Major this was a significant discovery, for it positively identified the Indian culture as Shinumo, for he had seen the Hopis using the willow reeds to make bread trays. Once the entire Colorado River had been populated by these people, but now, save for water pockets here and there, the land was as arid as the Sahara, and the Indian culture that had once been extensive had disappeared.

Before leaving the mouth of the Grand, the rations, which Dellenbaugh described as being reduced "to poverty bulk," were overhauled and evenly distributed among the boats, and daily rations were determined, the bacon ration being cut in half. The crew was beginning to tire after some three and one-half months on the river, and the first accident befell Stephen Jones, who wrenched a leg badly while stepping into one of the boats. Yet the Major knew that some of the worst lay ahead. Cataract Canyon into which they would soon plunge was full of "regular roarers," its coffee-and-cream-colored water plunging downward so violently that they could hear the great boulders being rolled along on the river bed—Dellenbaugh said it "sounded like distant thunder." Driftwood in the canyon lay in great piles, tree trunks pulverized into spongy masses of splinters; blocks of sandstone thirty to forty feet in diameter had come to rest on other boulders and had ground their way into them, two to three feet in, fitting as snugly as a hand in a leather glove.

But with the knowledge gained from experience the men went through Cataract Canyon without serious mishap. However, Andy Hattan made the mistake of putting his foot into his shoe one morning without first turning the shoe upside down. A scorpion that had gone there for warmth during the night stung him painfully, and it affected his health for some time to come. The water was cold now, as autumn came on, and the men shivered and their teeth chattered as they took the continual drenching that the Colorado imposed upon them.

Yet the beauties of the canyons never left them. Two nights before reaching the Dirty Devil they camped along a brief stretch of the river where it ran east and west. The moon arose, Thompson remembered, "directly in the east end of the canyon. The finest moonrise I ever saw. First the clouds became edged with silver while their marrow was blackened dark, then the cliff tops, while all was night around us and the canyon seemed a bottomless abyss. Then the clouds shifted and more and more of their shapes became illumined, the light crept down the cliffs, a little crescent of bright silver hung in the end of the canyon above a black depth of darkness. It then grew larger and larger and we and the canyon were flooded in the light of a full moon. The effect on the rapid below us was startling. Every drip of water glistened as it sprang in the air. Every wave caught a glow and the whole river seemed one dancing sea of light. Where the light fell on cliff, every crevice and crag was shown with startling distinctiveness, rendering the shadows more intense."

They reached the mouth of the smelly Dirty Devil on September 30, but this did not end their task. The Major's plans for a pack train to bring supplies there had not materialized, and the men had only their scant supplies until they reached the Crossing of the Fathers, another one hundred miles down. So the *Cañonita* was cached and most of her supplies placed in the *Dean* so that very little standing room was left in her. Beaman was to ride bow oar in the *Dean* so that Dellenbaugh could do his sketching of the canyon, and Clem Powell was to work the bow oars in the *Nell* so that Bishop could keep up with his map work. Hattan was to ride on the center cabin of the *Nell*. This redistributed the men who had ridden the *Cañonita*.

Their clothes were in rags, their shoes were worn out, their rations about gone. With apprehension they looked forward to their arrival at El Vado de las Padres, for if a pack train was not there they would face starvation. But on October 6, with relief, they sighted a stick with a white flag hanging from it, and soon they met Captain Pardyn Dodds and two prospectors, George Riley and John Bonnemont, with a good supply of rations: the lonely Crossing of the Fathers had been reached. Dellenbaugh hastily donned some new overalls and a new pair of heavy work shoes. The good food revived the men, but the severity of the long voyage was taking its toll. Steward, the geologist, was so sick that for several days he could not get out of bed nor keep anything in his stomach. On October 15 he recorded that he had "spent the worst night of [his] life"; however, the layover at the Crossing helped him to make a gradual, partial recovery. Jones's leg was bothering him, and by mid-October he was mentioning severe rheumatism that he was suffering in both his legs. Hattan, who had been stung by the scorpion, was pale and thin, and Bishop was developing pleurisy and having trouble breathing.

On Tuesday, October 10, the Major left for Kanab, but before starting on downstream the men remained in camp a few more days to rest and get their records in order. Some climbed up to the plateau to get the lay of the land.

On October 14 the men in camp heard a shout and saw an Indian standing, looking them over, on the rocks not far away. They beckoned to him and found themselves looking at a new kind of red man. He wore a red turban, a loose, unbleached cotton shirt, a woven sash at the waist, and "wide unbleached cotton trousers reaching a little below the knee and there slashed up on the outer side for seven or eight inches, bright woven garters twisted around [his] red buckskin leggins below the knee, and red mocassins with turned-up soles and silver buttons." Dellenbaugh further explained that he was a Navaho named Agua Grande and, with his son, his wife, and six others, was bound for the Mormon settlements to trade. Hamblin's treaty of the year before, in which the Major had been an active participant, had encouraged such ventures.

The Indians had forded the stream just below camp at the Crossing of the Fathers, and as soon as Agua Grande was satisfied with the peacefulness of these white men, he signaled for the rest of the party to come on in. Jones met the old chief and they hugged each other—Clem Powell said that he thought he saw a distinct resemblance, but Clem was none too fond of Jones. They found the Navahos a tall and dignified group, with at least one of them possessing a long, drooping, jet-black mustache. When they talked with each other they reminded Clem of a bunch of Dutch geese—"it was gabble, gabble, gabble." Thompson gave the chief a letter instructing Jacob Hamblin to meet the crew at the mouth of the Paria on October 25 rather than on November 1 because of the illness of several of the men. He felt that there was some chance that the letter might fall into

Hamblin's hands, for the Indians would be meeting other white men as they advanced toward the settlements, and in a sparsely settled country, Jacob Hamblin was an important white man. Then the crew, a little skeptical of the honesty of the Navahos, embarked and floated downstream a few miles, leaving the Indians along the bank to watch them disappear and to talk about those strange white men in boats for many moons to come.

On Monday morning, October 23, they rounded a bend and came in sight of the Paria River, the end of the boat journey for 1871. They pitched camp in a dense grove of willows, constructed some wickiups, and broke little trails from one to another. This was camp number 86, and they had been on the river 154 days. Two men, Steward and Jones, were sick, and Bishop was badly run down. But no one had lost life or limb, and topographical work sufficient to make a map of the river had been carried out. So far, the Powell Survey had done well.

The second part of the project began: the exploration and mapping of the plateau country of southern Utah—"Dixie" as the Mormons called it—and of Arizona north and west of the Colorado. This Sahara-like land is almost as desolate today as it was in 1871. Save for a few highways cutting through the canyons and along the ridges, it has remained for the most part uninhabited. In some sections the population has even declined, for the wandering subtribes of the Utes—Paiutes and Shivwits—are no longer around. Only the faint trails of rubber-tired Jeeps used by modern uranium prospectors, or the occasional appearance of a Mormon rancher, attest to the presence of human life. The region is fascinating—at places the mountains and plateaus rise to over 10,000 feet—but in general it should never be explored without the services of a guide. Just because the Powell men could always find water pockets or springs—often just in the nick of time—is no sign that the modern explorer can do the same.

Into this barren land the Mormons came, searching for valleys or pockets where water was available, there to make the desert blossom with the rose. They were like men transported out of the Old Testament. They came as settlers, as men of God, breaking the desolation that reminded them of the lands of the Bible. They laid out their towns, such as St. George and Kanab, with system and intelligence. They constructed little adobe homes, provided for their school houses and their ward assembly halls, obeyed the rulings of the local bishop. Fences soon protected the truck gardens of a half to a full acre that stretched out behind their homes. Irrigation ditches brought the heaven-sent water from its sources to the town where it ran down on either side of the street and sang a tinkling tune of joy and fertility and virility. Milk cows bleated and foaled their calves, and the bearded Mormon farmer kicked the calf aside and filled his pail with the warm white milk, and butter and cheese appeared on the tables. The soil welcomed grapes and peaches and melons of all kinds, and before many seasons the outposts of Zion, down in Dixie, were coming forth with crops of vegetables and fruits, milk and cheese. Wine was made from the grapes, and it tasted good. On the cold winter nights when the settlements lay alone under the star-flecked sky, the good Mormon people assembled at the ward building or at the schoolhouse (often they were the same) and danced to the strains of a fiddle until the wee hours of morning.

"As pioneers," said Dellenbaugh, "the Mormons were superior to any class I have ever come in contact with, their idea being home-making and not skimming the cream off the country with a six-shooter and a whiskey bottle." Kanab was a heaven compared to the typical frontier town—"a ghastly hodge-podge of shacks in the midst of a sea of refuse." The Mormons were a happy, vigorous, basically moral people building with their hands and their muscles, plowing fields and planting orchards, populating with the seed of their loins. Lusty and vigorous, they felt little loneliness in the desolate land: they had all that they wanted, including a final, basic ingredient—plenty to get done.

The Major and his men, Gentiles all, got along remarkably well with the men of Zion. The Mormons were different all right—so much so that the Navahos placed them in an entirely different category from all other white men—but the differences were more apparent to the Mormons than to the Gentiles. To

297

John Wesley Powell they were hard-working farmers. The Major had been raised on a farm. He knew their language.

This was the country, then, that the crew, still camped at the mouth of the Paria, would have to map. They knew that plans called for a continuation of survey work on through the winter, and so they waited impatiently for the pack train to come in with supplies and instructions. Meanwhile, maps were completed and exploration was carried out. Not until November 2, nearly two weeks after they had pitched camp at the Paria, did an old man appear with news that the pack train was up on the plateau. Thompson and Dellenbaugh climbed out to meet it. At first they saw nothing, Fred wrote, "that apparently had not been there for several thousand years," but eventually the train appeared in a draw. They led it down to the Paria, and a sudden increase in activity characterized the camp. On November 6 they headed out from the Paria (where the *Nell* and the *Dean* had been cached) northwestward toward Kanab.

The journey started out slowly. Packing was difficult, for learning to tie a diamond hitch on a mule was not easy after three and one-half months rowing a boat. Then there was the problem of the sick men. For Jones, who was still incapacitated with rheumatism, they found a gentle gray horse called "Doc," brought him to the sick man's willow-bough bed. Joseph Hamblin (Jacob's son) and Beaman lifted the sick man gently onto the horse and then wrapped him in blankets, for it was cold. Clem Powell snorted that Jones had "done nothing but grunt and groan, making a complete fool of himself." That day they reached the plateau, arrived at a "diminutive spring" with just enough water in it for the cook to make coffee and bread, gathered a few armfuls of sagebrush for the fire, and there made camp. The cold grew more intense, and the sick men—Jones with rheumatism, Bishop and Steward with pleurisy—suffered terribly.

The next day they were glad to reach Jacobs Pools, two of them about seven to eight feet long supplying clear, cold water, one for the stock and one for the men. About sunset of the next day they reached two large boulders that had fallen together to form a shelter. Down a little from the spot was an excellent spring. Here, at House Rock, as it was called, Bishop, Clem, Andy, and Fred encamped while Thompson took the ailing Jones and Steward on into Kanab. Fred accompanied the hospital train to the summit of the Kaibab Plateau. Then he returned, after drinking in the splendor of the view to the north and west.

Camp number three of their land operations was then made as comfortable as possible. "We immediately set up a stout 6 x 8 tent that was in the outfit brought from Kanab, and it made a snug sleeping place for the four of us," Dellenbaugh recalled. "Around the fire we rolled big stones for seats, and soon had the gulch in a homelike condition. There was an abundance of dead, fat piñon, which burned like a candle, and we could easily extend our reading into the evenings."

Wolves were a bother. They stole a side of beef which Andy had hung from a tree; they trotted along, licking their chops, as Fred took the horses to the spring. They stole pieces of leather and anything containing any grease at all. Bishop got so exasperated that he rigged up a trap with his Remington pistol, and soon he collected a sizable group of skins, only to have them all stolen by their "wolf relatives," as Dellenbaugh called the howling beasts that still lurked around the camp.

Still, even Bishop, nervous and slightly afflicted on his left side with St. Vitus's dance, was impressed by the beauty of the land. On November 26 he recorded a rare and lovely phenomenon that helped him forget his troubles. "Between our camp and the foot the Kaibab Plateau," he recorded in his journal, "the valley is about 2 miles wide. About 8 o'clock a dense cloud came over the Plateau and the valley was white with a mist of rain. Just at this point, the full, bright disk of the moon burst through the drifting Nimbii a few feet above the edge of the cliff east of us and in the broad band of mellow light that suddenly bathed the valley appeared a perfect lunar bow, a phenomenon not often seen. To us it was a beautiful sight. The light of the moon was so intense that newspapers could be read with ease."

On December 4, they left House Rock, climbed the 2,000 feet to the Kaibab Plateau, and then started northwestward toward

Kanab. Their route lay through a cedar and piñon forest. When they came to its western edge, the men were able to grasp the general outlines of the country they would be mapping.

> We saw again the magnificent, kaleidoscopic, cliff country lying to the north [wrote Dellenbaugh]. First about twenty miles away was a line of low chocolate-coloured cliffs, then a few miles back of this the splendid line of the Vermilion Cliffs, the same which began at the mouth of Glen Canyon and which we had skirted to House Rock Spring. From there the line continued northward till it passed around the north end of the Kaibab, when it struck southwesterly far to our left, where it turned back to the north again, forming one of the longest and finest cliff ranges anywhere to be seen. Above them and some miles still farther back, rising higher, was a line of greyish cliffs following the trend of the Vermilion, and still above these was the broken meandering face of the Pine Cliffs, frosted with snow, whose crest marks the southeastern limits of Fremont's "Great Basin," the end of the High Plateaus, and tops the country at an altitude of some 11,000 feet above sea level. A more extraordinary, bewildering landscape, both as to form and colour, could hardly be found in all the world. Winding our way down to the barren valley, in itself more a high plateau than a valley, we travelled [sic] the rest of the day in the direction of the great cliffs. The sun was just gone when we reached the first low line, and passing through a gap turned into a side gulch thickly studded with cedars, where we saw before us two white-covered waggons, [sic] two or three camp fires blazing, and friends. . . . The fragrance of coffee and frying bacon filled the sharp air, while from the summits of the surrounding cliffs the hungry chorus of yelping wolves sent up their wail of disappointment.[13]

This was Eight Mile Spring, so named for its distance from Kanab. And there lay a domestic scene in the style of southern Utah. Two large tents had been erected, one for the Major's family (for he had brought Emma and their three-month-old daughter down from Salt Lake), and the other for the Thompsons—the Prof, his wife, and her dog Fuzz, a brave little Dandie Dinmont terrier. This was to be the main camp for much of the

[13] Dellenbaugh, *A Canyon Voyage*, 164–65.

winter, and Dellenbaugh was most happy with it, for it had been months since he had been around such domestic surroundings. The wolves were just as bad as they had been at House Rock, though. They carried off two sacks of jerked beef from near Fred's blankets, and the night before that they had pulled a ham out from under Captain Dodd's sleeping head.

The day after their arrival, the Major showed up from Kanab, the first the men had seen of him since he left the camp on the Paria on October 10. Both Thompson and Bishop had complained bitterly about the long delay in getting the survey under way and had expressed discontent over the Major's apparent thoughtlessness about his men, left out in the barrens as they were while he decided what to do next. Now, however, Powell was ready to move. They were to establish a base line south of Kanab and push through their topographical map come snow or rain or drought.

16

The Great Plateau

ON DECEMBER 7, the Thompsons, Andy Hattan, Clem Powell, and Jones (who had nearly recovered from his illness), packed up and located a new camp south of Kanab, just below the Utah-Arizona boundary. Two weeks later Dellenbaugh joined them. It was cold, snowy, and rainy, but the tents, each with a conical, sheet iron stove, were comfortable. Andy cooked outside and served his "guests" on a large piece of weathered canvas, and Fred remembered the deserts they so often had—bread and Sorghum molasses, which was produced in abundance in Dixie. On December 26, after a Merry Christmas replete with Mrs. Thompson's plum pudding and a Mormon dance, work began on the nine-mile base line. Jones was still recovering from his illness and Bishop was discontented, but so far only John F. Steward had chosen to leave the party. So 1871 ended with a weather-beaten, loyal crew hard at work to accomplish a tremendous task.

The new year ushered in the earnest mapping of the plateaus. The broken terrain was every bit as difficult to work as the mountains of Colorado where Hayden's men would be lugging transits a year hence, and it was more difficult than King's strip

302

in the Great Basin. As for the territory being covered by Wheeler's men, it actually included much of the same country that Powell's Survey proposed to map.

But the Major's chief liability, or so it at first appeared, was not in the terrain, but in his men. Thompson, his chief geographer, knew topographical theory very well, but when he began the actual work he found the practice and the theory far apart. The experiences of all the men that first year were ludicrous, and Thompson, Jones, and Dellenbaugh had to go through a difficult process of on-the-job training before they reached a stage of acceptable competence.

For Bishop, the year began with a bitter complaint. He had not felt well for several months, he had not got along well with several members of the survey, and he felt that the Major had been sorely neglectful of the welfare of the men. On January 3, Bishop vented his wrath at Thompson's amateurishness in establishing a base line:

> Sent over in Utah to hunt a place for a lunatic-asylum—for if I ever see a lot of men working on a bigger piece of tomfoolery than this, measuring base line with 3 fourteen foot rods, I am going to petition the powers for an asylum for the insane.

But Powell's preliminary report to Joseph Henry indicated that much more thoroughness entered into the groundwork of the topographical project than Bishop acknowledged. Perhaps Bishop was cynical because he was nearly finished with his own map of the river, which was based upon astronomical readings with a sextant every forty-five miles, the meandering of the river, and triangulations back from the river twenty-five to fifty miles. Actually, Thompson's line was fixed with an astronomic transit and alignments were made with a theodolite. The latitude at the northern end of the line was determined with a zenith telescope, and the longitude was determined by means of telegraphic signals with Salt Lake City. Then the primary triangulation got under way, points being established every twenty-five to thirty miles, pyramids being constructed, and angles measured with a seven-inch theodolite. Secondary triangulation was then carried out.[1] The planning was basically sound and once the application of the textbook instructions had been mastered, the work went along in an acceptable way.

Thompson was in charge, the Major having left for Washington, and he gritted his teeth and prepared to do his best. It was winter, a time when Hayden, King, and Wheeler went into warm quarters, but the Powell Survey proposed to ignore the seasons and push ahead. Trips with pack trains to establish stations and sketch the land were made in all directions, and the work was of the same nature of that already described for Hayden and King. But there were a few differences.

The snow posed a feeding problem for the stock and a survival problem for the men. They had to look for campsites where the snow was shallow and bunch grass lay underneath, easily accessible to the stock. For his own comfort Fred made a pair of seamless leggings out of pieces of a heavy sack, and they served to keep his legs dry and warm. Sometimes the entire world seemed lost in virgin whiteness. On the way to Mount Trumbull, in Arizona, Fred stopped once in the forest stillness and listened to the "whispering sound . . . produced by the friction of the snowflakes on the pine needles . . . a weird, ghost-like language." Another time, they were returning from the Uinkaret Mountains, when, said Dellenbaugh:

> We were enveloped in a severe flurry one morning soon after starting. When we had gone about a mile and a half, the whole world seemed to terminate. The air was dense with the fast-falling snow-flakes, and all beyond a certain line was white fog, up, down, and sideways. A halt was imperative, as we knew not which way to turn except back, and that was not our direction. Descending from our horses we stepped out in the direction of the illimitable whiteness, only to find that there was nothing there to travel on. . . . Presently there were rifts in the white, and as we looked we

[1] Gregory, "Diary of Almon Harris Thompson," *Utah Historical Quarterly,* Vol. VII (1939), 134–38.

could discern, far, far below our position, another land. As the
storm broke away more and more, it was seen that we had arrived
at the edge of a cliff with a sheer drop of one thousand feet.[2]

The men did some unorthodox things in carrying out their
work. Once Thompson climbed a tree 125 feet high to look
around and get his bearings. Jones told of climbing a tree 40 to
50 feet high, drawing up the gradienter with a rope, and taking
his bearings with it "in a perfect gale of a wind." Once Andy
slipped and slid 1,500 feet in three to four minutes, passing over
a twenty-foot ledge in the process and landing up to his neck
in snow.

But in spite of their troubles they still made progress. On
February 9 they found the boundary line between Utah and
Arizona and planted a star at the spot. Where names were
needed, they either made them up from local phenomena or
used names of dignitaries, often men of Illinois.[3] By the middle
of May they had mapped the Arizona–Grand Canyon area, and
the territory in the southwest around Mount Trumbull and west
to the Nevada line. The time had come for them to turn their
attentions southeastward.

Somewhere northeast of Kanab, over completely unknown
and unexplored country, lay the Dirty Devil River, and cached
at its mouth was the *Cañonita*, which was to be rowed down to
the Paria. It fell to Thompson, Dellenbaugh, Jack Hillers, and
a man named Fennemore who was replacing Beaman as photographer to forge through the wilderness toward the site of the
cached boat. In mid-May they set out, making their way over
the Aquarius Plateau and the Henry Mountains, and by June 22,
having avoided some Indians and received directions from
others, they reached the mouth of the Dirty Devil. There they
found the *Cañonita* in good condition save for a single missing
oar. Dellenbaugh, Hillers, Fennemore, and a camp man named
Johnson then took it down to the Paria, where they arrived on

[2] Frederick S. Dellenbaugh, *The Romance of the Colorado River*, 307–308.
[3] Wallace Stegner, "Powell and the Names on the Plateau," *Western Humanities Review*, Vol. VII, No. 2 (Spring, 1953), 105–10.

July 13. Thus the second phase of the Powell Survey ended and the third phase, the completion of the trip down the Colorado, was about to begin.

For several weeks they remained at the mouth of the Paria waiting for the survey members to reassemble and complete preparations. Thompson had returned from the Dirty Devil to Kanab, and would subsequently be coming in with Jones and the Major; Clem Powell and Andy Hattan had come on ahead and arrived at the Paria on July 15. While waiting there, the boys made themselves at home with John D. Lee, of Mountain Meadows notoriety. He was an extremely vigorous man, with cattle and fields at Jacobs Pools and House Rock as well as at Lonely Dell, the name his wife had given to the home at the mouth of the Paria.

He had come down to the Colorado in December, 1871, accompanied by wife number seventeen, Emma. She already had four little children to look after, but within a month she was delivered of a daughter, Frances Dell, and in 1874, while John was in hiding from the law, she gave birth to still another daughter with the aid of her thirteen-year-old son. Emma was a strong-willed woman who, after her husband's execution in 1877, went on to become a famed frontier nurse.[4]

The Powell men worked on a dam for Lee and helped him till his fields. In exchange for this neighborliness, Emma often invited them to supper and fed them squash and melons and beef and homemade beer. Time dragged, however, and the boys swam and dozed, did some target shooting, cut each other's hair, and speculated about old Lee. Did he *really* have seventeen wives? And sixty-two children? And had the old coot really participated in the Mountain Meadows Massacre? Was he just a little bit crazy? Clem Powell thought so. Finally, on August 13, the Major arrived fresh from Salt Lake City and Washington, D.C. Then things got under way.

[4] Juanita Brooks, "Lee's Ferry at Lonely Dell," *Utah Historical Quarterly*, Vol. XXV (1957), 283–95. A picture of Lee's cabin faces page 283.

Only seven men remained to carry out the final task. These were the Major, Clem Powell, Dellenbaugh, Jones, Hattan, Thompson, and Hillers, who was about to embark upon a successful career as photographer. Bishop, Beaman, and Steward were not with them, although Bishop was still in Utah and Beaman was making an expedition on his own to the Hopi towns, actually crossing the river at Lees Ferry. The *Nellie Powell*, the boat in worst condition, was abandoned—although Lee used it as a ferry boat for years to come. The *Dean* was to be manned by Jones, Hillers and Dellenbaugh, with the Major sitting at his usual place in the armchair. Thompson, Hattan, and Clem Powell were to man the *Cañonita*.

On August 17 they started down Marble Canyon. Gradually the walls became higher—100 feet, 200 feet, by August 22, 3,500 feet, and a few days later at least 5,000 and in some places nearly 6,000 feet above them. The channel was fast, and often the boats made a mockery of the efforts the men made to control them. At one place the Major gave up. "By God, boys, we're done," he yelled at them above the roar of the foam, for he could see no hope at all from his vantage place astride the armchair. But the boats found their own channel, and made it.

At noon, sometimes, they found the ripened fruit of the cactus, "cactus apples," as they called them, which tasted like something between a fig and a tomato. They were a pleasant addition to their meat and flour diet. And where there was space on shore now, the willows gave way to mesquite bushes, and a watchful eye had to be kept for gila monsters, tarantulas, and rattlesnakes. Mostly, though, it was the river and the canyon walls, and there was no way out now, no way out at all, except down the river in the boats.

As they approached the Little Colorado, where the Grand Canyon began, the immense chasm became gloomier and the booming of the great river louder and more ominous than ever before. They arrived at the mouth of the tributary stream on the afternoon of August 22 and found no cause for celebration. "A stream about 3 rods wide by 2 feet deep and as disgusting

307

. . . as one ever set eyes upon," Clem Powell wrote in his journal. "Its waters are of a bright red and very salty, rendering it un-palatable."

They continued on, but the weather turned cold and rainy and the rapids became worse. On August 30 the rain and the rapids reduced their morale to a new low, and a rapidly rising river increased the danger they were in. Everything, everyone was wet through to the skin, and a tarpaulin had to be stretched over the fire to keep it going. The boats were tied to the cliff walls, and the men had to sleep on hard granite. "If the river continues to rise will have to lift them still higher," wrote Clem, "for if they go—God help us. . . . The party seems dead—nothing but work and danger, hard beds and worse food—a little bread, a few peaches, jerk [jerky] and coffee." Actually an ugly little many-legged worm had infested their jerked beef, making their meals of bacon fat, scorched flour, and beef almost unpalatable.

On August 31, it rained all day long, and the river continued to rise. The boats were swamped again and again, and to ease matters somewhat, many small items, such as Clem's dark tent, Jones's big straw hat, Andy's old coat and a pair of his breeches were thrown overboard. In one of the rapids Thompson was knocked overboard, but got back to safety. But finally they ran up to Bright Angel River, found a sandy beach, made camp, and slept deeply from sheer exhaustion.

The Colorado was as muddy now as they had ever seen it. On September 3 the *Dean* was swamped, two kettles, a couple of axes, and some other utensils were lost, and Jack Hillers was thrown six feet from the boat, landed in a whirlpool, was sucked under, stripped of his hat, shoes, and stockings before he got out. Then the Major landed in the same whirlpool and would probably have been drowned but for his life jacket. " 'Twas the closest call he ever had," Clem wrote, and Thompson agreed, saying that the river was the worst he had ever seen it. It was probably ten feet higher than it had been in 1869 when the Major had come down before.

On September 7 they arrived at the mouth of Kanab Canyon. Joe Hamblin was there with rations and mail for the men, and soon they felt better. But the news was not good. There were rumors that the Shivwits were on the war path and might be preparing an ambush for the Powell group. And the men were tired. The next morning at breakfast they were therefore none too surprised when the Major informed them that the trip was at an end. Nothing substantial was to be gained by continuing. The flag of the *Dean* was given to Dellenbaugh, of the *Nellie* to Steward (who was in Illinois), and of the *Cañonita* to Clem Powell, who mentioned the gift with warmth: "I will always keep it," he said.

Now the initial work of the Powell Survey, which had included the trip down the Green and Colorado in two parts, divided by a long season of work on the Great Plateau, rapidly came to a close. Clem Powell, Stephen Jones, and Andy Hattan left the survey for good. Thompson and Fred Dellenbaugh returned to Kanab, however, prepared to remain there at work on the map until it was completed. They expected it to take them well into 1873.

Those weeks at Kanab were difficult in the extreme for Almon Harris Thompson. Suddenly the moment of truth had arrived. It was apparent that the manner in which he had laid the base line, and the acceptance of such tricks as taking sightings from the tops of swaying pine trees, were going to result in a map that was far from perfect. "Swear on the outside about it—Old Boy— but thank God in your heart that I have not chucked the whole business into the fire," he wrote the Major in Washington early in the year. Three weeks later he reported that he was about to mail the map to him. "It is more work than I expected," he commented, "and does not satisfy me in accuracy." And writing a week later he added that "it does not satisfy me in many respects, but it is perhaps passable."[5]

And the map, on a scale of two miles to one inch, *was* a passable production, and when Fred Dellenbaugh trekked through the snow to place it on the eastbound train in February, 1873, he was sending the Major an excellent argument for a continu-

[5] National Archives, R.G. 57, Powell Survey, Letters Received, January 11, 1873; January 20, 1873; February 6, 1873.

ation of the survey. The last great unexplored area in the United States had now been examined. The Grand Canyon of the Colorado would soon become a tourist attraction without parallel in the entire world. And Major John Wesley Powell, with one arm and a courageous spirit, had written his name on the roster of America's brave men.

The preliminary map was completed in the winter of 1873. Yet Powell's survey continued until 1879, when it gave way to the United States Geological Survey. What was its nature during these nine years?

Administratively, the Powell Survey passed through two changes before the year 1879. In the first instance the change resulted from a congressional investigation; in the second it was merely a change in name.

The congressional investigation was held in the late spring of 1874, and the Major had worked behind the scenes to bring it about.[6] Parties of the Hayden and Wheeler surveys had clashed on July 9, 1873, in South Park, Colorado Territory, and when the Congressional Committee on Public Lands was informed of this duplication of activities, it opened hearings. In the course of the discussion, Hayden, Powell, Wheeler, Gardner, General Humphreys, and others testified. The committee concluded that all the Surveys should be continued, and about the only concrete proposal from the hearings was that Powell's survey should be placed under the administration of the Department of the Interior, where it became known as the Second Division of the United States Geological and Geographical Survey—that is, Hayden's survey. Powell still remained completely in charge, however, and was in no way subservient to Hayden. Yet the Major really emerged the victor in these hearings, for Hayden and Wheeler made a bad showing before the congressmen, while Powell succeeded in enhancing his status with the lawmakers.[7]

In June, 1876, when his survey was up for its usual appropria-

---

[6] Darrah, *Powell of the Colorado*, 211.

[7] *Geographical and Geological Surveys West of the Mississippi River*, 43 Cong., 1 sess., *House Report 612*, 17–18, 63, 72–73.

tions from Congress, Powell succeeded in changing its name to the United States Geological and Geographical Survey of the Rocky Mountain Region, and thus eliminating all indications of any subservience to the Hayden Survey.[8]

During these years, from 1873 until 1879, Powell's Survey functioned with never more than six to eight professional men and a few camp men and packers. Even the Major, although he made many trips into the field, spent most of his time in Washington, where he had lived since 1872. There he inspired the respect and the friendship of many of the powerful men of his generation. The limited size of his survey is revealed in a comparison of total costs. By June 30, 1879, the Powell Survey had spent $259,000—less by far than Hayden's $690,000, King's $368,000, and Wheeler's $449,000.[9] However, it had never concerned itself with any of the natural sciences save geology. The Major had no strong interests in botany, ornithology, or zoology. Little collecting was done in these fields. Nor did the Major publish much material in comparison with the outpourings of the Hayden Survey.

So in the remaining years, the work of the Powell Survey settled down to the humdrum tasks of topographical surveying and geological exploration that characterized the other Great Surveys. The glamorous activities had taken place from 1869 through 1872. After that the land was known and the problems were of a technical or a speculative nature.

In the realm of topography, Almon Harris Thompson stayed on with Powell. Thompson was capable, a devoted servant carrying out his tasks to the best of his ability, while his chief in Washington often neglected him. The aim was the mapping of the entire plateau region from the Grand Canyon northward to the southern boundary of the King Survey. The eastern boundary would link with the Hayden Survey close to the Colorado line. Westward the map would extend in many places all the way to the Nevada-Utah border.

[8] National Archives, R.G. 57, Hayden Survey, Letters Received, Townsend to Hayden, June 26, 1876.

[9] National Academy of Sciences, "Communication of John W. Powell," *A Report on the Surveys of the Territories*, 45 Cong., 3 sess., *House Misc. Doc.* 5, 22.

The poor fellow had his troubles. He could not find good packers ("Our boys don't amount to a row of pins in handling animals."), and he ran into difficulties in dealing with the Indians. When he made ready to come to Washington late in 1874, he informed Powell that he would consider the year's work a success, "but I have been geographer, topographer, packer, horseshoer, cook, and man-of-all-work to do it."[10]

In 1874, Powell hired Professor Harvey C. De Motte, an acquaintance of his from Illinois Wesleyan, as a topographical assistant. De Motte had come West with Powell in 1872, and so he should have known what the job expected of him. But he made a bad showing. "It is my *first* effort of the kind and as the work lay before me I felt like placing it in the fire and making another attempt," he apologized to Powell after his first years' work. He had failed even though he had a map by the King Survey to aid him.[11] He lasted only a year.

Ultimately, a small group of capable men did come to Thompson's aid. J. H. Renshawe, W. H. Graves, and Robert Bell all did acceptable work. And so Thompson, blessed with the patience of Job, kept at the task until it was finished in 1878. The maps placed him "in the front line of geographic explorers," and many of the maps are still in use and are the only ones available for some of the still remote areas of southeastern and southern Utah.[12]

It was in the important field of geology that the Powell Survey made its greatest showing. The Major was highly competent, and two of the professional geologists he employed were recognized as leaders in the field. These two men were Grove Karl Gilbert and Captain Clarence E. Dutton of the Ordnance Department of the U. S. Army.

The Major's principal geological reports were embodied in

[10] National Archives, R.G. 57, Powell Survey, Thompson to Powell, March 11, 1872; September 23, 1874.

[11] *Ibid.*, De Motte to Powell, November 9, 1874.

[12] Gregory, "Diary of Almon Harris Thompson," *Utah Historical Quarterly*, Vol. VII (1939), 9–10. The maps were never issued in an atlas such as Hayden or King produced, but they did accompany many of the monographs of the Powell Survey.

Part Second of his *Exploration of the Colorado River of the West,* pages 149–214, and in his *Report on the Geology of the Eastern Portion of the Uinta Mountains and a Region of the Country Thereto,* published in 1876 along with a folio atlas of the region. In volume they did not amount to much, but in content they opened entire new fields for geological investigation and incidentally revealed much about the mental capacities of their author. He spent very little time with fossils and cared little about the study of types of rocks. His mind dwelt upon enormous changes in the earth's surface, of uplifts of great blocs of earth, and then, through millions of years, of their wearing away by the forces of wind and rain, cold and heat, and the desire of all moisture to return to the level of the sea. He was an expert in physiographic geology. And he understood and explained changes in the earth's surface that less imaginative men completely missed, writing his explanations in beautiful, almost flamboyant style.

Why, he asks, did the Green River choose to flow right through the Uinta Mountains? Why did it not take an easier route through valleys north and east of the mountains?

> The answer is that the river had the right of way; in other words, it was running ere the mountains were formed; not before the rocks of which the mountains are composed, were deposited, but before the formations were folded, so as to make a mountain range. ... The river preserved its level, but the mountains were lifted up; as the saw revolves on a fixed pivot, while the log through which it cuts is moved along. The river was the saw which cut the mountains in two.[13]

The Major used new ideas and new phrases—*consequent valleys, antecedent valleys, superimposed valleys, base level*—and left the explanation and elaboration of them to a future generation of scientists. "A half score of younger men have elaborated, extended, and applied them; and they stand today for a division of the science so important that it is sometimes called the 'new geology,'" Grove Karl Gilbert wrote in 1903. "Geolo-

[13] Powell, *Exploration of the Colorado River of the West,* 152–53.

gists and geographers now recognize that each hill, hollow, and plain of the earth's surface originated by some process of change, and is therefore susceptible of explanation and interpretation. Whereas geologic history was formerly read in the rocks alone, it is now read not only in the rocks but in the forms of the land and the arrangement of the streams."[14]

Gilbert's own contributions to geology were hardly less than Powell's. This remarkable man, with his brilliant theoretical mind and vivid imagination, found his challenge in the questions raised by the geology of the Great Basin and the plateaus of Utah. They tested to the ultimate what he called his "guessing faculties"—and he won out, or at least many of his theories have continued to be considered valid in the light of half a century of additional research.

The pattern of his early life bore a similarity to the early experiences of Powell, Hayden, Meek, Hall, and many other nineteenth-century scientists. Gilbert was born in 1843 in Rochester, New York, the son of a portrait painter. Poverty was always close upon the heels of the family, but Grove Karl did finish high school, and in 1862 he graduated from the University of Rochester, where he had enrolled in most of the classical subjects. He had also done part-time work for Professor Henry Ward, a zoology instructor who augmented his income by running a "scientific establishment." It was filled with stuffed animals and a few prehistoric bones. Here Gilbert showed more than a normal interest in geology and paleontology.

After a year of schoolteaching at Jackson, Michigan, Gilbert returned to Rochester and worked full time for Ward. Then in 1868 the opportunity arose for him to break away from his humdrum existence. He went to work for the Ohio Geological Survey, where his drawings of geological phenomena attracted attention. Next he was offered work with the Wheeler Survey, and in 1871 he began a four-year affiliation with it. Gilbert trod the barrens of the American southwest during those years and formulated some ideas which did not come to fruition until many

[14] Quoted in "Necrology of John Wesley Powell," U.S. Geological Survey, *Twenty-fourth Annual Report*, 279.

decades later. Meanwhile, in 1872, while in winter quarters in Washington, he met the girl whom he later married and a man— a fiery man full of ideas—John Wesley Powell. These two men, one quiet and jolly and easygoing, the other dynamic and opinionated and brilliant, immediately got along, and as soon as Gilbert was able to sever his relations with the restrictive, red-tape-ridden army, he joined Powell's survey. It was a turning point in his life.[15]

Gilbert's first specific assignment under Powell was to investigate the Henry Mountains in southeastern Utah. Both men knew that these remote mountains, lying south of the Dirty Devil and west of the Colorado, represented "a limited system of disturbances, which interrupt a region of geological calm, and structurally, as well as topographically, stand by themselves." Gilbert emphasized that they are not even a range of mountains, but are "simply a group of five individual mountains, separated by low passes and arranged without discernible system." They rise from a plain 5,000 feet high to a height of about 11,450 feet, and by their altitude they create their own water supply, acting as "local condensers of moisture."

So the five mountains—named Ellen, Pennell, Hillers, Ellsworth, and Holmes—lying like "island mountains" in the desert, naked and isolated, waited for the examination of the earth scientist. Gilbert gathered together some mules and camp men and packers and set out. His long trip to the remote area was not without its reward. These mountains were different. For whereas igneous rocks usually rise to the earth's surface and spill out as lava, the lava of the Henry Mountains had acted in a different way. "Instead of rising through all the beds of the earth's crust," he wrote, "it stopped at a lower horizon, insinuated itself between two strata, and opened for itself a chamber by lifting all the superior beds. In this chamber it congealed, forming a massive body of trap." Gilbert called such a phenomenon a *laccolite;* today such formations are called *laccoliths.* And

[15] William M. Davis, "Grove Karl Gilbert," *American Journal of Science,* Fourth Series, Vol. XLVI, No. 275 (November, 1918), 669–81. A readily available essay on Gilbert is in Carroll Lane Fenton and Mildred Adams Fenton, *Giants of Geology,* 269–87.

this was the chief type of structure exemplified in the Henry Mountains. Obviously the intrusion of a laccolith created an enormous bubble in the earth's surface, and every stratum above it was uplifted, upbent, to "portray, more or less faithfully, by its curvature, the form of the body it covers."

From this simple beginning, Gilbert pieced together in intricate detail the geological history of the Henry Mountains, not only their laccoliths, dikes, and sheets, but the kinds of rocks and the weathering and erosion that they had undergone. He asked the eternal questions of why and when and speculated upon various possibilities. And he ended his monograph with several maps of these intriguing mountains, maps photographed from a model he had made of them. One photograph, called a stereogram, showed the Henrys as a series of great bubbles on the earth's surface.[16]

Gilbert was also the leading authority on the prehistoric Lake Bonneville (which he named), and in 1890 he published his definitive monograph on the subject. It was the result of field work that dated as far back as 1871, when he had been with Wheeler.[17]

When the consolidation took place, Gilbert stepped naturally into a position with the new U.S.G.S., and was for several years its chief geologist. As an administrator he was respected and deeply loved by his colleagues. He was the kind of chief who challenged his men, dared them to think boldly and differently. He wanted his men to be questioners and theorizers. The practical question for the teacher of scientists is, he once said, "whether it is possible by training to improve the guessing faculty, and if so, how is it to be done?" Gilbert did it by his own personality.

His own work included continued research on Lake Bonneville and the mountain ranges of the Great Basin. Toward the end of his life he worked on the problems of silt and drainage in San Francisco Bay. When he died in 1918, he was the modest

16 Grove Karl Gilbert, *Report on the Geology of the Henry Mountains*, 2–3, 18–21.

17 Grove Karl Gilbert, "Lake Bonneville," U.S. Geological Survey, *Monographs*, No. 1.

owner of numerous medals and citations, and his loss was keenly felt by the scientific world.[18]

A third geologist who was attached to the Powell Survey was Captain Clarence Edward Dutton of the Ordnance Department, U.S. Army. He was a Connecticut-born Yale graduate who had entered the army in 1862 at the age of twenty-one. At one time, early in his army career, he was detailed at Watervliet Arsenal in Albany County, New York, and there his interest in geology and paleontology was whetted through his acquaintance with R. P. Whitfield and James Hall. Later, stationed in Washington, D.C., Dutton continued his interests and came to know Henry, Baird, and Powell. He was encouraged to ask the army to place him on special duty with Powell, and beginning in May, 1875, Dutton began one of the longer special details in army history— he spent the next fifteen years with Powell and the United States Geological Survey.

In this position he devoted himself to the study of the plateau regions of Utah and the Far West, and he became an expert on the physical problems posed by the barren, canyon-scarred lands. He was also interested in volcanism and isostasy. But his greatest achievements were his reports: *Report on the Geology of the High Plateaus of Utah,* published in 1880, but under the auspices of the Powell Survey (U.S. Geographical and Geological Survey of the Rocky Mountain Region), and in 1882, as the second monograph of the U.S. Geological Survey, his *Tertiary History of the Grand Canyon District.* Most of the research for this report had been carried on during his years with Powell.[19]

As a geologist Dutton made some mistakes, but as a writer about geological phenomena he was at least equal to Powell. His descriptions possess some literary quality, and they also contain a human element that is sorely lacking in so much scientific reporting. Captain Dutton saw no reason why a report should not contain some descriptions of the land as it appeared now, with its present-day flora and fauna. So he proceeded to give

[18] Davis, "Grove Karl Gilbert," *American Journal of Science,* Fourth Series, Vol. XLVI, No. 275 (November, 1918), 671.

[19] George F. Becker, "Obituary of Major C. E. Dutton," *American Journal of Science,* Fourth Series, Vol. XXXIII, No. 196 (April, 1912), 387–88.

flesh and blood to the usual skeleton of a geological report. Riding across the Kaibab Plateau, he took time to describe "the winding glade, with smooth bottom richly carpeted with long green grass, aglow with myriads of beautiful blossoms. . . . Very sweet and touching now are the influences of nature. The balmy air, the dark and somber spruces, the pale-green aspens, the golden shafts of sunlight shot through their foliage, the velvet sward—surely this is the home of woodland nymphs, and at every turn of the way we fancy we are about to see them flying at our approach, or peeping at us from the flowery banks."[20]

And when, in his description, he finally arrived at the Grand Canyon ("in an instant, in the twinkling of an eye, the awful scene is before us"), he digressed from his geological studies to explain the best approach for the observer of this display of nature's power:

> The Grand Canyon of the Colorado is a great innovation in modern ideas of scenery, and in our conception of the grandeur, beauty, and power of nature. As with all great innovations it is not to be comprehended in a day or a week, nor even in a month. It must be dwelt upon and studied, and the study must comprise the slow acquisitions of the meaning and spirit of that marvellous scenery which characterizes the Plateau Country, and of which the great chasm is the superlative manifestation. The study and slow mastery of the influences of that class of scenery and its full appreciation is a special culture, requiring time, patience, and long familiarity for its consummation.[21]

Even after he returned to the army in 1890, Dutton continued his interests in geology, especially in volcanism and earthquakes. In 1886 he studied the Charleston earthquake and profited from the fact that, for the first time in all history, a man could coordinate the facts about such a catastrophe. This was possible because in 1883 the nation had gone on a standard time system. Dutton also journeyed to Mexico to study volcanoes, and he did some work on the Zuni Plateau in the American Southwest. But

[20] C. E. Dutton, *Tertiary History of the Grand Canyon District*, 140.
[21] *Ibid.*, 141.

he is most remembered for the two great reports he did for Powell. "Very few American men of science have possessed to so marked a degree that sympathy with the reader which is the secret of arranging ideas in the order in which they will be most easily grasped," wrote George Becker. But Dutton did possess it—and thus an army career man made his name in history as a great geologist.[22]

The work of Powell, Gilbert, and Dutton was of a consistently high order, and it was accomplished with the thoroughness that the coming age would demand of all scientists. Granted that they had one of the most intriguing areas of the world to investigate, their monographs remain to this day outstanding examples of scientific investigation and reporting. If nothing else had come from the Powell Survey, these monographs alone would have assured it of lasting recognition.

But besides geology the Major early manifested other interests in the plateau and desert country. He had always been interested in the Indians, and in fact in 1873 he had been a commissioner to the Indians of the Great Plateau. As the years went on, his concern for the Indians actually superseded his interest in geology, and the Major was the moving force behind the creation of the Bureau of American Ethnology in 1879, and became its first director.

In ethnology, Powell was aided after 1875 by James C. Pilling, another of his better appointees. Pilling, twenty-nine years old when Powell hired him, had enjoyed an excellent reputation in Washington as, of all things, a stenographer. He had taken testimony in law courts and congressional hearings and was respected for his accuracy, diligence, and efficiency. Pilling began working for the Major as a sort of secretary, recording the Major's notes in the field, and acting as a sort of editor in chief of survey publications. Then one of those unpredictable, fateful combinations occurred. Pilling found himself fascinated with ethnology, and his shorthand training made it possible for him to record accurately the words of Indian languages. With his

[22] Becker, "Obituary of Major C. E. Dutton," *American Journal of Science,* Fourth Series, Vol. XXXIII, No. 196 (April, 1912), 387.

speed in writing he could set down, as it was told, the weird mythology of these people of the sun and the wind. Working with the Indians of the plateau country between 1875 and 1880, and with Powell's help and direction, Pilling soon established his own reputation as an outstanding ethnologist, and his contributions to North American ethnology are today considered invaluable.[23]

An elaboration of the accomplishments of the Powell Survey would not be complete without mentioning the work of the photographers, journalists, and painters. The Major had difficulties with his photographers, although in the early years they were the only true professionals he hired. E. O. Beaman and James Fennemore both quit in the field. Then Clem Powell and Fred Dellenbaugh tried, and failed. Finally Jack Hillers, who had started with Powell as a boatman, acquired the proper techniques while in the field and finally made good. After taking views of the Grand Canyon and Kanab Wash, Hillers wrote the Major that "he was pleased with a good many, but some are not up to the mark." Then he added pridefully, "I think we done middling for Greenhorns." It had been so cold that his body had turned blue every night, and the water had been too cold for use in the photographic process.[24]

He remained with Powell throughout most of the years of the survey and then went with him to the U.S.G.S., where he was in charge of the photographic laboratory until his retirement in 1900. Hillers' greatest contribution was in the field of ethnology, for he left thousands of Indian photographs. Most of the negatives are on glass plates, each having two exposures 4x5 inches, suitable for stereoptican slides, and in spite of the hardships of pioneer photography the Hillers pictures have been described as "every bit as good as modern professional photography."[25]

[23] *Dictionary of American Biography,* XIV, 603. *National Cyclopaedia of American Biography,* XV, 55.

[24] National Archives, R.G. 57, Powell Survey, Letters Received, Thompson to Powell, February 7, 1872; April 18, 1872; May 10, 1872; Hillers to Powell, May 25, 1873.

[25] J. H. Steward, "Notes of Hillers' Photographs of the Paiute and Ute Indians Taken on the Powell Exploration of 1873," *Smithsonian Miscellaneous Collections,* Vol. XCVIII, No. 18 (July, 1939), 3. Gregory, "Beaman, Fennemore,

In 1873, Powell was accompanied on his excursions in Utah by a mediocre journalist of the New York *Times* and by the landscape painter Thomas Moran. The journalist was more interested in the Mormons than in the terrain, and used up many inches of space describing the squalor of the small Mormon farm home, complete with a dozen dirty urchins. He complained that only the husband and wife (or wives) slept inside during the summer, the children stretching out in a little house "of dog-kennel architecture" where they slept "like a spaniel."[26] Moran, however, made detailed sketches of the Grand Canyon and the plateaus, then returned east and in 1876 completed his magnificent painting of *The Chasm of the Colorado,* which was sold to Congress and hung for years in the Senate wing. In coloring and drawing his painting left little to be desired, and its topographical accuracy, without the distortion of a camera lens, made it, in the opinion of one authority, a work of great art.[27]

Such were the achievements of the Powell Survey in the realms of topography, geology, ethnology, photography, journalism, and art. Yet one other contribution must be mentioned—Powell's concepts of land utilization. The Major was a highly capable geologist and a proficient ethnologist, but the best measure of his brilliant mind was his grasp of the problems confronting settlers in the arid lands of the United States. He saw firsthand the fallacies of the land policies of his government and the frauds and criminal wastefulness made possible by them. In the arid lands especially, he had witnessed the shortcomings of the land program, and in his annual report for 1873, he devoted three pages to the subject of land classification of the area within his survey.[28] Just as in his knowledge of geology and ethnology, so in his understanding of the problems of the public domain, Powell became an expert within a few years after he

Hillers, Dellenbaugh, Johnson and Hattan," *Utah Historical Quarterly,* Vol. XVI (1948), 495–99.

[26] New York *Times,* August 7, 1873, p. 2.

[27] Charles E. Fairman, *Art and Artists of the Capitol of the United States of America,* 69 Cong., 1 sess., *Sen. Exec. Doc.* 95, 299.

[28] Powell, *Report of the Survey of the Colorado River of the West,* 43 Cong., 1 sess., *House Misc. Doc.* 265, 10–12.

put his mind to the problem. When he did set out to force a change, he knew what he was talking about. With the exception of his war record, his masterful grasp of the problem and his systematic presentation of it constitutes the most patriotic and brilliant work of his career.

A little background in American land policy seems necessary here. There are those who believe that the next great approach to the study of history will be a psychological one. If it is, some psychologist-historian is going to have a great day analyzing the history of American policies toward the disposition of the public domain. For although there was always a latent opposition to new giveaways, the consistent trend of United States land policy throughout the entire nineteenth century was toward a greater and greater generosity in the disposal of the public domain.

The trend is simple to trace. It starts in 1796 when the first land act provided for the sale of land at $2.00 an acre, with half the tracts to be disposed of in 640 acre lots; the other half were to go in larger tracts of 5,760 acres. In 1800 came the Harrison Land Law, "one of the most important measures in the history of the public domain," which reduced the minimum purchase to 320 acres at $2.00 an acre, payable in installments over a four-year period. The trend toward more leniency was now becoming clear, and the "buy-now-pay-later" characteristic of American life was already on its way to becoming a part of the national heritage. Moreover, when large numbers of settlers could not make their payments, "relief bills" were readily introduced in Congress to help them through their period of hardship. Shocking as the fact may be, this government has always been a welfare state to someone.

In 1820, on the heels of a brief depression, the price of land was reduced to $1.25 an acre—a rule of thumb charge that became the norm for over a hundred years—and the new law also reduced the amount of acreage that must be purchased to eighty acres. It also cancelled time payments.

As if these easy-credit, bargain-basement offerings were not sufficient, the idea of military bounty lands took hold. The pre-

sentation of gifts of land in the West to veterans was not new—
it had been done in colonial times—but now such gifts became a
part of the aftermath of every American war, including the
Indian wars. Finally, in 1855, a general act gave a bounty of
160 acres of land to any soldier or his heirs who had served in
any war after 1790, and a year later Revolutionary soldiers were
included in the giveaway. By 1907, bounty land warrants
amounting to 68,239,030 acres had been issued to American
war veterans.

Then there were grants for internal improvements and education and, beginning with the Illinois Central grant of 1850,
lush proposals for the railroads. For sharpies and speculators
there were the made-to-order Swamp Land Grants, the Timber
Culture Act, and the Desert Land Act, all passed upon faulty
information and with the encouragement and backing of interested, greedy pressure groups. To help settlers there were
Frontier Donations (simply rewarding early pioneers, as in
Oregon, with gifts of land), and finally in 1862 came the ultimate gift, the Homestead Act, whereby settlers could acquire
160 acres of land and, if they lived on it for five years, could claim
it as their own.[29]

Into the more arid regions of the United States came the expanding, land-hungry Americans. Some just crossed the arid
lands on their way to Oregon or California. The Mormons went
to the western slope of the Wasatch Mountains, gazed out upon
the dry land and the great, sterile lake lying out there like a hot
piece of glass, squinted their eyes from the brightness, and set
out to make their homes in the new Zion.

In 1859, a gold rush brought thousands to the eastern slope
of the Rockies. Every babbling brook, every rippling creek was
fair game for the prospector's pan and the fifty-niner's sluice
box, and by the 1870's the towns of Colorado Springs, Denver,
Boulder, Leadville, Black Hawk, and Central City, and a
hundred little mining camps hugging the canyon walls in the

---

[29] Roy M. Robbins, *Our Landed Heritage: The Public Domain, 1776–1936,*
16–34. Benjamin Horace Hibbard, *A History of the Public Land Policies,* 121,
132, 352, 385.

depths of the Rockies, supplied the population for Colorado Territory. And eastward on the plains in the 1870's ranchers grazed their lean herds of cattle on an open range that had barely quieted from the last snort of a mighty bison, or from the blood-curdling war whoops of a war party of Cheyennes. Railroads and homesteaders were working westward onto the high plains.

They came—saints and sinners, womanless miners, and nesters with thin wives beside them and dozens of undernourished children hiding behind the flaps of their covered wagons. But west of the one hundredth meridian, west of the twenty-inch rainfall line, west of the tall grass, there was a difference. The experiences of the pioneers on the Great Plains, as Walter Prescott Webb has pointed out in his classic study, *The Great Plains*, was well-nigh traumatic. Wives went mad in the lonely sodhouse country, where only the wind furnished sound by day and the coyote and the wolf joined in during the cold depths of the night. The children died of fever, the summers were stifling hot, the winters cold enough to freeze the lowing cattle so that sometimes the desperate plainsman took his best stock into the soddy with him. Grasshoppers by the millions hitched rides on the west winds which picked them up at their hatching places in the high Rockies and carried them to the croplands of the desperate pioneers, there to destroy a season's work, a season's hopes, a season's prayers. Until barbed wire was developed, cattle trampled the fields.

But something even worse was in store for the men of the high plains. Nature's handmaiden, climate, had played them a dirty trick. The decades of the sixties and the seventies were years of the wet side of the climatic cycle. Settlers went too far west, far beyond that magic zone where normal rainfall was sufficient for crops. And when the cycle changed once again, nature broke the farmer's spirit as the dry winds withered his crops and his hopes at the same time.

Powell had witnessed all this.

He had seen the nester starved out while the promoter, the

speculator, gained control of the land for his own selfish purposes. He had seen how ranchers had filed fraudulent homestead, pre-emption, and timber-culture entries, so that along creek bottoms and near water holes they had staked their claims and built their cabins, while their cattle grazed to the horizon on the public domain, and the small farmer was shooed out of the territory with shotgun promptness.

Or, closer to the Rockies, the entrepreneur had formed irrigation companies, whereby a smart man or a small company controlled the water resources of entire river and creek valleys and sold cool, sweet water for a fee to farmers whose thirsty crops would shrivel and die without it.

The Major had watched as miners denuded mountainsides and whole valleys of timber which was never theirs to take. He had seen frauds in registration, timber lands and coal lands going at the flat $1.25 an acre because no one checked to make sure that the land did not have such resources. He had witnessed great forest fires, two of them in Colorado, "each of which destroyed more timber than all that used by the citizens of that State from its settlement to the present day," and, since Indians were thought to start most of the fires, he advocated a closer control of the red men.

He witnessed the rapid depletion of the nation's natural resources, and his methodical scientist's mind was repelled by what he saw. He understood the human wastefulness, to say nothing of the misery, that was involved in a system that used water, timber, and grassland resources without any overall plan, that let men stake out 160 acres of land when at least 2,500 acres were the bare minimum necessary to eke out a living. The arid regions, he pointed out, constituted four-tenths of the area of the United States. With planning, there was no limit to what this area could mean for the rest of the nation.

Thousands of men who now own herds and live a seminomadic life; thousands of persons who now roam from mountain range to mountain range prospecting for gold, silver, and other minerals; thousands of men who repair to that country and return disappointed from the fact that they are practically debarred from the public lands; and thousands of persons in the eastern states without employment or discontented with the rewards of labor, would speedily find homes in the great Rocky Mountain Region.[30]

Even though it was almost too late, Powell demanded an end to unprincipled and unplanned exploitation and suggested that it was high time for some unit of government to provide for land classification, and for Congress to revise its land laws to better fit the arid regions. Land classification would specify lands as mineral lands, coal lands, irrigable lands, timber lands, or pasturage lands. The land laws should, he insisted, be changed so that irrigable lands could be organized as irrigation districts, that the fixed parcel of land should be eighty acres, and that the rights to water should inhere with the land. Water monopolies would thus be abolished and associations of men—those property owners making up the irrigation district—would meet in democratic manner and draw up their own bylaws and regulations. The fixed checkerboard pattern of land survey would be changed, for the tracts of land should all be accessible to the water.

Pasturage land, or ranchland as it is called today, should be allotted in a manner different, but more realistic than, the manner in use in the 1870's. According to the proposed "Bill to authorize the organization of pasturage districts" associations of men could organize these groups and each individual could select 2,560 acres as a pasturage homestead, and in no case could it be situated in such a way as to monopolize the supply of water.[31]

To the westerner, John Wesley Powell was beginning to sound more and more like a bureaucrat, like a late nineteenth-century brain truster, a government man out of Washington who proposed to change a situation which suited the powerful elements in the West to a T. It was the old clash between the rugged individualist who claimed that it was his kind "who made America"

[30] John Wesley Powell, *Report on the Arid Regions of the United States*, 29.
[31] *Ibid.*, 29–45.

and the cautious government planner, highly educated, who "knew" what was right and set out to tell the westerners how to settle their land.

Yet there were those who were impressed by his ideas. One such individual was Collis P. Huntington, hardly a government man by any stretch of the imagination, railroading—specifically the Central Pacific Railroad—being his business. Having read the news story of one of the Major's speeches on the subject of the public domain, Huntington sat down and wrote the Major a letter of support. "My own mind has been evolving something of the kind [of change in the disposal policy] for years," he wrote, "and . . . this company will not oppose, but will favor, any good and proper plan for a new system of surveys which shall allot and divide the land with due regard to the water without which it is valueless."[32]

There was no immediate result from Powell's *Report on the Arid Lands,* but it started men thinking, and within a generation the ideas which he first promoted brought about changes in the system of land survey and new thinking on the problem of irrigation and reclamation in the West. The Major's ideas also alienated many of the western men in Congress, who impatiently awaited the opportunity to put him "in his place." In May, 1894, long after the Great Surveys had been consolidated into the U.S.G.S., Powell resigned as its chief because of pressure opponents brought to bear, not so much on him as on his survey.[33]

All of this happened after the U.S. Geographical and Geological Survey of the Rocky Mountain Region had ceased to exist. It does not concern us here. But the way in which Powell's survey, as well as Hayden's, Wheeler's, and King's, came to an end is part of our story. For the end of the four Surveys and the creation of the U.S.G.S. was all of Powell's doing. As has already been shown, he brought about a congressional investigation of the four surveys in 1874. He brought the situation to the atten-

[32] National Archives, R.G. 57, Powell Survey, Letters Received, April 30, 1877.
[33] Darrah, *Powell of the Colorado,* 336–39. The details of Powell's resignation go beyond the scope of this book, but can be found in Darrah's biography.

tion of the Congress again in 1878, and this time he succeeded. The surveys were consolidated into a single unit. And after Clarence King had served one year as its first director, he stepped down and Powell replaced him.[34] By 1880, then, John Wesley Powell, a midwestern farmer's son without an earned degree, had achieved the highest position in scientific circles then attainable. He possessed tremendous power over the shaping of the government's policies toward scientific research. He had reached the top, and he knew it.

Generally, he is given credit for establishing the Geological Survey and placing it on so firm a basis that Congress could never abolish it. He is also credited with the establishment of the Bureau of American Ethnology, of which he was appointed first director in 1879 and remained as such until his death. (In 1877 he published *Contributions to North American Ethnology* under the imprint of the Powell Survey.) Dynamic, ambitious, and brilliant to the point of genius, it was a logical development that the Major would end his days studying the great questions of science and religion and the nature of things. He became a philosopher.

Yet if we leave the Major without mentioning some of his shortcomings we would be doing history an injustice. John Wesley Powell had his faults, and they were serious ones.

The historian who tries to tell the truth can never forgive the Major for publishing his *Exploration of the Colorado River of*

[34] Henry Nash Smith, "Clarence King, John Wesley Powell, and the Establishment of the United States Geological Survey," *Mississippi Valley Historical Review*, Vol. XXXIV (1947), 37–58. David H. Dickason, "Henry Adams and Clarence King: The Record of a Friendship," *New England Quarterly*, Vol. XVII, No. 2 (June, 1944), 229–54. Both of these essays demonstrate the weakness in writing of an event from the point of view of just one of the participants. Mr. Dickason, writing about King, gave him credit for founding the U.S.G.S. Mr. Smith began his essay by pointing out Mr. Dickason's errors and then proceeded to narrate the creation of the survey from a Powell-oriented point of view. In neither case did the writers adequately research the career, accomplishments, and virtues of Hayden or his survey. His side of the controversy was never investigated. Yet he had his arguments, and he numbered among his supporters many respected men. Mr. Dickason's failure to investigate the background of the matter is perhaps justifiable, for he was primarily concerned with the friendship of King and Adams. In Mr. Smith's case, no such excuse can be found.

the West as a true narration of a trip down the Colorado in 1869, when actually many of the events mentioned in the book occurred in 1871 and 1872 on the second Colorado River trip—a journey which he fails to mention at all. The historian can never forgive a man who chose to ignore any mention whatsoever of the brave men who went down the river with him on the second voyage. Dellenbaugh, Clem Powell, Jones, Steward, Bishop, Hattan, Hillers, Beaman, and Thompson deserved better treatment than this. Not only is there no valid excuse, but one wonders how a physical scientist, who makes such a fetish of truth, could ever compromise it as the Major did.[35]

The Major was a man with fiercely loyal friends and bitter enemies. He was terribly ambitious, and his scheming for the creation of a single survey was not altogether altruistic.

But how many men possessed his brilliance? How many men had his courage?

There he is now, a bearded man, without a right arm, sitting in an armchair tied to the mid-section of the *Dean*, floating down one of the most tumultuous rivers on the face of the earth. He is a curious man, questioning, thinking, guessing. There is a flash in his eyes denoting lust for life, love of nature; the creases around his eyes show the signs of laughter. He lives with an air of expectancy of what is around the next bend. And when there is nothing else to do, he pulls a book out of his rubber bag and reads aloud to his men *The Lady of the Lake*.

He was abundantly endowed with God's eternal spirit. The Major was unconquerable, unassailable, unlimited, in a special class with Columbus, and Galileo, and a handful of others.

They are the ones who have made all the difference.

[35] Stanton, *Colorado River Controversies*, 97–137. An entire chapter is devoted to Powell as historian.

PART FOUR

The Wheeler Survey:
Science the Army Way

17

Soldiers and Surveyors

PRIOR TO THE CIVIL WAR, the official, scientific exploration of the American West had been the work of the United States Army.[1] This was a natural prerogative, for by the time the new American nation was established, the necessity of good topographic maps for use by an army in the field had been well demonstrated.

Czar Peter the Great had first understood this need early in the eighteenth century. With his troops fighting enemies from the Sea of Azov northward to the Baltic, from Poland eastward into Siberia, Peter's armies had entered regions that were virtually terra incognita, and because of the lack of knowledge of the terrain, his armies had suffered reverses. So it was that in 1720 Peter ordered that surveys be made, maps be drawn, and districts be described. The plan was a success, and Napoleon, the Prussians, and finally the young United States adopted the policy of gathering maps, or having them made, for military purposes.[2]

In 1813, the Corps of Topographical Engineers was created, and it was this branch of the service that conducted much of

[1] See W. H. Goetzmann, *Army Exploration in the American West.*
[2] Captain George M. Wheeler, *Report upon the Third Geographical Congress and Exhibition at Venice, Italy, 1881,* 48 Cong., 2 sess., *House Exec. Doc. 270,* 90.

the exploratory work in the American West prior to the Civil War. Stephen H. Long, John C. Frémont, John W. Gunnison, Howard Stansbury, and Gouverneur K. Warren were just a few of the explorers of western America attached to the Topographical Engineers before that branch was abolished, a casualty of the desperate struggles of the Civil War year of 1863.

The war ended in 1865, but the policies of Reconstruction kept the army busy for several more years. When it did revert to peacetime duties, the generals discovered that the civilian surveys conducted by Hayden, Major Powell, and Clarence King had filled in the vacuum left by the army's withdrawal. Career men like General Humphreys felt that the service had been robbed of one of its few peacetime occupations. Therefore, partly to regain what it considered its rightful duties, and partly to conduct topographical work that more specifically suited its needs, the army established the United States Geographical Surveys West of the One Hundredth Meridian, under the command of a West Point graduate, First Lieutenant George Montague Wheeler.

On one of the rainiest, windiest, most miserable commencement days in the memory of local inhabitants, George Montague Wheeler was graduated from the United States Military Academy at West Point and commissioned second lieutenant, Corps of Engineers. There were thirty-nine graduates, and Lieutenant Wheeler should have held his head high, for he ranked first in philosophy and mathematics, second in engineering, sixth in mineralogy and geology, seventh in Spanish, eighth in ordnance and gunnery, ninth in ethics, and twenty-first in cavalry tactics; in general merit he ranked sixth. With this record did Lieutenant George M. Wheeler stand upon the threshold of his career. It was June 18, 1866.[3]

But the view of the future was as somber as the rain clouds hovering over the Hudson and the vine-covered buildings of

[3] Major George W. Cullum, *Biographical Register of the Officers and Graduates of the U.S. Military Academy at West Point, New York*, III, 65. New York *Times*, June 19, 1866, p. 8. *Rocky Mountain News*, July 3, 1866, p. 4.

the Point. The civilian population was tired of soldiering and uniforms, of drums and bugles. The coming age would be a civilian one, and the optimism of the Harvard and Yale graduates in that year of 1866 was every bit as justified as the pessimism of the young officers from West Point. What chance for glory in a lifetime career in a peacetime army?

Twenty-four-year-old Lieutenant Wheeler well knew what had happened since Appomattox. The demobilization of the best-trained, best-experienced, most modern army in the world had swept through the ranks like a tornado. What had been a military force of a million men in 1865 had dwindled to barely 25,000 regulars by 1867. One authority called the period that began in 1865 and ended in 1880 the army's Dark Ages.[4] It was so reduced in size that it could barely muster the energy to attract attention. When Congress annually considered its appropriations the army's cries were drowned in the clamor for economy. By the time Maximilian had been shot in Mexico and Radical Reconstruction was coming to an end, the American citizen had virtually swept the army out of sight and out of mind. It had been sent West to fight the Plains Indians, and there many a dedicated West Pointer spent the better part of an embittered career.

The pay was so poor—less than $14.00 a month for a private and commensurately bad all the way up through the ranks— that mostly riff-raff enlisted, and nearly one-fifth of the total army deserted each year.[5] And the work was dangerous at times, for the Plains Indians were a formidable enemy until the mid-1880's. Yet between skirmishes life was so *dull*. The army was housed in 169 posts, of which 130 were west of the Mississippi. The largest of these frontier forts was Fort Sill, in Indian Territory, with 550 men; most of the posts contained less than 100 officers and enlisted men and 40 of them contained less than 50 men.[6] Gossip and backbiting under such conditions of loneliness

[4] William Addleman Ganoe, *The History of the United States Army*, 309.

[5] New York *Times*, December 7, 1875, p. 2. In 1874, there were 4,600 desertions in an army of 25,000.

[6] *Annual Report of the Secretary of War for 1874*, 44 Cong., 1 sess., *House Exec. Doc. 1*, Part II.

and boredom could become simply maddening. Visitors to these lonely outposts told of the royal treatment they received, for even a dull visitor, even a bored English hunter, was at least something of a change from the humdrum existence.

Who, then, could have desired an army career in these Dark Ages of our military history?

First were those West Point graduates, career men prior to 1861, to whom the army was their only way of life. Such a man was Brigadier General A. A. Humphreys, chief of the Corps of Engineers, who had graduated from West Point in 1831. To him there was no other life than army life, no other way but the army way.

A few younger men graduated from the Point and chose the army career in spite of all its frustrations. To these men the military life had some kind of appeal. The order of it all, the way of doing things, the power, the travel, perhaps just their inertia—there were these reasons, and as many variations of them, as there were officers in the service.

Lieutenant Wheeler was one of those who chose to make the army his career. Shortly after his graduation he assumed his official duties as assistant engineer on the survey of Point Lobos and vicinity, in the San Francisco Bay area. On March 7, 1867, he was promoted to first lieutenant, and a year and a half later he was appointed engineer on the staff of the Commanding General of the Department of California, in which capacity he was soon to be engaged in some surveying and exploring.[7] It was in 1868 that he credited himself with having given the great plateau in southwestern Colorado, eastern and southern Utah, western New Mexico, and northeastern Arizona, the name which it bears to this day: the Colorado Plateau.[8]

By 1869—the year Powell first went down the Colorado, King worked eastward into Utah, and Hayden enlarged his survey

[7] Cullum, *Biographical Register*, III, 65. *Geographical and Geological Surveys West of the Mississippi River*, 43 Cong., 1 sess., *House Report 612*, 21.

[8] Captain George M. Wheeler, *Geographical Report*, Vol. I in *Report upon United States Geographical Surveys West of the One Hundredth Meridian*, 13. On page 23 of the same volume, Wheeler states that he named the plateau in 1871. Such discrepencies (and they are sprinkled throughout his work) reflect something of the man's capacities.

and moved into Wyoming—twenty-seven-year-old Lieutenant Wheeler was devoting his full energies to explorations and re-connaissances. In that year he worked mostly in southeastern Nevada, covering about 24,000 square miles of it, and in western Utah, where he covered about 400 square miles.[9] The principal aim of his exploration was not mapping or surveying, however, but rather an endeavor to find a more direct route for the transfer of troops from Idaho, northern Utah, eastern Oregon and Washington, southward to Arizona. The previous route had been by way of ports on the Pacific, southward by sea to California, and then inland again.[10]

But his operations in the field had given Wheeler an idea, and when he submitted his report on the work in Nevada and western Utah, he included suggestions for a general survey extending its operations throughout the West.[11] His recommendations, coming at a time when General Humphreys was keenly aware of the civilian surveys that had pre-empted one of the army's traditional peacetime activities, were promptly taken under serious consideration. The young lieutenant was called to Washington for consultation.

More was involved, however, than professional jealousy and inter-departmental rivalry. The army knew that the other surveys placed greatest emphasis upon geology, and their topographical work was co-ordinated to the needs of the geologist. The army had a different interest. It needed maps that stressed human developments—mines, farms, villages, roads, railroads, dams. It needed maps which gave the strategist "a thorough knowledge of the conformation, the obstacles and resources of a country." As Wheeler once emphasized, no military commander had ever succeeded "except by a thorough and free use of a full supply of accurate topographical maps, upon which [were] delineated all the natural and economic or artificial features, and of the means of transit over the territory to be pro-

[9] *Ibid.*, 22. For the exact itinerary, see 22n.

[10] *Geographical and Geological Surveys West of the Mississippi River*, 43 Cong., 1 sess., *House Report 612*, 20.

[11] Stanford University Special Collections, Wheeler Survey, Letters Sent, Wheeler to Joseph Henry, February 12, 1877.

337

tected or the region embraced within the scope of the military operations."[12]

What Wheeler was trying to make people understand was that a topographical map was more essential to a nation's security than the geological maps produced by Hayden, King, and Powell. The scientists' maps, he insisted, were "controlled by the theoretical considerations of the geologists," while the army maps would stress "astronomical, geodetic, and topographic observations, with map delineations of all natural objects, means of communication, artificial and economic features, the geologic and natural history branches being treated as incidental to the main purpose."[13]

These were the two arguments, then, that were advanced to warrant a new, a fourth survey out West: map work was the army's traditional task, and no one else was making maps that were suitable for army purposes. Furthermore, a man capable of administering an army survey was available and willing to shoulder the task. Wheeler was eager to continue the program, the rude beginnings of which had been made during his reconnaissance work in 1869. The Corps of Engineers therefore inaugurated a crash program (to use modern terminology) and sent a full-blown survey into the field in 1871.

Wheeler was placed in "charge of the exploration . . . of those portions of the United States Territory lying south of the Central Pacific Railroad, embracing parts of Eastern Nevada and Arizona." He was informed that the main object of his exploration was to obtain "correct topographical knowledge of the region traversed . . . and to prepare accurate maps of that section." At the same time, although topography was his principal concern, he was to ascertain "as far as practicable, everything relating to the physical features of the country, the numbers, habits, and disposition of the Indians who may live in this section . . . the facilities offered for making rail or common roads, to meet the wants of those who at some future period may occupy or traverse

12 Wheeler, *Report upon the Third Geographical Congress and Exhibition at Venice, Italy, 1881*, 48 Cong., 2 sess., *House Exec. Doc. 270*, 84.
13 *Ibid.*, 100.

this portion of our territory." Moreover, the survey was to note the mineral resources and, where indications justified, to make "minute and detailed examinations of the locality and character of the deposits." "The influence of climate, the geological formations, character and kinds of vegetation, its probable value for agricultural and grazing purposes, relative proportions of woodland, water, and other qualities which affect its value for the settler" were to be carefully observed. To aid him in the 1871 survey, Wheeler was authorized to employ ten assistants as topographers, geologists, naturalists, etc., plus the necessary number of packers, guides, and laborers; the total number of civilian employees was not to exceed thirty."[14] Fifty thousand dollars were allotted for the expedition.[15]

In the spring of 1871, Wheeler entrained from San Francisco for Halleck Station, near Elko, Nevada, and there assembled his men. Besides officers and enlisted men of the army, he employed a number of civilians at both laboring and professional levels. Grove Karl Gilbert, later with Powell, was with him, as was Archibald Marvine, later with Hayden. These two men worked up the geology while others collected botanical and zoological specimens. Timothy H. O'Sullivan, borrowed from the King Survey, was along as photographer. Frederick W. Loring, scion of a prominent Boston family, was along as "barometric observer and recorder," but in reality he was expected to chronicle the achievements of the expedition for the eastern press.[16]

This was Wheeler's biggest assignment so far, and on its success hinged the future of army surveys and his own future as well. The area of the survey in 1871—72,250 miles actually worked—embraced the dry wastes of central, southern, and southwestern Nevada, eastern California, southwestern Utah,

[14] Wheeler, *Geographical Report*, 31–32. I have quoted a letter from Humphreys to Wheeler.

[15] Lieutenant George M. Wheeler, *Preliminary Report of Explorations in Nevada and Arizona*, 42 Cong., 2 sess., Sen. Exec. Doc. 65, 4.

[16] Wheeler, *Geographical Report*, 660. Captain George M. Wheeler, *Geology*, Vol. III in *Report upon United States Geographical Surveys West of the One Hundredth Meridian*, 19–20, 193. Stanford University Special Collections, Wheeler Survey, Letters Sent, Wheeler to A. D. Lyle, 1878, 112.

and northwestern, central, and southern Arizona. This was not only barren and formidable ground, but it was one of the last bastions of Indian resistance. Aborigines of questionable character—Shoshones, Paiutes, Chemehuevis, Utes, Mohaves, Apache-Mohaves, and the Havasupai, Tonto, Pinal, Coyotero, Mescalero, and Arivaipa branches of the Apaches were still at large in 1871. Some of the worst of them, Wheeler wrote, "were those encountered in the lonely marches, away from either highways or trails." Many of them were quite ready to give to any lone surveyor, and especially to one in a blue uniform, their own special brand of torture. Some of the Utes and Paiutes north and west of the Colorado were of more certain friendship, and a few acted as guides, "pointing out the little hidden springs and streams, especially in the Death Valley country, Southwestern Nevada, and Eastern California sections." Yet just because of the Indian problem, the maps made by the survey promised to be of immediate use to the army.[17]

On May 3, the parties—for several different groups, each under command of an officer, worked at the same time—set about their tasks. The surveyors carried their sextants, chronometers, six-inch theodolites, gradienters, and pivot levels, field, prismatic, and pocket compasses, steel and linen tapes. Other men gingerly carried cistern and aneroid barometers and pocket thermometers. Odometers clattered along behind the more placid mules. Pack trains carried most of the provisions. The Wheeler Survey was operational.[18]

Nevada, Arizona, and western California baked in temperatures as high as 118 degrees that summer, and the men and their animals suffered in the dry, furnace-like atmosphere. Sometimes they camped by a dry stream, knowing that by midnight a substantial trickle of life-giving water would appear, only to disappear by noon the next day, a victim of the heat and evaporation. Often at midday the soldiers' eyes actually pained them as a result of the dazzling brilliance. Evening was a welcome relief,

---

[17] Wheeler, *Geographical Report*, 30, 34–35.
[18] *Ibid.*, 661.

for then the brightness faded and the land filled with softer shades of azure, and the ridges of the western hills flamed with the fiery gold of the setting sun. There was some danger from the Indians, but for the most part the topographical work was hard, routine, and exhausting.

An Ernest Ingersoll, a William H. Jackson, a Clarence King, or a John Wesley Powell would have found much to write home about, but Fred Loring, the Boston journalist, was a most unimaginative young man. The best he could do was pep up his reports by writing in a flippant style, stressing the humorous events of the expedition. He thought the Shoshone conference he attended was most interesting because the chief's mother-in-law was kept busy all morning bringing an old fruit can full of water to the Indian braves. Cowitch, the chief, dressed in buckskin trousers, a red and white flannel shirt, and an old dress coat with one tail missing, hardly raised Loring's fears of the dangerous red men. The Shoshone chief's crown, replete with crow feathers and buttons, and his two long braids tied with muskrat skins, and his forehead and cheeks painted with vermilion, only made him, in Loring's opinion, "frightfully grotesque."[19]

The young Brahmin was particularly critical of the Mormons he met, with "faces of the lowest class of the coarse foreign peasantry . . . or the hard, mercenary features of speculating Yankees . . . who had . . . invested in Mormonism, and rubbed most of the life out of their souls. And in the younger classes," he went on, "even a casual observer can see the results of polygamy. Not a face that shows a single admirable quality—avarice and sensuality predominating almost to the exclusion of other expressions." And, Loring asked darkly, "After Brigham Young, what?"[20]

Even the dangerous trip from Owens Lake into Death Valley and on westward to the Inyo Mountains failed to bring forth

[19] Frederick W. Loring, "A Council of War," *Appleton's Journal of Literature, Science, and Art,* Vol. VI, No. 124 (August 12, 1871), 182–83.

[20] Frederick W. Loring, "A Glimpse of Mormonism," *Appleton's Journal of Literature, Science, and Art,* Vol. VI, No. 124 (August 12, 1871), 214–15.

any writing that pulsated with danger, romance, or urgency. Loring found Owens Lake despicable, full of alkaline water, with a black band one foot wide and two inches thick around it, of flies which fed on the crust and fostered maggots, which the Indians ate. But he spent more time describing their disreputable guide, a forty-niner, bear hunter, and squatter. The guide told Loring how a friend of his, forty years old, had married an eight-year-old girl. When the Bostonian expressed disbelief, his reply was: "We develop in California, we do."[21]

Actually, the trip across Death Valley was a strenuous, desperate endeavor which could easily have ended in disaster. Wheeler, who rarely deviated from the official dullness of army reports, lost his military reserve in describing it. "The route lay for more than 39 miles in light, white, drifting sand, which was traversed between 5 a.m. and 6 p.m., the center of the desert being reached about meridian," he wrote. Two of the command succumbed near nightfall, but after they were revived, the march was continued in the moonlight until finally, between three and four in the morning, a "living stream" was found. "Other marches," he added "have extended from fifty to sixty or even eighty hours, with scarcely a single halt."[22]

The attempt to make a successful survey of this vast desert land, the importance of success to the army and to himself, taxed Wheeler's abilities to the utmost. Fragmentary news items paint an unpleasant picture of a commander who walked the narrow edge of disaster many times, committed many errors in judgment, and in a few instances resorted to inexcusable cruelty to maintain order and achieve his objectives. The problem these unpleasant news fragments pose is frustrating, for Wheeler never mentions the incidents in his annual reports, nor is other evidence available to substantiate or disprove the charges.

One clipping (the newspaper is in no way identified) indicates that Wheeler's topographer, Louis Nell, came close to losing his life, "being found, however, after two days' exposure,

---

[21] Frederick W. Loring, "Into the Valley of Death," *Appleton's Journal of Literature, Science, and Art,* Vol. VI, No. 138 (November 18, 1871), 574–75.
[22] Wheeler, *Geographical Report,* 45.

all senses but that of sight being gone." And another member was reported to have died of consumption.[23]

Still another news item is headlined "Where is Egan?" It accuses Wheeler of leaving a guide named Hahn to die, the guide's belongings having been found "near the head of Gold Mountain, near Death Valley, in a canyon which has no outlet." (Charlie Hahn and William Egan are listed as civilian guides in Wheeler's *Geographical Report*, 660.) This was merely preliminary to the question about Egan, who was supposed to have guided O'Sullivan and a man named Price, but who failed to return with them. The news item then continues:

> As incidents illustrating the character of the man placed in command of this expedition, we will relate two or three of his noteworthy operations, not forgetting to mention, incidentally, that all his civilian employees were induced to give him a power of attorney, conveying to him the right to represent them in anything which might be found. Did the Government fit out a private prospecting expedition?
>
> Near Belmont [a mining town in central Nevada] the packers lost a mule, probably allowing it to stray, as they were not very closely herded. A boy was found herding cattle, who was taken to camp and, by Wheeler's order, tied by the thumbs to an elevated wagon tongue, to make him tell the whereabouts of the lost animal. It is almost needless to add that the boy's tormentor succeeded in eliciting nothing but protestations of ignorance.[24]

A third incident reported in the same news clipping involved Wheeler and his relations with the Indians. He had requested four braves to lead a party seventy miles across the desert to purchase some mules, but the Indians had asked for what Wheeler considered an outrageous sum of money in return for their work. So Wheeler ordered all four Indians tied to the ground until they came down in their demands. One untied him-

---

[23] Bancroft Library (Berkeley, California), Wheeler Scrapbook, P-W 32, Vol. I. It is not known for certain that this scrapbook did belong to Wheeler, but the librarians believe it did, and I believe that only Wheeler could have chosen the clippings it contains.

[24] *Ibid.*

self, but was shot three times while trying to escape, later dying of his wounds. The other three then started out with a corporal and a private accompanying, having agreed to guide the soldiers to the mules. An hour later the white men returned with news that the Indians had successfully escaped. Impetuously, Wheeler took to the trail, was soon surrounded by a dozen Indians, and only the presence of an "Indian Charley"—a half-blood or a squaw man—saved his life. And finally the news item ends with this:

> The Wheeler Exploring Party . . . seems to have been composed of brutes, if not worse. Two guides taken from the Owens River region have [not] since been heard from, and the *Inyo Independent* broadly hints that they were murdered by members of the party. . . . Evidently the Wheeler Exploring Party has disgraced the U. S. service.[25]

Are these news clippings all from the same paper, all by the same editor? Do they reflect personal animosity backed up by unjust rumors? We do not know. However, Wheeler never referred to the deaths of Hahn and Egan, and in the absence of further evidence it is only fair to assume that the two guides were neither murdered nor abandoned by the members of the survey. O'Sullivan was an honorable photographer, and the young officers under Wheeler's command were not murderers. The matter of cruelty to the boy and to the Indians is more difficult to evaluate, yet again, it could be that the stories are the product of the imagination of a frontier editor who was embittered at the survey for reasons we shall never know. Or could it be that Wheeler did fall back upon military discipline and unnecessary cruelty in order to prevent his expedition from ending as a failure?

All of this is speculative, but the foolishness of Wheeler's next endeavor is self evident. He purchased three flat-bottomed boats in San Francisco, had them delivered by way of the Gulf of California to Camp Mohave, near where the California border

[25] *Ibid.*

runs into the Colorado, and then proposed to row, tow, or push them two hundred miles up the river to Diamond Creek, in the Grand Canyon!

Why? Powell had already been down the river in 1869 and was repeating the journey in the same season in which Wheeler proposed to carry out his plan. Lieutenant Ives had been up the river in 1858. But Wheeler ignored Powell, expressed faith in the statements of raftsman James White, and set out to conquer the Colorado from the bottom up. He insisted that the primary aim of the trip was to ascertain the limits of practical navigation up the Colorado. Other investigations—geological and topographical—and a compilation of statistics on the velocity of the river and its width were to be made.[26]

About thirty-five men began the journey, although only twenty of them reached the mouth of Diamond Creek. Besides Wheeler, the white men included G. K. Gilbert, T. H. O'Sullivan, and Fred Loring. Six boatmen and six enlisted men from Camp Mohave, plus the Indian chief, Captain Asquit, and thirteen of his Mohave brethren completed the party. Wheeler said that he had three boats and a barge, but a picture facing page 156 of his *Geographical Report*, based on one of O'Sullivan's photographs, shows four boats and a barge.

On September 16, 1871, the party set out, boatmen, soldiers, and Indians all cheerfully pulling the boats with tow lines. The next day they made fifteen miles. Wheeler concluded a treaty about rations with the Mohave employees and posted strong guards that night, for by then they had entered the land of the Paiutes, with whom the Mohaves had recently been at war.

By September 23 they were in the midst of Black Canyon, with walls rising 1,700 feet above them, so that for the first part of the day the sun's rays never reached the river, and, wrote Wheeler, "the moon is now so far increased that the last two evenings in the Black Canyon have been most picturesque and lovely." Yet there was something strange, something sinister about being down in the deepest crevices of mother earth, and

[26] Wheeler, *Geographical Report*, 169–70. Pages 156–71 deal with the trip and include an itinerary kept by Wheeler.

there were "points at which a stillness like death creates impressions of awe." Wheeler was glad to leave it.

By September 26 they had reached the foot of Boulder Canyon, and the next day, a little farther upstream, Wheeler ordered a day of rest. They cleaned and caulked the boats and the barge, and O'Sullivan and his roving photographic party, in their own boat, the *Picture*, caught up with them, with news of good photographic successes.

The journey continued, and by September 29 they were at the mouth of the Virgin River. Above it the current was so strong that even the white men had to jump into the water and help pull the barge. Rattlesnakes added to the danger along the shore. The Mohaves were getting "tired and lazy," and the barge lagged behind and reached camp by dusk, its crew exhausted. But by October 4, at camp 18, the expedition had reached "The Crossing of the Colorado," where a land party commanded by Lieutenant Lockwood joined them, mail was received, and the whole party stayed over for a day of rest. Then they crossed to the north side of the river, losing only one animal in the dangerous undertaking.

The Mohaves got hold of the dead horse and feasted upon it. All of them got sick, and they called in a local specialist, a Paiute medicine man. He spent the greater part of a day working over them, making life "hideous by his roars, screams, and moans." But the Mohaves did recover—sufficiently to try desertion for a third time. Wheeler induced them to remain "by dint of threats and persuasions."

Three crews of nine persons each were now chosen to continue the ascent of the Colorado. It was with difficulty that they progressed, but the scenery was indescribably grand. Not the least of the canyon's charms were the contrasts—desert and water, dazzling sunlight and cooling shadow, massive gorges and smaller tributary canyons. In these, sparkling cool water babbled down from springs, giving moisture to great, delicate ferns, soft as a baby's bed, of gentle, cool green colors, and delicately patterned. Yet, as Wheeler's journal recorded, problems were close by:

October 11.—Camp No. 23, below Disaster Rapid. . . . Portage is made, and the rapid near camp passed. Another appears within one fourth of a mile, then smooth water for a little distance, after which a powerful rapid that takes the strength of all the three crews. Then appears another stretch of fair water that brings one to the worst rapid of the trip. All the boats were brought up and lines thrown ahead. This rapid seemed long but not dangerous, however, but the first boat going into it proved differently. The first dash filled the boat with water, the second swamped it, and in this way the lives of two boatmen were endangered. The boat ran back against the rocks almost a prefect wreck, and its contents were washed down below the overhanging rocks. A stout case containing my most valuable public and private papers and data for a great share of the season's report, which for the first time had not been taken out of the boat at a portage, was lost, as well as valuable instruments, the astronomical and meteorological observations, and worse than all the entire rations of that boat.[27]

The next morning everyone save Gilbert and Wheeler was despondent, but the desires of these two men to reach Diamond Creek prevailed over the wishes of the rest of the party, and by sheer tenacity and courage Wheeler and Gilbert pulled their boat over the rapids and the others followed. Rations had to be cut, and the ascent became more and more tedious, with smooth sandstone on each side of the river. On October 16, at "Starvation Camp," the weary Wheeler wrote in his journal, "To-day it has often been necessary to climb as high as 100 feet to pass the tow-rope ahead." And by October 18 the boats were leaking badly. Success was almost literally in sight, however, for on October 19 they reached their destination, Diamond Creek. It had taken them thirty-three days to push, pull, and row the two hundred miles upstream. When they returned to Camp Mohave, they accomplished the distance in just five days, demonstrating emphatically the strength of the current.

As soon as the party was safely back at Camp Mohave, the unit disbanded. Timothy O'Sullivan started for Washington, D.C., with a large collection of negatives. These were to adver-

[27] *Ibid.*, 164–65.

tise to the world not only the beauties of the Colorado River but also the bravery of the men of the Wheeler Survey. Unfortunately, O'Sullivan lost nearly all of his negatives en route.[28]

Then the flippant Frederick Loring started for San Bernardino, California, on one of the crude stage coaches then in use in Arizona. It was hoped that he would publish his accounts of high adventure in places where such material would be read by important and powerful people. But on Sunday, November 5, 1871, the hopes of young Loring as well as Wheeler's dreams of publicity came to an abrupt end. Loring and two other men attached to the Wheeler Survey had climbed aboard the canvas-topped buckboard at Wickenburg. An hour or so later the wagon passed within four to five feet of a band of Mohaves who were hiding in the brush. Then the Indians fired. The driver, Loring, and one other occupant were killed by the first volley; the second round killed three more passengers including the other two Wheeler men, William Salmon and P. W. Hamel. To add to the drama of this "Wickenburg Massacre," two other occupants of the stage, both of whom lived, were a Prescott jeweler and one Moll Shepard, a "disreputable character," and one report claimed that the Indians got $25,000 from the stage and even hinted that the bandits were not Indians at all![29]

They actually were Indians, however, and Wheeler made use of one of the Mohaves of the Colorado River trip, Maimum, who had been fond of Loring, to ferret out the redskinned assassins. Some of the killers were found and later punished during General Crook's command of the Department of Arizona.[30]

In relating this incident nearly twenty years after it happened, Wheeler was still unable to control his rage over a government policy that envisioned an eventual control of the Indians on reservations. The "peace at any cost" policy toward them was totally unacceptable to him. "Unfortunately," he wrote, "the bones of murdered citizens cannot rise to cry out and attest the atrocious murders of the far-spreading and wide-extending

28 *Ibid.,* 168.
29 New York *Times,* December 6, 1871, p. 8.
30 Wheeler, *Geographical Report,* 35.

border lands of the Great West, and while the fate of the Indian is sealed, the interval during which their extermination as a race is consummated will doubtless be marked . . . with still more murderous ambuscades and massacres."[31]

Statements like this, his references to his treatment of the Mohaves on the Colorado River trip, and newspaper clippings such as those quoted above, all cast an image of Lieutenant George M. Wheeler that is far from pleasant. And with O'Sullivan's pictures lost, and Loring's descriptions of the Colorado River adventure buried in his grave, what chance had the army survey against an aggressive Powell or Hayden, a suave and polished King?

Yet, in spite of his hard luck, Wheeler had the power of the United States Army behind him, and with its help he found his future brighter than ever.

[31] *Ibid.*

18

Mapping the West

THE ACCOMPLISHMENTS of the Wheeler Survey in 1871 consisted of a ninety-four page report and a preliminary topographic map on a scale of one inch to twenty-four miles of the 72,250 miles covered in 1871. Thus a beginning had been made toward mapping a vast area whose dusky inhabitants were about as hostile as the dry and barren climate. Marvine and Gilbert had made good beginnings in their geological explorations, some photographs had been preserved by O'Sullivan, and some collections of flora and fauna had been gathered.

During some of the long and lonely marches, Wheeler had considered the problem of mapping the Great West, and by the end of the field season, December 4, 1871, his comprehensive plan had grown considerably from what it had been six months before. Now he envisioned (as he explained to General Humphreys) a general mapping of the entire United States west of the one hundredth meridian. The project was never printed, but, according to Wheeler, it "was a plan substantially for a complete connected continuous detailed topographic survey (with natural history observations) . . . to be in the main an aid to military administration and operations, to occupy 15 years, and to cost, in all, not exceeding $2,500,000."[1] The original plans were for the map to be on a scale of one inch to eight miles, but it was later changed to one inch to four miles. The area under consideration was to be divided into 95 rectangular divisions, each of which, when presented upon a scale of one inch to four miles, would require four sheets, each 19 by 24 inches in size. The approximate size of the area represented by each atlas sheet would be 150 miles in longitude by 120 miles in latitude, "or in square miles, approximately 18,000, corresponding to 11,520,000 acres."[2] The project, according to Wheeler, was approved by the Chief of Engineers and the Secretary of War and was adopted by the Committee on Appropriations, the money for the fiscal year 1872 being granted on June 10 of that year.[3]

After his plan was approved in 1872, Wheeler gave his organization the official title of the United States Geographical Surveys West of the One Hundredth Meridian, and, learning by experience, he gradually converted his haphazard reconnaissance into a methodical survey. In 1872 and 1873, however, his organization was still more of the former, covering great areas of land—72,500 square miles in 1873 alone. But by 1874, his survey had become thorough, painstaking, and methodical, and in that year it covered an aggregate of only 23,281 square miles, never again to cover more than 40,000 square miles in a single year.[4] Latitude, longitude, and altitude were determined by the most advanced scientific methods, the meandering system of tracing valleys and roads being reduced in total importance while triangulation and plane-table work were increased. Although in the early years he had conveniently left certain large areas un-

[1] Wheeler, *Geographical Report*, 45.

[2] *Surveys of Territory West of the Mississippi River*, 45 Cong., 3 sess., *Sen. Exec. Doc. 21*, 15–16. This was certainly an approximation. Multiplying 18,000 by 95 rectangles will give a total of 1,710,000 square miles, but Wheeler stated that the total area west of the one Hundredth meridian was 1,433,360 square miles—a difference of 276,640 square miles. He does not explain this discrepency.

[3] Wheeler, *Report upon the Third Geographical Congress and Exhibition at Venice, Italy, 1881*, 48 Cong., 2 sess., *House Exec. Doc. 270*, 485. *U.S. Statutes at Large*, Vol. 17, 367. The sum granted was $75,000.

[4] Wheeler, *Geographical Report*, 40–46.

surveyed "as inaccessible, or not immediately necessary to be known for military purposes," he became more consistent with time and mapped all terrain that lay in the path of his men.[5] In 1874 Wheeler added the task of land classification to the duties of the topographical corps, and by 1879 over 175,000 square miles in the West had been subjected to classification under the four categories of (1) arable or agricultural land; (2) timber land; (3) pasturage or grazing land; (4) arid or barren land.[6]

In terms of personnel Wheeler always had a sizable survey. The smallest number of men employed was in 1869, when he took along ten officers and other assistants and an escort of twenty-seven; the largest number used was in 1873, when the personnel numbered eighty-nine officers and other assistants, and an escort of seventy-nine men. From 1871 there were always more than fifty officers and assistants along—a respectable number for a general survey.[7]

From 1875 on, the operations of the survey were conducted in two divisions, designated as the California and Colorado sections, and each of them was further broken down into parties. Occasionally a natural history party would go its own way without a military man at its head, but usually every party was led by an officer.[8]

In determining the caliber of the army men, the commanders of the defensive military escorts need not be included, for they did nothing more than protect and guard, but the administrators and division or party leaders, of which there were about twenty, should be carefully screened. They led the survey parties, carried out the field observations, and were responsible for achieving the objectives which Wheeler established for them each spring.

[5] *Surveys of Territory West of the Mississippi River*, 45 Cong., 3 sess., *Sen. Exec. Doc. 21*, 13. Stanford University Special Collections, Wheeler Survey, Letters Sent, Wheeler to Humphreys, April 28, 1878.

[6] Wheeler, *Geographical Report*, 223.

[7] Stanford University Special Collections, Wheeler Survey, Letters Sent, Wheeler to A. D. Lyle, 1878.

[8] *Ibid.*, Wheeler to Joseph Henry, 1877. Military and scientific personnel for each season are listed in Wheeler's *Geographical Report*, 659–92.

They were of high caliber, for the Engineers traditionally took the brightest men. Nineteen of them were West Point graduates, young men, mostly from the classes of 1868 through 1875. Three of them—Rogers Birnie, Jr., Eric Bergland, and Thomas W. Symons—had ranked first in their respective classes at the Point (1872, 1869, and 1874). Four had graduated third in their classes, four had ranked fourth, and only three had ranked below nine—one at number twelve and two at twenty-one—and even so they were in the upper fifty per cent of their classes.[9]

The high quality of the personnel helps explain the achievements, especially in the realm of topography, that the survey accomplished in its later years. Among the records that still exist concerning the Wheeler Survey, there is practically no indication of troubles, conflicts, or controversies among the officers or between Wheeler and his military subordinates. This is significant and creditable to Wheeler, for in these monotonous volumes, containing thousands of pages of official correspondence, just such trouble would have been chronicled.

But if the officers worked in harmony, their continual transfers out of the survey just when they had learned enough to be of value was a constant problem for the commanding officer. In a letter on the subject to Humphreys, Wheeler pointed out in late 1875 that one of his officers had served four seasons, three had served two seasons, and nine had served one season—and now, for 1876, it appeared that he would have only two experienced officers with him (Bergland and Morrison), and all the rest would be new to the work. "Duty upon the Survey requires considerable experience with it," he emphasized, pleading that

[9] Cullum, *Biographical Register*, II. The following list includes the names of the men, their classes, and their class ratings. Eric Bergland, 1869, 1; Rogers Birnie, Jr., 1872, 1; Stanhope E. Blunt, 1872, 3; Eugene Griffin, 1875, 3; R. L. Hoxie, 1868, 3; D. W. Lockwood, 1866, 9; Henry H. Ludlow, 1876, 6; A. D. Lyle, 1869, 12; M. M. Macomb, 1874, 4; Philip M. Price, 1869, 4; B. H. Randolph, 1870, 21; A. H. Russell, 1871, 4; Thomas W. Symons, 1874, 1; Samuel E. Tillman, 1869, 3 (later commanding officer at West Point); George M. Wheeler, 1866, 6; Charles W. Whipple, 1868, 21; Willard Young, 1875, 4 (son of Brigham Young). William L. Carpenter does not appear on the rolls as a West Point graduate; he was both officer and entomologist, and he also served with Hayden.

some provision be made for officers to be granted longer assignments with the survey.[10] There is no indication that Wheeler's letter accomplished anything, and every season men had to be briefed anew about the organization and about the equipment, its care and use. This cut the efficiency of the otherwise capable military men that Wheeler had at his disposal.

In regard to scientific personnel, Wheeler's record is commendable in choice of men, if not in management. He hired Edward Drinker Cope as paleontologist in 1874, and Cope, Charles A. White, and Fielding Bradford Meek did much of the work in preparing the paleontological reports. John J. Stevenson, Jules Marcou, Grove Karl Gilbert, and Archibald Marvine spent some years with the Wheeler Survey. Joseph T. Rothrock, employed in the dual capacity of acting assistant surgeon of the army as well as botanical observer, became known as an outstanding botanist and a leader in the drive for forest conservation.[11] Henry Wetherbee Henshaw, Wheeler's ornithologist, later became the head of the Biological Survey in the Department of Agriculture. Both Rothrock and Henshaw found a haven in Wheeler's survey while their health improved.[12] Henry C. Yarrow, an army surgeon, likewise made notable contributions in zoology and ornithology.[13]

But this does not mean that Lieutenant Wheeler and his military colleagues commanded the respect of the scientists. For in fact, the old antagonism between army men and scientists loomed large in the Wheeler Survey. The army way and the way of science simply would not mix.

The scientists needed freedom, and restrictions of any kind curtailed their progress and of course ruffled their tempers. Cope, in 1874, had to disobey Wheeler's orders or else fail to

[10] Stanford University Special Collections, Wheeler Survey, Letters Sent, Wheeler to Humphreys, 1875.

[11] *Dictionary of American Biography*, XVI, 188. Joseph Ewan, *Rocky Mountain Naturalists*, 293. This book contains an excellent listing of early naturalists.

[12] *Dictionary of American Biography*, VII, 564. Ewan, *Naturalists*, 228. According to Ewan, Henshaw's appointment came on the recommendation of Spencer Baird, whom Wheeler had consulted in his search for an ornithologist.

[13] Ewan, *Naturalists*, 343.

make what he later considered his greatest discovery.[14] And scientists were asked to send in all manner of reports, the most irritating of which were "Progress Reports," which by their very name implied continuing progress and continuous results.

But there is another side of the coin, and it is tarnished too. The scientists could be a pretty difficult group of prima donnas for anyone to handle. Cope, for example, was always at war with the army, for he lagged in his manuscript preparations, protested when editorial changes were made, and even tried to include in the official publications several barbs pointed at his arch enemy and fellow paleontologist, Othniel Charles Marsh. Poor Wheeler, trying to get along with Cope, trying to be fair with him, and trying to be impartial, simply incurred the wrath of all.

Concerning one of Cope's more violent letters to him, following Wheeler's editing of Cope's report, the Lieutenant replied firmly, "I have to ask you to withdraw entirely the sentence in your letter that reads 'I think it could be shown to be a form of forgery.' Had your report, like the others, been received in good time, a careful consideration and comparison could have been made." Later Wheeler had to delete unfair references in Cope's report to that scientist's rivals. "I cannot permit that your report or that of any person received . . . shall by the slightest inference reflect upon anyone engaged upon similar work," Wheeler reminded him. "If you wish to reflect upon Prof. Marsh you must do it outside of reports published by this office." And again he reminded Cope that he could not insert new manuscript matter into the galley proofs. Finally, Cope even implied that Wheeler possessed some sinister reasons for not publishing his volume more promptly.[15]

Of course Cope was only half of the Cope-Marsh feud. Marsh wrote to Wheeler and implied that he was being unfair to *him*, and patiently Wheeler sat down and wrote Marsh a letter in which he stressed how he tried to co-operate with all the scien-

[14] Osborn, *Cope*, 201.

[15] Stanford University Special Collections, Wheeler Survey, Letters Sent, Wheeler to Cope, December 19, 1875; April 4, 1877; April 12, 1877; April 7, 1877; Letters Received, Cope to Wheeler, August 27, 1877.

tists, not just with Cope but with Marsh also, and he reminded Marsh that he had sent him several fragments of vertebrates. And they even fought among themselves within the survey. White, the paleontologist, protested that Cope sent him a bunch of fossils that were "worthless fragments."[16]

After spending three years with Wheeler, G. K. Gilbert asked to be relieved, but Wheeler "requested" the geologist to complete his report, since he had published almost nothing while with the survey. "I have ever sought to give to all the civilian specialists connected with the Survey, the utmost scope for individuality in the prosecution of their duties and preparation of reports," Wheeler protested to Gilbert, trying to defend the army position. But Gilbert went through with his resignation (although he did complete his report). When he requested permission to keep his notebooks, he was curtly informed that "it is not army policy to let the civilians keep the notebooks." Nor could Gilbert publish material outside of army publications until it had first appeared in official documents.[17]

In general ability, then, the personnel of the Wheeler Survey, both military and civilian, compared favorably with that of rival surveys. In fact, along with its packers, cooks, scientists, Army men, journalists, photographers, pack-jacks, jennies, mules, horses, tents, food supplies, survey equipment, heavy woolen clothing, hob-nailed boots, and the odor of horses, saddle soap, and unwashed humanity, the survey was not unlike Hayden's and King's. Only in its military leadership, and in its emphasis on mapping, was it different.

The chief journalist for the Wheeler Survey was William H. Rideing, who wrote for *Appleton's, Harper's,* and other magazines and kept the New York *Times* posted on the activities of the survey during the field seasons of 1875 and 1876. Rideing later published his newspaper articles in a little book entitled *A-Saddle in the Wild West: A Glimpse of Travel among the*

[16] Stanford University Special Collections, Wheeler Survey, Letters Sent, Wheeler to Marsh, January 24, 1876; Wheeler to Cope, May 3, 1875.

[17] Stanford University Special Collections, Wheeler Survey, Letters Received, Gilbert to Wheeler, June 7, 1874; Letters Sent, Wheeler to Gilbert, June 7, 1874; November 5, 1874; October 23, 1874.

Mountains, Lava Beds, Sand Deserts, Adobe Towns, Indian Reservations, and Ancient Pueblos of Southern Colorado, New Mexico, and Arizona.[18]

He was a New Yorker, a city man, and a reporter doing a job. From his descriptions we can piece together a picture of the Wheeler Survey in action. Rideing had arrived at Pueblo, Colorado Territory (a town, he said, "as Puritanical as a New England village"), early in June, 1875, there to meet the survey. Wheeler had already entrained for Los Angeles, where his California division was assembling. He had left the Colorado division to be split up into three parts, one each under the command of Lieutenants William Carpenter, William Marshall, and C. C. Morrison. The three topographers with the division—Frederick A. Clark, Frank Maxon, and J. S. Spiller—had already seen several seasons of service with Wheeler and were competent men.

The outfit, Rideing soon discovered, was hardly what pictures of tent-life at Wimbledon would lead the easterner to expect. The tents were of light canvas shaped like the letter *A*, each one three and one-half feet high, five feet long, four feet wide at bottom—pup tents, as they are known today. Bed consisted of a sheet of canvas, "with one rubber and three pair of woolen blankets stretched on the ground, which you share with as many grasshoppers, moths, centipedes, scorpions, and rattlesnakes as may choose you for a companion." You saddled your own mules, and your food was "seasoned with unlimited quantities of dust . . . said to sharpen the teeth and strengthen the stomach."[19]

The New Yorker accompanied Morrison's division, which pulled out of Pueblo on June 14, 1875. Their area of operations was to lead them to Fort Garland in the San Luis Valley of Colorado, south from there into New Mexico, westward into northern

[18] In 1872, The New York *Herald* ran at least one article on the Wheeler expedition (October 5, 1872, p. 10). In 1874, the New York *Times* assigned a reporter to Wheeler, and his articles are sprinkled throughout the newspaper for that year. I believe this reporter was Almont Barnes, listed in Wheeler's *Geographical Report*, 674, as "general assistant," the same title given Rideing. According to the Library of Congress Catalogue, Almont Barnes published six books during the period 1875–90, and although none of them deal with the West, this leads me to believe that Barnes was a reporter.

[19] New York *Times*, June 13, 1875, p. 13.

Arizona, then southeastward through northwestern and north-central New Mexico. Santa Fe would be more or less the center of their field of activities.

The outfit consisted of nine men and twenty-two mules. The mules reacted in the usual fashion to the first days on the trail, but they soon fell into line "behind that godsend of surveyors, the bell-mare," which in this case was a white horse ridden by a Negro cook. "A pack mule's only consolation," remarked Rideing, "seems to be in rubbing noses with the bell-mare, which receives all advances with an ill-humored snort and a contemptuous shake of the head."

The New Yorker was not carried away by Colorado's splendor. He found it dry and barren and thought that the "barrenest of our Eastern States appear gardens in comparison." Even the young ladies had suffered from the dry air, their beauty being shriveled and parched. Soon, however, the party began climbing into the Rockies toward Fort Garland, eighty-five miles to the southwest. The mountains were beautiful after all, and when they reached the crest of the Sangre de Cristo range, even the cynical city man waxed poetic. A day or two later the party reached Fort Garland, in the San Luis Valley of Colorado, nearly 8,000 feet high. There they were entertained by two pitiful companies of cavalry serving out their time in complete boredom.[20]

Garland's little rectangular group of squat, flat roofed, red adobe buildings struck Rideing as being a pleasant military establishment, but a lonely one. The nearest railroad was back at Pueblo, mail arrived by wagon twice a week, and travelers were rare. "Nevertheless not an item of discipline was omitted," said the *Times* man. "The reville was beaten [and the] guard was mounted and relieved in the fullest and neatest dress, and to inspiring music, even though six men were all the post could muster. Reports were submitted and received with the same pomp and circumstance as one observed in the largest army, and the sentries challenged with unremitted vigilance all who passed the gates." The routine was broken only by a very occa-

[20] New York *Times*, June 13, 1875, p.13; July 3, 1875, p. 3.

sional Indian scare, or by a more frequent search for an escapee from the guard house. The officers invited the survey men into their homes, which were crudely built but made interesting by the animal skins and relics of the chase which were prominently displayed on the floors and walls. But it was the beginning of the season, there was much work to be done, and the Wheeler men were soon on their way again.[21]

Moving southwesterly, the party headed for New Mexico. As they crossed the San Luis Valley, they marvelled at the massive distant peaks of the San Juans—and cursed at the prairie-dog-filled prairie over which they trod. The mountain wind tore at their clothing, and the silent land added to their feelings of isolation. In every direction, mountain peaks, snow-capped at this time of the year, rose up like islands from the plain over which they marched. The San Luis Valley was high, unreal, and unworldly. They were happy to leave it.

On the third day out of Fort Garland, they reached the Spanish-American settlement of Conejos, just north of the border, and boasting a Roman Catholic church built in 1856. Here Rideing was fascinated by the culture of the people, "a mixed race of Spaniards, Indians, and half-breeds," full of "Old World superstitions," where the principal instruction was given by a few priests "and blind fanaticism exhibits itself in the most extraordinary forms." He found the women fat and squat, but with the sweetest of all human voices, uttering *no sabe* and *quien sabe* "with a gentle, melting, longing intonation to be enjoyed." And the maidens, he added, "carry earthen vessels of water on their heads in the same manner that Rebecca did in the time of the patriarchs." Their last view of Conejos, as a new guide led the party southward, included "a native plowing a field with an iron-shod forked stick dragged by a pair of oxen."

Meanwhile, side parties were climbing the peaks, building pyramids, making their triangulations, while the main party was taking readings and meandering the route, making notes that would be of value to future travelers over the terrain.[22]

---

[21] Rideing, *A-Saddle in the Wild West,* 30.
[22] New York *Times,* July 19, 1875, p. 1.

After they had rested briefly at the little north New Mexican town of Tierra Amarilla, they set out for the dry and dangerous northeastern corner of Arizona. They were advised to fill their canteens and trust in Providence, taking along twenty-one days' rations. Soon they entered the mesa country, some of the great earth forms resembling "great iron-clads, with projecting rams at the bows," and the sandstone strata added blood red to predominately light yellow rock, with a dark green or a faint shade of blue appearing now and then. At the end of the second day they camped by a muddy creek, "with water of the color and thickness, without the flavor, of rich cream."

Then they came on bad weather, and for five days, as they headed through the rain for the Canyon de Chelly, they plodded through mud. There was no grass for the stock, and horrible sores appeared on the backs of their mules. Rattlesnakes were plentiful, and a dangerous centipede, about five inches long, one-fourth of an inch thick, light, watery looking with black claws, and poisonous wherever the claws touched the skin, had a tendency to take refuge in their bed clothes.

Soon they came upon the pueblo ruins that are today embraced in the Canyon de Chelly National Monument. They explored Pueblo Pintado (Painted Town) on the banks of the Chaco River, crossed the Chaska Range via Washington Pass, and, after the rigors of the desert, marvelled at the stately pines, the spreading cottonwoods, and the carpet of wild flowers— "bluebells of the tenderest blue; roses red, white, and yellow, of the most exquisite fragrance; large buttercups and daisies that might have wafted from English meadows; purple-flowered morning glories." When the party reached a clearing, they pitched camp and were almost immediately visited by Navahos, for they were on the reservation.

At first, Rideing wrote favorably of the Navahos, calling them "a peaceable tribe, a good-looking tribe, and an honest tribe as Indians go. The squaws," he noticed (for he had an eye for the women), "have wondrously fine arms and ankles, and flashing black eyes. Their laugh is low and musical and tender." But a

Beaman photograph
National Archives

Powell's expedition at Green River, 1871.

T. H. O'Sullivan photograph
National Archives

Start of the Colorado River Expedition (Wheeler Survey)
from Camp Mohave, Arizona, 1871.

T. H. O'Sullivan photograph
Smithsonian Institution

Canyon de Chelley (Wheeler Survey).

Fred W. Loring and his mule, "Evil Merodach," about two days
before his murder, as photographed by O'Sullivan.
From a stereopticon set produced by the U. S. Geographical
and Geological Surveys West of the One Hundredth Meridian.

Maiman, a Mohave Indian guide and interpreter who later
helped find the murderers of young Loring (O'Sullivan photograph).
From the stereopticon set described on the opposite page.

T. H. O'Sullivan photograph
Denver Public Library Western Collection

Distant view of Camp Apache, Arizona (Wheeler Survey).

T. H. O'Sullivan photograph
Denver Public Library Western Collection

Mining development somewhere in Nevada (Wheeler Survey, 1873).

T. H. O'Sullivan photograph
Denver Public Library Western Collection

Looking across the Colorado River to the mouth of Paria Creek
(Wheeler Survey, 1873).

reappraisal was not so favorable. "Before a person has been among them a week, a feeling of utter disgust and contempt for them overcomes him. They are mendacious, lazy, and filthy in the extreme. When they cannot find a chance to steal they will beg for dinner, tobacco, or anything else that is available. Most of them, too, are horribly tainted with diseases introduced by the whites, and as we approached Fort Wingate we met several squaws ordered away from the post on account of their loathsome condition."[23]

They shortly turned southeastward and reached Fort Wingate, about twelve miles southeast of Gallup. There they enjoyed their first substantial rest in six weeks. For five days they remained there before taking the field again with fresh stock, and for two weeks, as they explored the Zuni Mountains to the southwest, they enjoyed fresh water and a good, though limited diet. Then they came to some Pueblo Indian settlements, and Rideing found the Pueblos more to his liking than the Navahos. The party explored some of the extinct volcanoes west of the Zuni Mountains, marvelling at their symmetry and the beauty of the green cottonwoods and the pretty wild flowers that grew on the extinct floors. They worked for eight weeks in sight of 13,000-foot Mount Taylor (which is actually three summits). It was beautiful to look in their direction in the evenings, "when they glowed for a moment before a heavy haze of blue flooded them like a rising tide, and closed them in its folds for the livelong night."[24]

After skirting Santa Fe for three months, the expedition finally entered the town—"a full-grown settlement when New York was a baby in arms," Rideing said of it, "and . . . as hoary in wickedness as it is in age." It seemed so foreign. They entered by a narrow little street of one-storied houses, and women sat outside the doorways making cigarettes, pulling their shawls over their heads. At one point an eight-bull wagon team blocked the route, and "the Mexican drivers hissed and spluttered like

[23] New York *Times,* August 9, 1875, p. 1.
[24] New York *Times,* September 4, 1875, p. 1; September 19, 1875, p. 1.

so many frying-pans filled with gravy" as they tried to move it. The public square of Santa Fe was surrounded by stores, save on the north side, where the governor's "palace" stood. "Quite an active throng circulates on the plaza," Rideing noticed, "—fashionably-dressed civilians, military officers in blue and gold, rough-looking soldiers, weather-beaten emigrants and broad-hatted teamsters with raw-hide whips that crack like a pistol. There is a clanking of spurs on the sidewalk, and some dashing cavalrymen clatter around the corner." But the New Yorker was appalled at the completely amoral attitude of Santa Fe's best citizens, nearly all of whom gambled and caroused with "unfortunate women," and thought nothing of it.[25]

Before they left the wicked city, Carpenter's party came in, minus a couple of side parties, having already covered over 1,000 miles and surveyed over 3,000 square miles. But as his group rested, Morrison's took to the field again. On a warm morning—"an indolent, enervating, bit of Summer that had fallen into Autumn"—they headed northward. But soon the weather turned cold and damp, and Rideing came down with chills and fever. For a time he left the survey and stayed with a ranching family, but the boredom—and the yapping of their thirteen dogs—drove him back to Santa Fe and what medicines he could find there.[26]

He recovered and joined the party again east of Santa Fe. By then, Rideing had suffered through cloud bursts, wind storms, snow storms, centipedes in his bed, bacon and beans and pork and dried fruit as a steady diet, and he could almost consider himself an old hand. The news of the death of one of Wheeler's men in southern California from exposure did not phase him. Yet he could never quite accept the West. He still found sitting around an evening campfire a far cry from the pleasurable experience "which juvenile and inexperienced people" insisted it was. "The camp fire," he growled, "always reminds me of how cold my back is. . . . The smoke suffocates, the

[25] New York *Times*, October 10, 1875, p. 3.
[26] New York *Times*, October 13, 1875, p. 3.

flame scorches, and the flying sparks raise serious blisters on the exposed parts of the skin. The eyes smart and fill with tears, and the lungs labor under the astringency of the fumes that find their way into them. . . . And yet," he added:

When the supper is over and pipes are lighted . . . the yarn is woven busily on the spindle of ready tongues, and the brighter the blaze the more exciting are the stories involved. Lieut. Morrison is usually absent from these gatherings of wondermongers, and could you see through the darkness you would probably find him stretched out on a blanket star-gazing with a quadrant, and absorbed in his astronomical observations, which form an important part of the work of the survey. The scientific men are young and diffident, and are only heard in an occasional interrogation. So the burden of the conversation falls on the packers and the cook, who are fully qualified to carry it on to the length of a Chinese novel, while its range is limited to the Westward of the Missouri. There is Aleck who came to Colorado during the Pike's Peak excitement, and has since led a wild life stockraising in Texas, and prospecting for gold among the mountains from Harney's Peak in the Black Hills down to the spurs of the San Juan. Another member of our party is Juan, the Mexican, who has led a wilder life still, and has been in jail for selling cartridge lead among the Apaches, and another is Sam, an excellent sample of the roving young American adventurer, who fought through the latter part of the war, and coming out unscathed, has since been trying to dispose of himself among the freeshooters of ruffianly border towns. Then there is Nick, who has passed a good part of his young life buffalo hunting on the Plains, and Green Terril, the cook, an ex-slave, whose prime boast is that he 'never had enough liquor aboard to make him walk unsteady and never took the good Lord God Almighty's name in vain in all his life.' Which is a great deal more than most men who have spent fifteen years in Colorado and Nevada can truthfully say for themselves. The multitudinous episodes in the lives of these waifs, the patient industry of the gold-seekers, the nerve and daring of the huntsman, the fertile ingenuity of the scouts, and the recklessness of the frontiersman . . . afford topics for endless conversation, and when the resinous pine logs sing and the flames leap to their highest our pulses beat faster as we listen to the strange stories told with a simplicity that removes all doubts of their strict veracity.[27]

And so the little party kept hard at work into the cool months of autumn. Since leaving Pueblo, they had covered nearly 2,000 route miles in Colorado, Arizona, and New Mexico. When bad weather kept them in camp, the whole force worked on computations, and on the days when they did take the field, they were most likely to break into three detachments and, with the experience of a season behind them, accomplish nearly three times what a single unit could have done. But by now the New York traveler was getting anxious to return to his winter quarters near Times Square. He inquired about coach connections with the railhead at Las Animas, Colorado, and prepared to make his way home.[28]

So it was that at five o'clock on a cold, dark morning early in November he stood waiting under the patio of Chapman's ranch and hotel at Las Vegas, New Mexico, quite uncertain whether he could get a seat on the stage or not. Fortunately the coach arrived empty. Following advice, he bribed the conductor, the driver, and the station master each with six stiff drinks of whisky —and then forgot what he had bribed them for. He was about to climb aboard the rickety little vehicle when three "red-eyed, sallow, and sleepy-looking" Texas stockmen appeared out of the darkness, their night's carousing at an end. Yes, they too were going to Las Animas. " 'Four of you will just balance her,' said the driver, 'and we'll go sailin', sailin' (hic) along like a lovely (hic) little moonbeam. A-all b-board!' "

With fear and trembling Rideing squeezed into the coach and tried to make himself completely unobtrusive, if not invisible. "You probably have no idea," he said to his readers, "how jovial a ruffian a Texas stockman is—how infinite his profanity, how broad his sense of humor, how audacious and defiant all his in-

27 New York *Times,* October 31, 1875, p. 10.
28 New York *Times,* November 22, 1875, p. 2.

stincts." Compared with a Texan, a Bowery "butcher boy" was as tame as a lamb. But what was worse, the jolting coach livened them up, a bottle appeared, and for two hours the Texans drained the bottle, roughhoused until the compartment was a shambles. "I crouched in a corner apprehensively watching the elephantine play which threatened to crush me every moment. . . . The big-booted ruffians hugged, hit, and rolled over each other in wild glee, and as we jolted over the hillocks they bounced to the roof and came down like lumps of lead." Even the third Texan, the one who had turned Rideing's stomach at the very start by dressing a bullet wound in his abdomen "which he proudly exhibited . . . as the memorial of a recent combat near the borders of old Mexico," participated in the free-for-all. Finally their faces whitened to a deathly hue, and the smiles waned into the "idiotic vacancy of drunkenness."

The journey continued in agony over the drab plains of northern New Mexico. The coach was not a spacious Concord, but was smaller, "with two benches, six inches wide and three and a half feet long, stretched athwart. It was covered with canvas, and was without glass windows, the substitutes for them being blinds fastened with a buckle and a strap. The bottom was strewn with dirt and hay—principally dirt—and the seats were covered with leather." Two days and two nights were to be spent in it.

The first day the breakfast consisted of buffalo meat, eggs, and bread; supper, eleven hours later, was of fried pork, bread, and coffee. On the morning of the second day the scenery changed, and Raton Pass was crossed, and Trinidad, Colorado Territory, appeared, modern and "American" after the slow pace of the towns of Spanish New Mexico. At Trinidad they transferred to another, still smaller coach and added a fifth passenger—a Methodist minister. "The Texans," Rideing said, "had lost their spirits or they would probably have thrown him out of the window, but instead of that they determined to smoke him out. . . . They filled the foulest of pipes with the vilest of tobacco and puffed thick clouds into his face. They swore the roundest of oaths and sang the vilest of songs. The poor old gentleman coughed a mild protest, and complained that some of the songs, which would have choked the audience of a Water street dance house, were 'a little coarse!' "[29]

But on November 4, the Southern Overland Express pulled into Las Animas, Colorado, with its correspondent, its three Texans, and its man of the cloth. The fate of the stockmen and the preacher is unknown, although we may safely surmise that they did not end up in the same place. As for William H. Rideing, special correspondent for the New York *Times,* he dragged himself aboard the eastbound train, collapsed into a soft seat, and conjured up fantastic visions about how nice it would be to take wing and be in New York in time for a dinner at Delmonicos.

Yet he must have found something to his liking out West, for he spent the following season with another one of Wheeler's parties.[30]

William Rideing was no Mark Twain, and many of his attempts at humor fell flat. His writing had a general air of poorly concealed exaggeration, if not fabrication. Yet he was with the survey. The trouble was, he was with it without being a part of it. He did not share in the enthusiasm about new sights and new discoveries. Instead he complained about the hardships, wrote about the people he saw, and loved the opportunity to make comparisons between New York, or the humid east coast, and the dry and barren Colorado plains.

He lacked the boyish enthusiasm of an Ernest Ingersoll, a William Henry Jackson, a Clarence King, or a John Wesley Powell. Those men accepted the rigors of survey life without a whimper, for their interest lay in the thrill of new discoveries, the beauties of the virgin land.

[29] New York *Times,* November 4, 1875, p. 2.

[30] New York *Times,* August 14, 1876, p. 5; September 13, 1876, p. 5; September 24, 1876, p. 10; October 1, 1876, p. 4; October 9, 1876, p. 3; October 31, 1876, p. 3; November 5, 1876, p. 4; December 4, 1876, p. 2. Rideing was in southern Nevada and California, around Virginia City and Lake Tahoe, during this season.

In the course of their work, 1869 and 1871 through 1879, Wheeler's men listed the locations and examined some 219 mining districts and made "observations and delineations of the physical details of 143 mountain ranges, 103 groups of mountains, and 3 plateaux [*sic*] within the limits surveyed topographically, from among the 161 ranges, 196 mountain groups, and 41 plateaux [which he listed] for the entire mountainous area." Wheeler also claimed that his survey located and made profiles of 202 mountain passes, followed 90 rivers and countless streams, determined the heights of 395 peaks above 10,000 feet, and named many of them, explored 21 lakes, including Great Salt Lake, discovered "not less than 50 thermal and mineral springs," discovered one new species of bird, eight new reptiles, 32 new fishes, one new mollusk, and 64 new insects. These were but a minute part of the collections that were made in all branches of the natural sciences. He figured his total number of specimens, ranging from "rocks" through "archeology," and including natural science, at 61,659, all of which were placed in the custody of the Smithsonian Institution.[31] Such detailed statistics, available for none of the other surveys, speak well for army thoroughness.

Yet when the consolidation debate took place in 1878, it was immediately clear that just about everyone was against the Army and commonly agreed that the Wheeler Survey should be abolished. The scientists were the most hostile group of all. They wanted no army interference whatsoever with their pursuit of science.

The 1870's were years of great activity in the history of American science. Not only was it a period of much original research, but it was a time of trial and error in the administration of scientific activities. What was the government's roll to be in furthering scientific knowledge? No one knew, but the scientists were working to create a precedent of governmental aid embodied in a sound government bureau. The army, which had always

[31] Wheeler, *Geographical Report*, 137. Stanford University Special Collections, Wheeler Survey, Letters Sent, Wheeler to Humphreys, April 28, 1878.

considered itself as a leader in explorations, engineering, and science in general, thus had much to lose if it failed to get the scientists on its side. And the army failed miserably.

The hostility of the men of science was apparent at least by the time of the congressional investigation of 1874. They disliked militarism with all its restrictions and regulations, and they suspected the Wheeler Survey of being the instrument by which the army hoped to take over all the surveys. The discovery in 1873 that both Wheeler and Hayden were operating over the same area in Colorado's South Park solidified the opposition of the scientists and was used as the reason for bringing about the investigation in 1874.

Actually, Wheeler's party, under the command of Lieutenant William L. Marshall, entered an area where Henry Gannett's party of the Hayden Survey had been working for three weeks.[32] The result was an unpleasant investigation that accomplished very little—save that Wheeler was to work south of the most northerly of the Spanish Peaks (located northwest of Trinidad in southern Colorado).[33]

Was this infringement upon Hayden's area part of a plan to take over western surveys? It is not possible to say. The army plan, it will be recalled, provided for a complete survey of all the states and territories west of the one hundredth meridian. If there was duplication, and surely the army knew there would be, then the army men believed that when the cards were laid on the table, Congress would favor the army. If this was true, then the army error lay in underestimating the opposition. Powell, Hayden, and King had powerful connections in Washington.

The attitude of scientific men was best reflected by the geologist Josiah Whitney, who pointed out in 1875 that "thus far the field-work of Wheeler's Survey has been almost exclusively carried on in the same region in which Messrs. Powell and Gardner have been employed, and it is evident," Whitney stressed, "that

---

[32] Gannett, "Geographical Report of Henry Gannett," *Seventh Annual Report,* 670.

[33] *Annual Report of the Chief of Engineers,* 44 Cong., 1 sess., *House Exec. Doc. 1,* Part 2, Appendix LL, 935.

this has not been done without design. It has been, and probably still is, the wish of the engineer bureau to put a stop to all topographical work done in the region west of the one hundredth meridian, except such as may be under their own direction."[34] In the hearings of 1874, members of the Yale faculty, including Professors Dana, Brewer, and Brush, had memorialized the committee not to place the surveys under the War Department, and members of the Harvard faculty and of the faculty of the Massachusetts Institute of Technology also protested. So too did James A. Garfield on behalf of the American Geographical Society.[35]

Five years later, when a stronger move was made to bring about a consolidation, the Army Engineers did not have a chance, and their elimination from the field met with the approval of all their competitors. Yet in retrospect, this accomplishment of abolishing the Wheeler Survey, so happily acclaimed by Powell and Hayden and King—this great victory over the army— spelled defeat for the best interests of the United States. And this is why:

At a very moderate cost, probably of not over two million dollars, the Wheeler Survey could have completed its fifteen year project for the mapping of the territories and states west of the one hundredth meridian. "The field work," Wheeler wrote, "could have been completed by 1887, if not earlier."[36] Thus by 1887, plus five to six years for office work, the War Department could have presented the citizens of the United States with a reasonably accurate map of about 1,500,000 square miles. Under the guidance and administration of the United States Geological Survey, such a map has not yet been completed.

Would Wheeler's maps have been good enough for practical

[34] Josiah Dwight Whitney, "Geographical and Geological Surveys," *North American Review*, Vol. CXXI, No. 248 (July–October, 1875), 83.

[35] *Surveys of Territory West of the Mississippi River*, 45 Cong., 3 sess., *Sen. Exec. Doc. 21*, 73–75.

[36] Wheeler, *Geographical Report*, 692n. Wheeler spent a total of $559, 316, placing him next to Hayden in total expenditures. National Academy of Sciences, *A Report on the Surveys of the Territories*, 45 Cong., 3 sess., *House Misc. Doc. 5*, 22. Stanford University Special Collections, Wheeler Survey, Letters Sent, Wheeler to Humphreys, April 28, 1878.

purposes? Yes. As H. G. Wright, acting chief of engineers, stated to the committee in 1878, "The methods to be employed, and the degree of precision to be maintained, depend upon the actual and prospective requirements of the government, . . . the wants of the inhabitants, and of those who are looking toward the West with views of emigration or investment."[37] The army's aim, then, was for sort of an "outline map," based upon the best trigonometrical and topographical methods, exhibiting the chief geographical features. Then, as time went on, and certain areas became populated and required better, more precise, more detailed or minute maps, an accurate "framework map" would be available, and the more detailed survey could be accomplished quickly and accurately.

No sounder concept of needs, both for then and for the future, was heard at the hearings. But the logical arguments set forth by the army were lost among the scientists and the congressmen alike. In trying to save money by consolidation, Congress therefore literally threw away all the sound work that had been accomplished by Wheeler—and since 1873 most of his work had been of high caliber. Congress prevented the completion of a good, useful, overall map of the West and dismantled Wheeler's organization, which by 1878 was functioning smoothly and capably. Half a million dollars and the energies of all of Wheeler's topographers over a period of nearly ten years went for naught.

It is small wonder that Wheeler, promoted to captain in that year, broke down from the defeat and was on sick leave from 1880 until 1884. During this period, however, he was commissioned the delegate from the War Department to the Third International Geographical Congress and Exhibition at Venice, Italy. From this assignment came his *Report of the Third Geographical Congress and Exhibition at Venice, Italy, 1881,* in which he presented his case for control of explorations and surveys by the War Department.[38] He complained bitterly of

[37] National Academy of Sciences, *A Report on the Surveys of the Territories,* 45 Cong., 3 sess., *House Misc. Doc. 5,* 7.
[38] 48 Cong., 2 sess., *House Exec. Doc. 270.*

the destruction of his survey, writing that it was "suspended on account, it is believed, of persistent adverse claims set up by certain geologists and others in the name of science . . . the result of which has been a plain and positive step backward hitherto without precedent throughout the civilized world."[39]

In 1885 and 1886, back on active duty, the Captain was hard at work completing the final reports of the survey. By 1889, when his *Geographical Report* was finally published, Wheeler could list a total of 164 maps and 41 reports among the accomplishments of his organization.[40] Unfortunately, a single, bound atlas was never compiled, but seven final reports were published, beautiful examples of the bookmaker's art.[41] Wheeler was retired on June 15, 1888, for disability contracted in line of duty, and he died in New York City May 3, 1905, at the age of sixty-three.[42]

If Wheeler could have completed his mapping of the West, then his survey could have accomplished the most important goal of all. Destruction of his organization in a sense made most of his work of negligible value. The most practical achievement to come from the Wheeler Survey was due primarily to—of all things—an excruciatingly painful toothache, Lieutenant Marshall's toothache, to be exact.

It was in late November of 1873, and the Lieutenant was holed up at the mining camp of Silverton, in the San Juan Mountains of southwestern Colorado. His jaw was so swollen that he could hardly move it, and he was living on thick gruel that he could suck into his mouth from a spoon without moving his jaws. The nearest dentist was in Denver, 300 miles away over cold and stormy mountain terrain. But to Denver he determined to make his way just as rapidly as he could.

[39] *Ibid.*, 468.

[40] Wheeler, *Geographical Report*, 692.

[41] *Report upon United States Geographical Surveys West of the One Hundredth Meridian*, which was published over a span of fourteen years as seven separate volumes. Wheeler was in charge of all the reports, but he himself wrote only the first one, *Geographical Report*. Most of the other reports represented the combined efforts of several men.

[42] *Register of Graduates and Former Cadets United States Military Academy*, 157.

Cochetopa Pass was the logical crossing, but the desperate Lieutenant racked his mind to recall a depression among the mountains that he had seen earlier in the season, which might get him to Denver faster. He dimly recollected it, and with a packer named Dave Mears he headed for that depression. They found it, and in spite of his toothache he and Mears remained a day and a night at the top of the new pass taking thermometer and barometer readings; Marshall also sketched a profile of the area. Six days after leaving the summit they arrived at Denver, ahead of their main party that was coming in by way of Cochetopa Pass. The Lieutenant had found a route that cut 125 miles from the trip between Denver and the San Juan area, and that pass is known to this day as Marshall Pass.[43]

[43] Thomas F. Dawson, "The Godfather of Marshall Pass," *The Trail*, Vol. XIII, No. 4 (September, 1920), 5–12.

1879: The End of the Great Surveys

WITH THE END of the fiscal year 1879, all of the Great Surveys had ceased to function as active organizations, and a chapter in the history of American science had ended. The four surveys had flourished side by side during the 1870's because many men had displayed interest and determination in exploring the American West. A government that was caught without a policy, but with a general understanding that it should subsidize and encourage the advancement of science, had temporarily solved its dilemma by granting funds to all four surveys. (It had even subsidized others—several army surveys of a temporary nature and a survey of the Black Hills by W. P. Jenney and H. Newton in 1875. Many private natural history expeditions were also in the West during the 1870's.)[1]

Such a situation, which implied waste, competition, and extravagance, could not be allowed to go on for many years, and by 1878 the forces were organized to bring about a consolidation, an end to waste, and a boost to efficiency. Led by Major John

[1] Wheeler, *Geographical Report*, 718. Howard D. Kramer, "The Scientist in the West, 1870–1880," *Pacific Historical Review*, Vol. XII, No. 3 (September, 1943), 239–251.

Wesley Powell, but supported by most of the members of the scientific community, as well as by leading politicians, the Hayden, Powell, and Wheeler surveys were discontinued (King had already completed his work), and the United States Geological Survey was created. It is still functioning actively, and it commands high respect from statesmen and scientists alike.

It is unfortunate that the bitter controversy which accompanied the creation of the U.S.G.S. should have resulted, as it did, in a complete eclipse of its four predecessors. The Hayden, King, Powell, and Wheeler surveys were forgotten. Only Powell remained fairly well known as an individual, and then it was not for his survey, but for the specific achievements of his two journeys down the Colorado River and his subsequent work with the U.S.G.S.

Yet the Great Surveys accomplished much for science and for the nation. Because of their efforts, large parts of the American West were mapped with enough accuracy to be useful to miners, lumbermen, railroad builders, ranchers, and farmers. Not just dozens, but hundreds of place names were given to mountains, valleys, streams, and plateaus. The Great Surveys literally named the components of the new land.

For the first time, the vague stories about a land of geysers and hot springs were checked and the truth was established. For the first time, the rumors about "Aztec ruins" were investigated, and the true nature of the cliff dwellings of the Southwest was made known to a curious world. The awesome mystery of the Grand Canyon of the Colorado was investigated, described, and its awesomeness confirmed.

Photographs by Jackson, O'Sullivan, Beaman, and Hillers conveyed to the rest of the world the true look of the mountains and the other wonders of the West, and people were no longer deceived by the colorful lithographs, in vogue during the 1870's, that depicted the Rockies rising at sixty degree angles from the eastern plains. Moran's paintings of the canyons of the Yellowstone and the Colorado exhibited their true beauties in an age before color photography. Journalists like Ernest Ingersoll and even William R. Rideing wrote more accurate word pictures of the West than had previously been published.

The geologists established the general earth history of the West. They gave every mountain range its biography, and they visualized the West as it was, laid out the boundaries of the great inland seas (east of the Rockies) or lakes (Bonneville and Lahontan) in the Great Basin. They examined mines and traced veins of precious ores. And King exposed the greatest hoax ever perpetrated in the American West.

The paleontologists helped their fellow scientists fix the geologic ages, and Cope and Marsh, Lesquereux, Meek, and Leidy explored and examined and pieced together so that they soon knew the story of life, both plant and animal, in the West.

Botanists, zoologists, ornithologists, entomologists, conchologists, and other natural scientists even more specialized painstakingly collected specimens, classified them, and placed them on deposit at the Smithsonian, or in university collections throughout the United States. Ethnologists collected the myths, the languages, the tools of the primitive Indian tribes, to be thus remembered long after the tribes had forgotten their own culture or had themselves disappeared from the face of the earth. Because of the work of Powell and Pilling, Hayden and Stevenson, Gilbert and Dutton, the Hagues and Emmons, Coulter and Carpenter, Ridgway and Bailey, and many others, the flora and fauna, the geology, and the primeval cultures of the West were studied and pertinent materials deposited, so that advancing mankind need never lose the knowledge.

And so the greatest contribution of the Great Surveys was in the foundations they laid. For even down to this day it is from these bases that the complicated natural history of the American West has been gradually disclosed.

But, being human beings, we come back through interest to the men of the Great Surveys. They were the dedicated, quiet men of science. They were mature men, educated men, intelligent men—who never outgrew their childlike curiosity, their eagerness to discover what was around the next bend. Their reports, filled with drawings of fossils, birds, reptiles, geologic sections, and plants and flowers, lie in our reference libraries. The dust on them thickens, their bindings crack, and the interested researcher never comes.

Then was the work of the men of the Great Surveys all in vain?

Of course not. For these men shared in the beginnings. They pushed back America's first frontiers of science. Again, they were foundation makers. Not a textbook in geology or any of the natural sciences is published that does not embody the knowledge derived from the work of the men of the Great Surveys. Most likely the facts are stated without a citation, without a footnote to give credit. But Hayden's work, and King's work, and Powell's ideas, and Coulter's collections are all there. No student graduates in the natural sciences without in some way having built his knowledge upon the facts established by our scientists of the 1870's.

And finally we come back to the Western land. In 1867 men had asked, "What lies out there?" By 1879, thanks to the work of the Great Surveys, their question had been answered. Now a new question was on men's lips: "When shall we go there?"

For all the discoveries made by the Great Surveys had only confirmed an impression that the rest of the world had cherished for a long time: the American West is a wonderland.

Bibliography

Unpublished Government Documents in the National Archives

THE HAYDEN SURVEY:

Record Group 57. Records of the United States Geological Survey. This is the most valuable collection of material on the Hayden Survey. It contains much correspondence sent to Hayden from members of his survey and from other individuals, ranging from job-seekers to congressmen to scientists of other nations. Much of this material has been microfilmed and is now available at nominal cost.

Record Group 48. Records of the Office of the Secretary of the Interior. Hayden records are to be found in two of the divisions into which R.G. 48 is divided: the Patents and Miscellaneous Division, and the Lands and Railroads Division. The amount of Hayden material is small, consisting of some correspondence between Hayden and the Secretary of the Interior and some correspondence from scientists.

Record Group 49. Records of the General Land Office. This contains a little Hayden material concerning the years 1867 and 1868.

THE KING SURVEY:

Record Group 57. Records of the United States Geological Survey. The "Copy Book of Letters Sent by Clarence King to General

377

A. A. Humphreys, 1867–1879" constitutes all the King material in R.G. 57, but it is invaluable.

Record Group 77. Records of the Office of the Chief of Engineers. This group contains a small amount of material on King, including King's letters to Humphreys following the exposure of the diamond hoax.

THE POWELL SURVEY:

Record Group 57. Records of the United States Geological Survey. In this group are seven letter press books of Powell correspondence.

THE WHEELER SURVEY:

Record Group 77. Records of the Office of the Chief of Engineers. Orders, lists of personnel, and some correspondence from Wheeler to Humphreys are available in this group.

Since 1959, the material relating to the Wheeler Survey used by me at the Stanford University Library has been removed to the National Archives. This voluminous collection consists of official correspondence, letter books, and technical material.

MISCELLANEOUS:

Still Pictures Section. A large collection of photographic plates and negatives, not processed or identified, are in the custody of this branch, as well as hundreds of identified Survey photographs.

Cartographic Records Branch. Here are filed most of the maps of the Great Surveys, including preliminary maps, work sheets, plane-table drawings, and sketches.

Other Unpublished Materials

Crosby, Harry. "So Deep a Trail: A Biography of Clarence King." Unpublished doctoral dissertation, Stanford University, 1953.

Doane, William Croswell. Doane Papers. Library of the State of New York, Albany, New York. Contains some material concerning James Terry Gardner.

Emmons, Samuel Franklin. Emmons Papers. Manuscript Division, the Library of Congress. These include Emmons' diary of the trip into the diamond fields.

Farquhar, Francis P. Farquhar Collection. Bancroft Library, Berkeley, California. This collection contains some good material on King and Powell.

Holmes, William Henry. "Random Records of a Lifetime Devoted to

Science and Arts, 1846–1929." In custody of the Director of the National Collection of Fine Arts, New Museum Building, Washington, D.C. The first five of these sixteen volumes are useful for the study of the Hayden Survey.

Jackson, William Henry. Diaries. Custody of the Colorado State Historical Society, Denver, Colorado.

King, Clarence. Clarence King Collection. Huntington Library, San Marino, California.

University of Pennsylvania Archives. Philadelphia, Pennsylvania.

Redman, J. T. "Reminiscences and Experiences on My Trip Across the Plains to California Sixty-one Years Ago When I Drove Four Mules to a Covered Wagon." Manuscript, Huntington Library No. HM 20462.

University of Rochester Special Collections. University of Rochester Library, Rochester, New York.

Wheeler, Captain George M. Scrapbook. Bancroft Library, No. P–W 32, Vol. I.

Published Government Documents

In the course of research on the Great Surveys the following annual reports for the years 1867 through 1879 were examined: those of the Smithsonian Institution, the Department of the Interior, the Secretary of War, the Chief of Engineers, and the Hayden Survey. Embodied within the annual reports of the Chief of Engineers were those submitted by Lieutenant Wheeler and by Clarence King. Powell's reports, or information about his activities, appear in both the annual reports of the Smithsonian Institution and of the Department of the Interior. Also examined were many of the monographs issued by Hayden's and Powell's surveys as well as the magnificent final reports of the King and Wheeler surveys. The researcher is reminded of Laurence F. Schmeckebier, *Catalogue and Index of the Hayden, King, Powell, and Wheeler Surveys.* U.S. Geological Survey, Bulletin 222. Washington, 1904. He will also find useful the "Lists of Congressional and Departmental Publications," *Checklist of United States Public Documents.* Vol. I. Third edition. Washington, 1911.

Barlow, Captain J. W. *Reconaissance of the Yellowstone River.* 42 Cong., 2 sess. *Sen. Exec. Doc. 66.* Washington, 1872.

Bradley, Frank H. "Report of Frank H. Bradley, Geologist." In Hayden, *Sixth Annual Report* (Hayden). Washington, 1873.

Carter, Clarence Edward, ed. *The Territorial Papers of the United*

States. Vol. XIII, "The Territories of Louisiana-Missouri, 1803–1806." Washington, 1948.

Coues, Elliott, and Joel Asaph Allen. *Monographs of North American Rodentia*. Vol. IX, Hayden, *Monographs*. Washington, 1877.

Doane, Lieutenant Gustavus C. *The Yellowstone Expedition of 1870*. 41 Cong., 3 sess. *Sen. Exec. Doc. 51*. Washington, 1871.

Dutton, Captain Clarence Edward. "Report on the Geology of the High Plateaus of Utah." *U.S. Geographical and Geological Survey of the Rocky Mountain Region* (Powell). Washington, 1880.

———. "Tertiary History of the Grand Canyon District." U.S. Geological Survey, *Monographs*, No. 2. Washington, 1882.

Fairman, Charles E. *Art and Artists of the Capitol of the United States of America*. 69 Cong., 1 sess. *Sen. Exec. Doc. 95*. Washington, 1927.

Gannett, Henry. "Report on Astronomy and Hypsometry." *Sixth Annual Report* (Hayden). Washington, 1873.

Gardner, James T. "Sketch of the Methods of Survey in the Geographical Department." *Seventh Annual Report* (Hayden). Washington, 1874.

Geographical and Geological Surveys West of the Mississippi. 43 Cong., 1 sess. *House Report 612*. Washington, 1874.

Geological and Geographical Surveys. 45 Cong., 2 sess. *House Exec. Doc. 81*. Washington, 1878.

Gilbert, Grove Karl. "Lake Bonneville." U.S. Geological Survey, *Monographs*, No. 1. Washington, 1890.

———. "Report on the Geology of the Henry Mountains." *U.S. Geographical and Geological Survey of the Rocky Mountain Region* (Powell). Washington, 1877.

Hayden, Ferdinand Vandeveer. "Letter to the Secretary," embodied in each of the twelve *Annual Reports of the United States Geological and Geographical Survey of the Territories*. Washington, 1868–1883.

———. "Annual Report of F. V. Hayden" in each of the twelve *Annual Reports of the United States Geological and Geographical Survey of the Territories*. Washington, 1868–1883.

Hayden Survey. *Geological and Geographical Atlas of Colorado and Portions of Adjacent Territory*. Washington, 1877.

Holmes, William Henry. "Report on the Sierra Abajo and West San Miguel Mountains." *Tenth Annual Report* (Hayden). Washington, 1878.

Ives, Lieutenant Joseph C. *Report Upon the Colorado River of the West.* 36 Cong., 1 sess. *House Exec. Doc. 90.* Washington, 1861.

"James Stevenson." U.S. Geological Survey, *Ninth Annual Report, 1887–1889.* Washington, 1889.

King, Clarence. *Professional Papers of the Engineer Department, U.S. Army.* No. 18. Seven volumes plus atlas.

    I. Clarence King. *Systematic Geology.* Washington, 1878.

    II. Arnold Hague and Samuel Franklin Emmons. *Descriptive Geology.* Washington, 1877.

    III. James D. Hague and Clarence King. *Mining Industry.* Washington, 1870.

    IV. (Part I) Fielding Bradford Meek. *Palaeontology.* (Part II) James Hall and R. P. Whitfield. *Palaeontology.* (Part III) Robert Ridgway. *Ornithology.* Washington, 1878.

    V. Sereno Watson. *Botany.* Washington, 1871.

    VI. Ferdinand Zirkel. *Microscopical Petrography.* Washington, 1876.

    VII. Othniel Charles Marsh. *Odontornithes: A Monograph on the Extinct Toothed Birds of North America.* Washington, 1880.

Leidy, Joseph. "Notice of Some Worms Collected During Professor Hayden's Expedition to the Yellowstone River in the Summer of 1871." *Fifth Annual Report* (Hayden). Washington, 1872.

Lesquereux, Leo. 'The Flora of the Dakota Group." U.S. Geological Survey, *Monographs.* No. XVII. Washington, 1891.

———. "On the Fossil Plants of the Cretaceous and Tertiary Formations of Kansas and Nebraska." *Fourth Annual Report* (Hayden). Washington, 1871.

Macomb, Captain John N. *Report of Exploring Expedition from Santa Fe, N. Mexico, to Junction of Grand and Green Rivers of Great Colorado of the West in 1859 under command of J. N. Macomb.* Washington, 1876.

Merriam, C. Hart. "Report on the Mammals and Birds of the Expedition." *Sixth Annual Report* (Hayden). Washington, 1873.

National Academy of Sciences. *A Report on the Surveys of the Territories.* 45 Cong., 3 sess. *House Misc. Doc. 5.* Washington, 1878.

"Necrology of John Wesley Powell." U.S. Geological Survey, *Twenty-fourth Annual Report, 1902–1903.* Washington, 1903.

Peale, Albert C. "On Minerals, Rocks, Thermal Springs, Etc." *Fifth Annual Report* (Hayden). Washington, 1872.

Powell, John Wesley. *Survey of the Colorado River of the West.* 42 Cong., 2 sess. *House Misc. Doc. 173.* Washington, 1872.

————. *Report on the Lands of the Arid Region of the United States.* Washington, 1879.

————. *Report of Explorations in 1873.* 43 Cong., 1 sess. *House Misc. Doc. 265.* Washington, 1874.

————. *Exploration of the Colorado River of the West.* 43 Cong., 1 sess. *House Misc. Doc. 300.* Washington, 1875.

————. *Report on the Geology of the Eastern Portion of the Uinta Mountains.* Washington, 1876.

Raynolds, Brevet-General William F. *Report of the Exploration of the Yellowstone and Missouri Rivers, in 1859–1860.* 40 Cong., 1 sess. *Sen. Doc. 77.* Washington, 1868.

Rhoda, Franklin. "Report on the San Juan." *Eighth Annual Report* (Hayden). Washington, 1876.

————. "Topographical Report of the Southeastern Division." *Ninth Annual Report* (Hayden). Washington, 1877.

Stansbury, Captain Howard. *Exploration of the Valley of the Great Salt Lake of Utah.* 32 Cong., spec. sess. *Sen. Exec. Doc. 3.* Washington, 1853.

Steward, Julian H. "Notes on Hillers' Photographs of the Paiute and Ute Indians Taken on the Powell Exploration of 1873." Smithsonian Institution, *Miscellaneous Collections,* Vol. XCVIII, No. 18. Washington, 1939.

Thomas, Cyrus. "Agriculture of Colorado." *Third Annual Report* (Hayden). Washington, 1873.

Walcott, Charles D. "Ferdinand Vandeveer Hayden." U.S. Geological Survey. *Ninth Annual Report, 1887–1889.* Washington, 1889.

Warren, Lieutenant Gouverneur Kimble. "Preliminary Report of the Explorations of Nebraska and Dakota, 1855–57." *Annual Report of the War Department.* 35 Cong., 2 sess. *Sen. Exec. Doc. 1,* Washington, 1858.

Wheeler, Captain George M. *Report Upon the Third Geographical Congress and Exhibition at Venice, Italy, 1881.* 48 Cong., 2 sess. *House Exec. Doc. 270.* Washington, 1885.

————. *Preliminary Report of Explorations in Nevada and Arizona.* 42 Cong., 2 sess. *Sen. Exec. Doc. 65.* Washington, 1872.

————. *Report Upon United States Geographical Surveys West of the One Hundredth Meridian.* 7 vols. Washington, 1875–1889.

Bibliography

Books

Adams, Henry. *The Education of Henry Adams.* New York, 1931.

Baker, Virgil. *American Painting: History and Interpretation.* New York, 1950.

Bancroft, Hubert Howe. *Works.* Vol. XXVI, *History of Utah: 1540–1886.* San Francisco, 1889.

The Biographical Dictionary of America. Rossiter Johnson, ed. Boston, 1906.

Brayer, Herbert O. *William Blackmore: A Case Study in the Economic Development of the West.* 2 vols. Denver, 1949.

Brewster, Edward Tenney. *Life and Letters of Josiah Dwight Whitney.* New York, 1901.

Burlingame, Merrill G. *The Montana Frontier.* Helena, Montana, 1942.

Chittenden, Hiram Martin. *History of Early Steamboat Navigation on the Missouri River.* 2 vols. New York, 1903.

———. (Revised by Eleanor Chittenden Cress and Isabelle F. Story.) *Yellowstone National Park.* Palo Alto, California, 1940.

Clarke, John M. *James Hall of Albany, Geologist and Palaeontologist, 1811–1898.* Albany, 1932.

Clemens, Samuel L. *Roughing It.* New York, 1899.

Colorado: A Guide to the Highest State. "American Guide Series." New York, 1941.

Colorado State Planning Commission. *Year Book of the State of Colorado, 1948–1950.* Denver, 1948.

Cullum, Major George W. *Biographical Register of the Officers and Graduates of the U.S. Military Academy at West Point, New York.* New York, 1868.

Dale, Harrison Clifford. *The Ashley-Smith Explorations and the Discovery of a Central Route to the Pacific, 1822–1829.* Cleveland, 1918.

Darrah, William Culp. *Powell of the Colorado.* Princeton, 1951.

Davis, William B. *The Recent Mammals of Idaho.* Caldwell, Idaho, 1939.

De Lahontan, Baron (edit. by Reuben Gold Thwaites). *New Voyages to North America.* Chicago, 1905.

Dellenbaugh, Frederick S. *A Canyon Voyage.* New York, 1908.

———. *The Romance of the Colorado River.* New York, 1902.

De Voto, Bernard. *The Year of Decision: 1846.* Boston, 1943.

Dictionary of American Biography. Allen Johnson, ed. New York, 1928.

Driggs, Harold R., and William H. Jackson. *The Pioneer Photographer.* New York, 1929.

Dupree, A. Hunter. *Science in the Federal Government.* Cambridge, 1947.

Ewan, Joseph. *Rocky Mountain Naturalists.* Denver, 1950.

Farquhar, Francis P., ed. *Up and Down California in 1860–1864: The Journal of William H. Brewer.* New Haven, 1930.

Fenton, Carroll Lane, and Mildrid Adams Fenton. *Giants of Geology.* Garden City, 1952.

Ford, Worthington Chauncey, ed. *Letters of Henry Adams (1858– 1891).* Boston, 1930.

Freeman, Louis R. *The Colorado River: Yesterday, Today and To- morrow.* New York, 1923.

Fritz, Percy Stanley. *Colorado, the Centennial State.* New York, 1941.

Ganoe, William Addleman. *The History of the United States Army.* New York, 1924.

Gilbert, Grove Karl, ed. *John Wesley Powell.* Chicago, 1903.

Goetzmann, William H. *Army Exploration in the American West.* New Haven, 1960.

Hafen, LeRoy, and Ann W. Hafen. *The Diaries of William Henry Jackson.* Glendale, California, 1959.

Hague, James D., Edward Cary, and John LaFarge, eds. *Clarence King Memoirs.* New York, 1904.

Hall, Frank. *History of the State of Colorado.* Chicago, 1889.

Harpending, Asbury (ed. by James H. Wilkins). *The Great Diamond Hoax and Other Stirring Incidents in the Life of Asbury Harpen- ding.* San Francisco, 1913. Republished, Norman, Oklahoma, 1958.

Hibbard, Benjamin Horace. *A History of the Public Land Policies.* New York, 1924.

Holman, Louis A. *The Graphic Processes: Intaglio, Relief and Plano- graphic.* Boston, 1929.

Horan, James D. *Mathew Brady: Historian with a Camera.* New York, 1955.

Ingersoll, Ernest. *Crest of the Continent.* Chicago, 1885.

———. *Knocking Around the Rockies.* New York, 1883.

Irving, Washington. *The Adventures of Captain Bonneville,* New York, 1868.

———. *Astoria: Or Anecdotes of an Enterprise Among the Rocky Mountains.* New York, 1897.
Jackson, Clarence S., and Lawrence W. Marshall. *Quest of the Snowy Cross.* Denver, 1952.
Jackson, William Henry. *Time Exposure.* New York, 1940.
King, Clarence. *Mountaineering in the Sierra Nevada.* Boston, 1872.
Langford, Nathaniel P. *The Discovery of Yellowstone Park, 1870.* St. Paul, Minnesota, 1892.
Longfellow, Samuel, ed. *Life of Henry Wadsworth Longfellow.* Boston, 1891.
Merrill, George P. *The First One Hundred Years of American Geology.* New Haven, 1924.
Morgan, Dale L. *The Great Salt Lake.* New York, 1947.
Mumey, Nolie. *The Teton Mountains: Their History and Tradition.* Denver, 1947.
Nevada: A Guide to the Silver State. "American Guide Series." Portland, Oregon, 1940.
The National Cyclopaedia of American Biography. New York, 1898–1956.
Ormes, Robert M. *Guide to the Colorado Mountains.* Denver, 1952.
Osborn, Henry Fairfield. *Cope: Master Naturalist.* Princeton, 1931.
Pollack, Peter. *The Picture History of Photography.* New York, 1958.
Register of Graduates and Former Cadets United States Military Academy. New York, 1946.
Rideing, William H. *A-Saddle in the Wild West.* New York, 1879.
Robbins, Roy M. *Our Landed Heritage: The Public Domain, 1776–1936.* Princeton, 1942.
Robinson, Edgar P. *Painting in America: The Story of 450 Years.* New York, 1956.
Rodgers, Andrew Denny, III. *American Botany: 1873–1892.* Princeton, 1944.
———. *John Merle Coulter: Missionary in Science.* Princeton, 1944.
———. *"Noble Fellow": William Starling Sullivant.* New York, 1940.
Schuchert, Charles, and C. M. LeVene. *O. C. Marsh: Pioneer in Paleontology.* New Haven, 1940.
A South Dakota Guide. "American Guide Series." Pierre, 1938.
Stanton, Robert Brewster. *Colorado River Controversies.* New York, 1932.
Taft, Robert. *Photography and the American Scene.* New York. 1938.

Taylor, Emerson Gifford. *Gouverneur Kemble Warren: The Life and Letters of an American Soldier, 1830–1882.* Boston, 1932.

Watrous, Ansel. *History of Larimer County, Colorado.* Denver, 1911.

Wilkins, Thurman. *Clarence King.* New York, 1958.

Wittke, Carl. *Refugees of Revolution: The German Forty-eighters in America.* Philadelphia, 1952.

Woodard, Bruce. *The Garden of the Gods Story.* Colorado Springs, Colorado, 1955.

Articles

[In the course of research on the Great Surveys special use was made of the *American Journal of Science and Arts,* a veritable storehouse of information concerning science and scientists of the late nineteenth century and the *Utah Historical Review* (1947–1949), which contains the journals as well as biographical information on the members of the Powell Colorado expeditions.]

Adams, Henry. Editorial comments on the King Survey, *North American Review,* Vol. CXIII, No. 233 (July, 1871), 204.

Bartlett, Richard A. "The Hayden Survey in Colorado," *Colorado Quarterly,* Vol. IV, No. 1 (Summer, 1955), 73–88.

Becker, George F. "Obituary of Major C. E. Dutton," *American Journal of Science and Arts,* Fourth Series, Vol. XXXIII, No. 196 (April, 1912), 387–388.

Bishop, Captain Francis Marion (ed. by Charles Kelly). "Captain Francis Marion Bishop's Journal," *Utah Historical Quarterly,* Vol. XV (1947), 159–238.

Bradley, Frank. "Explorations in 1872: United States Geographical Survey of the Territories Under Dr. F. V. Hayden; Snake River Division," *American Journal of Science and Arts,* Third Series, Vol. VI, No. 33 (September, 1873), 194–206.

Brooks, Juanita. "Lee's Ferry at Lonely Dell," *Utah Historical Quarterly,* Vol. XXV (1957), 283–295.

Brown, Ralph H. "Colorado Mountain Passes," *Colorado Magazine,* Vol. VI, No. 6 (November, 1929), 227–237.

Chamberlain, Ralph B. "Francis Marion Bishop," *Utah Historical Quarterly,* Vol. XV (1947), 155–158.

Cope, Edward Drinker. "Ferdinand Vandiveer Hayden, M.D., LL.D.," *The American Geologist,* Vol. 1 (February, 1888), 111–112.

"Cyrus Thomas." *American Anthropologist,* New Series, Vol. XII (April–June, 1910), 337–343.

Darrah, William Culp, ed. "The Colorado River Expedition of 1869," *Utah Historical Quarterly,*" Vol. XV (1947), 9–18.

———. "Frederick Samuel Dellenbaugh," *Utah Historical Quarterly,* Vols. XVI–XVII (1948–1949), 497–499.

———. "George Young Bradley," *Utah Historical Quarterly,* Vol. XV, 29–30.

———. "Hawkins, Hall, and Goodman," *Utah Historical Quarterly,* Vol. XV (1947), 105–107.

———. "John F. Steward," *Utah Historical Quarterly,* Vols. XVI–XVII (1948–1949), 175–179.

———. "John C. Sumner," *Utah Historical Quarterly,* Vol. XV (1947), 109–110.

———. "Walter Henry Powell," *Utah Historical Quarterly,* Vol. XV (1947), 89.

Davis, William M. "Biographical Memoir of John Wesley Powell, 1832–1902," National Academy of Sciences, *Biographical Memoirs,* Vol. VIII (1915).

———. "Grove Karl Gilbert," *American Journal of Science,* Fourth Series, Vol. XLVI, No. 275 (November, 1918), 669–681.

Dawson, Thomas F. "The Godfather of Marshall Pass," *The Trail,* Vol. XIII, No. 4 (September, 1920), 4–12.

Dickason, David H. "Henry Adams and Clarence King, the Record of a Friendship," *New England Quarterly,* Vol. XVII, No. 2 (June, 1944), 229–254.

Emmons, Samuel Franklin. "Biographical Memoir of Clarence King," National Academy of Sciences, *Biographical Memoirs,* Vol. VI (1909).

Everts, Truman C. "Thirty-seven Days of Peril," *Scribner's Monthly,* Vol. III, No. 1 (November, 1871), 1–17.

Gardner, James T. "Hayden and Gardner's Survey of the Territories, Under the Direction of the Department of the Interior," *American Journal of Science and Arts,* Third Series, Vol. VI, No. 34 (October, 1873), 297–300.

———. "On the Hypsometric Work of the U.S. Geological and Geographical Survey of the Territories, F. V. Hayden, U.S. Geologist in Charge," *American Journal of Science and Arts,* Third Series, Vol. VI, No. 35 (November, 1873), 373–375.

Geikie, Archibald. "Ferdinand Vandeveer Hayden," *Nature,* Vol. XXXVII, No. 953 (February 2, 1888), 326.

Gregory, Herbert E. "Beaman, Fennemore, Hillers, Dellenbaugh,

Johnson and Hattan," *Utah Historical Quarterly,* Vols. XVI–XVII (1948–1949), 491–503.

———. "Diary of Almon Harris Thompson," *Utah Historical Quarterly,* Vol. VII (1939), 5–10.

———. "Stephen Vandeveer Jones," *Utah Historical Quarterly,* Vols. XVI–XVII (1948–1949), 11–18.

Hall, Andrew. "Three Letters by Andrew Hall," *Utah Historical Quarterly,* Vol. XVI (1948–1949), 505–507.

Harris, Harry. "Robert Ridgway," *The Condor,* Vol. XXX, No. 1 (January–February, 1928), 5–118.

Hayden, Ferdinand V. "The Hot Springs and Geysers of the Yellowstone and Firehole Rivers," *American Journal of Science and Arts,* Third Series, Vol. III, No. 15 (March, 1872), 161–176.

——— and F. B. Meek. "Notes on the Geology of the Mauvaises Terres of the White River, Nebraska," *Proceedings of the Academy of Natural Sciences of Philadelphia,* Vol. IX (June, 1857), 151–158.

———. "On the Geology and Natural History of the Upper Missouri Being the Substance of a Report to Lieut. G. K. Warren, T.E. U.S.A.," *Transactions of the American Philosophical Society,* New Series, Vol. XII (1863), 1–231.

———. "The Wonders of the West—II: More About the Yellowstone," *Scribner's Monthly,* Vol. III, No. 4 (February, 1872), 388–396.

"Henry Gannett." *National Geographic Magazine,* Vol. XXVI (December, 1914), 609–613.

Ingersoll, Ernest. "Rocky Mountain Cooking," *Scribner's Monthly,* Vol. XX, No. 6 (May, 1880), 125–131.

———. "Rocky Mountain Mules," *Scribner's Monthly,* Vol. XX, No. 2 (April, 1880), 929–936.

———. "Rocky Mountain Nights," *Scribner's Monthly,* Vol. XX, No. 2 (June, 1880), 219–224.

Jackson, William H. "First Official Visit to the Cliff Dwellings," *Colorado Magazine,* Vol. I, No. 4 (May, 1924), 152–160.

Jackson, W. Turrentine. "The Creation of Yellowstone National Park," *Mississippi Valley Historical Review, Vol.* XXIX (June, 1942), 187–206.

———. "Government Exploration of the Upper Yellowstone, 1871," *Pacific Historical Review,* Vol. XI, No. 2 (June, 1942), 187–199.

———. "The Washburn-Doane Expedition into the Upper Yellowstone, 1870," *Pacific Historical Review,* Vol. X, No. 2 (June, 1941), 189–208.

"James Stevenson." *American Anthropologist*, New Series, Vol. XVIII (1916), 552–559.

Kelly, Charles. "Walter Clement Powell," *Utah Historical Quarterly*, Vols. XVI–XVII (1948–1949), 253–255.

Keplinger, L. W. "First Ascent of Long's Peak," *The Trail*, Vol. VII, No. 8 (January, 1914), 13–15.

King, Clarence. "On the Discovery of Actual Glaciers on the Mountains of the Pacific Slope," *American Journal of Science and Arts*, Third Series, Vol. I, No. 3 (March, 1871), 158–160.

Kramer, Howard D. "The Scientist in the West," 1870–1880," *Pacific Historical Review*, Vol. XII, No. 3 (September, 1943), 239–251.

Langford, Nathaniel P. "The Ascent of Mount Hayden: A New Chapter in Western Discovery," *Scribner's Monthly*, Vol. VI, No. 2 (June, 1873), 129–157.

———. "The Wonders of the Yellowstone," *Scribner's Monthly*, Vol. II, No. 1 (May, 1871), 1–17; Vol. II, No. 2 (June, 1871), 113–128.

Liebling, A. J. "The American Golconda," *New Yorker*, Vol. XVI (November 16, 1940), 40, 48.

Loring, Frederick W. "A Council of War," *Appleton's Journal of Literature, Science, and Art*, Vol. VI, No. 124 (August 12, 1871), 182–183.

———. "A Glimpse of Mormonism," *Appleton's Journal of Literature, Science, and Art*, Vol. VI, No. 125 (August 19, 1871), 214–215.

———. "Into the Valley of Death," *Appleton's Journal of Literature, Science, and Art*, Vol. VI, No. 138 (November 18, 1871), 574–575.

Mattes, Merrill J. "Behind the Legend of Colter's Hell: The Early Exploration of Yellowstone National Park," *Mississippi Valley Historical Review*, Vol. XXXVI, No. 2 (September, 1949), 251–282.

Meek, Fielding Bradford, and F. V. Hayden. "Descriptions of New Fossil Species of Mollusca Collected by Dr. F. V. Hayden, in Nebraska Territory; Together with a Complete Catalogue of all the Remains of Invertebrata Hitherto Described and Identified from the Cretaceous and Tertiary Formations of that Region," *Proceedings of the Academy of Natural Sciences of Philadelphia*," Vol. VIII, No. 6 (November, 1856), 265–286.

———. "Explorations Under the War Department," *Proceedings of the Academy of Natural Sciences of Philadelphia*, Vol. IX (May 26, 1857), 117–148.

Mock, S. D. "The Effects of the 'Boom Decade,' 1870–1880, Upon

Colorado Population," *Colorado Magazine,* Vol. XI, No. 1 (January, 1934), 27–34.

"Obituary of General A. A. Humphreys," *Proceedings of the American Philosophical Society,* Vol. XXII, No. 117 (January, 1885), 48–71.

"Obituary of Sereno Watson," "*Scientific American,* Vol. LXVI, No. 15 (April 9, 1892), 233.

Powell, John Wesley. "The Ancient Province of Tusayan," *Scribner's Monthly,* Vol. XI, No. 1 (December, 1875), 193–213.

———. "An Overland Trip to the Grand Canyon," *Scribner's Monthly,* Vol. X, No. 6 (October, 1875), 659–678.

Raynolds, Captain William F. Letter preceding F. V. Hayden, "Sketch of the Geology of the Country about the Headwaters of the Missouri and Yellowstone Rivers," *American Journal of Science and Arts,* Second Series, Vol. XXXI, No. 92 (March, 1861), 229.

Samson, John. "Photographs from the High Rockies," *Harper's New Monthly Magazine,* Vol. XXXIX, No. 232 (September, 1869), 465–475.

Smith, Henry Nash. "Clarence King, John Wesley Powell, and the Establishment of the United States Geological Survey," *Mississippi Valley Historical Review,* Vol. XXXIV, No. 1 (1947), 37–58.

———. "Rain Follows the Plow: The Notion of Increased Rainfall for the Great Plains," *Huntington Library Quarterly,* Vol. X, No. 2 (February, 1947), 169–194.

Stegner, Wallace. "Powell and the Names on the Plateau," *Western Humanities Review,* Vol. VII, No. 2 (Spring, 1953), 105–110.

Toll, Roger W. "The Hayden Survey in Colorado in 1873 and 1874," *Colorado Magazine,* Vol. VI, No. 4 (July, 1929), 146–156.

Transactions of the Academy of Sciences of St. Louis, Vol. I (1856–60), 17, 107.

Whitney, Josiah Dwight. "Geographical and Geological Surveys," *North American Review,* Vol. CXXI, No. 248 (July, 1875), 37–85; No. 249 (October, 1875), 270–314.

Wilson, Allen D. "The Great California Diamond Mines," *Overland Monthly,* New Series, No. 43 (April, 1904), 291–296.

Bibliography

Bibliographical Additions to the Third Printing

A number of books and articles have been published on the subject since *Great Surveys of the American West* first appeared in 1962, yet most of the work has added little or nothing to the information contained in this book. Below are listed books and articles containing significant additions or varying interpretations to Great Surveys history.

Books

Richard A. Bartlett. *Nature's Yellowstone*. Albuquerque, 1974.

Orrin H. and Lorraine Bonney, *Battle Drums and Geysers*. Chicago, 1970.

William H. Goetzmann. *Exploration and Empire*. New York, 1966.

Aubrey L. Haines. *Yellowstone National Park, Its Exploration and Establishment*. *Washington*, 1974.

———. *The Yellowstone Story: A History of Our First National Park*. 2 vols. Boulder, Colorado, 1977.

H. Duane Hampton. *How the U.S. Cavalry Saved Our National Parks*. Bloomington, Indiana, 1971.

James D. Horan. *Timothy O'Sullivan: American's Forgotten Photographer*. New York, 1966.

Thomas G. Manning. *Government in Science: The U.S. Geological Survey, 1867–1894*. Lexington, Kentucky, 1967.

Wallace Stegner. *Beyond the Hundredth Meridian: John Wesley Powell and the Second Opening of the West*. Boston, 1953.

Bruce A. Woodard. *Diamonds in the Salt*. Boulder, Colorado, 1967.

Articles

Richard A. Bartlett. "John Wesley Powell and the Great Surveys: A Problem in Historiography," *The American West: An Appraisal* (ed. by Robert G. Ferris), Santa Fe, 1963. 37–47.

———. "From Imagination to Reality: With Moran in the Yellowstone," *Prospects: An Annual of American Cultural Studies*. Vol. III, New York, 1977. 111–24.

William M. Bueler. "Langford's Grand Teton Diary," *The American Alpine Journal* (1976), 471–76.

———. "Did They Climb the Grand?" *Off Belay* (June, 1976), 17–23.

Paul W. Gates. "Homesteading in the High Plains," *Aricultural History*, Vol. LI, No. 1 (January, 1977), 109–33.

William H. Goetzmann. "The Wheeler Survey and the Decline of Army Exploration in the West," in *The American West: An Appraisal* (ed. by Robert G. Ferris), Santa Fe, 1963. 37–46.

Index

Abajo Peak: 102
Absaroka Mountains: 34, 36
Academy of Natural Sciences of
    Philadelphia: 7
Adams, Captain Sam: ix, x, 243, 244n.
Adams, Henry: 124–26, 144, 148;
    with Emmons' party, 183; comments
    on death of King, 213–15
Adams, Robert, Jr.: 95, 105, 108
Agassiz, Alexander: 129
Agassiz, Louis: 15, 30, 106, 144, 181
Agua Grande (Navaho Indian): 295
Alder Gulch: 44
Aleck (character noted by Rideing):
    363
Allen, J. A.: 73
Alta Station: 192
American Fur Company: 7
American Geographical Society: 369
Amoy (China): 127
Antelope Pass: 172
Apache Indians: 93, 139, 163, 340–41;
    attack on Wickenburg stage, 348
Aquarius Plateau: 305
Arapahoe Indians: 131
Archean era: 207
Arches National Monument: 291
Arid lands: 321–27
Arivaipa Apaches: 341
Arizona strip: 274

Arkansas River: 21, 111; possible site
    of diamond fields, 189–93, 214;
    Powell's explorations in, 270ff., 284,
    296, 304, 337, 340, 358, 360, 364
Army Engineers: see Corps of
    Engineers
Arnold, Philip: 187ff., 202, 203;
    see also diamond hoax
Ashley, General William: 260 & n.
Ashley Falls: 286
Aspen, Colo.: 86, 110
Aspinwall (Colón, Panama): 154f.
Asquit, Captain (Mohave Indian
    chief): 345
Atlantic City, Wyo.: 26
Atlas of Colorado (Hayden): 103, 212
Atlas of the Fortieth Parallel: 207,
    211–12
Austin, Nevada: 164, 174
Aztec Indians: xi, 77, 374.

Bad Lands of Dakota: 6, 9
Badlands National Monument: 6n.
Bailey, William Whitman: 149, 154,
    162, 375
Baird, Spencer: 10, 32, 106, 120,
    143, 151, 268, 280, 317, 354n.
Baker, Captain: 114
Baker's Park: 115ff.; see also San Juan
    Mountains

393

Index

Green River Basin: 211

Green River City (Station): 28, 200, 235, 236, 238, 239, 251, 259, 263, 286; rendezvous for Powell, 241–44, 284–85

Green Terril (character described by Rideing): 363

Gregory Gulch: 74

Grizzly Peak: 110

Gros Ventres Mountains: 34

Grottoes: 260, 287; *see also* Winnie's Grotto

Grotto Spring (Yellowstone): 51

Gulf of California: 228, 246, 344

Gunnison, Capt. John W.: 334

Gunnison River: 94, 228

Gunnison's Crossing: 270, 283, 289, 290

Guyot, Arnold: 30, 100

Hague, Arnold: 149, 179, 185, 206, 375; education, 147–48; explores Mount Hood, 181; completes *Descriptive Geology*, 209

Hague, James D.: 123, 148, 149, 192, 207, 214, 375; education, 147; completes *Mining Industry*, 179; helps expose diamond hoax, 204

Hague, James D. and Arnold: 154, 178, 209

Hahn, Charlie: 343

Hall, Andrew (Andy, or Dare-Devil Dick): 241, 244, 248, 251, 253, 258, 266

Hall, James: 5, 6, 14, 15, 209, 210, 314, 317

Halleck, Maj. Gen. H. W.: 153

Halleck Station, Nev.: 339

Hamblin, Jacob: 276, 278, 290 guides Powell, 270ff.; concludes treaty with Navahos, 295–96

Hamblin, Joseph (Jacob's son): 298, 308

Hamel, P. W.: 348; *see also* Wickenburg massacre

Hamp, Mr. (political appointee with Hayden): 67

Harney's Peak: 363

Harrell, Mr. (Texas cattleman): 286

Harriman, Edward H.: 213

Harrison Land Law: 322

"Harvest of Death": 153

Hattan, Andy: 283ff., 290, 292–95, 299, 302, 305, 307ff., 329

Havasupai Apaches: 340

Hawkins, William Rhodes (Billy Rhodes): 236, 244, 266; early life, 241; describes clothing of party, 255

Hay, John: 124, 125, 213

Hayden, Ferdinand Vandeveer: xii, 32, 33, 39, 40, 43, 44, 51, 53, 72, 80, 107, 117, 135, 147, 208, 212, 220, 226, 267, 278, 314, 334, 336, 338–39, 349, 368, 374, 375; explorations in Dakota, 5–7; in Union Army, 8; awarded honorary degree, 9; heads geological survey of Nebraska, 10–12; publication policies, 29; early life, 41; describes Mammoth Hot Springs, 47; describes canyon of the Yellowstone, 50; marriage, 60; in Colorado, 76, 81; complimented by William Byers, 110; maps Holy Cross, 111; death, 119; thanked by state of Colorado, 120; *see also* Hayden Survey

Hayden Peak: 247n.

Hayden Survey (United States Geological and Geographical Survey of the Territories): xiii, 40, 48, 56, 59, 62, 77, 78, 89, 98, 108, 117, 302, 304, 311, 328n., 368; survey of 1867–68, 13–20; survey of 1870, 22–28; First Annual Report, 13; Third Annual Report, 20, 22; Fourth Annual Report, 28, 31; Fifth Annual Report, 57; critique of Fifth Annual Report, 58; permanent offices, 99n., 100; begins topographical work, 41; topographical procedures, 81, 82; first Yellowstone expedition, 36, 40–50; second Yellowstone expedition, 59–64, 69, 72, 73; clashes with Wheeler, 310; total costs of survey, 1867–79, 311

Hayes, Rutherford B.: 125

Heap, Capt. D. P.: 45

Hearst, George: 199

Henry, Joseph: 17, 62, 238, 278, 280, 303, 317; *see also* Smithsonian Institution

Henry, Mary: 62

Henry Mountains: 102, 291, 304, 315–16; *see also* Unknown Mountains *and* Grove Karl Gilbert

Index

Index

Index